Memento of the Living and the Dead

Memento of the Living and the Dead

A First-Person Account of Church, Violence, and Resistance in Latin America

Phillip Berryman

RESOURCE *Publications* • Eugene, Oregon

MEMENTO OF THE LIVING AND THE DEAD
A First-Person Account of Church, Violence, and Resistance in Latin America

Copyright © 2019 Phillip Berryman. All rights reserved. Except for brief quotations in critical publications or reviews, no part of this book may be reproduced in any manner without prior written permission from the publisher. Write: Permissions, Wipf and Stock Publishers, 199 W. 8th Ave., Suite 3, Eugene, OR 97401.

Resource Publications
An Imprint of Wipf and Stock Publishers
199 W. 8th Ave., Suite 3
Eugene, OR 97401

www.wipfandstock.com

PAPERBACK ISBN: 978-1-5326-9087-7
HARDCOVER ISBN: 978-1-5326-9088-4
EBOOK ISBN: 978-1-5326-9089-1

Manufactured in the U.S.A. 08/29/19

Contents

Preface | vii
Abbreviations | xi

1 Hollydale Boyhood | 1
2 Twelve Years a Seminarian | 12
3 Chafing under a Roman Collar | 39
4 San Miguelito, "Light of the World" | 55
5 First Steps in Chorrillo | 72
6 *Patria Grande*—My 1968 | 88
7 The Pastoral Turns Political | 106
8 Finding Our Way—With Twists and Turns | 132
9 Responding to Spiraling Violence | 155
10 Point of No Return | 182
11 Solidarity and Resistance | 207
12 "Too Many Orphans and Widows" | 234
13 Paradigms Lost | 256
14 Consumption Democratized? | 285
15 The View from Eighty | 300

Index | 311

Preface

"Don't come back to Guatemala. We have to leave as soon as possible," said Angie on the phone. "I'll meet you with the kids in Miami." I was in Nicaragua and had planned to go to Honduras and then return to Guatemala.

It was July 1980 and we had been living in Guatemala for four years, working for the American Friends Service Committee (AFSC), the Quaker-rooted peace organization. We had seen signs that we were under surveillance by Guatemalan military or police: a man taking our license plate number as Angie came out of the office of the umbrella organization of Catholic religious orders, mysterious phone calls asking for me, a suspicious person claiming to deliver flowers we hadn't ordered, and especially a man looking like a plainclothes police agent standing across the street from our house all day long—about once a week for a couple months.

We could be under suspicion for various reasons: travel to nearby countries, especially Nicaragua, where the revolutionary Sandinista government had been in power for a year; association with activists in church, labor, and peasant organizing; foreign journalists and representatives of human rights organizations visiting our house; or possibly documentation that I had done anonymously on political violence in Guatemala. None of these activities should be a crime, but increasingly people were being abducted and "disappeared," including two of the indigenous leaders of the project the AFSC had supported in the town of Comalapa.

Angie went with our daughters—Catherine, Maggie, and Lizzy, ages four, two, and two months—to stay with an American-Canadian couple for some protection. She and friends and colleagues spent hours burning our papers and files. Arriving at the airport on the morning of departure, she was told that their flight was cancelled. When she went back to the parking lot and got in the car, Angie realized that she was being followed by two men in a vehicle, even when she made diversionary turns. They stopped only when our friend with diplomatic license plates inserted his car in between them. She and our daughters caught an afternoon flight, and we rendezvoused in Miami late at night and flew to Philadelphia the next morning. In the next few weeks and months, some of our friends were abducted and disappeared; others went underground or into exile.

This memoir tells the story of how I came to that point and what happened afterward. It unfolds in stages, starting with my childhood in southern California, a seminary education, and two years as a young Catholic priest in Pasadena (chapters 1–3). That section prepares the ground by evoking pre–Vatican II Catholicism, as well as tensions and conflicts emerging at that time.

The next stage (chapters 4–7) covers my experiences as a young priest in Panama City, one year in the innovative parish of San Miguelito, and seven as pastor of Chorrillo, a teeming downtown poor neighborhood. A significant interlude is what I call "my 1968," when I studied in Quito and then traveled through South America by land, trying to understand the emerging situation. This was the period of the Latin American Bishops Council (CELAM) conference in Medellin (1968), in which bishops and theologians charted a distinctive approach for Latin American Catholicism, particularly the importance of solidarity with the poor. When I returned to Panama in 1969, the country was under the military rule of General Omar Torrijos. The abduction and disappearance of my friend Fr. Hector Gallego in 1971 led to a tense church-state conflict. Meanwhile, we sought to address housing conditions through barrio organizing efforts.

Angie and I fell in love and married in 1973, leading to the next period (chapters 8–12). We experienced firsthand the growing opposition to the Somoza dictatorship, and militancy in El Salvador and Guatemala, with consequent increasing repression. After our forced departure we settled in Philadelphia and spent the 1980s participating in the broad movement of opposition to the Reagan administration's ideologically driven policies of supporting murderous governments in El Salvador and Guatemala, and sponsoring the *contra* guerrilla army attacking Nicaragua. That work led to writing several books and translating others. In the period since 1990 (chapters 13–15) I have done freelance translation, and taught, researched, and wrote about Latin America, while trying to make sense of the post–Cold War world.

What has impelled me to write is a sense that I have been involved in significant events that deserve to be remembered, particularly what my generation experienced as a "springtime" period in Catholicism in the wake of Vatican II. In my case that period unfolded in Panama and elsewhere in Latin America, and I was involved in the struggle of Central Americans in the 1970s and 1980s and the movement of solidarity with them.

A thread running through this account is that of seeking to overcome poverty through social and economic development, which was memorably defined by Pope Paul VI and ratified at Medellin as "the passage from less human to more human conditions." Economic growth was not an end in itself but a means whereby people could overcome dehumanizing conditions and live more fully. Experiencing the effects of poverty in Chorrillo I was radicalized, as were others of my generation. We came to see poverty as systemic and reasoned that if this is what capitalism produced, some other system—perhaps socialism—might be called for. That concern didn't vanish with the end of the Cold War and the seeming triumph of capitalism.

Much of the story told here is of efforts to respond to widespread human rights violations, starting with the military dictatorships of the 1970s. That intensified with our years with the AFSC in Guatemala while monitoring events in neighboring countries. As murders at the hands of official forces and death squads increased, we sought to alert the outside world to what was happening.

The church in Latin America is central to this account. It was no accident that approximately two dozen priests were killed between El Salvador and Guatemala, including Archbishop Oscar Romero and Bishop Juan Gerardi. Priests and sisters were important protagonists in the story told here. A particular strand of the story is that of liberation theology, which arose in the crucible of these struggles. From 1968 onward, I got to know the theologians and from time to time translated their works and wrote on the movement. The questions they raised were my own questions, and this account follows developments over the decades. Another strand is the emergence of evangelical Christianity in Latin America.

In writing I have had various audiences in mind, those who experienced some of these events and younger cohorts for whom it may read like ancient history. I hope that these stories may give some sense of the horrors but also the hopes and yearnings of those times. On one level I am seeking to make sense of the events of my lifetime. I am likewise seeking to honor the memory of the people of my generation, particularly those who lost their lives in the struggle.

In reality these stories are not entirely ancient history. Central Americans fleeing violence today in their countries are portrayed as a threat or an invading force. This account may provide some perspective by showing some of the roots of the present crisis and the role of the United States in aggravating problems decades ago in the name of the Cold War.

The story told here may also shed light on Pope Francis, the first non-European pope, whose lifetime coincides with mine. As a young Jesuit, Jorge Bergoglio experienced a brutal military dictatorship, and as a priest and bishop, he made it a priority to spend time and work with the poor, along the lines of commitments made by Latin American Catholicism. His friends and colleagues include Argentine exponents of liberation theology, sometimes called the "theology of the people."

This is a memoir, an account of my experiences, as I recall them. The emphasis is on public events, not my feelings about them. It also includes some intellectual and cultural currents of the time. The story is told in the form of vignettes, typically of a few paragraphs, at the risk of leaving readers dizzied with frequent changes of locale. My aim is to show the intertwined nature of the events in different countries, including the United States, during the same time period.

In writing I have checked my memory against written sources, including my own. A number of people read drafts or portions of it and have corrected errors and made valuable suggestions: Angie Berryman, Frank Colborn, Betty Cotton, Tom Cotton, Mike Dunne, Elizabeth Ellis, Robert Ellsberg, Dick Erstad, Phil Evanson, Ricardo Falla, Terry Halloran, Don Headley, Bob Ledogar, Elly Ledogar, Milton Machuca, Jack Malinowski, Ellen McDonald, John McFadden, John McNamee, Jim Mulherin, Tom Quigley, Charlie Reilly, Juan Romero, John Ruthrauf, and Art Schmidt. Remaining errors or shortcomings are my responsibility.

This memoir is dedicated to our daughters, Catherine, Maggie, and Lizzy, and to our grandchildren, Francisco and Odile.

Abbreviations

AFSC	American Friends Service Committee
ANEP	(Asociación Nacional de la Empresa Privada) National Private Enterprise Association (El Salvador)
ARENA	(Alianza Republicana Nacional) National Republican Alliance (El Salvador)
ATA	American Translators Association
BPR	(Bloque Popular Revolucionario) Revolutionary People's Bloc (El Salvador)
CELAM	(Consejo Episcopal Latinoamericano) Latin American Bishops Council
CEPAD	(Comité Evangélico Pro-Ayuda y Desarrollo) Evangelical Committee for Assistance and Development (Nicaragua)
CFM	Christian Family Movement
CIA	Central Intelligence Agency
CIDOC	(Centro Intercultural de Documentación) Intercultural Documentation Center
CIF	(Centro Intercultural de Formación) Intercultural Training Center
CIIR	Catholic Institute for International Relations (United Kingdom)
CISPES	Committee in Solidarity with the People of El Salvador
CNBB	(Conferência Nacional dos Bispos do Brasil) National Conference of Bishops of Brazil
CNT	(Central Nacional de Trabajadores) National Labor Confederation (Guatemala)

ABBREVIATIONS

COEDUCA	(Comunidad Educativa Centroamericana) Central American Educational Community (Guatemala)
CONFREGUA	(Conferencia de Religiosos de Guatemala) Conference of Religious of Guatemala
CUC	(Comité de Unidad Campesina) Committee for Peasant Unity (Guatemala)
DENI	(Departamento Nacional de Investigaciones) National Department of Investigations (Panama)
EGP	(Ejército Guerrillero de los Pobres) Guerrilla Army of the Poor
FAO	(Frente Amplio de Oposición) Broad Opposition Front (Nicaragua)
FAPU	(Frente de Acción Popular Unificado) United Popular Action Front (El Salvador)
FDR	(Frente Democrático Revolucionario) Democratic Revolutionary Front (El Salvador)
FMLN	(Frente Farabundi Martí para la Liberación Nacional) Farabundo Martí National Liberation Front (El Salvador)
FPL	(Fuerzas Populares de Liberación) Popular Liberation Forces
GAM	(Grupo de Apoyo Mutuo) Mutual Support Group (Guatemala)
ICI	(Instituto Cooperativo Interamericano) Inter-American Cooperative Institute (Panama)
IFCO	Interreligious Foundation for Community Organization
IMF	International Monetary Fund
IPLA	(Instituto Pastoral Latinoamericano) Latin American Pastoral Institute
LASA	Latin American Studies Association
NAFTA	North American Free Trade Agreement
NCC	National Council of Churches
NGO	nongovernmental organization
ORDEN	(Organización Democrática Nacionalista) Democratic Nationalistic Organization (El Salvador)

ABBREVIATIONS

PCN	(Partido de Conciliación Nacional) National Conciliation Party (El Salvador)
PRI	(Partido Revolucionario Institucional) Institutional Revolutionary Party (Mexico)
PT	(Partido dos Trabalhadores) Workers Party (Brazil)
UCA	(Universidad Centroamericana) Central American University (El Salvador)
UDEL	(Unión Democrática de Liberación) Democratic Union for Liberation (Nicaragua)
UN	United Nations
UNO	(Unión Nacional Oppositora) National Opposition Union (Nicaragua)
WOLA	Washington Office on Latin America
WTO	World Trade Organization

I

Hollydale Boyhood

In 1950, the midpoint of the twentieth century, I turned twelve years old. At an idle moment, perhaps as I stared at clouds in the sky, it occurred to me that if I lived to the end of the century I would be sixty-two. I couldn't imagine what being that old would be like, presumably gray-haired and doddering, nor what the world would look like. For Catholics, twelve was the age of "spiritual adulthood," when you received the sacrament of confirmation (seven was the "age of reason," when you made your first confession and communion).

Despite its seeming pivotal placement, 1950 wasn't any more decisive than other years in the late 1940s or early 1950s. President Truman sent troops to Korea to halt communism, assumed to be a monolith controlled by Russia. The pope had also proclaimed it a Holy Year, and Catholics who went to Rome received a plenary indulgence (remission of all temporal punishment in purgatory). My uncle Clark Butterfield returned from Rome with photos and tales of visiting ancient shrines where stone steps had been worn down by countless pilgrims. He also brought rosaries and other items blessed by Pope Pius XII, whom he had seen from the crowd in St. Peter's Square.

* * *

We lived in a town then called Hollydale, located east of the Los Angeles River, surrounded by Downey, Paramount, Lynwood, and South Gate. Our house was typical of the time: wood construction with stucco walls, small by today's standards. Shortly after we moved in on my fourth birthday, Fr. Henry J. McHenry, pastor of Our Lady of the Rosary Parish, came to bless the house. When he had gone around the house, I said, "Father, you forgot something"—and he duly sprinkled holy water into the bathroom.

Housing construction had halted because of World War II, and there were still many empty lots, so you could see several blocks away. My memories of war years are fuzzy and few: my father putting on his air raid warden outfit in the dark and going out to make sure that families were observing the blackout, learning that a young man whom I had seen at the barbershop had been killed in combat, the neighbor woman weeping at the death of President Roosevelt, workers in the factory down the street leaving early the day the war ended.

My father was born Eduardo Berryman in 1915 in Rosario, Sinaloa, on the west coast of Mexico, south of Mazatlan. Rosario had been a mining town since colonial times, so it attracted foreigners with unusual names like Berryman. His father, Felipe Berryman, after whom I was named, ran a general store and was killed in an explosion caused by someone shooting at a rat and hitting dynamite when my father was only a half year old. My grandmother took him to Los Angeles when he was two. There she married Juan Camacho, who had come from Guaymas and who worked for the railroad. My father didn't speak English until he went to school. He grew up on Thirty-Seventh Street near Western and went to Manual Arts High School.

My mother, Katherine Butterfield, was born in Helena, Montana. Both of her parents were divorced and remarried more than once, and we never really got a clear idea of her side of the family. She was moved around as a child and attended many schools, largely in Southern California. She and my father met at a dance and were married in 1937. I was born in 1938, my brother Dennis in 1940, and Alan in 1943. This was our family until the late 1940s, when my sisters Claudia and Jean were born. Tom and Bob were born when I was in my late teens and in the seminary.

* * *

I was enrolled in Grove Avenue Elementary School and graduated from sixth grade in 1949. It was about a mile down Garfield Avenue and we walked back and forth. I was always the shortest and generally the youngest kid in the class. I recall playing kickball and dodgeball; field trips to the Griffith Park planetarium, the *L.A. Times*, and Langendorf Bakery (where I recall seeing and smelling a vat of rising dough); and feeling awkward at birthday parties. My mother went to school meetings and was active in the PTA.

The other students were children of families that had arrived from other states, especially Oklahoma, Arkansas, and the Dakotas, to work in the war manufacturing plants. Since my parents were longtime Californians and we were Catholics, I grew up feeling different from (and prejudiced against) the "Okies" and "Arkies" around us. The closest "Negroes" were a few miles away in Compton. There were some "Mexicans" in our parish, but I thought of them as other than us.

Much of the land in the surrounding areas was still orange groves and dairy farms. We regularly drove to a dairy in Downey where we smelled the cow manure as we bought bottles of milk in a metal crate. Occasionally when winter temperatures reached freezing, our nostrils went black from smoke we inhaled from oil burned in smudge pots in Downey to keep the citrus from freezing.

* * *

We were up shortly after 6 AM on weekdays, eating breakfast with the news on KNX or another L.A. radio station. My father left for work by seven, and my mother stayed home and worked, cleaning house, washing clothes and hanging them on the line, ironing, and working in the yard. The radio was on during the day, from Don McNeil's *Breakfast Club*, through midday soap operas and afternoon variety programs with Arthur Godfrey and Art Linkletter.

My father was a pattern maker, a skilled trade that he had learned at night school, and which was so valued for the war effort that he was deferred from the draft. At the time, however, I had little idea of just what he did. We ate dinner when my father came home, usually around 5 PM. It consisted of some form of meat, vegetables (canned peas or string beans), potatoes, and always dessert (cake, pie, canned fruit). Friday meant fish or macaroni. During grade school we were in bed by 7:30 (even when it was light outside) and listened on the radio to *The Lone Ranger*, *Red Ryder*, and *The Cisco Kid*; detective shows like Sam Spade; or variety programs.

* * *

I don't have strong memories of grammar school, as we called it. I must have been a teacher's favorite, doing schoolwork well and being short. I can't remember the names of most of my teachers, but do remember that Mrs. Smith, who taught fourth grade, was Mormon, and a descendant of Joseph Smith, the Church of Latter-day Saints founder. I can still sing the state song, "I Love You, California," which we learned that year.

The school building was set between a large fenced-in playground that stretched out toward Garfield Avenue and a somewhat smaller area where we could eat lunch under eucalyptus trees swaying in the wind. I usually took lunch in a paper bag (baloney sandwiches on white bread), but occasionally ate from the cafeteria, where we were served Diced Cream, ice cream in single-serving cubes, the latest thing in efficient packaging.

* * *

Since we were in public school, we attended catechism classes Saturday morning. Sometimes Fr. McHenry himself picked us up and drove us there. Teaching us at the church were two nuns in habits; I don't remember what they looked like, but one had a shrill voice. I did well at reciting catechism answers. "Why did God make you?" "God made me to know Him, to love Him, and to serve Him in this world and to be happy with Him in the next." Catechism introduced us to the reality of another world: God, Christ, the Trinity, angels and saints, commandments, sin, grace, and sacraments. I made my first communion at age seven and was confirmed before I was twelve. We went to monthly confession with our parents on Saturday afternoon and attended the Sunday 8 AM Mass—my mother saw going to any later Mass as an indication of some moral failing. She was in the Altar and Rosary Society, and my father in the Holy Name Society. Outside the parish we were surrounded by non-Catholics and were aware that others weren't like us.

Dennis and I were both altar boys, We memorized the Latin that we needed to respond to the priest, starting from the first moment, when the priest said, "Introibo ad altare Dei," and we answered, "Ad Deum qui laetificat juventutem meam." We had to learn when to move the book from the Epistle to the Gospel side (pick it up, carry it down the steps, genuflect, and carry it up to the other side), and when to bring the wine and water, then pour water over the priest's hands at the offertory, and place the gold-plated paten under people's chin at communion time. We walked or rode bikes to church when we were scheduled to serve at daily Mass.

Fr. McHenry was Irish and was almost always in a cassock. I remember one sermon in which he said, speaking of the church, "This is a terrible place!" That was a quote from the introit from the Mass for the dedication of a church: "Terribilis est locus iste!" A more accurate transition would have been that this was a fearsome place; if we really understood God's majesty we would be fearful. It reinforced the general notion that in church we should be respectful and keep silence and that the church meant serious business.

Fr. McHenry sometimes drove a carful of altar boys to the beach. Once Father told us to wait on the sand while he went swimming, and I was amazed that someone I viewed as an old man was such a good swimmer. As we were driving back we heard a radio news story about Henry Wallace, Roosevelt's vice president, who left the Democrats and ran as an independent left-wing candidate in 1948.

* * *

Our family sometimes went on a Sunday drive, such as to North Hollywood to see my father's parents, or occasionally relatives on my mother's side. The freeway system wasn't yet built, so we drove out on major arteries like Firestone/Manchester and Western Boulevards. On the way back my parents might swing through a wealthy part of town, such as the Los Feliz area, to admire the houses and yards. Our cars were Fords, including the 1949 sedan, which had something suggesting a propeller or a bullet in the center of the grille.

We also went on picnics, to places like the San Gabriel Mountains. A couple times we rented a cabin at Lake Gregory and did a bit of fishing with my father; I don't remember catching fish, however. We also went camping on the Merced River and in Yosemite.

For Fourth of July fireworks, we took blankets and went to South Gate Park, which was said to be a mile square. Once we went with my parents to the beach at night to go grunion hunting; grunion are small fish that spawn on the shore and can be picked up by hand.

HOLLYDALE BOYHOOD

* * *

Periodically we were taken to our grandparents, our father's mother and stepfather—Laura and Johnny, we called them for some reason—first to the house where my father grew up, and then after 1945 to a house in North Hollywood, which at the time had few or no other Mexicans. My father spoke Spanish with them. Laura's food was different from my mother's, especially tamales, including some that had raisins.

It was at their house in 1948 that we saw our first TV. Johnny boasted that it was the first in North Hollywood. What I remember is serials, especially one with Red Grange, the former football halfback, old movies, jalopy derby, and test patterns. We didn't get our own TV until around 1952.

We saw less of our other grandparents, even though Grandpa Butterfield lived in South Gate and Grandma Hazelet lived in a trailer park somewhere near Compton. Grandpa Butterfield had worked for the railroad. Around 1910 he had played catcher for a triple-A team in Minneapolis, and said when he was young the game was played barehanded.

Grandpa Butterfield and Grandma Hazelet both died within a year or two of each other around 1950. They were the first people I knew who died. Their funerals, held in mortuaries with a few sentimental Protestant hymns, briefly raised the question of the eternal fate of non-Catholics.

* * *

Late Sunday mornings after breakfast my parents tuned into *Peter Potter's Platter Parade*: the big bands (Dorsey) were still around, as were vocalists like Bing Crosby, Frank Sinatra, Jo Stafford, Peggy Lee, Nat King Cole, Frankie Laine, and the Mills Brothers, and novelty songs like "Open the Door, Richard."

On Sundays at around 1 PM my father often dropped us off at one of the two theaters in Downey, the Victory (nine cents) and the Meralta (twelve cents). They played double bills of non-first-run movies, along with newsreels, cartoons, and previews of coming attractions. We got our fill of detectives and singing cowboys, along with Abbott and Costello, and the Bowery Boys, as well as drama and melodrama. My mother monitored what we saw, no doubt checking the Legion of Decency list published in the archdiocesan weekly paper, which categorized movies into Unobjectionable for All, Unobjectionable for Adults, Objectionable in Part, and Condemned. We often went with the twins across the street, with our parents agreeing on drop-off and pickup. It gave my parents four hours or so of relief.

* * *

Although I have virtually no memories of the war (for people of my generation, "the war" has always meant World War II), my mind was filled with images from war movies: *A March in the Sun, Guadalcanal Diary, They Were Expendable, The Flying Tigers, Twelve O'Clock High,* and many others with the square-jawed types like John Wayne, Robert Taylor, and Gregory Peck, along with some more ordinary-looking types like Van Johnson and William Bendix. We played war in empty lots, throwing dirt clods as grenades. We also spoke and thought of "Japs" as enemies. Newsreels for years showed the ruin of European cities, refugees in camps, and displaced people lining up in the snow to receive food.

For months in 1948–1949, newsreels and the radio carried stories of the Berlin airlift as U.S. planes dropped food by parachute into the Allied section of occupied Berlin to overcome a Soviet blockade. The Russians were now an "enemy" assumed to be intent on world conquest, like the Axis that had just been defeated. In 1949 the USSR set off its own atom bomb. In 1950 *Collier's* magazine, to which we subscribed, portrayed in text and images what an atomic bomb would do to New York City.

My recollection of the late 1940s is of uncertainty, not of prosperity. I overheard my parents discussing strikes, particularly in major industries like coal and steel, but occasionally the possibility of a patternmaker strike. My parents saw things in the light of the still recent Great Depression. Although the economy grew after the war, prosperity and growth didn't feel normal until the mid-1950s.

* * *

Art Linkletter's daily radio show *House Party* had a segment in which children appeared and inevitably said amusing things. In fifth grade, I was one of five kids from Grove Avenue chosen to be guests. Before the show Linkletter and an assistant took us to lunch at the Brown Derby, where they engaged us in conversation, which unbeknownst to us was a quasi-rehearsal. My mother had told me to ask him for tickets for another of his shows, but only after the program itself. I did so at lunch, and they told me to ask him on the air. Now I understood my mother's instructions and was caught between two conflicting orders. When we went on, Linkletter went down the row conversing with us, getting laughs out of the female studio audience. He went past me without bringing up the tickets, so after the next kid, I interrupted, "Mr. Linkletter, my mother has been trying to get tickets to *People Are Funny* for two years now." Laughter from the audience. He said, "Tell her to put a stamp on it next time." More laughter.

* * *

During the summer we walked up the street and along the railway tracks smelling of creosote to Hollydale Park. There we could play pickup softball or workup (which didn't have two sides but you rotated through all positions from right field to pitcher and then joined the hitters until you were out and went back to right field) or participate in activities organized by a counselor, such as crafts (weaving plastic lanyards). An alternative was to go to the schoolyard at Grove Avenue School, which had similar programs. We regularly went swimming in public pools in Downey and South Gate Park.

We also went ice skating at a rink called Iceland in Paramount, which operated year-round, with afternoon and evening sessions. The live organ pumped out waltzes and tunes with strong rhythms, and we went around in free skating. The machine used for smoothing the ice after it had been gouged, the Zamboni, was developed there—named after the family who owned Iceland and were also Our Lady of the Rosary parishioners.

* * *

I used to spend time in our backyard looking up at the sky and watching clouds and planes, especially jets, which were then a novelty. I was fascinated by airplanes, subscribed to *Air Trails* magazine, and made model airplanes from kits. That meant laying out the plans; covering them with wax paper; cutting the parts for the wing, fuselage, or tail from balsa wood; pinning them over the plans and wax paper; attaching them with model airplane glue; letting the glue dry; and then removing the pins. Then the various parts were covered with tissue paper, and the plane itself was assembled. My father sometimes helped, and I also worked with neighbor kids. We took the plane to the school playground and gave the propeller a couple hundred winds and released it, hoping that it would fly evenly. My most ambitious project was a glider with a six-foot wingspan called the Floater. I also made at least one with a motor, which you flew in a circle maneuvering it with a handle connected to guy wires that manipulated the elevator flaps and thus took the plane up and down. My dad was very much involved in this one. It ended with an early crash. For some years I wanted to be a pilot. In fact, I didn't even board a plane until I was in my mid-twenties. With my nearsightedness and short height, I would never have been accepted.

* * *

The reading material in our house was primarily the *Los Angeles Herald*, a Hearst afternoon paper; *Collier's*, a general-interest magazine; some women's magazines; and *Popular Mechanics* and *Popular Science*. With my twenty-five-cents-a-week allowance I was able to buy comics (at ten cents apiece), and favored Captain Marvel over Superman and Batman. I also liked the dog stories of Albert Payson Terhune, and read lives of figures like Kit Carson and Daniel Boone. From the Hollydale Library, at the intersection of Main Street and Garfield, I checked out novels and nonfiction, such as accounts by Arctic explorers. I also discovered science fiction, particularly Ray Bradbury and Robert A. Heinlein, and *The Day of the Triffids*, which was serialized in *Collier's*. It describes a breakdown of civilization in which humans are under threat by mobile, carnivorous plants. (What I didn't realize then was that such fiction drew on unconscious Cold War fears.) From my parents' bookshelf I picked up the Berlitz *Brazilian Portuguese Self-Taught* and began trying to learn it until my father made fun of my pronunciation of *conversação*. In the sixth grade I decided to stop reading the "funny papers," as we called the comic section, and to concentrate on news and sports.

Around 1950 I read a magazine article with color illustrations, predicting that families in the future would all have private helicopters; it seemed like a logical step from having automobiles. Occasional classroom films extolled the wonders of steel, plastics, and soybeans.

* * *

For a year or so around 1950 I had a paper route, delivering the *Huntington Park Daily Signal* in Hollydale. The *Signal* was an afternoon paper that covered some national and international news, and primarily served subscribers in towns and cities southeast of downtown L.A. The paper boss delivered the bundled papers, and I folded them, put them in canvas bags that fit over my handlebars, and rode my route throwing the papers across yards and onto porches. The flight path of folded papers was unpredictable, and you could even "roof" them. Having a paper route also meant having to go each month to collect from customers, and also going out with the paper boss to a neighborhood and solicit subscription "starts," door to door, which I dreaded.

* * *

I was a Cub Scout (and my mother the den leader) and then joined the Boy Scout troop formed at our parish. Our first overnight outing was a hike along the sandy banks of the L.A. River (not yet cemented in) up to the Rio Hondo Scout Camp, where we stayed in open cabins and were supposed to do our own cooking. I read the Boy Scout Manual, absorbed Scouting ideals, subscribed to *Boys' Life*, camped with the troop at the Lake Arrowhead Scout Camp, and earned merit badges, but did not come close to being an Eagle Scout.

In the summer of 1952, after my freshman year in the seminary, our troop hiked the Silver Moccasin Trail, which runs fifty-three miles through the Angeles National Forest above L.A. I was senior patrol leader with around twenty Scouts and two men leaders. We carried dehydrated food, then a novelty. The trail starts in a canyon above Arcadia and rises to pine forest. We were resupplied halfway through where the trail crossed the Angeles Crest Highway. On the last day we went to Mount Baden-Powell (over nine thousand feet high), named after the founder of the Boy Scouts, making our way through patches of snow still around in June and ended in Wrightwood.

Along the way we learned the manly virtues of toughing it out on the trail and moving at the pace of others, like infantrymen in war movies.

* * *

We hung out and played with the twins across the street, who were Dennis's age, a year and a half younger than I. In the summer they returned to South Dakota where they were from, and we heard tales of pheasant hunting. One summer we heard that one had accidentally shot and killed the other. We had never been close to death, let alone one of a playmate. As it happened, at the time of the funeral Dennis and I were scheduled to spend the week in the Boy Scout camp at Lake Arrowhead. We could have been driven down and back, but my parents decided not to do so, perhaps to shield us from dealing with death. I felt a mixture of relief, shame, and guilt.

* * *

For seventh grade I was enrolled in St. Emydius (patron saint of earthquakes) School in Lynwood, about three miles away. Catholic schools were reputed to be more advanced than public schools, and in fact I had to learn some math in order to catch up. What was new was an emphasis on grammar and particularly diagramming sentences, and also a daily religion class. Our teacher in seventh grade was relatively young, with a postulant's habit, and the eighth-grade teacher, Sister Edmund, was of an indeterminate age. In one classroom debate I energetically defended General Douglas MacArthur, whom Truman had removed from his post as commander in Korea, and who didn't go quietly but used his popularity to gain sympathy in Congress and from the public.

* * *

The summer between seventh and eighth grades, some friends and I attended a retreat with the Salesian Fathers at St. John Bosco School in Bellflower. Retreats or missions were common in Catholicism at the time, but primarily for adults, not for twelve-year olds. The Salesians were an Italian congregation founded by St. John Bosco in the late nineteenth century, and they were initially devoted to street kids and education of poorer children. At this retreat, we were encouraged to ask ourselves whether we were called to be priests, and with two others I went to visit the Salesian seminary in Richmond in the Bay Area. The idea of entering the seminary was now taking hold.

How could I, at age twelve, possibly understand what it meant to be a priest? Within the Catholicism of the time, the most important thing in life was to die in the state of grace—that is, with no unconfessed mortal sin. The church had been entrusted with the "keys of the kingdom," and priests were crucial in this scheme: they and only they had the power to say Mass and to forgive sins in the confessional. No doubt I was influenced by the attention I had received from Fr. McHenry at our parish, and one of the priests at St. Emydius. Fr. Walter Martin took Bob Wagner and me sailing in Alamitos Bay.

Thus, by spring of 1951 when our classmates were choosing their high schools, Bob Wagner and I chose the junior seminary.

* * *

Was mine a happy childhood? I have memories of doing enjoyable things, some of which became part of my life, such as reading and outdoor activity, including hiking. We were occasionally spanked, but physical punishment was generally more of a backup threat. I can't complain of family dysfunction: my parents might have disagreements, but they didn't fight. I had buddies down the street and at school, and we did things together, like trying to build a Soap Box Derby car.

However, I don't recall my predominant feeling as a child as one of joy but rather one of worry, with the fear of doing something wrong or of being embarrassed. That was partly due to my short stature and my general feeling of inferiority.

From my parents, especially my mother, I acquired a concern for doing things properly. Her own childhood had been chaotic, at least in her retelling (both parents divorced and remarried, attending a couple dozen schools in different places). In hindsight I realized that she wanted to prevent us from having such a life.

I internalized a sense of the importance of obedience: to my parents, teachers and principals, priests and sisters, police and theater ushers, government officials—a kind of vertical structure going up to the president, the pope, and ultimately God. Life seemed to be a pretty serious business.

* * *

In the early 1950s Hollydale was incorporated into South Gate and ceased to exist as an independent entity. In the late 1950s my parents expanded the house and continued living there until they bought a larger house in the hills of Covina in the early 1970s.

The cluster of stores and businesses around the corner of Garfield and Main changed over time. Freeways destroyed portions of the neighborhood and cut off some streets. The area became Latino, as did large portions of Southern California. There is now a Salvadoran *pupusería* across the street from Our Lady of the Rosary church and school. But the houses in Hollydale look remarkably the same, after seventy years of wear and tear and remodeling. The nominal value of the house where I grew up is now almost a hundred times what it cost my parents (a forty-eight-hundred-dollar loan from Bank of America, which it took them decades to pay off). A juniper tree that

I brought home from school on Arbor Day and planted in our front yard eventually grew to over twenty feet high.

2

Twelve Years a Seminarian

In September 1951, when I and a hundred or so other freshmen entered the seminary in Los Angeles, we had a roadmap of the journey to the Catholic priesthood: six years in the minor seminary and six in the major seminary, covering high school, college, and four years of theology. As we were frequently told, the word "seminary" came from Latin *seminarium* (seedbed): the "precious seed of a vocation" to the priesthood had to be carefully cultivated. Seminaries were closed institutions, usually in the countryside. In high school our uniform was a white shirt, black tie, black (or navy) slacks, shoes, and coat, jacket, or sweater. Starting in college it was a cassock and Roman collar.

Seminary formation combined study, prayer, and recreation. The routine at the minor and major seminaries was quite similar. We were awakened around 5:45 AM, and went to the chapel for morning prayers, meditation, and Mass, followed by breakfast, and then a study period. Morning classes were continuous until noon prayers (Angelus), followed by lunch, a short recreation time, study period, and afternoon classes. From 3 to 5 PM we had recreation, when many of us played intramural sports, pickup games of the sport of the season, or perhaps tennis or handball. The period from 5 to 6 PM was for spiritual reading and prayers, followed by supper, another short recreation period, night prayers, further study, and lights out by ten o'clock. We ate our meals in the refectory (dining room) in silence while a book was read, unless the dean of discipline gave permission to speak. At no time in the day did we have to make any decisions about where we were supposed to be or what we should be doing.

At that time the normal path to the priesthood was through the minor seminary, starting in the ninth grade, as I did. Seminaries as an institution came from the Council of Trent in the sixteenth century, and the model of the minor and major seminary came from France. Although never stated directly, it was taken for granted that minor seminaries were intended to take in candidates for the celibate priesthood before puberty.

From the outset we knew that only a small fraction of those entering would make it all the way to the priesthood; over time most of our classmates dropped out, some after a year or two, and others after six or eight. Throughout the process, in conjunction with our spiritual director, we were supposed to discern whether we truly had a vocation—a calling from God to the priesthood.

* * *

Underlying the whole enterprise of the seminary was a mystique of the Catholic priesthood. The activity of the church—and hence of the Catholic priest—was assumed to be of the utmost consequence. The words of Jesus, "What doth it profit a man if he gain the whole world, yet suffer the loss of his soul?" were understood to refer to dying in the state of mortal sin, and thus being subject to eternal punishment in hell. The "immortal soul" was imagined to be something spiritual, animating the body but separate from it.

Catholics alone had the fullness of the "means of grace"—the sacraments and authentic teaching that were not available to non-Catholics. Individuals outside the church were not necessarily lost; they could be saved if they acted in accord with their conscience. The overall assumption, however, was that anyone's salvation was precarious: Jesus himself contrasted the "narrow gate" of salvation with the "wide gate" that leads to perdition. That was the accepted meaning of the theological adage "Outside the church no salvation."

Buttressing this system was a lively sense that beyond the visible natural world was another realm—supernatural—unseen but real, ultimately more real than the world around us. At our frequent Masses for the dead, with the priest wearing black vestments, we sang the "Dies Irae," the medieval hymn that conjures up the day of wrath when the trumpets will sound, and all creation will stand before God the judge, who will consult the book in which all is written. In our guilt we could only entrust ourselves to Jesus Christ. Each individual was said to have an individual "guardian angel." Angels were understood to be pure spirits (in that sense, closer by nature to God than humans), although they were represented in art as humanlike creatures with wings.

The Catholic Church and its institutions were assumed to have come from Jesus himself; the Last Supper was understood as a kind of "ordination" of the apostles, who then transmitted their episcopal powers in an unbroken chain to the present in what was called "apostolic succession." Especially important was papal succession: Pius XII, who by the 1950s had been pope for over a decade, was a link in a chain going back to St. Peter. Pius was a distant figure, whom we saw in black-and-white photos from Rome raising his bony fingers in blessing. Although according to official teaching the pope spoke infallibly only under very restricted conditions, the mystique of the papacy tended to make him a kind of oracle.

Whatever their own personal peculiarities, individual priests were playing an absolutely essential role in a drama of salvation, in the lives of individuals, and in the world itself. To the ordinary gaze, people going in and out of the confessional, whispering their sins or faults to a priest, might look peculiar; with the eyes of faith, what was at stake was of eternal importance. Although Catholicism sometimes seemed to be narrowly focused on avoiding sin and dying in the state of grace, at its best it held out the ideal of advancing toward holiness, like the saints.

*　*　*

For our first two and a half years, the junior seminary (formally Los Angeles College Junior Seminary) was in a three-story brick building at Third and Detroit Streets, a block from La Brea. The location was a few blocks from the Miracle Mile shopping district on Wilshire Avenue, the La Brea Tar Pits, and CBS Television City, built in the 1950s. Occasionally we could see the "HOLLYWOOD" sign through the haze on a hill to the north. On a holiday some of us walked to see a movie at the Grauman's Chinese Theater on Hollywood Boulevard, but such occasions were rare.

Coming in through the main entrance, you saw a more than life-size St. Peter in black marble, seated with the right hand raised as if in blessing. The hallways on either side were lined with classrooms, ending in one direction with the chapel at a right angle and the refectory in the half-basement below; at the other end was the auditorium, with a basketball court below. The playing field for touch football and softball was blacktop and thus led to scraped knees and elbows. The faculty residence was on the third floor, and the dormitories were converted classrooms with two rows of beds. A total of about ten classrooms was sufficient to accommodate all classes at any given moment, because each of us had the same schedule as our classmates.

Many of the seminarians were day students who arrived by car. Those of us from farther away were boarders. To go home Friday afternoon, I joined others taking the trolley bus down Third Street to downtown L.A. where the Pacific Electric (PE) station was located on Skid Row (Sixth and Main). From there I caught the Santa Ana red car and got off at Garfield Avenue, then trudged home with my battered blue metal suitcase and feeling conspicuous in my black tie and uniform.

With the move to the newly built Queen of Angels Junior Seminary in spring 1954 we all became boarders. It was built adjacent to the San Fernando Mission and in mission-revival style, like many other buildings in Southern California. In contrast to Detroit Street, which occupied less than a city block, we now had several acres for athletic fields. At one side of the complex was a large hall in which the entire student body met to study silently in the morning, the early afternoon, and before bed, under the watchful eye of a priest who monitored us. We slept in twenty-bed dormitories by our class group, overseen by an older student and a priest who was in charge of four dormitories.

The biggest change in the seminary process came with our move to the major seminary, St. John's in Camarillo, in the fall of 1957. Our high school graduation in 1955 was almost a nonevent: an evening in the chapel at San Fernando with our parents in attendance where we received diplomas, knowing that we would be back in the fall for fifth year. When we entered St. John's we were again at the lowest rung, symbolized by our places at the back of the chapel. For the next several years we witnessed the successive transition of fellow seminarians into ordained priests, as our assigned places moved closer to the altar.

St. John's was surrounded by farms and orchards, as befitted seminaries. Camarillo was a small town two miles away, known primarily for the psychiatric hospital—they were still sometimes called "insane asylums"—where people with serious mental illness were confined. (Charlie Parker had been an inmate in the early 1950s for drug addiction.) Because the seminary was roughly the same distance from town in the opposite direction, we frequently heard joking remarks about taking the wrong turn. The Camarillo campus was also in mission-revival style, with large athletic fields down the hill. The entire property was ringed by eucalyptus trees, and some citrus was grown on the grounds.

Rather than dormitories we now had individual rooms, with bed, table and chair, and sink; toilets and showers were still communal, but having one's own room made a great difference.

* * *

We prayed many times a day—starting with morning prayers, meditation, and Mass; a prayer before each class; the Angelus at noon; the rosary in the late afternoon before supper; and then night prayers, followed by the "great silence" during which speaking was prohibited until permission was given at breakfast the next morning. We also had occasional daylong retreats in silence and were given regular talks on the "spiritual life." The aim of all this was to make us prayerful, even "holy."

At the center of our prayer life was the Mass, primarily the daily "low" Mass, spoken quietly in Latin by the priest, which we followed in our missals. Because it was usually the feast day of a saint, and the texts were standardized following a few basic categories (martyr, virgin, confessor), the same few Gospels and other scripture texts were repeated day after day. Special occasions were marked by a high Mass, when we sang one or another of the Gregorian chant Masses. Occasionally we had a solemn Mass, in which a deacon and subdeacon stood with the celebrant and more altar servers were required, the entire action being coordinated by a master of ceremonies, who used a clicker to indicate when we should stand, kneel, or sit.

We were regularly assigned to be altar servers for faculty members when they said their daily Mass alone. We met with them in silence and proceeded to a side altar, answered the Latin prayers, served the wine and water at the offertory, and so forth, observing up close how they pronounced the Latin and how devout they seemed to be.

Some of the religious practices of that era have either disappeared or are far less prominent today, for example, the Benediction of the Blessed Sacrament, which was centered on displaying the eucharistic host under glass at the center of a gold-plated monstrance, with hymns in Latin. At the high point the priest made the sign of the cross over the congregation with the monstrance, and then placed the host back in the tabernacle. One devotional practice was the Forty Hours, which began with a Mass, after which the Eucharist was on display in the church overnight and during which we took turns spending an hour in silent prayer.

The rosary was also central to Catholic devotion at the time, recitation of Hail Marys and Our Fathers while meditating on one of three sets of "mysteries" of Jesus and Mary: joyful (centered on Jesus's birth), sorrowful (his death), and glorious (the resurrection). For each mystery you said an Our Father, ten Hail Marys, and a Glory Be. In saying the rosary, whether aloud in a group or privately, you didn't pay attention to the words you were saying, but were supposed to meditate on the mystery.

Benediction, the rosary, and other such devotions had been rejected by the Protestant Reformation as unscriptural and defended by Catholics in reaction. With the Vatican II reforms, the focus shifted to the liturgy, particularly the Eucharist, and such devotions are now regarded as private and optional, but in the 1950s they were still very much a part of our routine.

Prayer, we understood, wasn't simply repeating formulas or going through the motions: it was the "raising of the heart and mind to God." To what extent participating in constant prayers, however, actually made us prayerful may be questioned.

* * *

Although much emphasis was placed on avoiding sin and obeying the rules, the ultimate ideal was holiness. The Mass each day was usually the celebration of a saint. At noon meals the Roman martyrology, short accounts of martyrs in the early church, was read to us. We learned of the lives of the saints, such as St. Vincent de Paul, the founder of the Vincentians who taught us. He had begun as a conventional priest but devoted himself to the poor, founding hospitals, ransoming galley slaves, and starting a new type of religious order for women. Another figure was St. John Vianney, another Frenchman who devoted himself to hearing confessions. Another figure, not yet canonized, was Fr. Damian, who worked with lepers in Hawaii and eventually contracted leprosy himself.

The ideal was thus even heroic sanctity. However, at the same time we were told that true holiness could be achieved by carrying out one's ordinary duties. The example was St. Therese of Lisieux, the "Little Flower," whose life in a convent was uneventful and who died at an early age but who had achieved great holiness. Holiness meant seeking and doing God's will.

The theology of the time, which found its way into the catechism and in ordinary teaching and preaching, was that in addition to this visible natural order around us was an invisible but real supernatural order of grace that infused our souls. What was most important, the saving of souls, was not accessible to ordinary vision. That kind of dualism was not biblical and it disappeared after Vatican II, but it was still taken for granted in the 1950s.

* * *

With very minor exceptions, we all took the same classes for twelve years. Latin dominated the curriculum of the junior seminary. After grammar and vocabulary in freshman year, we went through Caesar's *Gallic Wars*, then Cicero, and finally Virgil's *Aeneid* in fourth year, and continued with Livy and Horace during the first two years of college. The procedure involved translating a passage for homework, turning it in, going over it in class, learning the new vocabulary and grammar, and moving on to the next passage.

This emphasis on Latin was practical: our philosophy and theology textbooks would be in Latin, and as priests we would be saying Mass and officiating the other sacraments, and praying the breviary, a mandatory hour-long prayer comprising mainly psalms—all in Latin. The Mass we attended daily was in Latin, as were some of our prayers. Each class began as the priest came into the classroom, went on his knees, and said, "Veni Sancte Spiritus" (Come Holy Spirit); we knelt and responded in Latin, alternating with the priest.

Those who entered the seminary after high school had to catch up; if they had taken Latin in a Catholic high school as was then common, that might be easy; otherwise it might take two years of work on Latin. These "specials," as they were called, had had experience in other schools, some in the armed forces or business, and seemed older and worldly wise to those of us in the twelve-year process. One of these specials was my uncle Clark Butterfield, who entered the seminary in his mid-forties after a career as a civilian employee for the Armed Forces and then as a technical writer, and was in the class behind me at St. John's.

Other than Latin, we took the standard high school courses of the time: algebra and geometry; general science, physics, and chemistry; U.S. history and world history; English composition; English and American literature; two years of Spanish; and classes in religion. In junior and senior years we had Greek: a year of grammar and vocabulary and then a year of translating Xenophon's *Anabasis*. Our religion courses were a non-technical presentation of Catholic dogmatic and moral theology. In the last two years of the junior seminary, that is, our first two years of college, we had survey courses in U.S. history, economics, sociology, American and British literature, and English composition. For each class we had a single textbook, often by a Catholic author—for example, literature surveys edited by Roy Deferrari, whose field was Latin but who was prominent in various fields of Catholic education. That reflected the defensive attitude of Catholics at the time, as a minority in a predominantly Protestant culture.

We had a regular round of written homework assignments, in-class quizzes, and exams. Only very occasionally were we assigned term papers, and then the emphasis was on the mechanics: take notes on index cards, organize the material, make citations properly; we acquired no sense of research itself, of posing a question and pursuing it. Although we received report cards, little emphasis was placed on grades, and hence the atmosphere was noncompetitive.

The curriculum was a form of liberal arts education, but it was all predetermined; we had no electives. We were not going to be scholars but parish priests, and thus the overall atmosphere was not intellectual, even anti-intellectual.

* * *

Our teachers in both seminaries were Vincentians, a religious congregation founded by St. Vincent de Paul in France in the seventeenth century, that specialized in running seminaries. These profs were generalists: Fr. Donald McNeil taught geometry and Greek; Fr. Thomas McIntyre taught a general science course to high school freshmen and an introductory economics course to college freshmen (using a very early edition of Samuelson, with which he disagreed); Fr. Bernard McCoy taught U.S. and world history in high school, and U.S. history in college, as well as an introductory sociology course. Any of the profs could teach a religion course.

The most memorable Vincentian in the junior seminary was Charles Barr—"Charlie" among ourselves—who taught Spanish. He had a sharp features, eyelids closed to a squint, and a shock of black hair, and he strode into the room and around the class with vigorous jerky movements. He kept the class on edge, for example, suddenly pivoting toward a particular student and saying, "*Tener* preterit, six forms!" The correct response was *yo tuve, tu tuviste, el/ella tuvo, nosotros tuvimos, vosotros tuvisteis, ellos tuvieron* (I had, you had, he/she/it had, and so forth). We thought he was crazy, but by being unpredictable he forced us to pay attention. Some of us enjoyed him, but he generated anxiety in others. More mechanically minded than most priests, Fr. Barr operated his own ham radio and did repair work on his car. He also taught drivers' education and first aid, illustrating both with stories from his own experiences.

A favorite of mine was the soft-spoken and bald Fr. William Ready (pronounced "reedie"), who taught English composition and literature. Perhaps because of his gentle manner and smile, even those who weren't especially interested in literature respected and liked Ready. He communicated his enjoyment of both classic and contemporary literature, and I found his responses to my writing assignments encouraging. The ruddy-faced and prematurely gray-haired Fr. Edward Virgits taught us Latin; Fr. Edward Brennan, algebra and geometry; and the somewhat sheepish Fr. Arthur Daspit, Latin and religion.

The priests lived in the same building as we did, albeit in separate quarters that we never entered. Seminary life enabled us to see examples of Catholic priests, some only a dozen years older than we were, without the barriers then existing between most priests and laypeople.

* * *

The third element in the seminary routine, alongside study and prayer, was recreation. The longest period was from three to five in the afternoon, when many of us played sports. Other designated recreation periods were after breakfast, lunch, and supper, varying between a half hour and an hour.

We played intramural team sports in season: touch football in the fall, basketball in winter, and softball in spring. That meant putting on sneakers, old pants, and T-shirt or sweatshirt, and getting to the field, playing, showering, and getting dressed in two hours. Our only uniforms were occasionally different-colored jerseys to distinguish one team from another. Since we were in Southern California, we could play outdoors all year.

In my first year or two I weighed less than a hundred pounds and was neither fast nor tricky, so I wasn't an asset to any team. Nevertheless the seminary ethos meant that I could play on intramural teams and would be placed where I could do least harm, on the line in football and right field in softball. If there was a B league, that's where I was.

We also played handball in either singles or doubles, barehandedly hitting a pink rubber ball the size of a tennis ball, played against walls with rules like those of racquetball. In San Fernando and Camarillo we had tennis courts and outdoor swimming pools. One year a few of us formed a polar bear club and swam until the water was so cold it made our heads ache.

My most pleasant memories aren't of leagues but of pickup basketball or even just shooting baskets and enjoying the sound of a swish. This was before players could dunk (not that I could have); the jump shot was relatively new, and a hook shot was common.

Those who didn't play sports could go to the recreation room where there were chairs and couches, pool and table tennis tables, and dominoes. Playing cards were prohibited, but some managed to play bridge using dominoes. Seminary culture divided to some extent along a line between athletes and nonathletes (e.g., opera fans). Smoking was permitted in the rec room and was common. We generally congregated in the rec room after supper.

Another form of recreation, especially after meals, was to walk around the grounds in groups of several seminarians. It's now hard to recall what we talked about in those groups, but it was partly kidding each other and perhaps about classes and profs. In principle we could join any group, but when we were at the low end of the six-year cycle we were careful not to intrude on our elders.

* * *

An obvious purpose of the seminary was to prepare us for a lifetime of celibacy: we were in an all-male society rehearsing for a life as Catholic clergy. Yet sexuality wasn't dealt with directly; it was not a topic in talks by the spiritual director, and we didn't talk about it among ourselves, except perhaps as implied in a passing joke.

In principle, our situation wasn't very different from that of unmarried lay Catholics, who were expected to avoid not only sexual intercourse but any form of sexual arousal, which if consented to was a mortal sin. During the 1950s, characterizing single people as "sexually active" would have sounded bizarre, certainly to Catholics but to many other Americans as well.

The San Fernando seminary had acquired from Spain a reredos, a large gilded background piece behind the altar. For many weeks a young woman in work overalls was painstakingly restoring it with a small brush. She never betrayed any sign that she was aware that her presence was a distraction for the eyes of adolescents praying the noon Angelus.

If sex itself was a distant rumor, homosexuality was even more so and was never discussed directly. Since childhood I had heard "queer" hurled as an epithet, but I would not have been able to explain to anyone what it meant: the notion of sexual acts between men would have been inconceivable. However, we were warned not to have "particular friendships," which was not really defined but meant a relationship between two of us that would be exclusive. Insofar as we dealt with sexuality it was likely to be in the confessional, where we might confess "impure thoughts," which unless they were consented to were merely "temptations." We were supposed to practice modesty, for example, wearing a bathrobe in the dormitory when changing in and out of pajamas.

Readers familiar with the sex-abuse scandals of the Catholic Church that have now been public for decades may find my portrayal here difficult to believe. If anything is now known about Roman Catholicism it is that a significant number of priests were sexual predators for decades; surely I would have observed signs of predatory behavior or perhaps of gay relationships. However, in all honesty I never saw such signs, and I was entirely taken by surprise at the first journalistic accounts of it in the 1980s and 1990s. That is equally true of my seminary contemporaries, whether they persevered to ordination or not.

Part of the reason must be the cultural impact of the sexual revolution. Until that moment, sex and sexual activity were private matters that entered into public discourse only obliquely. Here I am trying to convey what seminary life was like, but I am aware that what I say will sound unconvincing to those who came of age after the 1960s.

* * *

Both seminaries had a priest who served as dean of discipline. We had to get permission from him particularly for leaving the seminary grounds. More generally he enforced "the rule," which wasn't so much a document but the seminary routine itself. For example, we could not talk between night prayers and breakfast the following morning—the Magnum Silentium (Great Silence), as it was called. Visiting one another in our rooms was prohibited; our socializing was done in the rec room or out walking.

Above and beyond particular rules was a mystique of obedience. "Keep the rule and the rule will keep you" was one maxim we heard; we were also told that we couldn't go wrong obeying. The overall effect was to instill in us deference toward authority, both immediate and more distant. To obey authority was to obey God.

* * *

In high school I discovered the Modern Library, the series of cheap hardcover books ($1.25 and $2.50). The first two I bought were Dickens's *Pickwick Papers* and the writings of Thomas Jefferson. They and even cheaper Mentor paperbacks (thirty-five to seventy-five cents) made classic and modern literature (Hemingway, Eugene O'Neill, J. D. Salinger, and Graham Greene, as well as Tolstoy and Dostoyevsky) available.

One Friday afternoon while going home on the PE red car and reading *The Brothers Karamazov*, I came to the "Tale of the Grand Inquisitor." Jesus returns to earth and is arrested and brought before a cardinal who is an inquisitor. He lectures Jesus to the effect that the church has suppressed his message because ordinary people are unable to bear it, and has instead given them a religion within their reach. It is a critique of Catholicism, but really of institutionalized religion as a whole. It was momentarily frightening to find my seminary bubble punctured by literature. A similar experience occurred one day when some of us were in Pershing Square in downtown L.A. where orators could mount a box and address anyone who would listen. One speaker who was questioning the truth of Christianity seemed to have a better knowledge of ancient texts at that point than I did.

When I was home, I assiduously watched the Sunday afternoon CBS TV program *Omnibus*—"something for everyone," as the host Alistair Cooke explained: classic and contemporary plays, music, film. *Omnibus* dissolved boundaries between highbrow and popular culture, for example, with a film on the Watts Towers, which had been built by an Italian immigrant working alone over many years, which I had seen from a car window but never thought about.

* * *

Each day we had twenty minutes of spiritual reading in the late afternoon. In high school I read Thomas Merton's *The Seven Storey Mountain*, a memoir of his early life as a student and bon vivant, his conversion to Catholicism, and his decision to enter the Trappists, a religious order that observed complete silence. I then read *Seeds of Contemplation* and some of Merton's poetry.

Also in high school I bought a New Testament. This sounds unremarkable now, but at that time personal Bible reading was not common among Catholics. The catechism, the missal, and prayer books were deemed sufficient; personal Bible reading smacked of Protestantism. Catholic Bibles at the time were not translated from the original Hebrew and Greek but from St. Jerome's fourth-century Latin translation. I felt that reading the Gospels gave me direct contact with Jesus's words.

While still in the junior seminary I read Romano Guardini, *The Lord*, a series of reflections on the life of Jesus, and Henri DeLubac, S.J., *The Splendor of the Church*, meditations by the French theologian and historian. Both were addressed to nontheologians and were free of the narrowness common in conventional Catholicism at the time. They opened to readers the possibility of seeing beauty—splendor—in living the Christian faith in the church. Few readers were aware that DeLubac was under a cloud of suspicion from Rome. I also got some sense of postwar French Catholicism through a collection of writings of Cardinal Emmanuel Suhard of Paris. They proposed that France had been "de-Christianized" and that the church needed to see itself as in a missionary situation. On the surface that seemed to be far from the situation of Catholicism in Southern California, where new churches and schools were constantly being built for an expanding population, but at a deeper level it said something valid. Another source of an alternate vision of Catholicism was the monthly magazine *Jubilee*, which had fine black-and-white photography and ran articles and stories about liturgical art, Vietnam, artists like Georges Rouault, the Eastern rite churches, the Desert Fathers, and pieces by Thomas Merton, who was a longtime friend of the editors.

* * *

Music played a significant role in seminary life and for me personally. We used the *St. Gregory Hymnal* edited by Nicola A. Montani, an important figure in U.S. Catholic Church music in the first half of the twentieth century. Catholic musicians were then trying to weed out some of the more overwrought hymns of the nineteenth century, such as "Mother Dear Oh Pray for Me," a song to the Virgin with a waltz beat and trite rhymes. Montani and others were seeking to restore Gregorian chant to more common use, but generally with organ accompaniment which undercuts its character as a cappella and nonmetered music. Fr. John Cremins, a good-natured diocesan priest, came to the seminary to teach us classes and direct the polyphonic choir, in which I sang second tenor, and bass after my voice changed.

In high school I educated myself in the principles of music by reading books like Aaron Copland's *What to Listen For in Music*. That made me aware of rhythm, melody, harmony, and timbre, and especially musical form, such as "sonata form," as found in the first movement of symphonies, concertos, string quartets, and similar large works: the exposition of two contrasting themes, a development section in which they are explored through various permutations in different keys, and a recapitulation in the original key. In one of his *Omnibus* presentations, Leonard Bernstein analyzed the first movement of Beethoven's Fifth Symphony, using portions of the composer's notebooks and outtakes to shed light on the piece as we know it.

At the time classical audiences were still resistant to twentieth-century music, including Stravinsky, Prokofiev, Bartok, and Hindemith, and especially the twelve-tone or serial music of Schoenberg and Webern. The latter seemed to be a logical progression beyond late-Romantic chromaticism, but I found it difficult to discern the twelve-tone rows, perhaps because they were very hard for nontrained musicians to sing or even hear. While at home I listened to KFAC and occasionally went to chamber music concerts.

In another *Omnibus* lecture, Bernstein opened up what jazz was about, particularly showing the twelve-bar harmonic pattern of the blues, moving from the tonic (do), to the subdominant (fa), to the dominant (sol), and back to the tonic. He also pointed out that it was in iambic pentameter, and thus lines from Shakespeare could be turned into blues. Both classical music and jazz require active listening—to the form of the movement in classical music, and to melodic and harmonic improvisation in jazz.

In the mid-1950s I was in thrall to Bernstein, composer, conductor, pianist, educator, celebrity. He had moved beyond his boy-genius phase and had written symphonies and ballets with a brassy American sound. I shared the hope that he might write works that would enter the standard repertoire and place him in the company of acknowledged masters.

* * *

Going off to the seminary at age thirteen changed my relationships with my family. Although I came home weekends in high school and was around the house in the summer, I was already halfway out of the family. As my sisters Claudia and Jean grew up, they saw me as the older brother who came and went. My brothers Tom and Bob were born in 1957 and 1958 around the time when I moved from the junior to the major seminary. My summer activities also took me away from the family.

And yet I certainly wasn't fully grown up. I was still in school, and the money I earned was only enough for some expenses, so I was dependent on my parents. When at home I attended Sunday Mass with the family. I eventually got my driver's license, so that I could drive my father's pickup around Southern California, if it was available.

Around 1958 my father, who had been working in patternmaking shops since the war, opened his own shop. I came to appreciate how high-skilled my father's trade was. A patternmaker received blueprints from a foundry, typically for a part of an aircraft, from which he made a very exact model in wood, often with tolerances within thousandths of an inch. At the foundry, a core box of wet sand would be closed around that model, creating a reverse impression, which was then filled with molten metal, thereby leaving an exact replica. My father worked under tight constraints: each job was one of a kind, and he was in competition with other patternmaking shops. Over the years, wood patternmaking gave way to plastics, and more recently to computerized processes. Although I could appreciate his work, I didn't absorb much from him, at least at that time.

We still did some activities as a family, such as visiting my grandparents or other relatives, or going camping. For my fourteenth birthday my father took Dennis and me to climb Mount Whitney. I was surprised at how strong a hiker my father was.

* * *

In the seminary we didn't get the daily newspapers, except the sports page and perhaps a clipping of major news events, nor did we have regular television. The unstated reason for our seclusion seemed to be that we were to be focused not on the things of the world but on God. We were allowed to watch Bishop Fulton Sheen's Tuesday night program *Life Is Worth Living*, which earned surprisingly good ratings, even though it was vying with the very popular *Milton Berle Show*. Sheen looked at the camera with magnetic deep-set eyes in full episcopal attire and typically countered the errors of communism and secular philosophies with the truth of Catholicism.

The political events of the day largely passed us by. I recall watching the 1952 and 1956 Democratic National Conventions, which nominated Adlai Stevenson, while I was home for the summer. I don't recall any critical voices being raised about Senator Joseph McCarthy's witch hunts. That may be because McCarthy had intimidated many, including President Eisenhower, and he enjoyed passive support for a long time, notably among Catholics, as evident in the L.A. archdiocesan weekly paper *The Tidings*. His downfall occurred when after weeks of televised hearings he was finally challenged by the army's attorney, "Have you no sense of decency, sir?" What is now called McCarthyism was a nonissue in the seminary.

* * *

Each summer we had to decide what to do with three months of vacation. Besides keeping up with some practices, such as daily Mass, most of us found some work. Some got jobs in companies, some were hired by their pastor to work in the parish. In high school I worked in the kitchen at St. Francis Hospital in Lynwood, where two friendly Franciscan sisters hired seminarians. I also worked there on Saturdays during the school year.

I worked four summers at the archdiocesan summer camps. About half the counselors were seminarians, and so in some ways summer camp was a variation on the schedule and all-male camaraderie of the seminary. As counselors we were responsible for a group of boys in our tent and also for a particular program, in my case boating. That meant overseeing kids getting on rowboats and canoes and also repairing and painting them. I worked under Bill DuBay, three years ahead of me. We had long conversations, and from him I learned boat maintenance, such as repairing holes in canoes with fiberglass. In my third year I was in charge. At Camp St. Vincent de Paul in the San Fernando Valley, I was in charge of the camp store and running errands in the camp pickup.

Once at midday, late in the season while down at Jackson Lake, we saw smoke rising from over the hill. We hurried back to the camp and joined other counselors as we ran toward the forest fire with shovels in our hands, in my case still in swimming trunks. We tried to put out small flames by shoveling dirt on them; at one point we were being surrounded by flame and smoke and had to flee uphill. We then recognized the folly of what we were doing. Professional firefighters arrived, and the fire, which was largely in the brush area adjoining pine forests, lasted several days. We observed planes swooping in and dropping water. Zuni firefighters fought it for about a week.

I had imbibed a kind of psychology of "inside" and "outside," the "church" and the "world," the latter being a place of danger and temptation, and I obviously opted for safe seminary-like places to work. After St. Francis they were away from home, and in some case with fellow seminarians. I didn't get any inside experience in any industry or business. My reluctance to put myself in unfamiliar situations was reinforced by my shyness.

* * *

I spent the summer of 1958 with Fr. John Coffield at Dolores Mission, a parish that in recent years has drawn attention through the work of the Jesuits and particularly Fr. Greg Boyle with gang members ("homies"). The neighborhood, then known as "the Flats," lies below Boyle Heights and East L.A., bounded by First and Fourth Streets, the 101 Freeway, and some small factories adjacent to the L.A. River.

As a young priest, Coffield had gotten into trouble for liturgical innovations, and had then served for a dozen years in El Monte, where he worked with poor Spanish-speaking people. He was a chaplain for the Young Christian Workers and the Young Christian Students, movements that encouraged young laypeople to act on their own, which were suspect in Los Angeles and were then suppressed by Cardinal James Francis McIntyre.

I arrived on a Friday in June, the first day of the three-day parish fiesta or *feria*, a fund-raising event with food, music, raffle tickets, rides, and games. Coffield greeted me with a boisterous "Howya doin', buddy?" and I was handed the keys to a rattletrap panel truck and a list of addresses of *tortillerías* in East L.A. My task was to pick up packs of corn tortillas that had been promised to the *feria*. I didn't know my way around the area, and I'd never been to a tortillería. As I found out, tortellerías were small, hot, and noisy with the clanging of the machines. Somehow I managed to find them, communicate with my neophyte Spanish, and get the tortillas back to the parish. What sticks in my mind after all these decades was that act of handing me the keys and trusting me to fulfill that task; in the seminary we simply had to follow the rules and the routine.

The residents of the area were Mexicans or Mexican Americans and blacks, as well as descendants of Armenians and Russians who had settled the area in the early twentieth century. Four seminarians had come from Maryknoll in New York, and one or two more from our seminary. Our work was with children in the summer program. We also did parish census—knocking on doors inquiring if any people were Catholics, using five-by-eight cards to fill out information and register households. This was a common pastoral practice of outreach at the time, particularly relevant in Southern California, with people continually arriving and moving. Once a man in a gypsy (today, Roma) family invited me to dance with him to the loud music coming from the phonograph. "What's the matter, don't you like to dance?"

For supper we went a few blocks away to the house of a parishioner, whom we called "Tia" (aunt). The food was Mexican, and we spoke Spanish. We went downtown a couple times with one of her daughters to see Mexican movies, such as *Nosotros los Pobres*, with Pedro Infante, already a tragic heartthrob, after dying in a crash of a plane he was piloting. We were getting a glimpse of Mexican family life, although we of course were always the *seminaristas*.

The most important aspect of the experience was simply being with Coffield, seeing him say daily Mass or deal with parishioners. In the mornings he was often taking a course at a local college or university, in psychology or sociology, which was highly unusual for a diocesan priest. He also had interesting friends, such as artists or community organizers; moreover, he was a magnet for people with emotional problems. Perhaps as a result of his psychological training, Coffield was nondirective with us when we went to him for confession or counseling. Coffield was treating me as an adult, in contrast to the extended adolescence of seminary life.

That fall at a seminary retreat day, I concluded that I had to take charge of my own education. What we were getting in class wasn't adequate, and I would have to educate myself independently through reading and with my fellow seminarians. That decision was a result of the sense of responsibility that I took away from the summer with Coffield.

* * *

With the move to St. John's in Camarillo we had two years of philosophy, our assigned (not chosen) "major." The subject was taught by Fr. Patrick O'Brien from Latin manuals, starting with logic and epistemology, followed by ontology (study of being), cosmology (material reality), rational psychology (human beings), and ethics. The whole scheme assumed a logic: establish the premises and everything else follows. Although this was presented as Thomistic philosophy, we never read Aquinas. It was really contrary to the spirit of Aquinas, whose works are organized around questions, in which he discusses both sides and is always respectful even of those who hold contrary views.

The classic philosophers, including Aquinas, seek to introduce their students and readers into questions: at the outset of the *Metaphysics*, Aristotle says that philosophy begins with wonder. Seminary philosophy was largely a word game that entailed learning terminology thirdhand. Such spoon-fed orthodoxy codified in manuals would become even worse in theology.

The history of philosophy as taught by Fr. Bernhard DeVries was somewhat better. Although we used only a textbook, DeVries at least treated classic philosophers with respect and sought to provide context for their work. Doing a term paper on the American philosopher Charles Sanders Peirce helped me overcome suspicion of non-Catholic thinkers. Fortunately, the St. John's library had much to occupy me, including contemporary Thomists like Jacques Maritain and Etienne Gilson, but also Gabriel Marcel, classified as a Catholic existentialist, and Emmanuel Mounier, whose philosophy was personalist.

Our four years of college, split between the junior and major seminary, were accredited by the Association of Western Colleges. Delegations from the association occasionally visited the San Fernando and Camarillo seminaries, but we had little idea of what they inspected. In hindsight I imagine that the seminary must have resembled a fundamentalist Bible college, except that our bible was our Latin philosophy manuals.

* * *

Confined to the seminary I spent time in the library reading periodicals like *America*, *Commonweal*, and the *Saturday Review of Literature*, and conservative magazines like the *National Review*. At the time there was considerable interest in fiction by Catholics, such as Graham Greene and J. F. Powers. I worked my way through James Joyce, starting with *Dubliners* and *Portrait of the Artist as a Young Man*, eventually reaching *Ulysses*, which I read with the assistance of the guide by Stuart Gilbert, which indicated the layers of the structure, chapter by chapter. I also read Hemingway, Fitzgerald, Thomas Wolfe, and the young John Updike, including *Rabbit, Run*, and the Beats and Kerouac's *On the Road*.

The *Saturday Review* made me aware of art films—as opposed to Hollywood movies—and particularly the auteur approach to film criticism. Federico Fellini's *La Dolce Vita* was understood to be a critique of decadent celebrities and wealthy people. The Marcello Mastroianni character is torn between the empty life of partying and a serious life as a writer—while having his choice of attractive women. It was a glimpse into a world far removed from that of the seminary. Ingmar Bergman's *The Virgin Spring*, a legend set in medieval Sweden, was shocking for the rape and murder of a young girl at the heart of the plot. Toward the end, the girl's father looks heavenward and tells God, "I don't understand you."

At an art house theater in west L.A. I saw *The Naked Island*, said to be a tribute to the peasant parents of the director, Kaneto Shindo. The black-and-white film opened with a husband and wife carrying water to a boat in silence in the dark. The viewer eventually realizes that they are carrying it from the mainland to an island where they live. At one point the woman stumbles, spills the precious water, and is slapped to the ground by her husband. The story continues with little or no dialogue through a full day of their work, and then through the seasons for a full year, including the death of one of their two sons. The story was somewhat contrived: farming would be impossible if you had to haul all your water as portrayed in the film. But it remains a significant film portraying the hardship and dignity of subsistence farmers.

* * *

Growing up in Southern California, I thought "back east" started in Arizona. People in New York and New Jersey spoke an exotic form of English—at least in the movies. In 1959 I finally got a chance to see the rest of the country, first driving with my uncle Clark and other seminarians to Notre Dame for the Liturgical Conference, and then to Detroit to the house of my uncle Willis. From there I took an overnight Greyhound bus to New York, where I rendezvoused with my classmate Gerry Fallon on the steps of St. Patrick's Cathedral, and we began a round of taking the subway to places we had only seen in movies. We realized that with the money we had, we couldn't afford to eat at restaurants, so we snacked out of grocery stores and used our scarce cash to see the city.

The first night we went to Birdland, where we saw and heard a young and little-known Ramsey Lewis, who began with "The Way You Look Tonight," and a group led by the drummer Buddy Rich. Another night, while in a drugstore in Greenwich Village, I was startled and frightened to see what seemed to be two or three men with makeup and women's clothes. I had no framework for understanding it; this was a decade before Stonewall.

Our first afternoon we had taken a subway and gotten off arbitrarily at 125th Street and Lenox Avenue, unaware that it was the heart of Harlem, which we realized only when we had walked a few blocks and seen no other white people. Early one morning we walked over the Brooklyn Bridge and then went to see the Stock Exchange. We then went to Christie Street, the address of the Catholic Worker and went in. Unsure of what to do—say we're seminarians from California and want to meet Dorothy Day?—we sheepishly made our way out. At the Museum of Modern Art we saw Picasso's *Guernica* and the photo exhibition of *The Family of Man*, portraying people around the world in similar situations from birth to death.

Short of money for return bus fare, we found a car-delivery business in lower Manhattan and convinced the skeptical proprietor that we were reliable drivers. We were assigned a year-old red Oldsmobile convertible that we had a week to deliver to a serviceman in Monterey, California. We drove across New York state on a Thursday afternoon; spent a couple days in Erie, Pennsylvania, attending the wedding of a cousin of Gerry's; and continued driving across Route 30 (construction of the interstate system was barely under way) day and night. Somewhere in Nevada where you can see thirty miles ahead on the road, I pushed the accelerator until the speedometer read 105. We delivered the car and took a Greyhound back to L.A. It was a seminarians' *On the Road*—no drugs, no sex, but a red convertible and a full tank of gas.

* * *

In the fall of 1959 we began our studies of theology (dogmatic theology, moral theology, patristics, church history, canon law), which should have been the crown of a seminary education. Dogma was organized around various Latin treatises: in the first year, revelation and the church, that is, God has revealed supernatural truth and entrusted it to the church. There followed several tracts on traditional theological topics—the One God, Triune God, incarnation, redemption, grace, eschatology (judgment, heaven, hell)—which were taught in a two-year cycle, so that we were with the class immediately above or below us. The fourth year was devoted to the sacraments. Moral theology was organized similarly: a Latin manual, a first year on general principles, and the second and third years on various categories of sin, organized around the Ten Commandments and intended to prepare us to hear confessions.

Dogmatic theology was structured around propositions or statements of formally defined Catholic doctrine, for example, that Jesus had both a divine and a human nature, or that in the Eucharist bread and wine become the body and blood of Jesus through transubstantiation. For each proposition the manual presented errors and heresies, and then citations from scripture, council definitions, and quotations from the church fathers and theologians to prove the official teaching. It was entirely based on authority. At the beginning of each year, we were all assembled to witness our professors take the Vatican-imposed Oath Against Modernism, an alleged heresy from the early twentieth century.

Although the manuals sometimes cited scripture they were utterly unbiblical: individual verses were quoted out of context to prove defined dogma. Theology was presented as a set of timeless truths, with no sense of the process by which the doctrines had emerged. Normally four years of postcollege study ought to lead to an advanced degree or professional accreditation, but what we were taught was a giant Latin catechism, not graduate-level work.

My classmates generally accepted the situation, or endured it as necessary in order to become priests, and were turned off by what was presented as theology. Some of us, however, were aware of other currents of theology, particularly in northern Europe, although those currents were suspect in Rome and certainly in Los Angeles.

Two large works, Matthias Scheeben's *The Mysteries of Christianity*, written in the nineteenth century, and Emile Mersch's *The Theology of the Mystical Body*, after World War I, were especially inspiring. Neither questioned official teaching; instead they focused on connections between one mystery and another (incarnation and grace), and they revealed aspects of beauty—the "splendor" I had read about in Henri de Lubac.

In the second year of theology I taught myself to read theological French and German, using the method followed by a seminarian a few years older who had been sent for studies in Rome: get a book you want to read, plus a dictionary and grammar, and start on page one. At first you're looking up every noun and verb, but you begin to build up a vocabulary and by the middle of the book you can read whole pages: academic language is repetitious and is actually easier to learn to read than literature or colloquial speech. Working twenty minutes a day after breakfast I learned to read French in the fall and German in the spring.

Two Jesuits, the German Karl Rahner and the Canadian Bernard Lonergan, were crucially important. The first English translations of Rahner began to appear in 1960. Around 1962, I read his seminal philosophical work *Geist im Welt* (Spirit in the World). After an introductory section analyzing a passage in Aquinas, Rahner begins his exposition with a three-word sentence: *Der Mensch fragt* (Humans question). That laconic statement was a thunderclap. The official theology we were being taught was an endless drill of *answers* based on official church teaching. Here was a theologian, very rooted in Catholic tradition, who was making human questioning the basis of his philosophy and theology. His short book *Encounters with Silence* was a series of prayers that revealed him to be someone who shared in the uncertainties and perplexities of life.

Like Rahner, Lonergan made human knowing the starting point for his philosophy and theology, which were rooted in Aquinas but also in the contemporary world. His book *Insight: An Inquiry into Human Understanding* (1957) starts with the common human experience of coming to an insight and leads the reader through various examples in mathematics, physics, and everyday life. Human knowledge is constantly expanding; just view the books in a large library, with thousands of new ones coming every year. How does it all fit together? Lonergan's answer isn't some grand scheme like a giant encyclopedia but rather the inquiring human mind. By becoming explicitly aware of how we gather data, seek insights, and make judgments in different realms, we come to what he called "self-appropriation" as knowers. That was a powerful help to me and has remained so.

Some of us went underground intellectually. We dutifully studied our Latin texts, recited in class, and passed exams, while devoting our real energies to becoming familiar with the theological ferment elsewhere in the Catholic world. In dogma class I occasionally used questions as a way of undermining some of the teaching, but I calibrated my questions so as not to overantagonize Fr. Kenneally, who was the rector and had the power to decide whether we stayed in the seminary.

* * *

Our professors in the major seminary weren't scholars; they were teachers who followed the text. The one exception was Newman Eberhardt, C.M., the clacking of whose manual typewriter echoed down the hall from his room at the end of one of the residence wings. He gave magisterial lectures through five semesters of church history and two of patristics (early church fathers). He published his two-volume church history in the 1960s. Even those who had little taste for history appreciated Eberhardt's dedication. He described dramatic moments, such as arrival of papal legates in Constantinople, or Emperor Henry VI being forced to stand barefoot in the snow by Pope Gregory VII in the investiture conflict. In preparing for examinations, I compiled and memorized chronologies in order to put them in blue books. My own lifelong pursuit of history owes something to Eberhardt.

Decades later I realized that our church history course was a kind of apologetics, whose unspoken agenda was to demonstrate that whatever the failings of individual Catholics, including popes, the church itself had never erred in teaching faith and morals. However, even as Eberhardt was writing, that kind of church-history-as-apologetics was going out of fashion, as scholars took a more open and ecumenical approach.

Another Vincentian who was important to me was Charles Miller, who taught biology, public speaking, and preaching. On weekends he was active as a chaplain to laypeople in the Christian Family Movement. Once in class he presented some of his reflections on the Trinity and other aspects of Christianity, filling the blackboard with schematic diagrams. Whatever the merits of his ideas, he was actively raising theological questions rather than treating theology as a set of answers. In one private session with me he drew my attention to a flippant remark I had made in a blue book and forced me to pay attention to the attitude behind it.

Two Dutch Vincentians were decidedly different from the others. Bernhard DeVries, who taught history of philosophy, was slow and deliberate in speaking English. Andrew Willemsen spoke rapid-fire in teaching canon law and sacramental theology. Both were no doubt aware of progressive tendencies in Holland and elsewhere in Europe, but were cautious in the atmosphere of Camarillo and the Los Angeles archdiocese.

* * *

At Camarillo a new element was added to the seminary routine mentioned earlier (study, prayer, and recreation): work. Saturdays after lunch we had a designated period during which all of us were expected to be doing some sort of job, generally for no more than two hours. Lowerclassmen cleaned toilets, washed windows, and swept or mopped floors. In my early years I worked in the bookstore, which also entailed being open for sales on weekday evenings. Some were assigned to drive to town for particular errands; some cut other students' hair. Thus, the element of work in the seminary was a token amount.

My job was as music director for our next-to-last year. Normally that job would be assigned to someone who played piano or organ, but our class didn't have anyone. On a December night after the polyphonic choir had been caroling all day in hospitals and residences for the elderly, someone proposed we sing "Sleigh Ride" for fun. When the director was unwilling, I stepped forward and beat time, pretending to direct a piece that we now knew by heart. I was then picked as a kind of understudy to Brad Dusak and Peter Nugent, the student directors at that time.

As music director I led Gregorian chant at Sunday solemn Mass and vespers as well as other special occasions. For chant we had a three-inch thick book called the *Liber Usualis* (Usual book) published in Belgium, which had Gregorian notation (squares and diamonds on a different kind of staff without bar lines, because chant follows the Latin words and isn't metered). In the chapel we sat in wooden choir stalls, facing each other, as in a monastery. Directing polyphonic music, both in worship and Christmas caroling, meant looking at all lines of the score, understanding how they were related, getting the tempo right, and seeking the proper expression. I was an imposter, but I learned a lot.

In student entertainment events, I participated in several musical groups: a close-harmony quartet with Brad, Pete, and Joe George doing American standards and show tunes ("Moonlight in Vermont," "I Love Paris") and a folksong group along the lines of the Brothers Four. I also played second violin in a mariachi group put together by Pete to perform at seminary functions. We didn't take ourselves too seriously—he gave us the name Los Lamentables. However, when we played for braceros at a nearby labor camp we saw real tears in their eyes.

*   *   *

Although we were spending many years preparing to be priests, just what it meant to be a priest remained mysterious. Our seminary training offered no virtually practical pastoral training. At my home parish Fr. McHenry and later Fr. Bernard O'Reilly, both Irish, were pleasant enough, but I wasn't taken into their confidence and I didn't get a sense of their lives. Our seminary profs likewise lived in their own quarters behind closed doors. However, a few priests besides Coffield helped or inspired me in one way or another.

Fr. George Parnassus taught at Pius X High School in Downey and was in residence in our parish in Paramount. He was only about ten years older than I. His father was a well known boxing promoter in L.A., but he was soft-spoken, delicate, almost hesitant in speech, and always wore cufflinks. Perhaps I saw in him the possibility of pursuing intellectual interests while being a diocesan priest. He was relatively conservative, but he treated with respect my interest in matters like the liturgical movement. Perhaps most important, he took me seriously as an adult. Decades later, he was one of the first priests in L.A. to have an AIDS ministry, and was beloved as a pastor in West Hollywood.

When I learned that the Jesuit scripture scholar John McKenzie was staying at the rectory in a nearby parish in the summer, I went to see him to get his view about material I was reading. Besides scholarly work, he had published works accessible to nonscholars. At the time he was working on the *Dictionary of the Bible*, which he did himself, as opposed to the usual practice of enlisting legions of scholars to write highly compressed articles. I was struck that this well-known scholar and author was willing to take time with a seminarian. He had a wry sense of humor, and his life of scripture scholarship made him acutely aware of the distance between first-century Christianity and the Catholicism of our time, but he was content to serve that church as a priest.

Another Jesuit, Eugene Schallert, a sociologist at Santa Clara, gave a talk or two at St. John's. He recommended that we read the works of Jean Mouroux, a French theologian influenced by phenomenology and existentialism. I also saw Schallert at UCLA, where he was using computers (tape spinning on reels at that time) for some of his sociological research. He had a wide-ranging mind and at the time was exploring theology and Christian faith. When I expressed my dissatisfaction with the seminary education, he said, "Well, I've been in education for about forty years" (he was then in his mid-forties), "and how many great teachers have I had: two? three? four? That's about par for the course." That remark reinforced my sense that ultimately I was responsible for my own education.

In August 1962 Gerry Fallon and I spent two weeks in Merced in the Central Valley of California, with Jay Martin, the pastor, who was no more than thirty years old. He invited us there to staff a booth at the Merced County Fair as a kind of Catholic outreach. He was a young priest in action, intellectually curious (then reading Teilhard de Chardin). One evening he had a meeting in a living room of a half-dozen people, at least one a psychologist. I realized that there are interesting people even in an out-of-the-way place like Merced, and that a parish priest could interact meaningfully with them.

One opportunity to observe large numbers of clergy up close was to work at the annual priests' retreat held at St. John's each June, which I did two or three times. We spent a week cleaning floors, windows, and so forth, and then for three successive weeks waited on tables, cleaned rooms, and worked in the bookstore.

To our seminarians' eyes, it didn't look much like a retreat. The priests attended talks and prayed together, but it certainly wasn't silent and looked more like a clergy get-together. Those in attendance each week varied from seventy-year-old pastors and monsignors to young clergy ordained the previous year, so they naturally sought out friends from their age cohort. In the evening they gathered in one another's rooms to smoke, play cards, and drink whiskey. We picked up the empties when cleaning the rooms the next day.

* * *

We were encouraged to learn usable Spanish by going to Spanish conversation tables on Saturdays in the refectory or accompanying Fr. Beutler when he went to say Mass at the bracero camps. In the summer of 1960, two other seminarians and I spent a month in Montezuma seminary, near Las Vegas, New Mexico, in what would now be called an immersion language experience. Montezuma had been set up in the 1930s by the U.S. bishops to help the Mexican church then under government persecution, and it had continued to operate somewhat as an elite national seminary run by Jesuits. The neighbors around that part of northern New Mexico spoke Spanish and had been there for centuries, but many didn't have electricity or running water. Through that month I moved from speaking classroom Spanish to being at home in it.

Students were on vacation, so we didn't attend class; instead, we played soccer and baseball, went hiking in the nearby mountains, and kidded around with each other. At Montezuma I was introduced to pozole, the hominy-based stew or soup, which students prepared outdoors in a large pot. Conditions were more spartan than in U.S. seminaries. I was struck by the simplicity and approachability of a Mexican bishop visiting his seminarians, in sharp contrast to U.S. bishops in their chancery offices and cathedrals, with courtly ceremonies, surrounded by layers of clerical gatekeepers and managing millions of dollars in real estate

Impressed by the good spirits and seriousness of these seminarians, I returned to California wishing to prepare to be a priest in Mexico, where the need seemed great. My spiritual director, Fr. DeVries, who had worked in northern Brazil for many years, was sympathetic, but he advised me to get to ordination first and then think about going to Latin America. In the early 1960s, the Vatican was proposing that dioceses and religious orders in Europe and North America send 10 percent of their personnel to aid the Latin American churches, which suffered from an apparent clergy shortage while confronting challenges from Protestantism and communism.

* * *

The end of each year at St. John's was marked with the ordination of the Fourth Theology class and their departure into the ranks of the priesthood. That was preceded by various steps: ordination to the minor orders (porter, lector, exorcist, acolyte) and major orders, the subdiaconate at the end of Third Theology, and the diaconate before

Christmas in Fourth Theology. As the cardinal and other clerics processed into the cathedral for ordination ceremonies, we sang a polyphonic "Ecce Sacerdos Magnus" (Behold the great priest).

As subdeacons, we began praying the breviary or the office, the collection of psalms organized into seven "hours," recited and sung by monks and prayed silently by priests in Latin. It took about an hour, and failing to pray it was considered a mortal sin (like missing Sunday Mass or eating meat on Friday).

* * *

When we returned to the seminary in fall 1960, the presidential election was in its final phases. We watched the televised debates and shared the excitement that one of ours, a Catholic, was a candidate. Being contrarian, I resisted the notion of letting Kennedy's Catholicism influence my decision and in fact voted for Nixon. That election is now rightly seen as a key moment of U.S. Catholicism emerging from its cultural ghetto. During the Cuban Missile Crisis of October 1962 I attended a small meeting where we solemnly discussed what we could do in the event of a nuclear attack.

* * *

In August 1962 Bill Von Der Ahe, Wilbur Davis, and I spent a month traveling in Mexico. I was about to enter my twelfth and last year in the seminary, and they were a year behind me. It was Bill's car, and Wilbur had researched travel guides. For each of us it was an adventure to leave the familiar confines of Southern California and enter a foreign country.

After crossing the border we spent two or three days barreling through the harsh deserts of the north. Arriving in Guaymas, now in the tropics, we parked at Bahia los Carlos, where we slept on the beach and swam in the very warm water. In Los Mochis, then a modest town surrounded by irrigated fields, we went to the Catholic church and asked to see the priest, who graciously gave us an idea of his work. To some extent, we were exploring what role Mexico or Latin America might have in our future.

After leaving Mazatlan, we came to Rosario, the town where my father had been born. My grandmother's relatives lived in a hamlet called Potrerillos, a couple miles outside the town. The streets were unpaved, and the houses were of adobe with tile roofs. We arrived with no advance notice around dusk at the house of my grandmother's brother, Joaquin Echegaray. Since there was no electricity it was soon dark, and they were preparing to go to bed. They served us some beans and provided us cots in one of the rooms. When I asked a man where I could go to the bathroom, he shrugged, and so I found a place in the street to urinate, feeling exposed when lightning dispelled the darkness for an instant. The next morning we could see more clearly that the house was a kind of compound of several structures around a patio where animals and supplies were kept. At one point a hog came wandering through the house.

As it happened, the following day the priest from Rosario came to Potrerillos to say Mass, which we seminarians attended. At midday, before we were to continue on our trip, my grandmother's *comadre* Trinidad served us a special meal with many dishes, an astonishing array of food from people who to our eyes looked poor (no electricity, no indoor plumbing). In fact, I may have misjudged their poverty; they were driving a pickup truck, and Joaquin seemed to be an elder in the community. Even though we could understand Spanish, there were many basic things that we did not comprehend.

At San Blas on the Pacific Coast we hired a boatman to take us through mangroves. Puerto Vallarta, not far away, was already being slated for tourist development. One night, after driving through a powerful thunderstorm, we pulled off the road and slept in the open near the car. When we woke in the morning we found that some of our valuables had been stolen, and an official directing traffic at a bridge already knew about it and was amused. We heard mariachi bands in Guadalajara.

In Mexico City we stayed at the seminary of the Missionaries of the Holy Spirit. Rather than submit to the risks of wild traffic with no marked lanes, we took public transportation, especially *peseros*—vans and cars driving fixed routes on major thoroughfares in which the driver held out an upraised index finger signifying fare of one peso. We saw the Ballet Folclórico and went to the floating gardens of Xochimilco. In Cuernavaca we stayed at the Benedictine monastery, attended some recitations of the office, and ate lentils and bread in the refectory.

After around four weeks we drove nonstop north from Guanajuato, crossing into El Paso, Texas, where were could finally eat lettuce and trust the ice cubes, and then continued to Southern California.

* * *

It was only very late in our seminary career that we had any training in actually doing what priests do, and that was focused primarily on ritual actions. In spring 1962 we were ordained subdeacons, and in late fall, deacons. We were now clerics and could take on those roles at solemn Mass. In our last year we spent some time practicing saying Mass and role-playing in confessions. We had no classes in psychology, counseling, or management. We did have a semester class called The Gentlemanly Priest, from Fr. Kenneally, consisting largely of his advice on how to comport ourselves, and matters such as which forks to use for salad and dessert.

One area in which we received some training was in preaching. During the first two years of the major seminary we had class from Fr. Miller in public speaking, and then during theology we had classes in preaching. In order to get some practice and overcome stage fright we first addressed our class. From there we moved to speaking to the whole student body at a meal, where we had to make ourselves heard over the clank of silverware and plates being collected and piled.

At that time Fr. Miller and others like him were advocating plain speech in sermons as opposed to flowery Victorian rhetoric. His proposed method was to catch people's attention with the opening, then develop an idea connecting it with people's experience, and move toward the consequences or implications. Such preparation did not make us good preachers, but it gave us a method and some confidence.

* * *

During our second year at St. John's, Pius XII died and was succeeded by Angelo Roncalli, Pope John XXIII. A biography of Roncalli was read in the refectory, including the story of him walking barefoot to school to save shoe leather. We had begun theology when he announced that an ecumenical council would be held, the first since the nineteenth century. One of the books read to us was by a young Swiss theologian, Hans Küng, which expressed hopes for what might come from the council, particularly through rapprochement with Protestant and Orthodox Churches. The first session of Vatican II took place in fall 1962, our last year. We passed around copies of the articles in the *New Yorker* about the procedures, issues, and machinations of the first session, and particularly the leadership roles taken by northern European bishops and theologians rejecting the business-as-usual proposals from Vatican offices.

* * *

The flaws in seminary education and formation at the time are obvious. We were enclosed in an all-male society for a dozen years, creating a psychology of a "church" inside and a "world" outside, from which we were largely cut off. Our education was mostly learning from a single textbook per class. We received a smattering of a classical liberal education, but not really its spirit, unless we pursued it on our own, as some of us did. Much of the unstated agenda was to turn us into docile clerics.

At the age of twenty-five, I had worked at a series of summer jobs but had no real experience of actual businesses, and could point to few accomplishments of my own. We were prepared to perform the ritual actions expected of Catholic priests, but we had very little actual experience dealing with lay Catholics. Because we had suppressed rather than dealt with our own sexuality, we were still adolescents in some respects. Despite many hours spent in prayer we may not have been deeply prayerful. At some level I sensed these lacks and felt inadequate.

Yet I generally enjoyed my seminary years and don't regret them. That may be just the common psychological tendency of being reconciled to the course of one's life rather than having regret for roads not taken. I internalized a sense of seeking to discern my vocation that has remained meaningful throughout my life

MEMENTO OF THE LIVING AND THE DEAD

* * *

In our last year, considerable attention was devoted to preparing for ordination in ordering or even designing a chalice or vestments in the liturgically contemporary style. When he died, Fr. McHenry had passed on to me his chalice, made in Dublin in 1929, so I didn't have to make that choice.

Finally the time came, and on May 1, 1963, twenty or so of us processed into St. Vibiana's Cathedral in downtown L.A. At the beginning of the ceremony we prostrated ourselves in silence on the marble floor. We then arose, and at a particular moment Cardinal McIntyre anointed each of us with oil, and we then joined him around the altar concelebrating. The following Sunday each of us then celebrated his first Mass in his home parish. John Coffield preached; Walt Kelly and George Parnassus were deacon and subdeacon. The first Mass was then followed by a reception and meal. It had various features of a wedding, complete with reception line, gifts, and the celebration of a presumably lifelong commitment. It was a great occasion for Our Lady of the Rosary Parish and for the circle of parishioners close to my parents.

3

Chafing under a Roman Collar

Shortly after our ordination and first Mass, our class attended a clergy luncheon on the cathedral premises with Cardinal McIntyre, other bishops, and several hundred priests. We were now inside this fraternity for which we had been prepared through years of seminary life. At that meeting our assignments were announced; mine was to St. Philip the Apostle Parish in Pasadena.

Within a day or so I showed up there with my belongings: a couple of black suits, cassocks, some recreational clothing, a few dozen books, and some records. I was given a room on the second floor of the fully carpeted two-story rectory. The parish complex covered a block: church, school, rectory, convent, and asphalt schoolyard. The pastor was Monsignor William North, and the other assistant was Michael Dunne, who had been ahead of me in the seminary, now a four-year veteran.

Pasadena was the largest of a string of cities and towns up against the San Gabriel Mountains along the north side of the Los Angeles Basin. It was founded in the late nineteenth century and was known for the New Year's Day Parade of Roses and Rose Bowl game—and for a recent surf song by Jan and Dean, "The Little Old Lady from Pasadena." St. Philip's was located on the east side of the city and was newer than St. Andrew's Parish downtown. The church sat across the street from Pasadena City College. North of Colorado Boulevard were modest middle-class houses; moving south were mansions built in the early twentieth century. Cal Tech and the Huntington Library were both within the parish boundaries, as was a portion of very wealthy San Marino.

In anticipating our assignments, we knew that much would depend on the pastor to whom we were assigned. Monsignor North carried himself with a sense of dignity or self-importance. He had been editor of the archdiocesan paper, *The Tidings*, and was one of the cardinal's consultants, his inner circle. North relished his position of overseeing the apprenticeship of newly ordained priests. However, he entrusted the actual details to Mike, whom I had seen primarily from a distance in the seminary. He was vigorous, businesslike, and friendly, with a shock of prematurely gray hair that added seriousness. He had an air of assurance that I learned from him much later was somewhat deceptive. He guided me in fairly short order on how to carry out my responsibilities.

Parishes in L.A. at that time typically had three priests: a pastor age sixty or older, a middle assistant in his forties, and a younger assistant. St. Philip's had that same structure, but the curates were younger. After a year and a half Mike was transferred, and I became the senior curate when Frank Colborn, a year behind me in the seminary, who had studied theology in Rome, was appointed to St. Philip's.

My very first pastoral call was to take the sacraments to an older Colombian woman. Perhaps it was an omen, because at the time there were practically no Hispanics in the parish. Not long afterward, I officiated at her funeral, preaching in Spanish.

* * *

Mike and I were kept busy with a round of duties: say the early or noon Mass, take communion to the sick, and be in the confessional during the 8 AM and noon Masses. North insisted that his curates be out in the parish doing "census" from 10 to 11:30 AM and 3 to 5 PM. The parish had cards for all of the two thousand or so Catholic households in the parish with names of family members, ages, and perhaps some other data, such as whether they had children in the parish school. We would drive to a section of the parish, take out census cards, and ring doorbells. Because it was during work hours, very often there was no one home. The ostensible aim was to keep the parish records up to date, but it was a chance for us to meet parishioners outside the context of Mass, or to encourage "lax" Catholics to consider returning to the sacraments. I felt somewhat awkward doing it, but often enough I had what seemed to be worthwhile pastoral interactions with people.

We ate lunch and supper together in the rectory. In the evening, that included priests in residence, who were working with the archdiocese in vocations or the Catholic school system, or a Jesuit physicist who was doing graduate work at Cal Tech. The cook was a quiet older Irish woman named Bridget, whose last name I don't remember and, what is worse, may not have known even then.

After supper we typically had a meeting with a parish organization, such as the Legion of Mary, or taught the adult instruction class, or had appointments in conjunction with weddings or baptisms. Saturday mornings we had catechism classes for public school children in the school, and then we heard confessions from 3:30 to 5:30 PM and from 7:30 to 9 PM. On Sundays the parish had Masses from early morning to noon, and we were expected to hear confessions and distribute communion at Masses other than our own and to greet parishioners. Baptisms took place early Sunday afternoon, and on some weekdays we officiated at funerals. Somewhere in the midst of these activities we had to fit in praying the breviary.

These duties were centered around ritual actions: daily and Sunday Mass, confessions, sick calls, occasional benediction of the Blessed Sacrament. The Mass, still entirely in Latin, was at the center. St. Philip's had a system for Sunday sermons whereby one of us—Mike, the resident priest, or I—would preach at all the Masses, and hence had to prepare only every third Sunday. One could prepare better and hone the sermon over several Masses. The exception was the 10 AM high Mass celebrated by Monsignor North, who always preached at his own Mass.

Mike and I helped count the collection Sunday mornings and drove to deposit it in the bank afterward. Otherwise, we had no real involvement in the parish finance or administration, which Monsignor North handled himself, consulting with some lay advisers. He also reserved for himself dealing personally with wealthy or prominent parishioners, one of whom was John McCone, an industrialist and then director of the CIA (1961–1965), who was usually in Washington at this time.

We were thus kept busy from early morning until 9 PM or so at night, a roughly fourteen-hour day, with a break after lunch. One day a week we had off, after the morning Masses starting at around 9 AM, and we had alternate Sunday afternoons off, starting at around 1 PM. Thus, I was "Father Berryman" most of the week, dressed in cassock or black suit, except for my day off when I could drive away in my assigned parish Ford Falcon to visit my family or get together with other priest friends, provided I returned by a reasonable hour at night.

After playing sports in the seminary for a dozen years, I suddenly had no regular exercise. To stay in shape I used the Royal Canadian Air Force exercises, often doing them at 10 PM before showering and going to bed. During my first month in the parish, while shooting baskets with a teenager, I felt pain that turned out to be a herniated disk and wore a neck brace for three months. I had periodic back pain for decades afterward.

The parish supplied my needs: a place to live and three meals a day. I had use of the parish car for my day off. My income was a one-hundred-dollar check each month from the archdiocese, and money donated for daily Mass intentions and baptisms (usually five dollars) and weddings. Catholic apologetics at the time insisted that these were not payments for the sacraments but stipends freely given to the priest. I felt vaguely uncomfortable with these "stole fees," but I don't recall consciously giving them away. I had sufficient cash for my modest needs. Nor do I recall being concerned about health care. My recollection is that Catholic physicians and hospitals would treat "Father" free of charge, although I believe that we had medical insurance from the archdiocese.

One Sunday night when I was returning to St. Philip's, it struck me that the streets of Pasadena leading to the rectory looked familiar; the parish may or may not have been home, but it was where I now belonged.

* * *

Confession had been familiar to me since childhood, but now I was on the other side of the grille, seated in the dark, in a cassock with a stole over my shoulders. As a confessor, I would slide back a wooden cover, and the kneeling penitent would begin, "Bless me, Father, for I have sinned. It has been one month [or X months, or a week] since my last confession, and these are my sins." There followed a recitation list of sins or faults, most often "venial" (disobeying parents, losing one's temper, telling a small lie), but often enough "mortal" (missing Mass, birth control, premarital sex, or sexual arousal). The penitent ended with an admission of repentance, I would assign a penance (typically saying a few Our Fathers or Hail Marys, or both), and pronounce absolution, in Latin, while the penitent said the Act of Contrition.

Being a good confessor meant listening sympathetically, being appropriate and helpful in any remarks or questions, and doing so briefly. At its best, confession may have helped Catholics to be conscientious in their dealings with their families and others and to deepen their faith and spirituality, but for many it didn't foster a mature Christian moral vision.

Shortly after the end of Vatican II, the notion of being condemned to hell for missing Mass or eating meat on Friday lost credibility, and the number of penitents dropped dramatically. Only a small fraction of practicing Catholics now go to confession regularly, even though church authorities insist on its importance. During my time in Pasadena, however, confession was still a regular feature of parish life, and neither I nor anyone else was questioning it.

* * *

Days off were important because it got me away from the morning-to-night routine of the parish and always being "Father Berryman." Even at a concert or movie on days off, however, I was often in my black suit and Roman collar. I tried to get together with other priest friends, sometimes individually, sometimes in a group. We might go hiking or to a movie or concert or for dinner. It wasn't always easy because our assigned day off (Tuesday, Wednesday, or Thursday) was often not the same as those of our friends. One Monday a month a group a group of younger priests in our area would gather at the Northwoods Inn in Monrovia for noontime hamburgers and beer.

Our closest friends were other priests of our own cohort or close in age. That was partly a carryover from the seminary and partly the clerical subculture. We had a sense that as priests we had things in common with each other that laypeople didn't have, certainly the sacramental powers and responsibilities, but also expectations that we were supposed to meet. Our relationships with laypeople could be friendly, but our relations were always those of priest and parishioner, not close friends.

What bound our loose-knit group together was our desire to be good priests. Just what that meant, we were trying to figure out as we went along. On the whole, we didn't want to simply be like the older generations of priests. Some of them were admirable, but our general impression was that they were often authoritarian or short-tempered, or lacking in zeal, or operating out of routine. A symbol to me was priests spending hours on the golf course. My friends and I intended to be different.

On my day off I sometimes went to the Benedictine monastery in Valyermo, in the high desert over the mountains, for a kind of one-day personal retreat. Sometimes I went to a park to read, or to the beach by myself.

* * *

John XXIII died in 1963, and his successor Paul VI pledged to continue with the Council. The middle two sessions (fall 1963 and 1964) took place during my time at St. Philip's. From journalistic accounts and books, it was clear that something important was happening, but where it all would end was not at all clear.

In December 1963 the full text of the first Council document, the decree on the liturgy (*Sacrosanctum Concilium*), was published in the *New York Times*. The text was cautious, first affirming that in principle the language of the liturgy was Latin, but then opening the door to the use of the vernacular under the guidance of church authority. The key idea was that the way the Mass and the sacraments were celebrated should be reformed so as to bring out their true nature. In 1964 the Epistle and Gospel began to be read in English, and soon the celebrant began facing the people at a tablelike altar. At the Liturgical Conference in St. Louis in 1964, we took part in an experimental Mass with some of the text in English. We also sang music composed by African American priest Clarence Rivers, especially his haunting song "God Is Love," which owed something to Gregorian chant and the Gelineau psalms and had more than a hint of the blues. Next to me at the final Mass was Tissa Balasuriya, a Sri Lankan who soon became a pioneer in forging an Asian Catholic theology.

Much of the commentary in the Catholic press at the time was on the liturgy, particularly to what extent it would be in the vernacular, and on ecumenism—to what extent the Catholic, Protestant, and Orthodox Churches could overcome their disunity. I don't recall paying much attention to the news in 1964 that Paul VI had removed contraception from discussion. Any change in church teaching seemed inconceivable, because artificial contraception was assumed to be against the "natural law" as then understood, and so firmly part of official teaching that it could not be reversed.

The topics that the bishops were discussing had to do primarily with church matters: scripture and tradition; the liturgy; ecumenism; possible renewal of the diaconate; the roles of bishops, priests, and laypeople; the meaning of religious life. At the suggestion of Belgian cardinal Leo Joseph Suenens, work was begun on the topic of the relationship between the church and "the world," and it was circulating as "Schema XIII," but its decisive importance was not yet recognized.

The assumption in the Archdiocese of Los Angeles was that the Council would not bring significant change. Swiss theologian Hans Küng was prohibited from speaking in the archdiocese, as was the Jesuit archbishop Thomas Roberts of Bombay. In spring 1964 Daniel Berrigan, then a young Jesuit poet and theologian, was scheduled to speak at a Catholic women's college and was prohibited from doing so. The sisters managed to obey the letter of the prohibition by canceling his speech in an auditorium but letting him speak unofficially in a basement venue at the scheduled time. I attended on my day off and found myself unable to understand what he was saying, partly because of his elliptical poetic expression, and partly because I was tired and dozing after a day of skiing.

* * *

Despite my limited time, I read about developments at the Council and in theology. I made my way through Rahner's *Hörer des Wortes* (Hearers of the word), an early work that develops a philosophy of religion grounded in the notion that human beings are created open to God, capable of receiving revelation. I turned particularly to scripture study and biblical theology. The theology we had been taught in the seminary used isolated sentences from scripture to "prove" Catholic doctrine. Biblical theology was an invitation to enter into the Bible's own categories, which were different. For example, the model of "obedience" in the Bible is Abraham, who obeys God's call to go out, not knowing where it will lead; it isn't primarily docility to a hierarchical superior. The French Benedictine Celestin Charlier spoke of the need for developing a "biblical culture."

One evening at the invitation of Bill DuBay I went to Westwood to meet with John A. T. Robinson, an Anglican bishop whose book *Honest to God* had recently been published. Robinson's concern was that "modern man" can no longer believe in a God "up there." Drawing on Paul Tillich, he proposed that God be understood as within our inner depths; he also borrowed the notion of a "religionless Christianity" from Dietrich Bonhoeffer. Robinson's ideas weren't new, particularly to academic theologians, but he wrote in plain English and his book found a wide readership, suggesting that many ordinary believers were interested in alternatives to Sunday-school imagery of God.

* * *

Although the 1960s were under way chronologically, the full force of "the sixties" was yet to come. It was the Camelot era, when a young president and his glamorous wife symbolized a can-do spirit, even if he was not succeeding in translating that sympathy into major legislation. Martin Luther King wrote his "Letter from Birmingham Jail," and the March on Washington took place in 1963; the Free Speech Movement emerged at Berkeley, and the Beatles and the "British Invasion" came in 1964.

Influential books—Michael Harrington's *The Other America*, Rachel Carson's *Silent Spring*, and Betty Friedan's *The Feminist Mystique*—were sowing the seeds of what later became movements around poverty, the environment, and feminism. Even though the United States had been meddling in Vietnam since the mid-1950s, the troop numbers were still small, and most Americans were little aware of it.

In November 1963 I attended a debate on the American presidency at the Hollywood Palladium between William Buckley, the conservative editor of the *National Review*, and the comedian Steve Allen. I had been informed of the event by one of its organizers, Michael Gazzaniga, a grad student at Caltech whom I had come to know in preparing for and officiating at his marriage. He and a fellow grad student had organized three such debates on U.S. politics between leading liberal and conservative figures. What I remember of that night is a role reversal: Buckley played the comedian and Allen the straight man. I was also impressed that two grad students around my age were able to organize events of such importance, and couldn't imagine myself doing so. Gazzaniga went on to become a leading neuroscientist, particularly on the basis of split-brain research, and to write several books interpreting the field for general readers.

That event on a Sunday night is etched in my mind because the following Thursday President Kennedy was shot to death in Dallas. I learned about it as I arrived at the rectory after hearing schoolchildren's confessions. Like the rest of the nation we were shocked, and our routine no longer felt normal—especially when two days later Jack Ruby shot and killed Lee Harvey Oswald on live TV. We watched the televised funeral on the rectory's black-and-white TV, a kind of national liturgy accompanied by Samuel Barber's *Adagio*.

President Lyndon Johnson harnessed the nation's grief to push for the Civil Rights Act of 1964 and the package of policies constituting the War on Poverty. Opposing him in the 1964 election, Senator Barry Goldwater embodied a new, self-confident kind of conservatism, but Johnson solidly defeated him in November 1964. For a brief season, it seemed that a movement akin to the New Deal might be uniting the nation to address its unresolved problems.

* * *

Several films from the period stand out in my mind as reflecting trends in society. *Dr. Strangelove* made zany fun out of nuclear war shortly after the United States and the USSR came to the brink of starting one during the Cuban Missile Crisis. It was great fun (Slim Pickens plummeting down astride an H-bomb like a bucking bronco), but it exposed the madness institutionalized in our world.

With elegant sets and music, *Tom Jones* sought to catch the picaresque sense of the eighteenth-century novel. Albert Finney lustily played the title role, romping merrily through exploits, mainly sexual, albeit off-camera. I viewed it with several other young priests, all of us laughing in our clerical garb. In *The Pawnbroker* Rod Steiger played a hard-bitten Jewish pawnshop owner in Harlem. In the course of the story the audience learns that he has closed himself off to other human beings as a result of his experience in the Holocaust, particularly the loss of his wife. His performance and the film won admiration and prizes. It was a landmark film because of brief female nudity, allowed by the Production Code, because it was artistically appropriate. Although it was condemned by the Legion of Decency, the film was well received by critics in Catholic publications, signaling a cultural change under way.

In *The Gospel According to St. Matthew*, Pier Paolo Pasolini followed the Gospel incident-by-incident with literal directness. Its sobriety and silence were worlds apart from the beards-and-sandals and overwrought musical scores common in Hollywood biblical epics. It was filmed in the Italian hill country using largely nonprofessional actors and captured well the starkness of the Gospel narrative. As a communist (and, as later revealed, a gay man), Pasolini had no use for official Catholicism, but that made his naturalistic black-and-white take on Jesus all the more striking. In one scene Jesus is walking alone on a trail in an open field when he encounters a man coming toward him, and Jesus simply says, "The kingdom of heaven is at hand; repent and believe the gospel," and keeps moving. Perhaps the church had something to learn from the Pasolinis of the world.

* * *

Rectory living meant being under the same roof as your boss. Monsignor North and I more or less got along, provided I was carrying out my expected duties. He treated me with a condescending paternalism as "the young man." We sometimes had conversations in his suite on the second floor, with overstuffed furniture, where he would often be smoking a cigar. As a subscriber to *America* and *Commonweal*, he was aware of events elsewhere and ideas in circulation. Judging from his preaching, his own theology was that of the Council of Trent, with some literary flourishes: he was fond of saying that God writes straight with crooked lines. If I mentioned anything that was not approved in Los Angeles, he dismissed me with a harrumph.

My relationship with Mike and the resident priests was friendly, but I was not really taken into their confidence. The sisters were in habit and lived in the convent across the yard. Our dealings were always as "Sister" and "Father," and always in conjunction with the school (the film *Doubt* with Philip Seymour Hoffman and Meryl Streep captures the situation well). My social life outside the parish was with fellow priests with whom I had become friends in the seminary.

St. Philip's parishioners were typically Catholic families headed by well-paid professional men with stay-at-home wives whose children attended Catholic schools. Those attending daily Mass were primarily retirees, some living within walking distance of the church. My contacts with them were cordial but not close. My most personal interactions were with people I saw regularly over a period of time, such as couples preparing for marriage, particularly if one of them was a non-Catholic who was taking instructions in order to be baptized. I enjoyed the opportunity to get to know them a little bit and be part of their life at this happy moment, including the rehearsals. To them I was probably a pleasant, young, short-statured priest doing his job. The bride in one marriage was an actress on a TV sitcom, which brought extra media attention and a photo story about the event in a Hollywood fan magazine.

One of my assignments was to be the Newman Club chaplain for students at Pasadena City College (PCC). The Newman Movement was then trying to move beyond its existing approach of seeking to protect the faith of Catholic students from the secular environment of the university toward one of helping them advance toward mature faith as young adults in higher education. Students at PCC were all commuters and spent no more time on campus than necessary. Monsignor North didn't think I should devote much time to it. The assigned faculty liaison was Margaret O'Donnell, who was also a parishioner and was very helpful to me. Each semester we had a handful of students and organized some regular discussion groups, in which I tried to present the view of Catholicism then developing from scripture scholarship and theology. It was one of the bright spots in my work in the parish, but I have no idea whether it had any impact on the students in their later lives.

* * *

In the seminary we had had no training in psychology, either in theory or in counseling practice. In fact, Catholicism was generally suspicious of or hostile to psychiatry and psychology; Bishop Sheen often used Freud as a foil. In the mid-twentieth century the image of psychiatry in the general public was dominated by psychoanalysis, whose clients spent years on the couch at great expense. The films of Hitchcock, Bergman, Fellini, and others were consciously Freudian. In the early 1960s, most psychiatrists could still trace their lineage to Freud through his disciples (Adler, Jung, Sullivan, Horney, Eriksen). However, other forms of humanistic therapy (Gestalt, Rogerian) were emerging. Their theories were not based on treatment of neurotics or psychotics, but psychologically healthy individuals. It was still "talk therapy" rather than treatment based on neuroscience and drug research, which was yet to come.

Despite official disapproval, some theologians and others found connections between psychology and Catholicism, and some priests, such as the Dutch Adrian Van Kaam and the French Marc Oraison were practitioners. While in the seminary we read and discussed among ourselves books like *Counseling the Catholic* by Fr. George Hagmaier. Coffield had taken courses in psychology at local Catholic colleges.

As priests we found ourselves in counseling situations, particularly if we showed any empathy. From time to time we encountered people who had serious emotional problems, and we were looking for help in responding to such situations. In spring 1964 our classmate John McFadden arranged for several us to meet regularly on our day off with a therapist named Bill Kuhnhardt in Claremont. We shared informally some of the situations we were facing in dealing with people who came to us. He helped us recognize the signs of serious emotional disturbance that would call for directing the person to professional help. He also sought to make us more aware of our own feelings and reactions, which inevitably would affect our pastoral contacts.

One day Kuhnhardt took us to a nearby psychiatric hospital to witness electric shock therapy, which was then common. He warned us that what we were going to see might be disturbing. It was clear that the patient, an adult man, thought the treatment was helpful to him. When the shock was administered, the man's limbs trembled and stiffened for a few seconds, and his trunk rose from up the bed in an arc.

Being an idea person more than a people person, I envied my priest friends who seemed to have greater empathy and more counseling skill. Not surprisingly, many of my contemporaries who left the priesthood became counselors and therapists.

* * *

On the last Sunday in May 1963, when I had been at St. Philip's less than a month, I went to Wrigley Field in downtown L.A., to hear Martin Luther King speak, sitting in the stands by myself in my Roman collar. In doing so, I opted not to take part in May Devotions (procession, rosary, Benediction of the Blessed Sacrament) along with the other clergy in the parish. It was my Sunday afternoon off and I was within my rights, but the choice reflected a tension between competing visions of what being a Catholic priest meant.

Since the mid-1950s, the focus in the civil rights movement had been on ending legalized segregation in the South, starting with the 1954 Supreme Court decision in *Brown v. Board of Education* and then the 1956 Montgomery bus boycott, followed by freedom rides and sit-ins in the early 1960s. Nonviolent struggles were being waged along these lines, with the participation of black and white volunteers who went south, including some church people. The force of national public opinion, and occasional action by the federal government, was being brought to bear on the South with its long-standing legalized segregation.

Now attention was turning to de facto segregation elsewhere, which in California meant housing discrimination. Most areas of Southern California had only infinitesimal numbers of nonwhites; blacks lived de facto in segregated neighborhoods. Catholic bishops were speaking out on these matters, and individual priests and sisters were visible in these actions, although not yet in large numbers. In Los Angeles, Cardinal McIntyre prohibited priests from being involved, and those who did so faced discipline.

In 1962, as an assistant pastor in Northridge, Bill DuBay spoke at a Sunday Mass against housing segregation. At the end of the Mass, the pastor rose in the pulpit to apologize to the congregation. When a visiting Kenyan bishop invited Bill to go work in his diocese, partly because of his innovative work in catechesis, Bill went to the cardinal with the request. McIntyre asked him how he had become interested in "those people," that is, Negroes. Bill's request was refused, but he was transferred to Compton: the logic was, we have some of "those people" here for you to work with. As an illustration of McIntyre's mind-set, in receiving a group of prominent Southern California black Catholics concerned about discrimination, he told them that he had met "your cardinal" at the Council, meaning Cardinal Rugambwa of (then) Tanganyika.

In 1963 the state legislature passed the Rumford Act, which prohibited discrimination in selling or leasing property on the grounds of race, religion, or other categories of identity. However, in 1964 the California real estate lobby counterattacked with Proposition 14, which would enshrine the right of property owners to not sell or lease to anyone at their own discretion. This appeal to freedom made sense to many people, particularly since the arrival of minorities in previously all-white neighborhoods often drove property values down and provoked white flight. Although it was couched in the language of property rights of individuals, Proposition 14 would have further legalized existing de facto segregation. It seemed to be a moral issue that required that the church take a stand, and some bishops in the rest of the state did so.

A small group of lay activists calling itself Catholics United for Racial Equality (CURE) had been pressuring the cardinal for a year by carrying out demonstrations at the chancery office and near his residence. DuBay was close to the group, one of whom was Al White, who had spent years with us in the seminary, but as a priest DuBay wasn't involved in the demonstrations.

For months, a number of us priests—primarily younger but including John Coffield—found ourselves discussing what we could do, both informally and in meetings convoked for that purpose. Some of us did participate in a march with Dr. King in downtown L.A. one Saturday. Through Coffield we had met John Howard Griffin at the house of Emil Seliga, a lay activist on integration. Griffin, a white novelist from Texas, had undergone skin treatments to make himself appear black. He then spent several months traveling in the Deep South and published his experiences in *Black Like Me* (1961), which became a best seller and was made into a film. Griffin was deeply Catholic and became a good friend of Thomas Merton, with whom he shared an interest in photography. My recollection is of a large man, reticent by nature, who nevertheless felt impelled to share what he had learned.

Pete Beaman, a priest a few years older than us, took Griffin to St. John's Seminary on a Sunday in the spring of 1964. Griffin gave an impromptu presentation to several dozen seminarians. No permission had been sought, and when the rector Fr. Kenneally found out, he called students in one by one for interrogation. At least one was expelled, some left on their own, and others were disciplined, including having their ordination to the subdiaconate postponed.

That incident demonstrated how intertwined were the issues of racism, conscience, and obedience to church hierarchy. Proposition 14 seemed to be a clear-cut moral issue. Polls showed that it had considerable support, and thus it seemed all the more important that there be a clear voice from the church—meaning church leaders. Just what we could do, however, was unclear. One day we spent several hours at John McFadden's family home in Altadena discussing the matter with no resolution.

In conjunction with some of his friends in CURE, DuBay decided to take a bold step. He would hold a press conference announcing that he was sending a telegram to Pope Paul VI denouncing Cardinal McIntyre and asking that he be removed for "malfeasance" in office for not giving leadership on racial discrimination and suppressing those who sought to do so. Bill phoned me and several other priests asking us to join him, but none of us did. We agreed that some kind of a stand should be taken, but we weren't convinced that this was what was called for. I hid behind the fact that I was scheduled to be in Camarillo on clergy retreat.

The press conference was held the following Thursday and was reported on the evening news and carried across the nation and overseas on the wire services. This was a very early instance of public dispute between a priest and his bishop over a matter of this kind. Reporters sought out Terry Halloran, who said that he agreed with Bill's complaint but not with his means, and thus both he and Bill were temporarily prohibited from functioning as priests.

When I phoned Bill after returning to Pasadena, his first words were, "Come on in, Phil, the water's fine," inviting me to join him. On Saturday night I went to see him at the apartment of Robert Kaiser, a *Time* reporter who had been covering the Vatican Council. Bill seemed to be intoxicated with the publicity battle. A week and a half later, however, Bill and Terry knelt before the cardinal and renewed their promise of obedience to him in the presence of hundreds of priests on retreat.

In November, Proposition 14 won decisively, with 65 percent of the vote—in other words, a majority of voters asserted their right to refuse to sell or lease to minorities. However, the U.S. Supreme Court later ruled Proposition 14 unconstitutional.

* * *

In summer of 1964 I took my two weeks of vacation in northern Mexico as a priest volunteer with the Latin America Mission Program (LAMP). LAMP had been started by priests and laypeople in the Bay Area as a channel for northern California Catholics to assist the church in Mexico on temporary assignments. Behind it was the notion then being promoted from Rome that the wealthy churches of Europe and North America should help the Catholic Church in Latin America with personnel and other resources.

After a week of orientation at the program's headquarters in Mexicali, I was assigned to serve as a priest in Algodones, then a small hamlet in a corner of Baja California, not far from Yuma. My task was to perform baptisms, teach catechism, and preach a mission in the evening. Accompanying me was a university student volunteer.

We were in a harsh desert area in August; one afternoon the temperature reached 114 degrees. Some of the area was used for irrigated agriculture, and one evening we went for supper to the house of a local grower. Some of the local people must have worked there. On the whole, however, I'm sure I understood little of life in the community.

My sharpest memory is of officiating at the burial of an infant. I said the Mass and read the funeral prayers over the wooden coffin made there, and we walked to the cemetery, where the casket was lowered into the grave. The mother was shrieking and trying to throw herself into the grave but was restrained by other family members. Someone threw a clod of dirt onto the casket, then others joined in and rained dirt clods into the grave. Presiding over funerals at St. Philip's had not prepared me for something like this. That child's death would have been prevented had he or she been born on the other side of the border, not many miles away. The matter-of-factness of the whole procedure, all handled by the people, and the lack of any of the cushioning of death performed by funeral homes left a strong imprint on me.

Conversing with local men I found that some had been to the United States. "Where?" I asked. "Gary, Indiana," they said. To me, Gary, Indiana, conjured up *The Music Man*, but years later I understood that they were part of a century-long pattern of Mexicans crossing into the United States to work temporarily.

In hindsight, it was absurd for me to go to Algodones for a few days, even if I had passable Spanish. I could perform ritual actions—say Mass and baptize, officiate a funeral, and preach a homily—but I certainly could not engage with the people with any real understanding of their situation.

After those two weeks of testing the waters, I informed the chancery office of my interest in going to Latin America as a priest.

* * *

In late 1964 I was informed that Mike Dunne was being transferred. He had gone to the chancery office to request it, primarily because he realized that living under the authoritarianism of Monsignor North was psychologically damaging to him. By that time he had been at St. Philip's for over five years, and a transfer was in some sense normal. North wasn't happy because Mike's request reflected badly on him. At the time it was treated as a routine transfer; only many years later did I learn how it had happened.

Replacing him was Frank Colborn, who had been in the L.A. seminaries for his college years and had then been sent to study theology in Rome. In a sense I now had seniority, but we were both simply junior curates and we divided our duties.

* * *

In January 1965 John Coffield decided to leave the Archdiocese of Los Angeles in protest, primarily over the church's failure to oppose racial discrimination. He was pastor of

Ascension Parish, southwest of downtown, then a black neighborhood. The archdiocesan authorities were willing to let him go and were assured that he would be accepted in the Archdiocese of Chicago. However, when the parish wanted to organize a farewell celebration, they pusillanimously allowed only a small clergy luncheon.

That prompted parishioners and other Coffield supporters to act on their own. They rented a recreation center in a public park for an entire Sunday. I managed to arrive in the middle of the afternoon and was struck by seeing how many people had come, no doubt hundreds over the course of the day, reflecting his years of work in El Monte, Dolores Mission, Ascension, and elsewhere. The religion section of *Time* ran a story on his "exile" and on the situation of the archdiocese.

* * *

That same month Monsignor Benjamin Hawkes, the chancellor and McIntyre's right-hand man, phoned and asked me how my intentions of going to Latin America were proceeding. I hadn't been pursuing it actively, but the authorities were now encouraging me. They apparently saw me as a potential DuBay, whom they regretted not having allowed to go to Kenya when he requested.

As it happened, the Catholic Inter-American Cooperation Program (CICOP) was going to hold its annual meeting in Chicago later in the month. CICOP conferences were organized to foster and coordinate North-South church cooperation in implementing the Vatican's call for church personnel to go to Latin America. Two thousand people, including notable figures from the Latin American church, attended. A major presence was the raspy-voiced Cardinal Richard Cushing of Boston, who strongly supported sending priests, even if he may not have comprehended all the subtleties. Latin American speakers were sharing their understanding of the challenges of their societies. The implication was that cooperation was not simply a matter of sending personnel, and certainly not to set up U.S.-type parishes and schools.

Unlike those representing institutions, I was there on my own, looking for a way to go to Latin America. My classmate John McFadden had alerted me to the work of Leo Mahon and a team of priests from Chicago who had gone to Panama City in 1963, and were pioneering new pastoral methods, based on forming small lay-led neighborhood church communities. One evening I went to a presentation for Chicago priests, where Leo told the story of what they were doing. He sketched a very different vision of what a Catholic priest should be: not primarily a performer of ritual actions but one who forms Christian community. His vision of the church seemed to square with what I was intuiting through reading scripture scholars and theologians. I was smitten by that vision, and by Leo himself, then about forty years old, who could communicate in plain terms, enjoyed a good laugh, and was very much admired by his fellow Chicago priests. Archbishop Tomas Clavel of Panama

City was at CICOP with Leo, and we agreed that I would come to Panama in late June, after officiating the marriage of my younger brother Al.

* * *

Like a number of my fellow priests, I had concluded that it was immoral to keep silent about racial discrimination and I should do something to take a stand, even though I was now going to be leaving for Panama. With some trepidation, I prepared a moderate sermon for Sunday, May 9, writing the full text rather than simply a set of notes. After an introduction using a *Peanuts* cartoon strip, I presented data on housing discrimination in our region of Southern California (virtually all white communities and a black ghetto in the older portion of Pasadena) and ended by saying that this was not God's will, and that we should do something about it.

After I had preached at two or three Masses, North confronted me in the sacristy: "What the hell is going on here?" A parishioner must have complained. He preached for the rest of the morning, riffing on Mother's Day—which in fact it was. Afterward there was stony silence between us, and I left because it was my Sunday off.

Twelve years of seminary training and the mystique of the Catholic priesthood had conditioned me to be docile and to defer to authority, since that authority was deemed to come from God. At the same time, I had been aware of intellectual and pastoral currents elsewhere, even in other dioceses in the United States. My circle of priests had been struggling to figure out what we should do. The sermon was a protest and affirmation of my own conscience; now I would have to face the consequences.

On Monday I was phoned from the chancery office and told to be there the next day at 10 AM. When I showed up I was ushered into a room with Cardinal McIntyre and other bishops and monsignors. The cardinal's first words were, "Fr. Berryman [Beh-wee-man, in his pronunciation], when were you thinking of going to Panama?" I said that I had planned to go after officiating at my brother's wedding in June. I was then told that I had two options: go to Panama immediately or take an assignment as a chaplain at Notre Dame Academy, a Catholic girls' high school on the west side of Los Angeles. No reason was given for why this was happening. When I attempted to bring this up, McIntyre became agitated: "We won't go into that! If we do, it will be worse!" and repeated it. Bishops Manning and Ward and various monsignors present were silent or nodded.

I said that I needed to consult with my spiritual director and my family. I went to see Andre Auw at the Passionist monastery in Sierra Madre and then to see my parents and decided to accept the assignment to the girls' school. On Wednesday John McFadden and I moved my belongings out of the rectory and across town. North still wasn't speaking to me, but he expressed surprise to John at how quick I was moving, thus hinting at some remorse on his side. I took up residence in the school, where I had a room adjacent to the chapel. My only duty was to say a 6:30 AM Mass for the sisters, and of course I was to have nothing to do with the students.

DuBay, who at this point had been appointed chaplain at St. John's Hospital in Santa Monica, had contacted the media, so reporters and TV crews arrived. I outlined the sequence of events and let them speak for themselves. Archdiocesan officials claimed it was a "routine transfer." The *National Catholic Reporter*, then in its first year, also devoted a story to it.

Friends came by to see me, and my father let me use his pickup—so for a month and a half I was able to travel around the Los Angeles Basin saying good-bye to friends. Otherwise, I spent the time reading and writing.

During this time the Johnson administration sent ten thousand Marines to the Dominican Republic, ostensibly to restore order or perhaps prevent "another Cuba." I took the administration's reasons at face value and gave it little importance. In fact, the troops were there to suppress a movement that had arisen to restore to the presidency Juan Bosch, who had been democratically elected in 1963, but had been overturned in a coup within months. The Marines stayed for a year and oversaw elections in 1966 that installed Joaquin Balaguer, a previous puppet president under Rafael Trujillo, the longtime dictator assassinated in 1961. Balaguer's brutally repressive regime lasted a dozen years. Although I was about to go to Latin America, I took for granted a U.S. right to intervene in its "backyard."

Shortly before leaving for Panama I had another appointment with the cardinal, who was now pleasant, recalling his experience passing through the locks of the Panama Canal on a ship in the late 1920s. He said, "You go down there and be a good pweest." I also went to see North, who was likewise cordial and wished me well.

4

San Miguelito, "Light of the World"

When I stepped off the plane after an overnight flight from L.A., I was hit with a blast of hot, moist tropical air at 6 am—this was going to be different from Pasadena. Fred McTernan drove me to the archdiocesan seminary where I joined two dozen other people who were participating in a three-month pastoral institute. The San Miguelito project had been attracting dozens, even hundreds, of visitors each year, primarily priests and sisters from Europe and North America going to work in Latin America. The parish had organized the institute to enable such people to participate in the parish and learn its methodology and underlying theology.

San Miguelito was then an area of twenty-five thousand people on the outskirts of Panama City. The central districts comprised new housing developments, primarily modest cement-block houses on small lots built by the government housing agency with international aid. The adjoining areas were filling up with migrants from the countryside who occupied the land, particularly up hillsides and in marshy areas, and built temporary shacks and then over time more permanent homes.

The priests and the parish office occupied three of the new houses, just downhill from the church property. On that property an innovative structure had just been built, not a conventional church but a parish center that could serve for both Mass and community meetings. It had a large octagonal roof supported by pillars on the outside, big enough for several hundred people, and open to allow a breeze to flow and commanding a view of the surrounding neighborhoods and the city. At the main Mass Sunday morning, people sat on wooden benches encircling the altar. The liturgy began with processional music in Panamanian folk idiom: *Vamos, vamos todos a la misa* (Let's all, let's all go to Mass). This sounds unremarkable now but it was practically unheard of at the time.

I was now "Padre Felipe," a member of the San Miguelito team, for the first three months taking part in the pastoral institute until early afternoon and accompanying visits and meetings in the evening. The ideals that I had been pursuing in theology and scripture study now seemed to be embodied in this pastoral experience that I had joined.

MEMENTO OF THE LIVING AND THE DEAD

* * *

In a 1962 memo to Cardinal Albert Meyer, Fr. Leo Mahon had proposed that the Chicago archdiocese contribute to the Latin American church by sponsoring an "experimental parish" staffed with priests and sisters. In responding to the Vatican's appeal for the churches of Europe and North America to send personnel to Latin America, it wouldn't be enough to staff existing parishes or to try to install a U.S.-type parish, because the pastoral situation was quite different. Five percent or fewer of Latin American Catholics attended Sunday Mass, mainly older women and children. The people's own Catholicism was centered primarily on the intercession of the saints or the Virgin Mary for their needs and problems.

Leo's proposal was to emphasize training "laymen in functions formerly performed by priests," especially catechesis, and "the use of the liturgy as the main vehicle of instruction and commitment." It could be summarized in four principles:

1. Work with men first, and then with their wives and other women.
2. Have a basic course called the Family of God in small neighborhood group discussions connecting basic human experiences to scripture.
3. Move toward a basic conversion, through a weekend retreat (*cursillo*).
4. Form a neighborhood-based church community and expand it through the basic course and cursillo.

His surprisingly specific proposal was based on pastoral work that he had done in Chicago with Puerto Ricans starting in the 1950s. Through pastoral experience Leo had concluded that family was the most meaningful aspect of the lives of Puerto Ricans. Together with Maryknoll sisters Mary Xavier and Maria de la Cruz, he had developed an entire adult catechesis around the experience of family: God is our Father, Christ is our brother, baptism is birth, the Eucharist is the family meal, and so forth. Each session began with a discussion of the human reality, such as the birth of a child, and led into one of the sacraments. Connecting it all was the overarching metaphor of family, seen as church, embodied in this here-and-now group of people.

With preliminary approval from Cardinal Meyer, Leo visited several sites in Latin America and settled on San Miguelito, on the outskirts of Panama City, partly through the invitation of Auxiliary Bishop Marcos McGrath. A government agency was then constructing a new housing development of thousands of new cement-block houses in a standard form, offering long-term mortgages at rates affordable to low- and moderate-income families (but not the very poorest). The people were largely migrants from the interior of the country, as with millions of people elsewhere in Latin America. People who had taken such a step, Leo reasoned, might be more open to innovation in their faith as well.

SAN MIGUELITO, "LIGHT OF THE WORLD"

When Leo and two other priests arrived in February 1963 they immediately attracted attention. They switched out of white cassocks into black pants and a white shirt with a cross on the lapel, a novelty at the time. They lived in the same type of house as everyone else, and during the first two months they had to line up with buckets to get water from delivery trucks until they had running water at home.

Their first Sunday Mass took place under a makeshift shelter and was attended by women, children, and dogs, but virtually no men. Later that day Leo came across some men playing dominoes and drinking outdoors and got into a conversation with them. Octavio Pinto, a self-employed house builder, became intrigued when Leo said they weren't there to teach catechism or put up a church building but "to start a revolution." Within a few weeks they had Family of God courses going in four sectors, and by the middle of the year they held a mission on three successive Sundays, preached by Jesus ("Chu") Rodriguez, a Puerto Rican layman with whom Leo had worked in Chicago, and Sunday Mass was attracting large numbers, including men.

Shortly after their arrival, Leo and the team published a widely circulated position paper—a manifesto—outlining what they intended to do and the rationale behind it. That and successive reports drew a constant stream of visitors, primarily North American and European priests and sisters on their way to assignments in Latin America, often after spending some months in Cuernavaca at the language and cultural training center run by Msgr. Ivan Illich. Leo and the team sometimes used the expression "San Miguelito, Light of the World." This experimental parish was showing the way.

* * *

Panama was—and still is—the smallest country in Latin America in terms of population, then about a million and a half people. Geographically, the country is an isthmus, extending from Costa Rica in the west to Colombia in the east. It is narrow: it was an hour's drive from Panama City on the Pacific Coast to the city of Colon on the Atlantic. Cutting the country in half was the Canal Zone, a ten-mile swath of land occupied by the United States, containing the canal itself and a number of U.S. military bases. About half of the population lived in Panama City and its environs, and the other half in the "interior," the portion between the Canal Zone and Costa Rica. With its mix of peasant agriculture and some large commercial farms, the interior resembled other rural regions in Latin America. About forty miles east of Panama City the highway halted and gave way to a roadless jungle extending to Colombia.

Despite the small population, Panamanians exhibited considerable ethnic and cultural diversity. The interior was populated by descendants of people from colonial times, including slaves. Three indigenous groups (then known as Kuna, Choco, and Guaymi) retained their language and ways of life, while living in marginal areas. Many in Panama City and Colon were descendants of West Indians who had come to work on the canal at the beginning of the twentieth century, along with Chinese, Jews, and immigrants from the Middle East. Panamanians are culturally similar to Puerto Ricans, Dominicans, Cubans, and others from the Caribbean and the coasts of South America. They are boisterous and informal, their diets are rice-based, their music is linked to dancing, and in their speech some consonants almost disappear.

In colonial times Panama was a transit point for gold and silver brought from South America, taken across the isthmus on pack mule, and then shipped to Spain in convoys. Panamanian identity has been shaped by the country's location between the Atlantic and the Pacific Oceans and between North and South America. Four centuries of trade had left their mark on people, at least those near the transit areas.

After independence in the nineteenth century, Panama was a province of Colombia, but Panamanians felt that they were ignored by far-off Bogota, and some advocated independence. Their chance came in 1903, when President Theodore Roosevelt, finding the Colombian government balking at the U.S. offer to continue the construction of a canal begun by the French, sent warships to shield Panamanians and enable them to proclaim independence. A treaty was then signed in New York, with no Panamanians present, ceding to the United States the rights it would have "as if it were sovereign" for ninety-nine years. After completion of the canal, admittedly a great wonder of engineering, those who had labored on it had to leave, and the Canal Zone was entirely occupied by U.S. civilian Canal Zone employees and military personnel. The Americans lived in large houses with well-manicured lawns, while most of the zone itself remained undeveloped.

Many Panamanians were employed by the canal or on the military bases and earned good wages by Panamanian standards, so much so that Panamanian GDP per capita was on a par with those of Argentina and Venezuela, far above the Latin American average. However, the price Panamanians paid for this relative prosperity was the indignity of knowing that the most distinctive feature of their country was in the hands of an occupying power.

In January 1964, a year and a half before my arrival, Panamanian high school students had marched into the zone attempting to raise the Panamanian flag alongside the U.S. flag—as was their right by treaty. They were met by hostile students and parents. Fighting broke out, and violence escalated. In these "flag riots," as they were called in news accounts, twenty-one people were killed, mainly Panamanians shot by U.S. military snipers firing into Panama City. The Panamanian government broke off relations, but when I arrived they had been restored, and issues of nationalism seemed dormant.

* * *

The Catholic Church in Panama displayed weaknesses rooted in its history. Only about forty of the country's two hundred priests were Panamanian; the largest number were from Spain. When Archbishop Tomas Clavel was appointed in 1964, he was the first Panamanian to head the archdiocese in 150 years. Many of the priests in the archdiocese were members of religious congregations. Church personnel were disproportionately serving the urban middle classes in schools and parishes. The vast majority of Panamanians did not attend Mass regularly; their Catholicism was expressed in devotions to saints or to the Blessed Virgin in terms of their own needs.

Some clergy were less than welcoming to the San Miguelito team, whose nonclerical garb and use of the Bible initially created suspicion. The refusal by the Chicago priests to accept money for Mass intentions or baptisms, weddings, or funerals—which were a significant source of their own income—was taken as a rebuke. However, Archbishop Clavel firmly supported the San Miguelito team.

* * *

When I arrived in mid-1965 the experiment had been going for over two years, hundreds of people had participated in the local Family of God groups, and the parish had a solid cadre of men and women leaders. The full-time parish team numbered about a dozen, between priests, sisters, and full-time laypeople.

The San Miguelito experiment had made important innovations in relating Christianity to Panamanian culture, including a Mass with Panamanian folk music. The parish had staged a Passion Play in contemporary form—for example, Jesus was dressed in peasant garb and wasn't crucified but was taken before a firing squad for his "revolutionary" message, the Jerusalem authorities wore business suits, and the Roman soldiers donned National Guard uniforms. The story was told partly in a *décima*, an elaborate kind of sung verse dating from colonial times.

Lillian Brulc, an artist from Illinois, was painting on one surface of the open structure used for Mass and other community activities a large mural depicting the "liberation of a people." On one side were men carrying heavy stone blocks, alluding to slavery in Egypt; in Diego Rivera fashion some of the exploiters looked like priests. On the other side was a small circle of people resembling a Family of God group; in the center was a man with his arms outstretched along a round wooden branch on his shoulders, suggesting the crucified Jesus.

Notable Panamanians in business and government came to the Passion Play and sometimes to Sunday Mass. Foreign visitors also came to visit, often spending a few days to observe the parish and talk with team members.

* * *

The Hermanos (brothers) were a key feature in San Miguelito, an all-male group of two or three dozen men who met Monday nights. These men had completed the basic

Family of God course and were themselves conducting courses in their sectors. The Monday night meeting was devoted to planning, evaluation, and preparation.

Leo would lead a discussion of the meeting theme for the week. He might begin by asking what happens at a family meal. Individuals would name common or favorite Panamanian dishes, or describe the family at the table. The discussion would eventually lead to the insight that a meal does more than nourish the body, it knits a family together. Toward the end, the New Testament account of Last Supper would be read, indicating that the Mass originally arose in the context of a meal, albeit a special meal. The discussion fit into the larger family metaphor running through the course and linking the sacraments to human life.

On Tuesday, Wednesday, or Thursday these same men in twos and threes organized and led a meeting in their own neighborhood, accompanied by a priest or sister. At the Monday night meeting they reported on the previous week's meetings, and a tally was made of the total number of people participating, thus giving a sense that cumulatively their own neighborhood groups were part of a larger movement, even a "revolution." This focus on men, based on the earlier work in Chicago, was intended to break the centuries-old attitude and practice in which church participation was regarded as a female activity. In fostering camaraderie among the Hermanos, the San Miguelito team was tapping into machismo to change the sense of what the church was about.

Leo and the team saw the Hermanos as being potential candidates for ordination to the diaconate. The notion of a restoration of the diaconate was circulating among theologians and became enshrined in Vatican II. However, Leo and the team also thought it would make sense that married laymen at some time could be ordained to preside the Eucharist in small community settings. If that were to come about, the role of the full-time celibate priest might be more akin to that of a bishop in early Christianity, an "overseer" of a number of house churches.

* * *

The weekly courses in neighborhoods were followed by a weekend retreat or cursillo, an adaptation of the *Cursillo de Cristiandad*, which had been developed in Spain and spread to Latin America and elsewhere, primarily among the middle and upper classes. The cursillo ran from Friday night to Sunday afternoon and consisted of singing and camaraderie, and several talks combined with small-group discussion. A key moment came on Saturday night, when a layman gave a presentation about sin and repentance, drawing on his own story. The portrayal was that of a darkness-to-life experience, a shift from an old self, marked by drinking, marital infidelity, and overall irresponsibility, to a new self who was now in love with and faithful to his wife and children, and who no longer needed to get drunk. Participants were invited to make a similar change in their own life; the evening ended with a penitential ceremony with the opportunity to go to confession.

Sunday morning presented the positive counterpart, joining the Christian community, being united in the Eucharist, joining the cause of Christ to pursue the kingdom of God. The cursillo song "De colores" was a kind of anthem—expressing the conviction that with Christ one's life was "in color," like a rainbow or the countryside in spring. Participants left the cursillo on an emotional high.

This process resembles the conversion that takes place when Latin American males join a pentecostal church: they renounce their former ways, particularly the macho behavior of drinking, womanizing, and domestic violence—along with their Catholicism. They are also initiated into a new alternate community that will support them in their change of life, and they themselves immediately become missionaries of their newfound faith. The San Miguelito conversion was different in the sense that people remained Catholics, albeit marked off from those who were simply Catholic by birth. They didn't totally renounce liquor, but rather getting drunk. Those who made the cursillo could become active members of the parish in their neighborhood and in attending the lively Sunday Mass.

Leo regarded this type of internal conversion as crucial. During the team's first few months they had brought together a group of men who formed an organization to deal with community issues, the Christian Men of San Miguelito, which quickly grew to 450 members, but then fell apart. The reason, Leo believed, was the lack of a sufficient internal conversion of the participants. Such a focus on conversion may appear moralistic, but it enabled men to start taking charge of their own lives in a new way. It also helped them move toward a more companionate type of marriage relationship.

The cursillo might also look like emotional manipulation—especially the Saturday night direct appeal for conversion—but at some level many men were perhaps unconsciously ready to move away from the macho behavior and image that they were expected to maintain. One man I knew was embarrassed by the fact that he had always been faithful to his wife; such were the pressures to live up to the macho image. The Family of God course and the cursillo were tapping into an unconscious desire of the men for a different kind of life, and the parish movement constituted a countercommunity.

* * *

Participating in the pastoral institute were twenty-five or so people, half of them Europeans and North Americans working in various Latin American countries, several Latin Americans, the priests and sisters of the team, and several laypeople. Like others around the continent they were increasingly aware that the problem facing the church in Latin America wasn't simply or even primarily a "priest shortage." They had committed themselves to this three-month course because they believed that San

Miguelito was developing a pastoral model that was based on the New Testament and that worked with ordinary Panamanians. However, it wasn't a method that could be applied mechanically but very much a mystique.

Unlike conventional pastoral institutes, which would have lectures on sociology or other social sciences, scripture, liturgy, pastoral theology, and so forth, here the format was a three-hour session in the morning (with a coffee break) based entirely on a Bible passage or two, which prompted a freewheeling discussion led by Leo. Over the course of three months we made our way through the biblical history of Israel (Abraham, Moses and the Exodus, the kingdom and the prophets) and then to the Gospels, Acts, and portions of the other New Testament writings. A thread running through the course was the formation of the people of Israel, and then the formation of the new people, the church.

A discussion of Moses and Exodus might lead to the relationship of a leader to his people. Examples were drawn from Panamanian or Latin American history or events in San Miguelito itself. It wasn't a fundamentalist reading; the work of scripture scholars and theologians served as background, but the emphasis was on connecting the major narratives and themes of the Bible to human experience. Don Headley, a Chicago priest familiar with contemporary theology and scripture scholarship, assisted Leo in the course.

In leading the discussion, Leo gravitated toward the laymen: Fidel Gonzalez, who was from Las Tablas in the interior of Panama, and two from Chicago, Jesus Rodriguez, a Puerto Rican, and Jesus Garcia, a Mexican. He was more interested in these laypeople because they had far more life experience than, say, someone like me who had been a seminarian and then a parish priest. He was genuinely interested in what they had to say: when the discussion took an unexpected turn, he followed it. Another forceful participant was Cecilia Dolan, a Maryknoll sister from Argentina. The discussion could easily move from an apparent tangent, to a tangent on that, and yet again, before coming back to the scripture passage that was the takeoff point. Often these tangents delved into traditional practices or beliefs, or turns of phrase in common speech. Leo was modeling how we should be, curious to learn from ordinary people.

Because of recurring themes, particularly the formation of a people (Israel, the church, San Miguelito), participants gained a key for reading the scriptures, connecting them to ordinary life, and an open-ended spirituality. This may sound unremarkable today because the three-year cycle of readings in the Catholic liturgy since Vatican II provides a thorough exposure to the Bible, but it was novel at the time. Leo exemplified a fresh way of doing theology. He respected academic theologians and was familiar with current theological trends, but his gift was to find ways to make theology come alive in dialogue with ordinary Panamanians.

Leo took seriously the humanity of Jesus in the Gospels, that is, that Jesus was like us and that our human experience is a pathway to understanding him. That led to the notion that Jesus's life was the most authentic human life, and that in following him and his ideals, we would be living our lives most authentically. That notion has been a commonplace in theology and in preaching for decades, but it wasn't in the mid-1960s, and Leo could express it in the Panamanian vernacular. In the institute I observed him in action, asking probing questions, enjoying the way the conversation proceeded, his imagination often fired with a new idea.

The course was held in the seminary building in the hills of Las Cumbres, about a twenty-minute drive from the parish. In the later afternoons, the participants, including me, accompanied groups in the various regions of the parish visiting neighborhoods, knocking on doors to invite people to a meeting, and attending the meeting held in someone's small yard or living room.

The Sunday Mass with several hundred people on benches in the open area with a view of the surrounding neighborhood was a kind of high point of the week and proof of the validity of the method. The main celebrant was usually Leo, and his sermon brought out something fresh in the scripture readings and related it to developments in the community.

* * *

I was now part of the San Miguelito team, which comprised five other priests, five Maryknoll sisters, and some laypeople. The other priests were John Greeley, who had arrived with Leo in the beginning; John Enright, also from Chicago; Mark Sheehan, a Benedictine from New Jersey; and Fred McTernan, a former military chaplain from Newark who focused largely on logistical matters. Paul Meyer, another Benedictine from New Jersey, a convert from Judaism, was also part of the community. We lived in three government-built adjoining houses across the street from where the main church structure stood.

By the time I arrived, Bob McGlinn, one of the three original priests, was working with rural people some miles away and was not using the team's pastoral methodology. He didn't have a vehicle and seemed to spend much of his time simply reaching people on foot or by river. At the time, he struck me as quirky and something of a loner, but perhaps he had opted to get some distance from Leo's strong personality.

The Maryknoll sisters had arrived around the beginning of 1965, after an earlier group of sisters had not worked out. The superior was Maria de la Cruz Coronado, a Mexican American from Los Angeles, who had worked with Leo for five years in Chicago. Cecilia Dolan was originally from Buenos Aires and spoke Argentine Spanish and English with a brogue. Together with Graciela Hernandez, Maura Cambra, and Beatriz Cardenal, a Nicaraguan, they lived in community a few streets away. The sisters worked primarily with women who had entered the parish program. Because women were generally at home during the day, the sisters had more day-to-day contact in the neighborhoods than the priests.

Pastoral activity was divided by areas, with some team members working in the original core of government-built housing and others in areas where people were building their own houses, often in swampy areas or hillsides reachable only by steep trails. In these areas, roads were unpaved, and some families didn't have running water or electricity. The team now met daily from 8 to 9 AM for a scripture meditation or discussion, similar to what had been done in the course. The initial passage typically led to a wide-ranging discussion connecting the reading to ongoing life in the parish.

Contrary to my experience in Pasadena, I now seemed to have found my place in Panama. The pastoral work we were doing, evangelization and formation of small communities gathering in houses, seemed to echo the New Testament and yet it was rooted in Panamanian culture. No longer wearing clerical clothes, I attended a community Mass rather than saying one daily, and I didn't hear confessions. The ongoing growth of the community and the constant flow of visitors from Europe, North America, and Latin America seemed to validate the experiment.

I don't recall us paying much attention to the final session of Vatican II, which took place at this time. The majority of bishops had prevailed over the conservatives, led by the Roman curia, but few of the documents had yet been published. At San Miguelito we assumed that we were already anticipating what the Council bishops were proposing. We did watch Paul VI on a grainy black-and-white TV as he addressed the United Nations and spoke in Yankee Stadium, urging peace in both places, in one of the first of the modern papal journeys.

My social life was with other priests on the team, going out to a restaurant for Italian food or Argentine steak on a plank, going to a movie downtown, or perhaps a day at the beach, an hour or so away through the Canal Zone and into the interior.

* * *

By this time Leo was rethinking and modifying the basic Family of God course. Rather than being structured on the sacraments as family events, the discussions were focused on certain key realities in human life. The first discussion began with a simple question: is there injustice in the world? People came up with various examples from public life, history, and personal experience. Eventually the Genesis account of Cain and Abel was read, as an archetype of the evil that human beings do to each other. Although the term "original sin" wasn't used, this reading represented a shift away from the conventional notion of something transmitted from Adam and Eve by procreation.

One of the livelier discussions began by asking participants to picture a *velorio* (wake). "Suppose I'm dead and in a coffin. What's happening?" The participants would then describe the scene of a traditional *novenario* or nine-day observance: the men playing dominoes outside the house, the women inside praying the rosary or serving coffee and sandwiches. The discussion leader then presses: "What's happened to me? Where am I?" Invariably, people would say that you are gone, that death is final. At some point, the leader would read a scriptural passage on the resurrection, thus confronting traditional cultural notions with this core biblical claim and how it should inspire the way we live.

Another discussion would be about relations between men and women as understood in the culture, particularly the notion that it is normal for men to be out drinking and having other sexual partners while women were expected to be at home taking care of the children. As the saying goes, *El hombre es para la calle, y la mujer es para la casa* (Men are for the street and women for the home). Then scriptural quotes emphasizing the equality of men and women were read, again challenging popular beliefs and assumptions.

In another session the questions would be aimed at what it means to be a full human being and would lead to the proposal that Jesus lived the fullest human life. In this instance Christian faith was seen to be a fulfillment of human yearnings. One of the later discussions led to the image of the first Christian community in Jerusalem as described in Acts, and the final one presented the image of redeemed humankind in the heavenly city in Revelation.

The course was still called the Family of God, but it was now built on fundamental human existential concerns rather than a somewhat forced structure based on the sacraments. It was very interesting to see Leo's mind at work as the themes for the revised course were being worked out. The result was a richer vision that drew on scripture and tapped into people's lived experience. It also demanded some adjustment on the part of those who had become accustomed to the simplicity of the original course, in which the answer to every question seemed to be that God wants us to be united as brothers and sisters.

* * *

In 1966 the original parish was subdivided into sectors that became parishes, with a priest-and-sister team in charge of each. At San Miguelito the identity of the priest was no longer centered on performing rituals or sacraments, but on forming Christian community. Leo and the others were not questioning celibacy for themselves: he thought that priest was married—firmly committed—to the community.

What then was the role of the sisters? Their work was primarily in the formation of women. It was also said that their presence was a challenge to the men of the community. These were attractive women who were nevertheless vowed and not potential sexual partners. The notion was that they embodied what being a woman meant or could mean. As later became clear, these notions of being a priest and sister could serve as a kind of ideology, obfuscating what was happening.

By this time Cardinal Meyer had died and was replaced by Cardinal John Cody. Meyer had understood the pastoral spirit of San Miguelito, but Cody was an imperious hierarch with little theological or pastoral sense. He didn't think the priests should live in houses like other people and pressed Leo to have a new complex built above the church, with space for meetings, a dining room, and residences for priests and visitors. Leo acceded, and the expensive construction was under way.

* * *

The approach in San Miguelito wasn't simply a method or a style; it raised fundamental pastoral and theological questions. Panamanian and Latin American Catholicism existed in two fundamental forms, those who regularly attended Mass, particularly a small middle-class elite educated in Catholic schools, and a much larger group of poor people whose Catholicism was much more centered on devotions to particular saints and images, often in terms of their immediate needs. Priests spent much of their time in ritual actions, Mass, baptisms, funerals, and weddings, and their income was dependent on those duties.

In the New Testament, being a Christian means hearing and accepting the gospel, being converted, and joining the Christian community through baptism. That was the case during the first three centuries, but with the formation of Christendom in which society itself was deemed to be Christian, infants were baptized and could go through their lives without ever hearing the gospel as "good news" and having to make a personal decision.

For several decades European theologians had raised the issue of people being raised in nominally Catholic countries and never making a personal decision to accept the gospel. In the late 1940s two French priests published *France: Pays de Mission?* (France: mission country?) arguing that the mass of industrial workers were pagans in a fully pagan milieu and needed to be approached in a missionary spirit. Such questions had generally not been raised in Latin America, with the interesting exception of Chilean Jesuit Alberto Hurtado, who worked among the poor and who in the early 1940s published *Es Chile un País Católico?* (Is Chile a Catholic country?). In the 1960s, Uruguayan theologian Juan-Luis Segundo proposed that most Latin American Catholics were in a pre-Christian stage.

The San Miguelito approach was, in effect, an attempt to restore something of the process of early Christianity through an evangelization embodied in the basic course, and a conversion in the cursillo, followed by adherence to a local Christian community or church. It assumed that people had not really been confronted with central dimensions of the gospel, such as the resurrection of Jesus as a pledge to his followers. (Technically, it was perhaps a blend of evangelization and catechesis, since it was building on an adherence to Catholicism as people understood it.)

This was all understood as building church. Taken literally, that implies that the church doesn't exist. That was in fact what Protestants said or assumed, that is, that traditional Latin American Catholicism was superstition, not biblical Christianity.

Not surprisingly, the San Miguelito team was sometimes accused of being Protestant or heretical.

Was the San Miguelito experiment aimed at *renewing* the Catholic Church in Panama? Or did it assume that the church—at least as understood in the New Testament—didn't really exist and had to be "built"? Often enough the language of Leo and others implied that "church" in a theological sense did not really exist.

This seemingly theoretical issue came to a head particularly around baptism of infants. Baptism was a major cultural event in family life, particularly in the choice of godparents. Infant baptism seemed theologically problematic: continuing to baptize children without adult evangelization perpetuated a pastoral and theological contradiction.

While still at San Miguelito I submitted an article on the topic to *Concilium*, the international theological journal edited by the major Vatican II theologians and published in several languages. I argued that the theological shift toward a focus on God's universal saving will should lead to a rethinking of infant baptism, especially in Latin America. The editors proposed that I reshape it with less emphasis on the theology of salvation, and more on pastoral practice. I did so, and the article was published in 1967. I described the typical situation and the pastoral contradictions.

Within a few years Latin American Catholicism was at least aware of the problem, that is, that many parents who presented their children for baptism were themselves not evangelized. A common solution was to require that parents and godparents attend two or three instruction classes for the sacrament. That was not really satisfactory, since the parents' desire for the sacrament was being used as leverage, and two or three instructions under such conditions were scarcely evangelization. Years later church documents called for a "re-evangelization of the baptized," an awkward expression that at least acknowledges the problem of faith transmitted by culture without conscious personal option.

* * *

For the second pastoral institute scheduled for the first three months of 1966, Leo asked me to assist him, as Don Headley had done for the first course. Approximately twenty-five participants came for the course from Peru, Chile, Brazil, Central America, and the United States. The procedure was quite similar to that of the first institute, moving through the Bible with freewheeling discussions in the morning, and participation in the parish in the evening and on weekends. Participants from these institutes implemented what they had learned in Choluteca (Honduras), Recife (Brazil), and elsewhere.

Leo and I met each evening to prepare the next day's session, he typically in his *guayavera*, smoking a cigar and making notes on a yellow pad. We would go over the scripture for the next day and anticipate where the discussion might go. Spending time with him enabled me to appreciate his pastoral genius. Leo combined mystique and organizational ability (he was from Chicago), and he was able to spot leadership potential in individuals (Octavio Pinto, Fidel Gonzalez, Ramon Hernandez, Severino Hernandez) and develop it. He didn't work alone but with a large team, including sisters and laypeople. However, it is not unfair to the others to say that the driving spirit was that of Leo himself. He had a strong personality; the only person on the team who could stand up to him was Cecilia Dolan.

Once as we were standing in the observation area on the roof at the Tocumen airport (we frequently drove to the airport to pick up visitors and see them off) a jet accelerated down the runway and then shot into the air at a sharp angle. He turned to me and said, smiling, "Who says men can't be gods?" It was a spontaneous remark, questionable if examined closely. However, it expressed a delight in collective human ingenuity, and he meant it not just about engineers and pilots but about the people of San Miguelito. On another occasion, he was speculating that perhaps people needn't be active in the local Christian community forever; perhaps after receiving some formation they would move on—"graduate," he called it. He didn't pursue the thought further, but it amounted to boldly questioning the underlying assumptions of the entire San Miguelito enterprise.

One night when we had been preparing the next day's session, he said to me, "You're a smart guy, but you've got to learn more from the people." Although it stung a little bit, the remark stayed with me and shaped my own later options. Leo was only a dozen years older than I, but he was a kind of father figure to me, although I wasn't conscious of it at the time.

Toward the end of this second course, as an exercise, Cecilia Dolan, an American Jesuit working in Peru, and I were assigned the task of composing a "canon," as the eucharistic prayer was then called. The canon was still in Latin and still prayed silently by the priest, although it was expected to be recited aloud in the vernacular in the renewed liturgy then being prepared in Rome. Based on themes from the course discussions and models from ancient eucharistic liturgies, we composed a canon invoking the story of Israel, thanking God for leading us out of slavery and into freedom, and for raising up prophets, and finally for Jesus himself. I did the basic draft in English and Cecilia put it into Spanish, and the canon began to be used in the parish. In 1967 it was published in the journal *Cross Currents*, alongside seven other experimental eucharistic prayers. It was rendered moot by Rome's publication of new eucharistic prayers in 1968.

* * *

In February 1966, in the middle of the course, the newspapers reported the death in combat of the Colombian priest Camilo Torres. From an upper-class Bogota family, Torres had returned to Colombia in 1960 after earning degrees in theology and sociology in Europe, and served as a chaplain to university students while doing research on issues in both rural and urban Colombia. Over time he became radicalized politically, and by 1965 was promoting the Broad Front, a political coalition intended to unite the majorities, bypassing the existing Liberal and Conservative parties. In writings and manifestos, he posed a radical challenge to Christians: revolution was necessary in order to achieve a just society. Under pressure from the archbishop, he agreed to cease acting as a priest; he then joined the guerrillas of the National Liberation Army (ELN) and was killed in combat. Camilo Torres soon became iconic, like Che Guevara, a symbol challenging Catholics to follow their convictions to the ultimate consequences.

His example posed the question of the relationship between the church (and priests) and politics. According to the San Miguelito vision, the proper role of the priest was to form Christian community, not to be involved directly in politics, and particularly not to be a caudillo-type leader. The influence of the church on politics had to be indirect, as a result of laypeople acting. That would apply to Torres as well, however much one might sympathize with his intentions. That neat separation of church and politics would soon be challenged by liberation theology, and in San Miguelito itself.

Panamanian politics had all the trappings of democratic government: a president, political parties, elections, Congress, and government ministries, but ordinary people regarded it as representing the interests of the elites, called in Panamanian slang *rabiblancos* (white tails), and to be corrupt. Some ordinary people and intellectuals were vaguely sympathetic to the notion of "revolution," as was true elsewhere in Latin America, but the heavy U.S. military presence in the Canal Zone, and the dependence of many people for employment there, made Panamanians quite unrevolutionary. Leo and the team used the language of revolution to refer to Jesus and to their aims in the parish, but it remained a metaphor.

To me the team's use of the language of revolution looked like tapping into people's resentment with traditional politics and their vague yearning for a more just society, but then utilizing that feeling to involve them in what was a church movement. I wrote a paper arguing that "revolution," such as what was happening in Cuba and was being attempted elsewhere, was serious and that we should be alert to the difference between a real revolution for which people risked and lost their lives, and a metaphorical use of the term. The paper was intended only for circulation among the team members, but I got some feedback from Maryknollers in Guatemala who a year or so later would be involved with revolutionaries there.

* * *

In 1966 a group of people had invaded land in an area near the university called Veranillo. The government housing agency proposed that these people be settled in

San Miguelito on lands with urban services and be given help in building permanent houses. They were allotted a hillside above the church structure. A lottery was held on Saturday morning to assign the lots, and people went to work putting up temporary structures. By Sunday night they had settled into Nuevo Veranillo. This was an early instance of a government working with "invaders" as opposed to sending the police. People received a plot with a cement platform and a loan for some building materials. They also had piped-in water and eventually sewer service. Over a period of years they could buy cement, sand, cement block, and roofing materials, and build the house at their own pace. I followed this process through the eyes of the Peralta family, whom I came to know pastorally.

* * *

I once represented San Miguelito at a two-day gathering of American Protestant ministers at a beach retreat. Some were missionaries, but most served congregations in the Canal Zone. My presentation of what was being done—particularly the use of the Bible—the attempt to emulate the New Testament communities, and the methodology must have seemed unlike their understandings and experience of Catholicism, but also an indication that a new era was beginning in the wake of Vatican II. It gave me a window into the situation of Protestants in this Catholic country and also an awareness of the island of the United States in the Canal Zone. Ken Mahler, a Lutheran, and Ned Webster, an Episcopalian, and their wives became friends.

* * *

At a meeting of the Hermanos, Fred McTernan made a presentation of the parish finances as part of a step toward instituting some form of financial contribution by parishioners. Even though the people could hardly be expected to pay anything like the full cost of the parish operations, something more than the negligible sums of the Sunday collection would signify commitment. As he went over various items, such as salaries and vehicles, he mentioned in passing a monthly cost of liquor (over a hundred dollars, as I recall). I realized that this was more than the monthly salary of many of the Hermanos. The cost represented hospitality to visitors, including the Hermanos themselves, who if they stopped by in the evening might be offered a gin and tonic or rum and Coke.

That realization fostered a vague disquiet that I was feeling not so much over San Miguelito as over my involvement in it. Money didn't explain the success of San Miguelito, which was the result of a pastoral vision and the team carrying it out. Nevertheless, priests and religious elsewhere had no such hefty foreign funding. I was especially uncomfortable with the new buildings on which Cardinal Cody had insisted.

While I enjoyed being part of a highly successful pastoral initiative that was drawing wide attention and seemed to be the answer to the yearnings I had felt since seminary days, I also felt like I was riding along with a juggernaut. If we wanted to find a valid pastoral method, it had to be closer to the situation of other Panamanian parishes. At a less conscious level, I probably wanted to get some distance from Leo's forceful personality.

Leo informed me that Archbishop Clavel was looking for a priest for the parish of Nuestra Señora de Fatima, in the barrio of Chorrillo in downtown Panama City, adjacent to the Canal Zone. It was a very crowded slum in an area that many Panamanians feared and avoided as dangerous. One day I went down on the bus and walked around there. I didn't feel entirely comfortable with the noise, smells, and density, but I met with Clavel and agreed to become pastor.

* * *

Before making the move I returned to Los Angeles for a month to visit with my family and friends. As the flight approached LAX at night from the south in a half-hour descent along the coast, I could see the Southern California basin lit up all the way to the mountains. It was obviously far larger and more powerful than all of Panama. During my visit I was reminded of the gap between even ordinary suburban homes and the self-built shacks up in the hills of San Miguelito, as well as the ordinary concerns of people in both societies. It was the "reverse culture shock" often felt by missionaries or Peace Corps volunteers, but in my case it was only temporary.

While in L.A., I attended a reunion with my seminary classmates. We were now three years into our priesthood, and I was excited by the San Miguelito vision and my prospects of starting out as pastor in Chorrillo. My classmates could expect to be in their fifties before becoming pastors. At the gathering I sensed a growing distance from them. More than one seemed to be in therapy mode, interpreting everything in terms of feeling, as though their new prophet were Carl Rogers. Toward the end of the evening, someone proposed going to a go-go bar. I don't know whether anyone did, but it indicated to me that they were adrift in their priesthood while I was enthusiastic at the prospect of starting work in Chorrillo.

While home I spent time in the backyard reading the newly published documents of Vatican II, in a new paperback, each introduced by a Catholic, and followed by a commentary by a non-Catholic, attesting to the ecumenical hopes of that moment. The newest element was *Gaudium et Spes*, the document on the church in the modern world, which broke new ground by identifying the Catholic Church with humankind as a whole, rather than emphasizing a separation or conflict between "church" and "world." The task ahead seemed to be to implement the work of the Council, and I felt fortunate to be in Panama where that vision had been remarkably anticipated and embodied.

5

First Steps in Chorrillo

Chorrillo was situated on the opposite side of downtown Panama City from San Miguelito, just before the bridge across the canal leading to the interior. It was bounded by the Canal Zone, the Pacific Ocean, and other barrios of downtown Panama City. Outsiders regarded Chorrillo as a dangerous slum, and few went there unless they had a specific reason.

The most obvious feature of the area was the housing: two-story wooden structures, one family to a room, with twenty to forty rooms per house. The houses were built around patios that contained communal sinks, toilets, and showers, and were separated from the adjoining house by an alley a yard or so wide. In a survey we found that 151 people were living in a house next to the church. These houses had been built as temporary barracks for workers forced out of the Canal Zone in 1913 when the canal construction was being completed. They soon filled with families, and the structures themselves were still in place a half-century later.

In the 1950s Fr. Guillermo Sosa, a Panamanian priest, had come to Chorrillo, founded the parish, and spent a decade there, having a large, solid church built with funds he had raised from benefactors. I met him only once or twice, but by all accounts he was a kind and pious man who helped people and was especially devoted to children. He had gone to work in the interior and had been succeeded by two priests, one Panamanian and one Spanish, each of whom had brief tenures, perhaps because there were few demands for weddings, funerals, or other traditional activities of priests. No parish organizations were operating, and so I inherited a relatively blank slate, but not as blank as San Miguelito when the Chicago team arrived.

According to the census, fourteen thousand people lived in the parish boundaries, most of them on three streets, Calle 25, Calle 26, and Calle 27. The church sat on Calle 26, not far from the sea wall along the ocean, from which a fishing cooperative operated. Given the tropical heat, windows and doors were usually open, and people had no real privacy. The characteristic feature of Chorrillo was street life: cars and buses and blaring radios, people hanging out, various smells.

Contrary to the stereotypes of outsiders, *chorrilleros* were generally law-abiding citizens like people elsewhere in the city. About 20 percent of heads of household worked in the Canal Zone and on U.S. bases, 20 percent for the Panamanian government, 40 percent for private companies, and 20 percent were self-employed. Many men were low-ranking members of the Guardia Nacional, whose headquarters was in Chorrillo. As is common among the poor, a significant number of households were female-headed. The people in the barrio reflected urban Panama: migrants from various provinces in the interior, descendants of the Jamaicans who had come to build the canal, members of Panama's indigenous groups, and people of Chinese descent. They were more urban than the people of San Miguelito, and many had been in Chorrillo all their lives.

Besides the crowded wooden housing there were three large apartment complexes in the parish, in which people had several rooms with their own plumbing and some privacy, varying between working-class and middle-class. Although they were territorially in Chorrillo the residents generally did not regard themselves as chorrilleros.

I had come to Chorrillo intending to implement the kind of pastoral work that I had learned in San Miguelito, but with some obvious differences: I was in an established parish in a neighborhood fifty years old, I wouldn't have the same resources, and I wasn't Leo Mahon.

* * *

After my first Sunday Mass a man introduced himself, and I learned that he lived on Calle 27 behind the church. "Don Toti," as I soon realized, was well known in Chorrillo because he sold *raspados* (snow cones) from his wooden cart, shaving the ice from a solid block by hand and pouring colored syrup over it. He agreed to go visiting with me, and we held the first Family of God discussion group in the patio of his house the following Friday evening. Through other casual contacts I did the same in two other areas of the parish. As in San Miguelito, the sight of this new "Padre Felipe" not in clerical clothes knocking on doors and inviting people to a discussion was a novelty. By the end of my third week we had groups doing the "basic course" in three areas.

Rather than applying the San Miguelito approach so quickly, I might have been better advised to spend some weeks or even months just getting to know the barrio. However, the door knocking and visiting entailed in organizing these groups helped me overcome my shyness and was itself a good way to get into the barrio and to meet people.

The natural place for holding meetings was in the patios of houses. Given the population density, it was enough to invite the people from the house where the meeting was to be held and in a couple of adjoining houses. I would first get the agreement of some people in the house to host a meeting, determine the day, and inform neighbors. On the day of the meeting, we went knocking on doors reminding people and set up chairs or benches in the patio, running an extension cord with an extra lightbulb if necessary. Then we sat and conversed casually until we had a quorum of eight or ten people, at which point we began one of the course sessions. This was the reformulated San Miguelito basic course, based on common human experiences and concerns, leading to a scripture passage that might reaffirm or challenge that experience.

One of those initial groups was organized in the Huerta Sandoval apartment complex. The buildings were concrete and well maintained, and people living there were of a kind of middle class, working in management or technical positions. People lived in closed apartments and were more private toward their neighbors than those in the rest of Chorrillo. We met in an open space outside one of the buildings.

Three or four months after my arrival, nineteen men from Chorrillo participated in a cursillo organized by San Miguelito. Some of them then began to go along as we moved into new sections with the basic course. As in San Miguelito the wives or partners of the men were soon part of the movement. Early parish leaders included Roberto and Encarnacion Batista, whose wedding I officiated very early on; Joaquin Melgar and his wife, Leoncia; and Gabino Hernandez, a Canal Zone worker and his wife, Chela.

* * *

One day during my first month in Chorrillo, while having lunch in San Miguelito, I got into a conversation with a Chilean literature professor, Jose Bulnes Aldunate, then teaching in Puerto Rico. He had come from CIDOC, the think tank in Cuernavaca set up by Ivan Illich. He spoke animatedly, a classic Latin American literary intellectual, with a broad view of the region. He came back to Chorrillo with me, and we continued talking for hours. At one point as we walked along the ocean, he recited Ruben Dario's "Ode to Roosevelt" (written in 1904), familiar to nationalists throughout Latin America but not to me at that point. The poem first acknowledges the power of the United States with its locomotives and electricity, embodied in its big-game-hunter president, but it then goes on to contrast the might of the North with the spiritual qualities of Latin Americans, warning that the peoples of the continent will resist.

At my invitation, Bulnes came back a night or two later and had a discussion with six or eight men whom I had been able to invite. He had recently been an observer at the elections in the Dominican Republic held under the guns of the U.S. Marines whom Lyndon Johnson had dispatched a year earlier. They had been sent to put down a movement to restore the democratically elected president Juan Bosch, who had been overthrown in a coup. The intervention was justified in the United States as preventing "another Cuba," but it led to many years of repressive rule under President Joaquin Balaguer. Just how the session with Bulnes fit into pastoral work in Chorrillo wasn't exactly clear, but I seized the opportunity, which may have opened horizons for the group of men that night.

FIRST STEPS IN CHORRILLO

* * *

For two years I lived in an apartment built into the church complex, upstairs from a space that served as the parish office. A woman named Sara who had worked with the previous priest continued to cook me breakfast and lunch, and left something for supper. Mike Barnes, a seminarian who had been traveling in South America and had visited San Miguelito, stayed with me for several months as he tried to figure out his next steps. Andres Lascano, a young man from San Miguelito who was thinking of going into the seminary, also came to Chorrillo. They accompanied some of the pastoral work, and so we were something of a community, if not a team.

I regularly went to San Miguelito, typically to talk with Leo and stay for lunch, and so I followed developments there over the next several years. Hundreds of people a year were still visiting. Through Leo I also got a sense of what was happening elsewhere in the church in Panama and in the United States.

Jorge Altafulla, the Panamanian pastor in San Miguel—another downtown area similar to Chorrillo—and I became friends. We went to each other's house for lunch about once a week. He had received a degree in liturgy from the Institut Catholique in Paris and was interested in theological and pastoral developments. Although I was associated with San Miguelito, other clergy understood that I was operating under constraints similar to theirs. At this time I was receiving one hundred dollars a month from the Archdiocese of Los Angeles, with which I was able to meet my needs, including maintaining a car, first a 1955 Chevy and then a VW Bug, both bought used from servicemen in the Zone.

My image of what was happening in the United States came largely through *Newsweek* or stories in the Panamanian newspapers or sometimes from Armed Forces Radio, which mostly broadcast from the Canal Zone current popular music; I had no TV. I spoke only Spanish morning to night, and Chorrillo and Panama were my horizon.

* * *

In Chorrillo the street sounds began at around sunrise, which was 6 AM year-round. People had to get up early to get to work or to get children off to school, where the morning shift ran from 7 AM to noon; a second shift went from 1 to 6 PM. An elementary school operated across the street from the church, and uniformed children came and went. High school students took buses to schools elsewhere in the city.

Women were occupied morning to night cooking three meals, each of which began from scratch since most did not have refrigerators. Cooking was done on a two-burner propane stove. Diets were simple and repetitious: rice, noodles, yucca (cassava), bread, a bit of meat or chicken, sometimes soup or stew. When not cooking, women were often hand-washing clothes in buckets, rinsing them, and hanging them out to dry on lines running over the patio from balconies.

Families typically had one room. For example, Joaquin Melgar and his family lived on the ground floor of a house on Calle 26, in the middle of the barrio. To get to their room you entered from the street and crossed a patio. The family consisted of Joaquin and his wife, Leoncia, and her mother, plus their three children (a boy and two girls) and sometimes a visitor: six or seven people, and all their belongings. The ceiling wasn't especially high, but they had a kind of loft arrangement over the top part of the room. The room was generally dark because the only natural light entering was from the patio. Rooms on the second floor had more natural light.

Out in the street were businesses of various kinds and a movie theater, where the double bill changed every day. Vendors cooked and sold *frituras*, deep-fried bits of fish, meat, internal organs, yucca, or dough. Others sold bags of cut-up pieces of mango, or soda poured into plastic bags with a straw, or green coconuts, after chopping off the top with a machete and inserting a straw to drink the liquid.

Chorrillo was the turnaround point for buses and *chivas*, smaller vehicles with wooden benches. From the barrio you could go to almost any point in Panama City without a transfer. The parade of buses coming down Calle 27, turning and heading back out, was continual, with their speakers blaring current and classic popular tunes. Buses themselves were painted brightly with depictions of saints or superheroes.

Panamanians, at least of the popular classes, eagerly played the lottery and similar games. Some barrio residents sold lottery tickets for a living. People went shopping for particular numbers that they felt would be lucky, for example, the last two digits of the four-digit winning number, which would still give a prize. The drawing of the winning four digits was televised on Sunday mornings. The contents of dreams were understood as offering clues to winning numbers, and people could go looking for the number to buy for the Sunday national lottery, or possibly for *la bolita*, a daily clandestine lottery (the numbers racket), whose winning two-digit number became known mysteriously at around 8 PM. Once while accompanying a funeral procession arriving at the cemetery, I noticed a buzz among the mourners as we approached the grave site: those who had gone ahead had noted the registry number of the grave, and it had been passed down along the line.

Although the barrio had a reputation for being dangerous, only once in seven years did I have a problem, when a youth attempted to pick my pocket from behind and I instinctively pushed him away. There was some talk of *maleantes* (hoodlums) in the barrio, but on the whole, chorrilleros themselves didn't complain of crime. Because of many "eyes on the street," the barrio was safe enough for its residents, contrary to its reputation elsewhere.

Panama has only two seasons, the "winter" or rainy season from April to the end of the year, and the "summer" or dry season in the first three months. Christmas thus came at the beginning of the dry season and Holy Week around its end. Schools were out during the dry season. We also suspended courses during the dry season. Temperatures were remarkably the same all year long, with highs in the mid eighties and lows in the mid seventies. I never wore a long-sleeved shirt, let alone a jacket.

Why wasn't I indignant over the housing in Chorrillo, the extreme crowding, the lack of privacy, the fact that people were crammed one family to a room with no indoor plumbing of their own? Why didn't I spearhead a movement to draw attention to the injustice? That was probably because I arrived with the theology—or perhaps ideology—and method of San Miguelito, which entailed working to build a Christian community, not to use the power of the church to address social problems.

A somewhat more subtle reason, one not conscious at the time, may be that I didn't experience life in Chorrillo as so dehumanizing. I enjoyed and appreciated the humanity of the people around me. They were not as poor as subsistence farmers in the interior. They were in the cash economy, although they lived day by day, often literally as the man doled out to his wife money for the day's expenses. I felt content as a priest attempting to work pastorally in their midst.

* * *

Unlike San Miguelito, where the team devoted itself to first building a core community and only then put up buildings, Fatima was an existing parish where I was expected to serve as the priest. Daily Mass was sparsely attended, and even at Sunday Mass it was perhaps three dozen or so traditional Catholics, largely older women. Very few people came for confession. Funerals occurred regularly, sometimes filling the church far more than on Sunday if the person was well known.

Typically several children were presented for baptism on Sunday, often around the time of the child's first birthday. Parents sometimes brought children who were ill, with the hope that baptism might be effective where medicine had not yet worked. A key element was the choice of *padrinos*, godparents, who besides accepting responsibility for the child became *compadres* of the parents. The word *compadre* (or *co-madre*), which has no English translation, refers to a fictive kinship between parents and godparents that is very important in Latin American culture. The *padrino* was responsible for putting on the baptism party, which was a major occasion. People sometimes asked wealthy or powerful people to be godparents, calculating that in the future they might call on them for help when in a bind.

Although I regarded infant baptism without evangelization and adult commitment as theologically and pastorally problematic, the people were not responsible for the fact that Catholicism was taken for granted as part of Panamanian culture, and baptism was considered a normal rite of passage. My option was to celebrate it as well as possible and to take advantage of the opportunity to get to know people, particularly by stopping by the party in the afternoon.

People viewed priests as having special powers. At some parishes they lined up to have a priest pray a *responso* (short prayer), for which they paid him twenty-five cents. I was sometimes asked to bless objects, even a vehicle, or sprinkle holy water at a ribbon-cutting event. Although I found such cultural Catholicism ambiguous and was tempted to challenge it, I learned to restrain my inclinations.

At the time, religion was taught in public schools, and so teachers sometimes wanted to take classes for accreditation purposes. I modestly tried to open their minds to a more biblical understanding of Christianity.

For the first Christmas we decided to do, before midnight Mass, a dramatization of Mary and Joseph traveling to Bethlehem. The crowded streets of Chorrillo were a natural theater, with hundreds of people coming out on balconies to watch. In the procession we sang traditional Spanish Christmas carols. What drew the most attention was the horse on which Mary rode—which we had obtained through the Guardia Nacional. In May 1967 for the feast day of Our Lady of Fatima, we organized a procession through the barrio with her image, singing hymns and praying the rosary. What struck me were males ogling the girls from the sidewalk and making remarks; we didn't have such street processions again.

Although traditional Panamanian Catholicism, centered on devotions to saints understood as intercessors for immediate needs, seemed far from biblical Christianity, my status as "Padre Felipe" gave me entrée into the barrio: virtually everyone was Catholic, and I was their pastor.

* * *

Through 1967 we continued to hold the basic course in different sections of Chorrillo. Although the patio discussions were on serious topics, the meetings themselves were social occasions. Before the discussion itself we would talk about all kinds of topics for a half hour or more. The overall process was one of getting to know people and the situation in different parts of the barrio.

The work was not unalloyed success. The first group, which started on Calle 27 behind the church, initially seemed to be going well. We saw each other regularly and played softball on Sundays. After a few months, however, the men in the group dropped out of participation, perhaps because of the influence of the informal leaders. I later thought that it may have been the strong demands of conversion presented at the cursillo, particularly that of marital fidelity. However, perhaps I was too mechanical in applying what I had learned in San Miguelito and should have been more alert to their situations.

Starting with a few respected neighbors in the house was important, as was the atmosphere between neighbors. A half-dozen people seated in a circle was usually sufficient to begin; others might drift in or listen from a balcony. In one group on Calle 25 we had a large patio, and seventy-one people attended the first meeting; subsequent attendance varied from twenty-five to forty, but attendance of between ten and twenty was more the norm. Rain or unexpected events could derail a meeting. Meetings didn't always work. TV programs were a constant competition, for example, *telenovelas* or *The Fugitive* with David Janssen. One evening we had gathered when word came that Martin Luther King Jr. had been shot dead. We continued discussing Dr. King, who was well known in Panama, but didn't hold the scheduled discussion.

Through one of the early courses I had come to know a young man at the Huerta Sandoval apartments, and we had become friends. When we held the first cursillo entirely by ourselves, that is, without help from the San Miguelito team, I asked him to become its leader. He resisted but reluctantly agreed to do it. After that he drifted away from the parish movement. I should have been more pastorally alert to him and his needs rather than pressing him to serve my concerns.

Unlike San Miguelito, which had a team of a dozen—between priests, sisters, and full-time laypeople—I was working alone with a cadre of men somewhat like the Hermanos. For a while in 1967 two sisters from a Panamanian congregation came regularly to the parish with the thought that they could be assigned there, but that did not happen.

Around 1968, this kind of pastoral work was given the name *comunidades eclesiales de base*: "grassroots ecclesial communities" or "Christian base communities." When Leo and the team began in San Miguelito in 1963, the approach seemed to be unprecedented, although it later turned out that similar efforts were being made in Brazil, Colombia, and elsewhere. The key element of base communities was a group discussion connecting the scriptures and the experience of ordinary people, aimed at forming an ongoing active Christian community. The starting point could be exploration of a basic human experience as in the Family of God course in San Miguelito, leading to a scripture passage, or it could be the reading of a scripture passage then explored by the participants, drawing on their life experience.

This method could easily lose the element of genuine dialogue and become simply a means for getting to the point that the leader had in mind in advance, favoring "right" answers and discouraging "wrong" ones. It then became a kind of catechism in the pejorative sense, indoctrination as opposed to discovery. The remedy was to be genuinely interested in what people had to say, even if it did not seem to lead in the right direction, and to be fascinated by the life experience and intelligence behind it.

By the 1970s, this kind of pastoral work sometimes took on a political dimension, as when peasants began to discuss land tenure and even organized to press for their rights. However, at this early stage the incipient base-community movement was pastoral in nature—that is, the aim was to build a community of committed adult Christians. For two years I assumed that it was not my role as pastor in Chorrillo to become directly involved in the most obvious problem in the barrio: the housing conditions.

Over time, something like the Hermanos of San Miguelito was formed in Chorrillo, and a cadre of leaders, primarily men but some women, took shape. The group wasn't large, perhaps a core of a dozen or so who were most active and another dozen or two who were involved. Our Sunday Mass with lively, with guitar music played by Gabino Hernandez and Joaquin Melgar. We instituted coffee and rolls after Mass as a social occasion for those attending.

* * *

We started the Christian Family Movement (CFM) in the parish as a way of continuing formation after the basic course and cursillo. In Latin America the CFM was largely middle-class. I wrote discussion guides that I thought were more adapted to the situation in Chorrillo. Eventually we had three groups of people meeting in different parts of the neighborhood.

In mid-1967 I attended a meeting in San Jose, Costa Rica, for priests and religious organized by lay leaders of the movement, perhaps with the aim of recruiting more priests as chaplains. We heard presentations on the situation of the family in our region. One morning we filled a theater downtown for a cineforum presentation of the prize-winning Claude Lelouch film *A Man and a Woman*, with Jean-Louis Tritignant and Anouk Aimee. Both protagonists are recently widowed and reluctant to become romantically engaged but toward the end of the film they begin to make love, suggested more by fast-cut cinematography than graphic portrayal. In the discussion that followed, some predictably pointed out that it was a sinful encounter, while others drew attention to the beauty of love—presumably the pedagogical reason that the lay couples running the meeting had scheduled the film.

My host was a Costa Rican lawyer who had been a representative in Congress. I was struck by the relative modesty of his house, his wooden office, and his rattletrap car. One evening he played LPs, introducing me to Carlos Gardel, the Argentine tango composer and singer from the 1920s, and shared his enthusiasm for other Latin American music.

While driving me around the city he gave me a short version of the Costa Rican national myth: we've always been hardworking because in colonial times we didn't have slaves. Family farming rather than large plantations was the typical form of agriculture, and so when coffee export started in the mid-nineteenth century, the benefits were shared more widely, which paved the way for a more egalitarian ethos in the country. A decisive event was the disbanding of the army after the 1948 civil war, making it possible to put resources into schooling and health care rather than troops and weaponry. For most of its history the country has had an orderly democracy. What he said was true, but when he said that the country was 98 percent white (by implicit contrast with Panama and Nicaragua on either side), I was bothered by an undeniable if perhaps unconscious racial edge.

FIRST STEPS IN CHORRILLO

* * *

When Vatican II closed in December 1965, there was little hint of the turmoil to come. The immediate task seemed to be one of implementation, most notably the new vernacular liturgy. Theologians focused initially on ecclesiology, the theology of the church, particularly the implications of the retrieval of the biblical image of the "people of God," and more generally the sense that Christians are fundamentally equal: any office in the church, such as serving as priest or bishop, is a function for the community, not a power that places them over their fellow believers.

Lumen Gentium, the document on the church, viewed matters from the standpoint of the Roman Catholic Church, and was most sympathetic to the Orthodox Churches and the historic Protestant Churches. Those of other faiths seemed ever further out in concentric circles. In contrast, the document on the church in the modern world (*Gaudium et Spes*) emphasized what all human beings have in common. Although not so clearly stated in its texts, the Council clearly reflected a shift away from the literal understanding of the adage "outside the church no salvation," visualizing the church as an ark of salvation in a sea of damnation, toward much greater trust in God's saving will toward all people. From the beginning, the Council aimed to recognize and overcome the anti-Semitism that was present over the centuries and which culminated in the Holocaust. This anti-Semitism had deep roots in European culture, reinforced by the notion that Jews were Christ-killers and that Christianity had replaced Judaism. *Nostra Aetate*, which evolved into a statement on the church and non-Christian religions, emphasized the common roots of Christianity and Judaism, which remains a part of God's plan.

At first glance, the document on revelation (*Dei Verbum*) seemed to be about a long-standing dispute between Catholics and Protestants over scripture and tradition. In hindsight, however, it meant that scripture would now be at the center of Catholic theology and preaching. The neo-Scholastic categories of theology that I had been taught in the seminary soon disappeared.

Theologians and scripture scholars were raising questions over the literal existence of angels and demons or the meaning of original sin: was it a stain on the soul transmitted by generation, or a tendency to evil common to all people and reinforced by institutions and culture? Beyond matters of individual doctrines, theologians in Europe and North America were taking up issues like secularization and atheism, and the difficulty of communicating the faith to "modern man" (in the sexist language of the time). A significant effort was the "Dutch catechism," a simply written summary of Christianity interpreted in humanistic terms (which soon encountered objections in the Vatican). In 1966 *Time* ran a cover story on the "death of God" theology, linking together a number of disparate figures, largely non-Catholic. Things seemed to be increasingly up for grabs.

Although these developments didn't appear directly relevant to life in Chorrillo, I followed them through the *National Catholic Reporter*, the journal *Concilium*, and books that I ordered from Blackwells in Oxford. When I read Rosemary Ruether's *The Church Against Itself* (1967), I offered to review it for the *NCR*, primarily to force myself to come to terms with its contents. Situating herself in a tradition of dialectical theology, Ruether went beyond Roman Catholic categories to raise fundamental questions about the church's purpose. In my review I likened it to a change in jazz style in the postbop period that was initially simply called the "new thing." Ruether was taking ecclesiology into a different realm.

Invited by a group of middle-class Panamanian laymen, I gave a talk on Martin Luther, emphasizing that in many respects he had been correct, and that Roman Catholicism was learning from the Reformation several centuries later. In early 1968 I was invited to present developments in ecclesiology to a group of English-speaking priests in the Canal Zone. Shortly before the presentation I received Hans Küng's book *The Church* and found that it reinforced what I had in my notes.

* * *

In late 1966 Charles Davis, a British theologian and *Concilium* board member, announced that he was leaving the priesthood and marrying, and he soon he published a book spelling out his critique of the church. At the time I was surprised—even shocked—but before long, others were taking similar public steps, and many of my contemporaries in Los Angeles were leaving the priesthood. News stories carried reports of conflicts between priests and bishops, especially after Pope Paul VI reaffirmed clerical celibacy (1967) and the ban on contraception (1968), rejecting the recommendation of the majority of a commission appointed to study the issue. The pope apparently feared that a change in church teaching on birth control would weaken papal authority. Since most married Catholics soon rejected that teaching, often with the support of priests, the effect was the opposite, an undermining of papal authority, at least on matters of sexual ethics. Priests found themselves with a conflict between teachings they were expected to uphold publicly and in the confessional, and their own conscience. Leaving the priesthood had once been inconceivable; it was now increasingly becoming a live option.

Initially these controversies did not affect me very much. People in Chorrillo didn't go to confession, and birth control wasn't regarded as a moral issue; the only time I ever encountered a question on contraception was from a Catholic-educated middle-class woman. In Latin America, celibacy was initially posed not as a demand that existing priests be allowed to marry, but rather as a proposal that the ordination of some married men—like the Hermanos—might make pastoral sense; a renewed diaconate could be a step in that direction.

FIRST STEPS IN CHORRILLO

In 1967 Leo invited me to go with him to a conference on the priesthood organized by the incipient Association of Chicago Priests to consider what was becoming recognized as a crisis in the Catholic priesthood. The conference was organized around some public lectures, including one by Leo, and two days of closed discussions by a core group of about forty, including the theologians Edward Schillebeeckx and Bernard Häring, and two well-known Chicago priests, sociologist Andrew Greeley and Msgr. John Egan. Greeley painted a possible picture of a future evolution in the United States in which priests come to resemble ministers in mainline Protestant churches. One question was that of the "hyphenated priest" (e.g., a priest-psychologist): if the priestly ministry was now being understood in terms of a function in a community rather than sacramental powers, how much sense did that make?

The night before I flew to Chicago, I was in a room in Chorrillo conversing with three or four people around a table, after the scheduled meeting had failed to reach a quorum. When I said something about the emerging idea of what the church should be, Beto, our host, said, "If that's true, the church should be the avant-garde of humankind" (*la vanguardia de la humanidad*). A night or two later I found myself in a reception meeting Schillebeeckx, who had expressed the same idea using a similar expression. The fact that an ordinary man of Chorrillo had intuitively leaped to the notion of one of the most prominent Catholic theologians confirmed my sense that it was theologically fruitful to be where I was.

* * *

Pope Paul VI's *Populorum Progressio* (1967) was another in a line of documents on Catholic "social doctrine," but unlike the previous ones, which had arisen out of concern over the impacts of early capitalism in Europe, this one focused on what was now being called the "Third World" (Latin America, Asia, and Africa) and its economic and social development. It drew on the work of a French Dominican named Louis-Joseph Lebret, who helped draft the document before he died. In an early passage the pope defined development as the "passage from less human to more human conditions." Less human conditions included extreme poverty and exploitation; more human conditions included acquiring sufficient goods to live with dignity, becoming educated, cooperating with others for the common good and seeking peace, and it continued all the way to faith and union with God. The encyclical envisioned a continuum from meeting basic material needs to the ultimate destiny of human beings, quite the opposite of the dualism that had reigned for centuries and that was still taken for granted in many church circles. This "development humanism," as it was called, was quite meaningful for me and many of my contemporaries.

In one paragraph the encyclical raised the question of whether revolutionary violence might be justified, and answered that the result would be worse than the evil it intended to correct. However, the wording seemed to leave a loophole: "except where there is manifest, long-standing tyranny." Many Latin American observers took the position that such was the case on their continent. I attended a one-day lay-organized meeting in Panama to discuss the encyclical, and toward the end of the day when a straw vote was taken on whether revolution would be justified in Panama, a majority of those attending said yes. That vote attested more to a vague sympathy with revolution throughout Latin America than to actual conditions in Panama.

A group of fourteen bishops, half of them Brazilian, wrote a response to the encyclical, which became known as the "Letter of Third World Bishops," broaching the possibility that socialism might be more effective at achieving development for the poor than existing systems—and that, if so, it should not be condemned. I laboriously typed a stencil of excerpts and cranked out a mimeograph machine and distributed it. In Argentina a nationwide movement called Priests for the Third World was formed.

* * *

For my first couple years in Panama, I paid little attention to its Central American neighbors. Panama didn't have much connection with them; its currency was the dollar, and its economy was based on the canal and on U.S. bases, not primarily on its agroexports, mainly bananas. Panamanian license plates bore the grandiose slogan "Bridge of the World, Heart of the Universe," reflecting its geographical position at the nexus of North and South America and its connection to world trade.

However, starting in 1967, I began to learn something of these geographically close countries, particularly on a monthlong trip to Mexico and back, driving up with Jorge Altafulla, and returning with my classmate Gerry Fallon. Along the way we had misadventures: in Costa Rica my VW Bug was broken into and Jorge's belongings stolen; we had to have expensive repairs done to the suspension in San Salvador from damage done by the unpaved highway in western Panama; after an accident on a slippery mountain highway in Mexico, we had more repair work in Cuernavaca, and had to deal with the police and the courts.

In El Salvador we saw young priests such as Ricardo Urioste, pastor of Miramonte, a new housing development, and Monsignor Arturo Rivera Damas, who arrived for a meeting of a small group of priests who worked with JOC (Young Christian Workers). Our host in Guatemala was Blase Bonpane, a Maryknoll priest whom I had gotten to know during my summer at Dolores Mission in Los Angeles. Guatemala was then under a wave of repression, especially in the countryside; traffic police in Guatemala City had bulletproof vests. Blase took us to see Padre Chemita, an outspoken priest who said he was under a death threat.

At the end of the year, three Maryknoller priests, Tom and Art Melville, and Sister Marian Peter (Margarita Melville), were discovered to be in contact with the guerrillas and they had to leave the country, as did Blase, who had been working with university students along with Marian Peter. They then left Maryknoll and had long careers as activists and academics in the United States.

Crossing into Mexico from Guatemala, I was immediately struck by what seemed to be the larger proportions of buildings, roads, and businesses, and that impression stayed with me. Viewed from Mexico, Panama and the other countries in the isthmus were tiny. In Mexico, we stayed with priest friends from Los Angeles who had gone to work in Cuernavaca around the time I went to Panama. The bishop of Cuernavaca was Sergio Mendez Arceo, then known mainly for the restoration of the cathedral by removing saints' statues and side altars and recovering earlier colonial paintings, and generally simplifying the interior to focus attention on the altar, and for mariachi music at the Sunday liturgy. My friends were questioning their priesthood and soon resigned.

* * *

In March 1968 I was in Managua for a Catechetical Week, invited by Sister Julieta of the Sisters of St. Agnes and Fr. Felix Quintanilla. Julieta had recently received a degree in catechetics in Paris. Participants came from around Nicaragua, including American Capuchins from Bluefields on the Atlantic Coast. This was one of many such meetings in the years after the Council, as priests and sisters were searching for ways to implement Vatican II. Julieta may have invited me because I was attempting adult catechesis work under circumstances similar to those of an ordinary diocesan priest, and perhaps because I could articulate the underlying theology. The conference was held in downtown Managua, low-rise buildings which would be destroyed in the 1972 earthquake.

The country had then been ruled by the Somozas since the 1930s, to the point where the dynastic dictatorship seemed permanent. In such a tiny country, a personal dictator could control everything and felt omnipresent, as though he were the uninvited guest at any social gathering.

Once in the early afternoon during the Catechetical Week I went out to a park and lay down on the grass in the shade of a tree to take a little nap so as not to doze in the afternoon sessions. I was awakened by a man tapping my foot and telling me to get up. Why? I asked. He explained that the police would pick me up. When I was unconvinced, he insisted, "We drunks have to stick together." A little later I was seated on a concrete bench when a man came up and sat beside me and struck up a conversation, which led to the poet Ruben Dario, whose statue was nearby. *Where in the United States would someone brag about a poet to a visiting stranger?* I asked myself.

Julieta arranged a dinner one evening at the house of a well-to-do Nicaraguan couple. The husband was the manager of Kodak operations in Managua. The house was sprawling and open so as to let in breezes and obviate the need for air-conditioning. In the middle of the meal I naively asked, "And what do you think of the experiment in Cuba?" thereby triggering a testy exchange. By "experiment" I really meant that we should be open to considering whether the Cuban revolution might benefit Cubans and offer possibilities for others. However, I had sabotaged whatever Julieta had in mind when she arranged the encounter with the young gringo priest from Panama.

* * *

Many, perhaps most, of the European and North American priests and sisters who stopped in San Miguelito on their way to assignments in America were coming from Cuernavaca, where they had spent three or four months at the CIF (Intercultural Training Center), set up by Ivan Illich, studying Spanish and learning about Latin American culture and society. Whenever expatriate church personnel gathered, Illich's name was likely to come up. Leo Mahon had also been in periodic contact with Illich.

Today Illich is known primarily as the author of *De-Schooling Society* (1971) and several other radical anarchist critiques of society written shortly afterward. However, at the time he was a Catholic priest in good standing, albeit a gadfly. Born in Croatia, he had followed an unusual path to the priesthood, including studies in Rome. He had worked as a priest in New York and had been the vice rector of the Catholic University in Puerto Rico until the bishops there had him dismissed. In the early 1960s he came to Cuernavaca, where he founded CIF and CIDOC a think tank and a documentation center.

In the early to mid-1960s Illich organized some meetings of young Latin American theologians, in which they were raising the question of whether their continent might have its own theological questions requiring its own responses. At the time, Catholic theology was still spoken of in the singular, which in practice meant European theology. Those meetings sowed the seeds of liberation theology several years before the term itself was coined.

Over time Illich came to see it as his mission not so much to train missionaries as to force them to question their own motives, aptitudes, and attitudes, and indeed the very nature of the missionary endeavor. He had recently stirred up controversy with two articles: "The Seamy Side of Charity," which challenged the very premises of development aid, and "The Vanishing Clergy," which questioned the existing model of priest and proposed a radically different one. Part of my reason for going to Mexico in 1967 was to meet Illich directly and question him.

Arriving at CIDOC during the morning outdoor coffee break, I introduced myself, and he replied, "You are Berryman!" He then invited me to walk around the grounds, and he replied to my questions with irony: we should pray that Paul VI remained in office a long time and was not replaced by some liberal "reformer": things needed to get much worse before they got better.

It felt like I was being treated with condescension, as though he were giving ten or twenty minutes to the young gringo priest out of courtesy. When I asked him about theology, he asked me to name five books I was reading. I hesitated, "I don't know . . . but I appreciate Rahner so much that I bought the *Lexikon für Theologie und Kirche*" (a ten-volume encyclopedia coedited by Rahner). He stopped in his tracks: "Thees eees tooo goood to be true," he said in his Dracula-like accent. He said that the *Lexikon* and Kittel's *Wörterbuch* (a reference book of key biblical words) were his only theological works, and he kept them by his bedside. Instantaneously, I had ascended into the ranks of those to be taken seriously. He took me into the library, showed me some books and monographs, and wrote down the names of theologians with whom I should become familiar (Gustavo Gutierrez, Juan Luis Segundo, and Jose Comblin, as best I can remember).

* * *

By the end of 1967 the work in Chorrillo seemed to have achieved some successes: seventeen basic courses had been held throughout the parish territory, with hundreds of participants. Eighty or more had participated in the weekend cursillos, two of which we had organized from Chorrillo. The Sunday Mass was lively and was in Spanish (a year before the new vernacular texts were out and permission was given), although it was nothing like the large celebration in San Miguelito. The Christian Family Movement was serving as a kind of ongoing house church. However, from what was reading, I sensed that something was stirring elsewhere in Latin America.

In April 1968 Jose Gomez Izquierdo, an Ecuadorian priest who was visiting San Miguelito, came to say Sunday Mass in Chorrillo because I had a very swollen infected foot and wasn't able to do so. Over breakfast afterward, when I expressed my interest in developments elsewhere in Latin America, he told me about a pastoral course organized by the Latin American Pastoral Institute (IPLA) sponsored by the Latin American Bishops Council (CELAM), which was beginning the next day in Quito. Pepe, as everyone called him, was one of the main organizers of IPLA, and he invited me to take part.

Within ten days I had discussed the situation with a core of parishioners, received permission from Archbishop Clavel, and arranged for Felix Valenzuela, a Spanish Augustinian priest and the national chaplain of the Christian Family Movement, to take my place in the parish. I was bound for Quito.

6

Patria Grande—My 1968

THE IPLA COURSE WAS held in a three-story building that housed the Ecuadorian bishops' conference. Over half of the participants were Ecuadorians, but others included Mexicans, Argentines, Colombians, Central Americans, a Chilean, and a Spanish laywoman—I was the only gringo. Twenty-five or thirty of us were living in the building, eating meals together, attending class, and having a daily Eucharist; a similar number of Ecuadoreans were staying elsewhere in the city and commuting for classes. It was like being back in the seminary—with no exams or grades.

CELAM institutes for liturgy and catechesis were operating in Chile and Colombia. This new institute would be devoted to pastoral ministry itself, although these areas obviously overlapped. These institutes were sponsored by the Latin American bishops, but there was no stress on hierarchical authority or doctrinal orthodoxy—nor was either being questioned. It was an instance of clergy and religious retooling in the wake of Vatican II.

At breakfast the day after my arrival, I noticed the Ecuadorian way of serving coffee, very thick and strong, which you then cut with hot milk or water. "Hola, Felipe," someone greeted me. He looked like a Christian Brother, but I didn't remember his name. He reintroduced himself from the previous evening: Bishop Leonidas Proaño of Riobamba, one of the course organizers. I was chagrined at not having remembered the name of a bishop, but he didn't take it personally. He is recognized as one of the outstanding Latin American bishops of that time, particularly for his decades of work with indigenous people.

* * *

The course consisted primarily of one- or two-week sessions by specialists from different disciplines, who lectured in the morning and the afternoon, with some class questions or discussions. The earlier courses were more in the area of social sciences or history, and later in the course more directly related to theology and pastoral activity. We were there from May until early December with a long break in the middle for the CELAM conference in Medellin, which took place in late August and early September.

Two Ecuadorian Jesuits, Alfonso Gortaire (anthropology) and Estuardo Arellano (sociology), gave some general notions from social science that might be useful for analyzing pastoral situations. Colombian Noel Olaya gave a course in scripture. For some reason, he and I hit it off, and he even tutored me a little in Hebrew—unsuccessfully as it turned out.

An Argentine layman, Enrique Dussel, very enthusiastically gave us a broad-strokes course in the history of the Latin American church. Dussel had spent a year or two in Nazareth with the Little Brothers of the Poor, and more recently had been doing archival work in Spain, researching the church in colonial times. Many of the characteristic themes that would appear in his dozens of volumes in philosophy, history, and theology were already present in these lectures.

The most idiosyncratic of our professors was the Uruguayan Jesuit theologian, Juan Luis Segundo. He was working on a series of books on five topics (church, grace, our idea of God, sacraments, and evolution and guilt), which grew directly out of his ongoing dialogues with a group of middle-class Catholics in Montevideo. The Spanish title of the series was Theology for an Adult Laity, which reflected his characteristic concerns, particularly the fact that the Catholic Church could no longer rely on support from society and the culture, as it had for centuries. His assigned topic was ecclesiology, and unlike others who generally gave lectures, he spent a good deal of time eliciting our understandings of the church before presenting his own. He was friendly with us and had a deep belly laugh.

Carlos Alvarez Calderon, a diocesan priest from Lima, gave a course labeled "philosophy," much of which, as I recall, had to do with *concientización*, the process of bringing people to critical awareness. Pepe Gomez did a course on media, and Segundo Galilea, a Chilean, presented one on Latin American spirituality.

As is evident, the professors were largely male clergy and religious. There was no discernible common theological, political, or pastoral line or framework, although they had a mutual concern of applying Vatican II to Latin American situations. It was a moment of expectation and hope. Most of the profs were involved in preparation for the impending CELAM meeting at Medellin and some served there as *peritos* (experts).

* * *

The professor who made the greatest impression on me was Jose Comblin, a Belgian-born theologian who lectured on the Theology of Development. Comblin had thick glasses, spoke Spanish slowly and deliberately, and was both shy and friendly. After spending ten years as a priest in Brussels, he came to Latin America seeking "a church with a future," as he later explained. He worked first in southern Brazil, then in Chile teaching theology, and he was now working with Archbishop Helder Camara in Recife, in northeast Brazil. His theological training had focused on scripture, but at

Louvain he had acquired the practice of delving into history. He was already publishing on widely varying areas of theology.

While at IPLA Comblin was being denounced in Brazil as a "foreign subversive" because of a confidential background paper he had written for Helder Camara for the Medellin meeting that had been leaked to the Brazilian press. Among the various topics he addressed was that of revolution, which was in the air throughout the hemisphere. He wrote primarily to provide some conceptual clarification; the document was in no sense a manifesto or call to arms. His mild manner in person made the charges against him all the more ludicrous. Stuck in Quito for several weeks, he continued to clack away on his manual typewriter, and he counseled some participants in the course, particularly two Mexican sisters working in a rural diocese. Sympathetic bishops using backchannel contacts with the military government arranged for his return to Brazil after a month and a half or so.

Comblin exemplified for me how intellectual work need not be done in an academic setting and could be related to pastoral activity. Years before, he had written a two-volume theology of peace in French, moving from scripture to the problems at that time, particularly the Cold War and the emergence of the Third World nations. In 1962 he published some articles intended as a crash course in recent theology for Chilean bishops to enable them to prepare for Vatican II, surveying kerygmatic theology, "nouvelle theologie," existential theology, theology of history, and so forth, with references to Jungmann, Rahner, Danielou, Schmaus, Congar, Haring, Liege, Thils, Leclerq, Mouroux, Fessard, and others. It was then published as *Hacia una Teología de la Acción* (1962) and ended with the suggestion that the heterogeneous movements in theology seeking to come to grips with contemporary society were striving, perhaps unconsciously, to enable Christians not merely to believe but to act for change in the world.

* * *

Through occasional outings and daily liturgy and meals together, we became a community, albeit a temporary one. With the Argentine priests we learned to drink mate, the bitter, tealike beverage sipped from a gourd through a metal straw and then refilled with hot water and passed to another person. It was a way to socialize in the late afternoon.

Fault lines appeared between the more traditional—those emphasizing church teaching or discipline—and the more radical, who emphasized social justice. Such differences could be reflected in the intercessions at the evening Mass in the small chapel: "Lord, may we have the courage to follow the gospel to its ultimate consequences" (Lord, hear our prayer). "Lord may we always remain faithful to the truth you have revealed and entrusted to your church" (Lord, hear our prayer).

Over time, some of these differences generated tensions among us. Matters came to a head almost halfway through the course as we hashed things out in a meeting. The two Argentine priests, Santiago and Angel, were at one pole, and some Ecuadorians at the other. We realized that the differences were to some extent cultural: the Argentines told us that insulting one another face-to-face even with vulgar language was the way they did things. People in the highlands are more nonconfrontational, even deferential. I felt in the middle and gravitated toward Chencho Alas from El Salvador and Gumersindo Cabrera, a Guatemalan. Insight into the cultural roots of our differences helped smooth things over for the rest of the course.

More generally I got some sense of differences between Latin Americans, such as between Colombians living within their very Catholic culture and two Mexican sisters in a country with a half-century of government hostility toward Catholicism. In particular I was struck by the difference between highlands (Andean countries, Mexico) and lowlands (Caribbean and Central American) cultures. Highlands people are relatively more reserved and traditional; people in the lowlands are more outgoing and informal. That difference is evident in music—the guitar and flute sounds of Andean music as opposed to tropical *salsa*, which is dance music. The percentage of couples cohabiting out of wedlock is notably higher in tropical areas. That may partly be because the Catholic Church was historically weak in coastal areas, in comparison to the highlands. These same differences can be found within countries, e.g., the difference between Bogota and Cartagena in Colombia, or Quito and Guayaquil in Ecuador.

* * *

At this time some intellectuals were speaking of Latin America as a *Patria Grande*, a Great Homeland, echoing Simon Bolivar, who had dreamed that all Spanish-speaking America would be a single confederation. Even before his death, that dream was shattered by power struggles between regional warlords that led to the dozen and a half countries that formed after independence. The yearning for a united Latin America was especially strong among revolutionaries in the 1960s: Ernesto "Che" Guevara, an Argentine and leader of the Cuban revolution, had been captured and executed in Bolivia the previous year during a failed attempt to ignite a South American revolution. The Catholic Church was itself a force for unification, as evidenced by CELAM itself and this pastoral course. I imbibed some of this sense of a continent-wide destiny over the course of 1968.

While in Quito I read a large cultural history of Latin America by Colombian German Arciniegas, and a sweeping work on the process of civilization by Brazilian anthropologist Darcy Ribeiro. Works by economists like Celso Furtado of Brazil introduced me to Latin American economic thinking, which was questioning the premises of "development"—that is, that "underdeveloped" nations should follow in the footsteps of "developed" nations, with their assistance and tutelage. These economists were arguing that it was more accurate to conceive of the world as divided into an industrialized center and a nonindustrialized periphery, which was dependent on the center and to which it had been assigned the role of supplying raw materials. The causes of poverty were structural. The nations of the periphery would never catch up; they had to break free of control by the rich countries, through revolution if necessary. This approach came to be called "dependency theory."

The boom in Latin American fiction was on: *Cien Años de Soledad* (One Hundred Years of Solitude) had been published the year before. I found Garcia Marquez's short stories as interesting as his novels because they reminded me of Panama. In a dialogue in Lima, Garcia Marquez and Peruvian novelist Alvaro Vargas Llosa agreed that in Latin America the most extraordinary things happen every day, and fiction had to find ways of expressing that. Thus emerged magical realism.

* * *

One afternoon we were taken to see a monument on the equator, which is what the word "ecuador" means. Because it is nine thousand feet high, Quito enjoys a springlike climate year-round. That made it a pleasant place to be, in comparison to Panama. A fifteen-minute bus ride would take me to the colonial downtown, with its several large churches and plazas. In downtown Quito I was struck by seeing indigenous men in the open-air market being hired to carry a heavy load of vegetables or fruit uphill on their backs to a car or truck, and then being paid a coin. Only indigenous men did this work. Sensitized by the U.S. civil rights movement, I told other course participants it looked like racism to me, but they didn't agree. Decades would pass before the term "racism" would be applied to treatment of the indigenous in Andean society.

I sometimes took the nine-hour bus ride bus from Quito down to Guayaquil for the weekend and stayed with Pepe Gomez, who was then living in a small community of priests downtown. Guayaquil is a manufacturing city, roughly as large as Quito. It is coastal and culturally more akin to Panama than to the indigenous highlands of Ecuador. Having these two large cities, sharply different from each other, made Ecuador unlike many Latin American countries, with their single large city dwarfing the others (Mexico City, Lima, Santiago, Guatemala City). Pepe's pastoral activity included a weekly radio show and a regular column in a newsweekly, in which he commented on national affairs. The people in Guayaquil, he said, claimed to have the *panteón más alegre del mundo* (the liveliest cemetery in the world). Grave sites rivaled one another with large architect-designed tombs in a variety of styles. On November 2, the Day of the Dead in Quito, I saw many families place flowers and having what looked like a picnic by the graves of departed loved ones.

Jose Maria Velasco Ibarra was again running for president; he had served four terms and had been removed by the military in all of them. As I stood in a large crowd in a plaza waiting for him to speak, I asked the indigenous man next to me why he was so popular. "*Es el hombre*" (he's the man) was his answer. This was an instance of Latin

American populism, a gut-level identification between the people and a charismatic leader. Arnulfo Arias was his Panamanian equivalent, who also won in 1968 and was deposed by the military.

IPLA participants were encouraged to do some pastoral work. I decided to try a Family of God course in a poor hillside neighborhood of Quito, populated by indigenous people. An Ecuadorian priest and I visited, and held three or four weeknight meetings, but the effort soon foundered. Quito wasn't Panama City, where windows and doors are open and street life is lively; houses in Quito are solidly built to withstand the cold, people dress in sweaters, and the streets are quiet. I shouldn't have assumed that, with a little bit of knocking on doors, outsiders could bring neighbors together.

My strongest memory is of being in the home of our host after a meeting failed to attract a quorum, when he invited me for supper. The lighting was by candle or kerosene lamp, not electricity. These people were so poor that they could only afford soup—but they shared it with me.

* * *

The year 1968 was the high-water mark worldwide of the sixties as a cultural and social phenomenon: massive anti–Vietnam War demonstrations in the United States, the assassinations of Martin Luther King and Robert Kennedy, the Russian invasion of Czechoslovakia, massive demonstrations and strikes in France, the massacre of student protesters in the Plaza de Tlatelolco in Mexico City, followed by the Olympics City where U.S. athletes raised their arms in Black Power protest. The originally French word "contestation" was being used to refer to the phenomenon of challenging the present order. Quito was an island of relative tranquility.

One reflection of the general spirit was the formation of priest groups in Peru, Colombia, Brazil, and elsewhere, on the model of the Third World Priests formed in Argentina in 1967. Manifesto-like statements by priest groups were being issued, and a month or two before the Medellin conference, several hundred priests from around Latin America signed a joint statement. These documents generally made observations about society, notably the great inequality between the poor majority and the few rich, and then some observations on the pastoral situation. Latin American priests weren't challenging celibacy or the contraception ban, but the institutional church's identification with the status quo in an unjust society.

* * *

Classes were suspended at IPLA for a month in August and early September when Pope Paul VI went to Colombia, where he gave a number of speeches to different groups and addressed the bishops, opening the CELAM conference. This was an early instance of the papal travel extravaganzas that have become common in the past half century. Colombia may have been chosen because it was far more Catholic, at least institutionally and culturally, than other Latin American countries. It had more priests per capita than other countries, the great majority Colombian, and a well-developed Catholic school system.

I took the bus to Bogota, where Noel Olaya had arranged for me to be hosted by a family. At one of the large open-air events I came across Fr. John Cremins, our music teacher from the seminary in Los Angeles. Since he was there by himself and not familiar with the city, I accompanied him to various events. On Saturday morning we went downtown toward the Plaza Bolivar where the pope was going to speak, but the crowds were so great that we could only get into a side street. When Paul VI emerged on a balcony to address the crowd, people around us were pushing and shoving. When he finished and withdrew, the crowd dispersed, and we found that our pockets had been thoroughly picked (John was in a Roman collar).

While in Bogota I sought out the papal nuncio to Cuba, Monsignor Cesare Zacchi, in a north Bogota neighborhood where he was being hosted. I wanted to see whether he could help me get to Cuba to see the revolution firsthand. Travel to Cuba was very difficult for Americans at the time. Zacchi had a more positive stance toward the revolutionary government than the Cuban bishops, whom the government regarded as "counterrevolutionary," because in the early days of the revolution, religious events such as processions had served as de facto counterrevolutionary rallies. Zacchi's charge from the Vatican was presumably to work toward some long-term rapprochement. He was courteous and indicated vaguely that he would inquire, but nothing came of it.

* * *

After the pope's departure about 150 bishops chosen by their fellow bishops met for two weeks in Medellin, and with the help of around 100 peritos in theology, pastoral ministry, liturgy, education, and so forth, they applied themselves to the task of applying Vatican II to Latin America. The set of sixteen documents they produced became a magna carta for Latin American Catholicism that inspired a generation of priests, sisters, and laypeople. Prominently in the introductory document, they quoted the long passage of Paul VI about development as the passage from "less human to more human conditions," explicitly linking it to the exodus from Egypt. A key biblical theme was thus invoked to make human social and economic development integral to the church's mission.

Each individual document began by attempting to read the "signs of the times," made some theological-pastoral judgments, and proposed commitments or lines of action. The documents themselves were organized in a similar order, starting with human development (justice, peace, and so forth), moving to pastoral activity (e.g., catechesis), and then finally the church and its structures (priests, religious, and so forth). The implication was that the church must be organized to carry out its mission, which includes serving the world. This "see-judge-act" approach, borrowed from Catholic Action, now became known as the "Medellin method" and was widely applied at the local, diocesan, and national levels.

Much of the impact of the Medellin conference came from particular passages that were often then cited, particularly in the diagnosis of society. The dire poverty (*miseria*) affecting so many people was called "an injustice that cries out to the heavens." In various passages, the bishops spoke of inequality, oppression, dominant and oppressed sectors, neocolonialism, distorted international trade, capital flight, tax evasion, indebtedness, the international imperialism of money, the arms race, and institutionalized violence.

True development was not simply a matter of economic growth; people were to be "agents of their own development." The bishops described three different mind-sets with regard to issues of faith and social responsibility: "traditionalists," "developmentalists," and "revolutionaries". They showed traditionalists little sympathy, identifying them with privilege and a "bourgeois mentality." "Developmentalists" were regarded as technocratic and viewed as narrowly concerned about production. "Revolutionaries" were described as those who "question the economic and social structure. They desire a radical change in goals as well as implementation. For them, the people are and must be the subject of this change in such a manner that they take an active part in decision-making for the reordering of the entire social process. This attitude can most frequently be found often among intellectuals, scientific researchers, and university people." Revolutionaries were thus defined positively, not in terms of violence.

The document on the poverty of the church began by noting problems of the dependence of clergy on fees at the time of sacraments. Reflecting the hand of Gustavo Gutierrez, the document stressed three points, somewhat in tension:

1. According to the scriptures, poverty is an evil.
2. Poor people tend to be more open to God and their fellow human beings than the well-off.
3. Christians are called to a voluntary poverty of solidarity with the poor.

Stressing that poverty is an evil ran counter to the common notion that it reflected God's will. The document provided a rationale for what came to be called "the preferential option for the poor."

In more specifically pastoral issues, a recurring theme was the problem of a Christianity transmitted by custom and not by evangelization and adult commitment. Thus the bishops called for a "re-evangelization" of the baptized. In connection with education, they spoke of concientización and "liberating evangelization." The influence of Paulo Freire could be seen at various points, and indeed at least one of Freire's associates was among the experts. More than once the bishops used a term that had just been coined: *comunidades ecclesiales de base* (ecclesial grassroots communities), often called in English "Christian base communities." The bishops suggested that parishes could become a network of such communities. These church leaders indicated that they were aware of a crisis in the priesthood, in seminaries, and in religious life.

The Medellin documents provided a vocabulary and framework for new approaches to pastoral work. When I visited Panama in September before returning to Quito, I found that the Medellin texts were being typed onto stencils and run off for people to have in their hands, since full publication would take a few months. What I scarcely noticed was that the typing and mimeographing were being done by nuns and other women. Virtually no women had been involved in the Medellin process, except in such ancillary roles. The voice in the documents, as prophetic and visionary as it might be in some places, was male and clerical.

* * *

About a month after the bishops' meeting, Argentine Jesuit Santiago Franck and I took the bus from Quito to Medellin for a gathering on nonviolence. Two dozen or so activists from various countries were hosted by Fr. Gabriel Diaz at the parish of Santo Domingo Savio, then a muddy, poor barrio on a mountain ridge overlooking the city a thousand feet below. We met in a rustic, open brick structure then being built to serve as a church.

Jean and Hildegard Goss-Mayr, who had been present at Vatican II lobbying for nonviolence to be on the agenda, made presentations. Jean more fiery—"Jamais la guerre!"—and Hildegard cooler and more analytical. Hector Merino, an Argentine, and his wife were followers of Lanza del Vasto, an Italian disciple of Gandhi who had founded the Community of the Ark in France in 1948. Glenn Smiley was a Methodist minister and lifelong pacifist who had been with Martin Luther King Jr. in the very early days in Birmingham. While the Goss-Mayrs and Merino spoke of nonviolence in terms of principles and spirituality, Glenn told stories of campaigns.

This was an early instance of efforts to promote explicit nonviolence in Latin America among activists. In a time when revolution seemed to be the route to a fundamentally different type of society, Latin American activists regarded nonviolence as tantamount to counseling the oppressed to accept their fate. For the next several years the Goss-Mayrs patiently held workshops and advised groups on nonviolence, particularly in Brazil. Latin Americans were in fact practicing nonviolence in strikes and demonstrations, but it would be decades before many activists would consider embracing it in principle.

* * *

At IPLA we weren't tested and didn't receive grades, but we were assigned to write a "monograph." I opted to write on the priesthood and ministry. My intention was to look for information on the early church and then to draw conclusions for priestly ministry for Latin America. A small book by J.-P. Audet, a Canadian theologian, made me aware that the very notion of a "priest" as a mediatorial figure is alien to the New Testament, in which it is assumed that priesthoods have come to an end in Jesus Christ. It was only in the fourth century, as Christianity became a public religion after Constantine, that the figure of the "presbyter" began to be described in a "priestly" language and to be seen as having a mediatorial role. From there it was a logical step to justify celibacy on the grounds of cultic purity: the hands that touch the sacred mysteries must be pure. That notion was still influential, at least as implicit background, in the idea of the priesthood that I had imbibed in the seminary, but it has been quietly dropped since Vatican II.

I presented the theological proposal that the priest's role is to form Christian community and offered some reflections on aspects of Latin American culture and society (quoting Pablo Neruda at length) that might call for specific qualities in ministers. A Colombian fellow student edited my Spanish.

My reasons for picking this topic may have only been partially clear to me. On one level, I was aware of a crisis in the priesthood and hoped to make a contribution in Latin America. At a less conscious level I must have been questioning my own status as a Catholic priest. Juan-Luis Segundo kindly read the manuscript but did not encourage its publication. Carlos Lohle, who headed an important publishing house in Buenos Aires, was likewise friendly but noncommittal. I don't recall any supervision by by IPLA staff, and I suspect that our monographs eventually went to a landfill.

* * *

By midway through the IPLA course, I had decided to complement my studies in Quito by moving through South America to observe firsthand the pastoral situation in the various countries, traveling down the Pacific Coast to Chile, crossing the Andes, and going as far as northeast Brazil. Through IPLA and San Miguelito I had contacts in a number of locales and leads on places to stay. In preparation for Brazil I took a dozen one-on-one classes in Portuguese from a teacher at the Centro de Estudos Brasileiros in Quito, mainly to get a handle on pronunciation, since the vocabulary and grammar are very similar to Spanish.

In early December I took a bus from Quito to Guayaquil to see Pepe Gomez, then continued to the Peruvian border and down the coast to Lima. Next I spent a week or so in Peru, visiting various places in the highlands (Cajamarca, Cuzco) and Arequipa. At the Peruvian border I crossed into Arica, Chile. Rather than spend two days or more on a bus going through desert, I opted to fly to Santiago. After three weeks or so there, I took the bus over the Andes to Mendoza and Buenos Aires, crossed the Rio de la Plata to Montevideo by hydrofoil, then moved on to Brazil: Porto Alegre, Sao Paulo, and Rio.

When I went to the Rio bus station, intending to go to Recife (a forty-eight-hour trip), I was told there were no buses for two or three days. Unwilling to just remain in Rio, I asked for a ticket in the general direction and got one for Belo Horizonte, with only a vague idea of where it was. After landing in the wee hours and a few hours sleep in a cheap hotel, I caught another bus for Teofilo Otoni, a city I had never heard of. I finally got back to the Atlantic at Salvador, where I caught another twenty-four-hour bus to Recife. It was like wanting to go from Miami to Boston by bus, but detouring through Knoxville, except that the roads weren't interstates but two-lane highways.

Traveling by bus gave me time to read the books I was buying and to appreciate the grandeur of the geography, from the arid deserts of southern Peru and northern Chile, where nothing seems to grow; to Santiago, where apricots were ripening in December as they would in June in California; to going over the Andes near Aconcagua, the highest mountain in the hemisphere (three thousand feet higher than Denali in Alaska); to crossing the estuary of the Rio de la Plata, which is dozens of miles across.

I spent few nights in hotels; almost everywhere I stayed in religious order houses (Colomban fathers in Lima, Holy Cross in Santiago, American Oblates in Sao Paulo) or parishes. Often they were connected to people I knew, but in some instances I simply knocked on the door, introduced myself, and was welcomed. That is how I stayed at a Franciscan house in Ipanema, the beach neighborhood in Rio made famous by the Antonio Carlos Jobim song, "The Girl from Ipanema." I only went to the beach late one afternoon for an hour.

My hosts were usually well informed. They could give me a good overview of the country, its history, and present situation, and suggest other people to contact. The fact that I could travel so freely attests to the clerical culture of the time, but also to a shared feeling in the postconciliar era that we were all embarked on a common enterprise of renewal of church and society.

* * *

I was now able to see the homelands of different Latin Americans I had known in Panama and Ecuador. People in the Southern Cone (Chile, Argentina, Uruguay, and southern Brazil) were primarily descendants of Europeans, with relatively few indigenous people. Their histories were marked by cattle ranching, so beef was central to the diet. At noon I saw Argentine factory workers having a lunch of steak and wine (which were quite cheap—I could get a steak on a board, salad, bread, and a glass of wine for a dollar or so).

Big as it was, Brazil reminded me of tiny Panama in some ways. A taxi driver in Rio told me that, in Brazil, "There are four women for every man," the same idea I had heard in Panama, except that there it was said to be seven. Men used this bit of folk sociology to justify machismo and infidelity. Another similarity was Carnival. I saw the beginnings of it with marching bands in Rio two weeks before Ash Wednesday. During Carnival itself, the country closed down from Saturday to Tuesday night. By that time I was in Recife, where customs were somewhat different than in Rio, more mass celebration than spectacle. Part of the activity was to throw talcum powder or water at strangers.

At this time Sao Paulo was one of the fastest-growing cities in the world. The streets were filled with VW Bugs and buses manufactured in Brazil; clusters of twenty-five-story apartment buildings could be seen in all directions. Yet Fr. Virgilio Leite took me to a village outside of Joao Pessoa where researchers had found that all the children had parasites.

In Santiago I spent a Sunday afternoon conversing on all types of issues with workers in a *población*, a shantytown of wooden shacks. We were outdoors, standing in a circle while sipping from and passing around a plastic glass of red wine half diluted with water. They seemed better informed about world affairs than the average American, for example, about the Vietnam War. In a country like Chile, world affairs were more prominent in the media than in the United States, where they appeared only insofar as the United States was involved or affected. At La Peña de los Parra, a place for folk and protest songs in Santiago, I heard Angel and Isabel Parra, children of Violeta Parra, who had collected folk music and composed her own songs, especially the haunting "Gracias a la Vida," before taking her own life in 1967.

Politically, the situation varied from country to country. Peru was in the first months of a leftist military government, but the implications were not yet clear. In Chile many people were disillusioned with five years of Christian Democrat government and were seeking more radical solutions. Argentina was under military rule, which was being opposed by Peronism, itself split into right and left factions. Brazil had been under a military government since 1964, but the worst days were just beginning. A JOC (Young Christian Worker) chaplain seemed crushed. He didn't offer any detail and may have been suspicious of a gringo priest showing up on his doorstep, but I had the sense of pained helplessness from him. Years later I learned that, just at this time, priests and religious were helping activists escape to neighboring countries to avoid being captured and tortured, but I felt no hint of that at the time.

* * *

In Lima I sat in on a gathering of foreign clergy with Jorge Alvarez Calderon; his priest brother Carlos had been an IPLA prof. Peru had attracted a large influx of priests and sisters from Europe and North America, particularly as the result of an active nuncio, and through the Boston-based St. James Society, supported by Cardinal Richard Cushing. In some instances they had set up U.S.-style parish operations without much reflection. Now they were questioning what they should be doing, with guidance from the Alvarez Calderon brothers and Gustavo Gutierrez.

Gutierrez was emerging as a leading figure among young Latin American theologians. I went to see him where he was then living, at a convent in Lima. He had returned from studies in Europe and had been a chaplain to university students. In a talk to priests in Trujillo he had recently proposed the need for a "theology of liberation," and he was now developing those ideas further. His writings bore the mark of these pastoral discussions. In Buenos Aires my host was Santiago Franck, a Jesuit who had been with me at IPLA. We went to see a priest in a working-class neighborhood who was a member of the Third World Priests and proudly showed a pamphlet he had just written, depicting Jesus on the cover looking like a revolutionary.

"Contestation"—a challenge to both political and church authority—was in the air. A group of priests in Chile had recently occupied the cathedral challenging the cardinal. It seemed to be a part of the worldwide phenomenon of the 1960s.

I found that contestatory spirit challenged in Montevideo, however, at the offices of *Víspera*, a review of Christian leftists with a continent-wide circulation. While I was conversing with Cesar Aguiar, the editor, an older man jumped into the discussion and attacked European progressive theologians like Küng and Schillebeeckx and Cardinal Suenens, particularly on contraception, but also on the papacy. His name was Alberto Methol Ferré, and he was argumentative, perhaps especially upon seeing me as a gringo priest. He insisted that Latin Americans should not follow the European progressives in the general mood of anti-institutionalism and what he called Malthusianism. Rather than attacking the "institutional church," Latin Americans should work to bring the church on the side of the poor. This was an early instance of Latin American church intellectuals taking critical distance from European progressives. Methol Ferré continued to write broadly about church and political matters, and some years later was a friend and confidant of Jesuit Jorge Bergoglio, the future pope.

In Montevideo I went to the Centro Pedro Fabro, a Jesuit think tank whose most illustrious member was Juan Luis Segundo. The center was one of a number of such Jesuit interdisciplinary teams that were being created in Chile, Colombia, Venezuela, Central America, and elsewhere, with the aim of utilizing their training in various disciplines not in universities but by being directly involved in society, as public intellectuals and in conjunction with active laypeople. It was the Southern Hemisphere summer, and I spent a couple days with them at their modest beach house. That they should have a beach house struck me as unusual, but in fact many families in Montevideo had some kind of beach place. Uruguay was and still is unusual: a welfare state had been set up with the government of President Jose Batlle y Ordoñez in the early years of the twentieth century, the country was highly secular with many people not only nonpracticing but unbaptized, and it had enjoyed a widely shared prosperity based on the export of beef and wool.

Entering Brazil forced me to start learning to navigate in Portuguese, thinking in Spanish but having the words come out in another language. People were generally patient with me, and they didn't think I was a gringo, but rather perhaps Spanish. In Rio, a Franciscan priest invited me to say Mass at Nossa Senhora de Fatima Parish in a favela, high in the hills. The name of the parish was the same as mine in Chorrillo, and I began the homily with that fact. After the Mass I was given a tour of the favela and eventually had lunch with a large group of neighbors, who perhaps thought having the gringo priest from Panama was a novelty. Despite the differences, I felt a kinship between these people and those in Chorrillo.

A priest in a middle-class parish in Rio said he had tried to work with base communities meeting in apartments, but that it was difficult. That was a hint that the base-community model might reflect particular circumstances and might not be as universally applicable as some assumed.

In Recife I spent a week with a team of priests and sisters from Detroit in the neighborhood of Nova Descoberta. Team members had participated in one of the pastoral institutes in San Miguelito. Archbishop Helder Camara came by, and people gathered around this diminutive figure in a white cassock. To my surprise he led a group of people, mainly women and children, in the rosary. That struck me as quite at odds with my image of him as a champion of social justice, but I was assured that that was quite natural for him. He was very much at home with poor people and was traditionally pious.

At that time Helder was proposing the formation of a continental movement of nonviolence, and I sat in on a meeting where he and a committee were working on the idea. That initiative didn't prosper, perhaps because nonviolent movements can't be started from top down, but must grow organically out of actual struggles.

That week I also went to Joao Pessoa, a city two hours north of Recife, primarily to see Bishop Jose Maria Pires, whom I had met in Bogota during the eucharistic congress. He was one of the two black bishops in Brazil, among an episcopacy of three hundred or so.

* * *

In Santiago a day or two after Christmas, I went with my seminary classmate John McFadden to see Paulo Freire, about whom I had been reading. Freire was an educator in northeast Brazil who had achieved fame by devising a method whereby illiterate peasants could be taught to read and write in a matter of weeks. Rather than treat them like first-graders and give them the equivalent of Dick-and-Jane readers, he assumed that they were adults with a great deal of knowledge and experience; what they lacked were the linguistic tools to decode writing.

The "Freire method," as it was called, was based on a series of group sessions, each of which started with a single poster-sized image and a single word. For example, an early session began with an image of a house. The leader asks, "What do we see here?" "A house" (*casa*). From there the leader would ask about what is in the house, how it was made, what it means to people.

After a half hour or so of such discussion, the leader would present the word *casa* divided into its syllables—*ca-sa*—and people would learn the connection between the sound of the word, which they knew, and the letters in the word. Before the session was over they would see that changing a letter could yield other words, such as *cosa* (thing), *casi* (almost), or *cada* (each). Participants learned to write the letters and the words in their notebooks. Within a few weeks they would have learned the entire alphabet and, in principle, could read (or write) any word. It helped that Spanish and Portuguese are quite phonetic, that is, that the written and spoken language correspond well.

The aim of the Freire method was not simply literacy, but literacy as a tool by which poor people could become aware of their dignity and press for their rights. The overall process was called *concientización*, often translated into English as "consciousness-raising" (but sometimes left in Spanish or Portuguese). Freire conceived of the process as a kind of "emergence" from a "submerged consciousness" to a "critical consciousness." Peasants typically have a submerged consciousness in the sense that they have been conditioned to believe that what they think or say is of no value; after all, they're illiterate—hence the importance of the first part of the discussion for people to express their ideas and to have them valued.

In the early 1960s Freire had worked in northeast Brazil with the peasant leagues until the 1964 military coup, when he was jailed and then exiled, along with many other activists, politicians, and intellectuals. He had now been in Chile for several years and was working at ICIRA, the land reform agency. He told John and me that he was beginning a course on "Concientización and Evangelization" at ICIRA the day after New Year's, taking advantage of the beginning of the (Southern Hemisphere) summer vacation, and said I would be welcome to take part. Freire himself was a believing Catholic—unlike many leftists, who were secular—and he was personally interested in the potential of concientización for church work.

Participating in the course, which went for two and a half weeks, were around thirty church people, mainly Chilean. Since the Freire method was built on dialogue, I was surprised to find that Freire lectured between 8 and 10 AM. After the lecture, and especially in the afternoon, we did group work with others on his staff. Once I overcame my surprise, I was pleased with the lectures, which were more interesting than a group discussion among us would have been. Speaking Spanish with a Portuguese accent, he elaborated on what was available in his books (*Education as the Practice of Freedom* and *Pedagogy of the Oppressed*). The lectures were largely about the philosophical and pedagogical underpinnings of his method. With his thick glasses and unkempt beard, he looked like a guru, and he himself joked about a "Paulo Freire myth."

Freire criticized what he called the "banking" model of education, in which it is assumed that the student is an empty receptacle like a piggy bank into which the teacher "deposits" contents. Rather, he said, both teacher and student are "educator-educatee": they are investigating the world together. The role of the teacher is to point and prod, for example, to get the campesinos to reflect on the meaning of a house, moving from more material aspects such as how it is built to what it means. The leader might have the participants note that they had usually built their own homes, which rather than being regarded as a mark of their poverty should be understood as a tribute to their skill. When the same sort of questioning was applied to matters like land tenure, the Freire method was deemed subversive.

Like other Latin Americans of that generation, Freire assumed that Latin America and the world were on a path toward a qualitatively different kind of society, and he interpreted history in terms of his concepts. For example, under the populist regimes of Peron in Argentina and Getulio Vargas in Brazil, people had come out of "submerged consciousness" to a "naïve consciousness" in the sense that they had begun to see the social origins of their poverty and oppression, but they placed their trust in populist leaders and their organizations. The further stage of critical consciousness would be that of revolutionary movements.

Freire was a philosopher as much as an educator. His lectures were full of references to various sorts of theorists, particularly phenomenologists and heterodox Marxists. He often mentioned what he was reading (e.g., Andre Malraux's *Anti-Memoires*); offered observations on his wife, Elza, or his family; or made comments on the differences between Chilean and Brazilian culture.

Freire would soon become an icon of educational reformers around the world. He spent the fall of 1969 at Harvard (where John went to be tutored by him for a month). Starting in 1970 he worked for the World Council of Churches, based in Geneva, until he was allowed to return to Brazil a decade later.

The parallels between the Freire method and the "family of God" approach being used in Panama are clear. Freire mentioned with admiration what he had observed in the pastoral work of Monsignor Robert Fox in New York, in which discussions were launched with a photograph rather than a drawing. In Paulo Freire I encountered a great humanist, one who believed that whatever philosophers since Plato have asserted about "man" is valid for a campesino or a chorrillero.

Many church people and activists throughout Latin America over the next decade or two utilized a Freirean approach. It enabled outsiders to begin to work with poor people on a village or urban barrio and to engage with them in a respectful way, to explore their situation in their own terms, and to help lead them to take steps to change that situation. When used skillfully and sensitively, it could help people to come to a better sense of themselves and their capabilities and to unite them in pursuing common goals. However, a discussion leader could also go through an ostensibly Freirean dialogue mechanically, starting with, "What do we see here?" and directing the discussion, especially by praising "right" answers and ignoring "wrong" ones, in a way that could be manipulative or become like catechism or indoctrination.

To celebrate the end of the course, a party was held among the participants and friends of Freire, including a number of fellow Brazilian exiles.

* * *

One of the participants in the Freire course was an Australian priest named Joe Broderick. He was from a prominent Melbourne family of successful Irish immigrants, had entered the seminary and priesthood, and then went into the Vatican diplomatic service, where he had assisted nuncios in Pakistan and then in the Dominican Republic. He was now traveling freely through Latin America, and he had stopped at IPLA on his way to Peru. The first night we met in Quito we went to a theater where the Roman Polanski dark comedy *Cul-de-Sac* was playing. He and I laughed out loud, to the consternation of the sparse Ecuadorian audience, which was largely silent and perhaps mystified. He also attended the meeting in Medellin on nonviolence, organized by his friend Gabriel Diaz. He found me a place to stay in Lima and set up some of my contacts, including one with a young Peruvian novelist in Cajamarca.

In the early 1970s Ivan Illich turned to Joe and said, "You should write the book on Camilo Torres." With that mandate he obtained lodging in a monastery outside Bogota and spent two or three years working on the book, including interviewing the military officer who had led the pursuit and fatal ambush of Torres. Although the book was based on thorough research, it was written in a novelistic style. When published in 1975 it sold only modestly in English, but the Spanish translation sold many thousands of copies. By then Joe had married and had a family and had put down roots in Colombia, where he penned political graphic comics, wrote more books, and became a fixture on the political and literary scene.

* * *

When I returned to Los Angeles for a visit in spring 1969, I had not set foot in the United States for three years, and I had seen the sixties primarily through the pages of *Newsweek*, pop music, and films. I felt part of a Latin American Catholicism that was searching for its own voice, and I identified with Latin America, not only with the people with whom I had been working in Panama but with a larger sense of solidarity with the region as a whole and a sense of its destiny.

My parents picked me up at LAX, and even as they were driving me home, something I said, possibly about Vietnam, triggered an angry reaction in my father. I felt a sense of alienation that continued through the month I was in California.

For the previous two or three years, the parish in Chorrillo had been receiving a modest monthly amount, under one hundred dollars, from a mission circle in a parish in Tustin, in Orange County, under a program of the Archdiocese of Los Angeles. The donations went into the parish coffers for expenses. I was invited to Tustin for a weekday evening Mass followed by a potluck. The Gospel happened to be that of the parable of the Rich Man and Lazarus, on which I briefly preached. Attending the potluck were a few dozen people, including some youth. I began with some slides from my recent trip, including photos of Rio favelas. My comments reflected my view of Latin America after a year of study and travel.

The first question was from a high school student who asked what could be done for people "down there": send clothes? My maladroit reply to her was something to the effect that given the heat Panamanians didn't need a lot of clothing, and that it might be better to examine U.S. foreign policy. The next question began, "Well, if our help isn't appreciated . . ." The questions grew increasingly hostile, although polite. As the evening was ending, I said that they needn't feel obligated to continue sending money, but that we could simply have a friendly parish-to-parish relationship.

Not wanting to leave things on a sour note, a few days later I phoned one of the couples and said I'd like to get together with the mission circle. The woman said, "We decided we'd like to keep it on a friendly basis," in a distinctly unfriendly tone. With some insistence on my part, she agreed to meet, so I drove to Tustin one night to speak with three couples or so. While waiting on the porch, I could hear some unhappy comments, perhaps over changes in the church, a loosening of "the rules," and the behavior of clergy and religious. Our discussion took place with chilly cordiality.

At the time I felt justified, and I attributed their attitude to their U.S. middle-class milieu (Orange County, after all). Later I realized that I should have been more sensitive to my audience, just as I would be with Panamanians. This experience suggested that alongside the well-publicized sixties generation was a parallel "countersixties" phenomenon, the reaction of people to changes in their world, and a harbinger of the coming culture wars in society and the church.

* * *

Although my 1968 study and travel started through a contingent set of events—Pepe Gomez coming to Chorrillo to say Mass—I had been sensing that significant developments were taking place elsewhere in Latin America, in theology and in pastoral practice. Suddenly I had a sabbatical, although I didn't think of it that way. My travel was like the Grand Tour that British and northern European aristocratic gentlemen once took through Italy, Greece, and elsewhere upon completing their formal schooling. IPLA, travel, and Freire helped me situate my subsequent work in Panama and Central America within the wider hemispheric context.

7

The Pastoral Turns Political

"We're now under the military boot," Felix Valenzuela had written me in a letter while I was still in Quito; by March 1969 when I returned, Panama had been under a military government for almost a half year. Felix and a fellow Augustinian had been serving the parish in my absence, and working with couples through the Christian Family Movement.

Two sisters soon came to the parish: Marta Torres, a Maryknoll from New York who had worked in the highlands of Guatemala for several years, and Mary Ray, a Franciscan. Marta began working with youth and Mary with women. They were joined by Ellen (Jennifer) McDonald, another Maryknoll sister who had been a secretary for Bishop Mark McGrath in the Diocese of Veraguas in the interior, handling his voluminous English correspondence. She moved to Panama City to continue in that capacity after he was made archbishop of Panama City. The sisters formed a small community and lived in the quarters that I had occupied over the church office. I joined them for breakfast after the daily Mass and for lunch at midday. We were a team but were working along separate lines.

I moved to a one-room apartment on Calle 27, a two-minute walk from the church, on the second floor of a cement-block building located below the broad avenue that divided Panama City from the Canal Zone. The apartment building was set in the midst of the wooden buildings of Chorrillo, but was it was solid and afforded some privacy. The previous occupant was a Peace Corps volunteer from whom I bought a two-burner propane stove and a refrigerator. A bookshelf, desk, typewriter, radio/cassette player, and a fold-up bed filled the room.

IPLA and my travels had broadened my pastoral vision beyond that of San Miguelito. As articulated at Medellin and as I had observed in my travels, the struggle to move from less human to more human conditions was central to the church's mission. In Chorrillo that meant addressing the conditions of the barrio. For the next several years we took up housing conditions and worked with women and youth. We had little hint of the complications and conflict to come.

* * *

The October 1968 coup that overthrew President Arnulfo Arias less than two weeks after his inauguration was driven primarily by self-interest, not ideology. Arias had been planning to replace top National Guard officials with his own loyalists, since his two previous presidencies had ended in coups, but the Guard leadership moved preemptively to depose him. It took a year or more for Omar Torrijos to emerge as undisputed leader, and for the regime's ideology to be defined.

Although labor unions and university students made some protests, it was in San Miguelito that the coup encountered the most active resistance. A small group of leaders from a recently formed civic group first gathered secretly to discuss the situation. They then organized a meeting with dozens of representatives of all sectors of San Miguelito, who resolved to present to the new government a manifesto with their demands. The manifesto was mimeographed at the parish and clandestinely distributed and presented publicly to the government. When they received no reply, the group organized a nonviolent march, which began with fifty people but grew as they marched down a hill, where they were met with armed *guardias* telling them they could not pass. When they insisted, the officer in charge phoned Torrijos, who said that they could continue accompanied by guardias. The main organizing work was done by lay leaders, notably Ramon Hernandez, but Leo was present and involved; he drove the bundles of manifestos around in his car trunk for distribution. Subsequently they were called to a meeting at National Guard headquarters, where Torrijos drew Leo aside, made some threats, and then returned to the delegation of leaders, who were not cowed. The result was a series of discussions between the San Miguelito group and two government ministers.

Then one Sunday morning, Torrijos arrived in a helicopter for Sunday Mass, went up to Leo, shook hands, and asked if he could go to confession, which he did in full view of the congregation. During Mass he received communion and stayed afterward in discussion with the leaders. Leo concluded that Torrijos was impressed by the self-assurance of these ordinary Panamanians.

Like other Latin American militaries, the Panamanian National Guard had been founded to maintain internal order, not fight foreign wars. The democracy overthrown by the coup provided orderly transfer of power through elections and served as a tool for elite rule, not as a vehicle for the aspirations of ordinary people. The Panamenista Party overthrown by the coup was the personal vehicle of Arnulfo Arias, an old-style populist who was a contemporary of Peron, and was the only party with a mass following.

Torrijos emerged as the head of the government only after he eliminated rivals, particularly exiling Colonel Boris Martinez. In December 1969, while Torrijos was in Mexico at a horse race, other military officers attempted a coup. When Torrijos was informed, he phoned loyal officers and flew back to Chiriqui at the western end of the country, where he was met by the base commander, Major Manuel Noriega. Torrijos and his supporters then organized a triumphal caravan driving through the interior toward the capital. I followed the events by radio in my apartment. Torrijos's vigorous response enhanced his macho image and solidified his control over the Guardia Nacional.

Ideologically, Torrijos was a left-wing nationalist and populist. That set Panama apart from the right-wing military governments then coming to power elsewhere (Brazil, Chile, Argentina, Uruguay). Torrijos was similar in several ways to Hugo Chavez, who for over a decade used oil revenues to impose populist policies in Venezuela until his death in 2013. Both Torrijos and Chavez were born in the countryside to schoolteacher parents; both were nationalistic and tapped into people's resentment of traditional elites and were effective communicators with crowds. Both rose through the ranks in the military, had engaged in combat with left-wing guerrillas, and at a crucial moment took part in a coup. (In Chavez's case the 1992 coup failed and he was put in jail, but upon release he took on the Venezuelan political class.) Both disbanded the existing political system and reshaped a new one to assure their own power. Both sought to use the power of the state to benefit the poor and pursued a nationalistic independent foreign policy that included friendly relations with Cuba. However, Panama is about a tenth as large as Venezuela in population and has no oil; its "oil" was the canal and the Canal Zone, which at that time were in the hands of the United States.

Immediately after the coup, dozens of leftists were imprisoned, and some died in prison. However, over time the People's Party (Moscow-aligned Communist party) made an alliance with the regime and supported Torrijos during the 1970s, while other leftists continued to be persecuted. For people in Chorrillo, all this was largely spectacle, even though the headquarters of the Guardia Nacional was located in the barrio and many low-level guardias lived there.

* * *

A few weeks after the coup, Archbishop Clavel resigned and left Panama, with no public reason offered. The military government may have regarded him as being in opposition, because during the election he had participated in a civic committee that pressed for an honest vote-counting procedure. He apparently felt overwhelmed by his responsibilities. Clavel moved to Mexico and then to Southern California, where he served as auxiliary bishop, for Latinos in particular, and was widely appreciated.

Replacing him was Marcos McGrath, who had been bishop of Veraguas in the interior since 1964. McGrath was born in Panama, the son of a Canal Zone employee from the United States and a Costa Rican mother. He went to boarding school in the United States, studied in Chile and then Notre Dame, and then entered the Holy Cross congregation, earned a doctorate in Rome, and after ordination taught theology in Chile. Thus, McGrath had spent his formative years and early adulthood outside Panama, and to many he was known as "Mark." By temperament he was reserved, and in that sense not especially Panamanian in the sense of carnival-loving—but not all Panamanians fit the stereotype.

In 1961 he was made auxiliary bishop in Panama City and then in 1964 the first bishop of Santiago de Veraguas in the interior. At Vatican II he was among the network of bishops and theologians who led the progressive majority. In a speech during the third session he urged that the document on the church in the modern world consider not only charity but economic and social development. He was also one of the leaders at Medellin and was a vice president of CELAM. While archbishop of Panama he continued to be involved with international church events.

My contacts with McGrath were primarily at clergy meetings or other formal occasions. He was supportive of our work in Chorrillo and occasionally came by for events. His own theology could be described as postconciliar mainstream. However, he was open to emerging more critical views. I shared with him some of my exploratory writings, and he passed on to me items of interest.

* * *

In May 1969, at the end of the dry season, we began to address housing issues directly. The starting point was people's immediate complaints about houses that needed repairs: balconies or stairs in danger of collapsing, toilets or other plumbing not working. We began with meetings in two houses, and then helped the people organize to deal with rent collectors, management companies, owners, and public officials, particularly the *corregidor* of Chorrillo, whose office was at one end of the barrio near the cemetery and the prison. Maryknoll sister Gail Jerome spent two months in Chorrillo and helped lay the groundwork for organizing, particularly by conducting a house-by-house census in a part of the barrio that provided data on households, numbers of people in houses, where they worked, and so forth.

A house across the street from the church was in danger of falling down, and we sought to have it condemned. When it finally collapsed, only three families were still living there. In another instance, when the owner of a house attempted to raise rents, we helped the people organize to resist. Eventually authorities stepped in and rather demagogically rejected the owner's request. This initial organizing work reached around fifteen houses (perhaps three hundred households), and representatives from them formed a Committee for Improvement of Chorrillo.

Doing this organizing was a core group, primarily of men whom I had known before going to IPLA and some youth. We met at the parish offices on Monday nights and used parish mimeograph machines. I accompanied the group but did not take the lead in the discussions in the houses or in dealing with public officials, since that would have been inappropriate for a priest and a foreigner. My role was to foster and develop leadership, not act as a caudillo.

In the preparatory stages I did some sessions with the group, attempting to give them a sense of Freire-style concientización, not simply the technique but the spirit behind it. This focus on a dialogue with people served as an antidote to the common image of a leader as someone who gives speeches, similar to party politicians.

* * *

Marta Torres worked informally with youth through 1969, initially becoming friends with them, especially those in the areas closest to the church. That meant hanging out in the streets, visiting them, and welcoming them into the sisters' residence adjacent to the church. Soon there was a group of twenty-five or thirty youth calling themselves Jóvenes Unidos (United Youth).

Marta and Mary left Chorrillo after about a year, and another Maryknoll sister, Geraldine O'Leary, arrived and took up work with youth. She was joined by Angela Brennan in 1970, who began working with women.

* * *

Some months after the initial resistance to the military coup from San Miguelito and after Torrijos had emerged as the undisputed head of the government, he and Leo Mahon became friends. Leo used to meet with him at the Guardia Nacional headquarters about once a month. Each admired something in the other: Leo thought Torrijos genuinely wanted to do something for ordinary and poor Panamanians, and the general appreciated what he saw in San Miguelito. In our conversations Leo sometimes gave me a glimpse into their relationship. Early one afternoon I went with Leo to see Torrijos in a windowless inner sanctum of the Guardia Nacional. I don't remember what was discussed, and the contact was relatively brief.

In 1970 the government proposed that San Miguelito be made a special district, with some administrative autonomy. That made sense, since the population in San Miguelito continued to grow to the point where it was a sizeable city in itself. The aim was that people of the area would have a voice and some self-determination in the area's future development. However, once the district was set up and began to do hiring, tensions arose with the parish. The district understandably saw leaders developed in the parish as potential employees, and a few did accept positions. Rivalries and power clashes ensued. Leo and Torrijos stopped meeting and a distance grew between them.

* * *

A crisis arose in the San Miguelito team in 1969 when Mark and Graciela, who had been working together in one of the parishes, realized that they were in love and returned to the United States to marry. Not long afterward John Greeley returned to

Chicago. For the next several months, he and Adela wrote letters back and forth sorting out their own feelings. That priests and sisters on the team fell in love should not have been too surprising, since there were many such cases in the United States by this time, and also among church personnel in Latin America.

Leo and the team may have been blindsided by their own theological conceptions, according to which the priest is married (definitively committed) to his community. To Leo, that idea—which is only a metaphor—was quite meaningful. Where the sisters fit in was not so clear. The team's theology—or ideology—had been devised before feminism had any impact within Catholicism.

Facing this crisis, Leo had meetings with the team and with the sisters and proposed that the remaining sisters would return to working as a team. The sisters refused, insisting that they should be recognized has having a shared ministry as co-pastors with the priests. Leo then decided to terminate the Maryknoll sisters as part of the team, and the sisters left in early 1970. John and Adela were married and lived in Chicago for decades, as did Mark and Graciela in northern New Jersey.

I followed this process primarily through the eyes of Leo, as I saw him every few weeks. It was obvious to me that in the end the decision was made by the men—by Leo—and that for all the talk of equality, the sisters were ultimately powerless.

* * *

In early 1970 the Irish American journalist Gary MacEoin made Panama his first stop on a journey through Latin America. In the seminary I had read *Nothing Is Quite Enough*, his memoir of life in an Irish Redemptorist seminary in the 1920s, which was acclaimed in Catholic circles in the 1950s. Much of the story is of fond recollections of seminary life, but toward the end he is abruptly told that he has no vocation and is dismissed with no explanation. He eventually found his calling as a journalist and writer, working in the Caribbean and then in New York. He covered Vatican II and played a key role in publicizing the majority report on contraception, which Paul VI had ignored. He had decided to stop in Panama, partly in order to line up contacts in the various countries, based on my travels a year earlier. I helped him arrange interviews in Panama. After initially staying in my one-room apartment he opted for a hotel room downtown where he could write.

How could he presume to write anything about Panama on the basis of a four-day visit? I wondered. I had been in the country for over four years and I still felt there was much I didn't know. I posed the question to him on his last night as we were eating at a Chinese restaurant.

"Well, now," he said in his brogue, "in a book of, say, sixty thousand words, how much will be devoted to Panama? Three or four paragraphs?" I was initially chagrined, but I realized that as important as Panama was to me and to Panamanians, it was a very small country. Even at the outset of his journey, he already had in mind the end product, a compact book portraying developments throughout the continent for English-speaking readers.

Over the next three months I read his dispatches in the *National Catholic Reporter* and then *Revolution Next Door* (1971), which presented vignettes of situations in different countries, and particularly disillusionment with the results of conventional development and yearnings for more radical approaches. Although Gary was already white-haired and looked old to me, he was vigorous and lively, and our friendship and occasional collaboration lasted for another three decades until his death in 2002. Observing him at work helped demystify writing and writers.

* * *

By 1970 we had decided to move beyond emergency situations like collapsing balconies to pursue possibilities of more dignified housing for the people of Chorrillo. We were partly inspired by activists from Marañon, a similar area in downtown Panama City, who had formed a barrio-wide assembly to defend themselves from plans by the government housing agency to demolish their neighborhood in the name of urban renewal—and who urged us to do the same.

We began in the section on Calle 27, behind the church, and organized meetings in individual houses or a cluster of smaller houses. Gerri O'Leary had drawn a poster depicting a scene in Chorrillo: a house, patio, kids playing, people hanging out, a full clotheslines, the reservoir of the gas company in the back, all very crowded together. The leader, generally Roberto Batista, began in Freire-like fashion by asking, "What do we see here?" That would trigger a series of commentaries on Chorrillo, inevitably focusing on the more negative aspects: crowded houses, no privacy, noise, disputes, fights, unsanitary conditions, and infectious disease.

At some point he would ask whether there were some positive features about Chorrillo. People then said that it was close to people's employment, people knew one another, and many had lived there for many years, even their entire lives. Despite the stigma from outsiders, people had a certain pride in being chorrilleros. Toward the end, he would ask questions like, Who is responsible for the situation? Where will Chorrillo be in 1980? Who can change the situation? That would lead into a proposal to form a barrio organization or assembly.

After holding meetings in nineteen houses on Calle 27, covering one sector, we organized elections, with ballots for everyone over eighteen years old. The two people in each house receiving the largest number of votes became representatives of that house. The Assembly of Chorrillo started to meet each month, sometimes with guest speakers, as the house-by-house organizing moved on to other sections.

By December we had reached the whole barrio and had an Assembly of Chorrillo with two representatives for each house (or more for the largest houses), totaling almost two hundred people, although just fifty or so tended to show up for meetings.

Through the process we identified a number of people respected by their neighbors who had latent leadership capability.

* * *

One Saturday Gerri and I went with the youth group to the gym at Colegio Javier, the Jesuit high school, with the idea of helping them prepare sociodramas. We then posed a barrio situation for them to dramatize: the *cobrador* (rent collector) is coming. They threw themselves into it with gusto, portraying what happens, such as a cobrador flirting with women and playing tenants off of one another. Soon they were performing this sociodrama in the patios of the houses. They then moved on to dramatize other situations: parents and children, women and men, mental disabilities, health issues, treatment by the police. They were invited to make presentations outside Chorrillo and on TV.

We combined several of these skits and, adding some slides that I took of the barrio, presented it in a popular theater festival at the University of Panama. Raul Leis, an activist, writer, and dramatist who often worked with the Jesuits, provided guidance at some points. One by-product was a sense of pride in being chorrillero.

* * *

Angela Brennan, who had come to Chorrillo after several years in the highlands of Guatemala, had opted to work specifically with women. In 1971 she visited house to house and organized meetings of women to discuss what they could do. In one initiative, women from the barrio went to the Santo Tomas Hospital as volunteers. Over time they decided that they wanted to set up a preschool.

In January 1972 Angela and three other women— together with women in a middle-class area of the city—took part in a course in the Montessori method together with women in a middle-class area of the city and became certified Montessori teachers. The structure built previously for community meetings was enclosed with cement blocks and a chain-link fence that let in light and air. For two or three months, people came on Sundays to make benches and other furniture and then painted them. In 1972 they opened the Childhood Development Center, which wasn't a daycare program but a genuine Montessori school with the appropriate educational materials. In the first year, forty children were taking part in two morning sessions. By 1973 that had increased to sixty children, and there were morning and afternoon sessions. Besides Angie, the school was staffed by women of Chorrillo who had earned their Montessori certificates, and the work was largely voluntary. The emphasis on child-centered development had ripple effects on attitudes toward children.

* * *

Our parish activities were akin to what was being done in many places in Latin America, seeking to participate with people in addressing their problems, especially poverty and its effects. Our pastoral rationale could be drawn from the Medellin documents, which assumed that the church was to be involved in the transformation of Latin America, moving from less human to more human conditions, which the circumstances seemed to require.

We could have continued some form of evangelization or catechesis as we had been doing before I went to IPLA, and we might have done so if we had a larger team. A more charismatic pastor or one with greater organizational ability, might have managed to do so, but I found myself largely absorbed in responding to situations as they arose.

The church building, which was quite large, was little used outside of Sunday and daily Mass. Given how crowded Chorrillo was, we thought some of its space could be made available to people in the community. In order to do so, we decided to free up the space of a dedicated baptistry in the back of the church off to one side of the entrance and make it available for youth to gather and also to do homework. To do so we moved the baptismal font up toward the altar area. The youth group took over the former baptistry, brought in some books, and began to use the space. It soon became a hangout for them during the evening and into the night. One effect was to desacralize the church space.

This group, led by several university students, soon split from the previous group (United Youth) and called themselves Youth for the Improvement of Chorrillo. They wanted to be independent of Gerri O'Leary and me. We had superficially friendly relations with them, but Gerri and I were not privy to their internal decisions and activities. Over time we could deduce that they had political ties, apparently with the People's Party (communist), which had a covert working relationship with Torrijos. A group with its own hidden political agenda was thus operating on parish property.

* * *

On June 9, 1971, Hector Gallego was abducted by force in Santa Fe, Veraguas, and was never seen again, triggering a church-state confrontation that lasted several months. Hector had come to Panama in 1967 as a recently ordained Colombian priest from a peasant family near Medellin. He began as pastor in the town of Santa Fe, two hours by unpaved road from Santiago de Veraguas, the provincial capital. Mild-mannered and soft-spoken, Hector lived simply in a thatched hut like the campesinos and began visiting dozens of hamlets in the outlying areas of the parish. Working in conjunction with the diocese, Hector trained leaders of Bible discussions and encouraged those outlying communities to unite and mobilize.

Realizing that they were at the mercy of local intermediaries in Santa Fe for selling their crops and buying goods they needed, they formed a cooperative that opened its own stores. Traditional power holders. particularly Alvaro Vernaza, a rancher who was also a cousin of Omar Torrijos, began to feel their position threatened. One indication of the growing independence of the peasants occurred when they decided against the traditional way of celebrating the feast of Sts. Peter and Paul, which was a moneymaking opportunity for merchants in the town. Hector was then arrested and held briefly on false charges. Torrijos met Hector a time or two and expressed some sympathy for his work, but also cautioned him not to move too fast.

I had come to know Hector through the Maryknoll sisters Elsie Monge and Laura Glynn, who worked with the Juan XXIII Center doing informal peasant education in the diocese. In March 1971 I went with four youth from Chorrillo to take part in a work camp with the campesinos, as well as with some university students from Panama City led by a Jesuit. We were there to clear some land that the cooperative had acquired on which it intended to cultivate coffee collectively. Those of us from the city had never used machetes and soon our hands had blisters; we weren't there primarily for our labor but to experience rural life and express solidarity with campesinos. We worked in the mornings, and in the afternoon and evening we had discussions and sang. This was Hector's utopian vision of a future society in which divisions between countryside and city and between manual and intellectual work would be overcome. However, we were accused of being guerrillas, and the guardia came and detained the head of the co-op.

Although our situations were quite different, I felt a strong kinship with Hector, perhaps because we were both working with poor people and were limited in the means at our disposal. When Hector came to Panama City, he sometimes stayed with me, and he did so a few days before his disappearance. On that occasion we went to see the Costa-Gavras film *Z*, about repression under the Greek military dictatorship.

In May 1971 the campesinos gathered to protect a woman whom one of the local caciques was trying to push off a plot of land she had occupied for years. A couple days later Hector's hut was set on fire while he was sleeping, but he escaped. Left homeless, he was sleeping at the home of Jacinto Peña, one of the co-op leaders, on June 9, when two men in uniform came asking for him. When he appeared in the doorway, they took him away. Soon the word was out, and Bishop Martin Legarra and others began to make inquiries. As the days and weeks went on, rumors flew. One version was that Alvaro Vernaza had arranged to have Hector abducted, possibly in order to have him deported, but he was so severely beaten that he could not be released. By this time the relationship between Leo and Torrijos had soured, but Leo went to see Torrijos, and found him drunk and weeping, apparently powerless to resolve the crisis.

At some point Hector was disappeared; one rumor at the time was that he had been dropped into the ocean from a helicopter. Years later the blame was placed on then Colonel Manuel Noriega, who as the head of G-2 (Intelligence) was the second most powerful figure in the country, and was presumably involved. In 2018, DNA testing on remains found at a Panamanian military base were identified as Hector's.

The disappearance of a priest shook Panamanian society and triggered a national crisis. The bishops pressed for information. A haunting protest song was composed and sung at weekly vigils held at the Iglesia del Carmen, a landmark church in the city. Clergy meetings were held, and Catholics rallied, including elite and middle-class groups whose traditional political activity had been suppressed but who could now protest against the regime under the banner of the church. Conspicuously absent were two or three nationalistic Panamanian priests who had ties within the regime.

The moment of greatest tension came a month after Hector's abduction, when four large processions from different directions converged at a major intersection in Panama City on a Sunday at midday. All the bishops, headed by McGrath, concelebrated an outdoor Mass. Had the crowd marched toward the headquarters of the Guardia Nacional, a very serious standoff or repressive violence could have ensued; government troops were prepared for such an eventuality. However, after the Mass the crowd dispersed, and any threat to the government dissipated, even though Hector's cause remained prominent in church circles for many months.

On October 11, the third anniversary of the 1968 "revolution" (as Torrijos called the coup), a holiday was declared, work was suspended, and supporters were bused in for a large progovernment demonstration. No mention was made of Hector Gallego, but the televised all-day event was plainly a show of force in response to the church movement. By early 1972 the hierarchy and the Torrijos government had moved back from sharp confrontation, perhaps discreetly assisted by the papal nuncio.

People in Chorrillo, except for those most involved with the parish, did not participate actively in the demands for the truth about Hector Gallego. Most people were not strongly identified with the institutional church and remained spectators. Despite my friendship with Hector and indignation at his disappearance, the confrontation struck me as somewhat artificial: the Catholic Church was not the great defender of the poor, nor was the Torrijos government their great oppressor. As with many things in Panama, the reality was more ambiguous.

This was an early instance of what soon became common in Latin America, the abduction, murder, or disappearance of a priest or sister by shadowy forces supporting the existing power structure.

* * *

During the post-Medellin period, church pastoral work frequently provoked threats and violence from the powerful. In El Salvador, my IPLA classmate Chencho Alas, the pastor in Suchitoto, a half hour north of San Salvador, had irked local notables by his work developing leadership among the peasants. In January 1970 he was abducted at noon in San Salvador, where he was attending a conference on land reform at the university. His captors blindfolded him and drove off.

When the word got out, peasants demonstrated. Archbishop Chavez went to the military authorities and demanded that Chencho be returned. His captors eventually left him alone in his underwear on a mountain, from which he made his way to safety. He told me the story when he stopped in Panama on his way to Trinidad and Tobago, where friends had invited him to recover. His abduction was followed by two decades of violence against priests and church personnel in El Salvador.

Not long afterward, some former IPLA participants invited Jose Comblin to give a course in Nicaragua, and Jorge Altafulla and I drove together to participate. Upon arrival in Managua, we learned that the Somoza government authorities had not allowed Comblin to deplane and had sent him on to El Salvador. We drove another day to San Salvador, where we were told that the meeting would be held at a modest beach resort owned by the brother of Monsignor Ramon Vega. In a meeting room within earshot of the waves crashing on black sands, Comblin delivered a series of lectures on "theology and politics."

These incidents were occurring at a time when the Catholic Church was seeking to extricate itself from an older type of implicit politics of support for the status quo. For example, it was still common for governments to hold an annual Te Deum in the cathedral. The Te Deum is a hymn of praise to God for which composers had devised elaborate settings. The text was beside the point, however: a Te Deum provided a solemn ritual whereby bishops and government officials and other dignitaries confirmed one another's authority in the cathedral in a Catholic country. Likewise, in the 1970s, military dictators were fond of dedicating their country to the Virgin Mary under her various titles. The symbolism was then being called into question, but such practices declined only slowly.

The church's official position seemed clear enough in principle: the church promotes the common good, and in that sense it is "political," but it does not engage in partisan politics. In real situations, however, that distinction was not so easy to maintain. Is opposition to a dictatorship partisan, or is it for the common good? Does it matter whether the dictatorship is on the right or the left? Is dictatorship only of an individual autocrat or can it be collective, for example, of the army high command? Work by church people with the poor was triggering political reactions, particularly when that work took the form of consciousness-raising, helping people come to a sense of their own dignity and rights and to organize.

In Chorrillo we were now tackling the obvious problem of housing, at first in pressuring administrators and owners to make needed repairs and then to explore possible ways to enable the people to have adequate housing. But why were people in such housing? Was there something systemic in Panamanian society that caused such an outcome? And what about the Canal Zone and U.S. bases: Was that an "occupation" of Panama? Was poverty ultimately due to the socioeconomic system itself, capitalism, and the role of the United States in maintaining it? What—if anything—should be the church's role in response? *And what should I do about it?*

Such questions were in the back of my mind as I went about the more immediate tasks in Chorrillo. These questions also impelled me to continue to read historians and social scientists, particularly works by Latin Americans.

* * *

In 1971 a social worker from the Ministry of Health came to Chorrillo proposing that a health committee be formed. The minister of health was Dr. Jose Renan Esquivel, a pediatrician who had previously headed the Children's Hospital. He wanted to move beyond a doctor-centered model of health care to a community-centered approach under the rubric "Equal Health for All." "Diseases aren't in the hospitals." he said. "They're in the communities." Under that rationale, he pressed for safe drinking water, breast-feeding, better nutrition, and getting physicians and other health personnel into the community. Working with him now was Cecilia Dolan, the Argentine Maryknoll sister, who after the sisters' forced departure from San Miguelito had earned a master's degree in public health and had returned to Panama—to the annoyance of Leo Mahon.

The ministry perhaps intended to take advantage of the organizing that had been done in Chorrillo in the previous two years. Esquivel agreed that a key health issue in Chorrillo was overcrowding; a health committee could be a vehicle for addressing housing. In the wake of the tension generated by the Hector Gallego conflict, working through the Ministry of Health could allay suspicions. I sensed a danger that the group might become absorbed in health-related tasks and lose the focus on housing, but they opted to go along with the proposal of forming a health committee as a vehicle for addressing housing as a health problem. To do so they had to win an election against other slates, made up of sports figures or traditional political leaders, and they did so decisively.

Esquivel showed his approval by coming to Chorrillo, and he invited committee president Roberto Batista and others to accompany him in visits to the interior to meet other health committees. However, the physician who headed the local clinic in Chorrillo did not share Esquivel's vision and was not convinced of the importance of community involvement. At one point the committee concluded that refuse in the streets was a health problem and made efforts to get trash bins installed around the barrio. The youth group prepared a sociodrama contrasting how receptionists and physicians were solicitous of the well-off and disdainful of the poor. The group was invited to make presentations outside Chorrillo.

The example of Esquivel and Cecilia Dolan illustrates how honest, good-willed people could serve in the Torrijos government, which some would simply dismiss as a dictatorship. The democracy overthrown by the coup was primarily a game for the elites, not a channel for ordinary citizens to defend their interests. The Torrijos regime that replaced it did not practice widespread systematic torture and murder, as became common in Latin America by the mid-1970s. Torrijos did not enrich himself in the manner of personal dictators like Somoza in Nicaragua or Trujillo in the Dominican Republic. He spent a lot of time helicoptering to remote rural communities in the interior, listening to people present their problems, and ordering concrete projects like roads or bridges.

In terms of housing, the people of Chorrillo would have preferred some plan whereby they could remain there in decent housing at an affordable price. That suggested replacing the existing housing with concrete apartment buildings four stories or so high and maintaining the existing density. Even bare-bones apartment buildings require expensive structural reinforcement and infrastructure. A key question was whether such units could be built and made affordable without entailing a disproportionate subsidy. The alternative would be to identify land elsewhere on which individual houses could be built more cheaply. Assisting in these explorations was the architect Jorge Riba, who had headed IVU (the Institute of Housing and Urbanism) in the 1960s and who now had his own architecture firm and a teaching position at the University of Panama. For over a year the health committee explored these possibilities, while never really dispelling the suspicion by the government that they might be in opposition, because of their association with the parish.

* * *

One night in February 1971 I was in the back of the church when I saw one of the youth from next door, Luis Valdes ("Caneo"), running, and a man chasing him, gun in hand. I went running after them, figuring that he was a plainclothes agent of the DENI (National Department of Investigations). Caneo and the agent bolted up the stairs into the sisters' quarters. There I confronted him, said I was the pastor, asked for ID, and he left. This had happened during a *batida* (sweep), the raids made on a house or set of houses, in which young males were arrested. The families would then have to go and get them released, paying a fee.

The health committee sought to address this practice, first going to the DENI, but the people felt they were treated rudely. The minister of justice came to Chorrillo, and when he was asked about the raids he said the barrio had to be cleansed of criminals. When people objected, he left in a huff in the midst of a tropical downpour. Colonel Manuel Noriega, head of G-2 (Intelligence), then came, and after listening to the people he said he would call off the batidas if the people would say who the criminals were. Their reply was that they wouldn't be *sapos* (toads; slang for informers), and that that was the job of the police. The fact that the people of the barrio would have confrontations with national officials over these matters underscores how small Panama is.

* * *

From time to time a man whom I knew as "Mingo" came to see me. He didn't live in Chorrillo, but some people there knew him and thought he was a little crazy. He always had several days' growth of beard and didn't have a regular job. He said he had been in Coiba, the notorious island prison off the Pacific Coast, and claimed to have known Floyd Britton, a left-wing leader who had died at Coiba in 1969, presumably after being beaten by the guardia. The Torrijos government worked with the People's Party, but independent leftists were suspect, if not persecuted.

Why did Mingo stop to see me? I wondered. Perhaps I was just a sympathetic ear, but I couldn't exclude the suspicion that he or others who dropped by might be informers of some kind. Someone pointed out to me that Panama was a "Beirut," a place of information gathering and intrigue. In addition to Panamanian government agencies, multiple U.S. intelligence agencies were at work: aside from the CIA, each branch of the armed forces in the Canal Zone had its own intelligence service. The presence of so many agencies seeking intelligence prompted some Panamanians to supply information for money. Americans occasionally came to the parish expressing interest in our work; some may have been gathering intelligence. Since we had nothing to hide, we weren't concerned.

* * *

In 1972, after ruling by decree with no legislature for over three years, the Torrijos government announced plans to form a new legislature, an assembly of 505 deputies, one for each of the country's administrative districts, called *corregimientos*. The vast majority of the corrigimientos were in the countryside; only about 10 to 15 percent were in greater Panama City, where half of the population lived. The obvious aim was to create a legislative body comprising predominantly docile rural people, loyal to Torrijos. He may have seen it as a way of improving life for campesinos in neglected rural hamlets. Those who opposed the military government on principle and called it a dictatorship dismissed the scheme out of hand.

If the housing activists had proposed a candidate for the assembly, they would almost certainly have won, given the their grassroots strength, but they decided not to, perhaps questioning the scheme's legitimacy and in any case realizing that it would distract from their efforts to address housing. Others recognized an opportunity, and Elias Castillo, a university student whose family had a store on Calle 26, decided to run with Gustavo Melgar as his alternate. Both had emerged from the organizing that led to the barrio assembly in 1970. The Youth for the Improvement of Chorrillo, which used the space in the back of the church and had murky political ties, worked to support Elias, who was elected to represent Chorrillo.

When the assembly—"the 505," as it was called—convened after the national election, Elias was elected its president. A young man in Chorrillo who had emerged through our organizing work was now the president of the Panamanian legislature.

THE PASTORAL TURNS POLITICAL

* * *

The Medellin conference unleashed intense exploration and questioning throughout Latin America. National episcopates and dioceses organized workshops for clergy and religious, often inviting theologians and pastoralists like Edgard Beltran from Colombia, Jose Marins from Brazil, and Segundo Galilea from Chile. Bishops conferences issued pastoral letters. Pastoral practices and the theology underlying them that had seemed controversial in San Miguelito five years before now had the endorsement of the Latin American episcopacy.

Books with collections of articles by theologians and activists were published. Topics raised in publications and meetings were the need for a Latin American theology, the relationship between theory and practice, violence, involvement in grassroots struggles, the relationship between Christianity and Marxism (and between Christians and Marxists), and class division. More pastoral topics included spirituality and popular religiosity. Protestants like Jose Miguez Bonino and Emilio Castro were involved, and the Protestant organization ISAL (Church and Society in Latin America) was a major sponsor of such encounters. This activity was especially intense in the Southern Cone (Argentina, Chile, and Uruguay). Brazilians were not yet prominent, partly due to the military dictatorship's level of repression.

Formal and informal networks were being created to communicate ideas. On a visit to Panama in 1970, Nicaraguan Jesuit Fernando Cardenal asked me to serve as contact in Panama for such networking. That may have been why, a few months later, Fr. Louis ("Mike") Colonese, the coordinator of the annual CICOP gatherings, invited me to Colombia for a meeting cloaked in considerable secrecy. Church-related people from a dozen or so countries met outside Bogota. Each made a presentation about his country (my recollection is that we were all male), the political and economic situation, as well as the situation of the church (taking it for granted that "church" meant the Catholic Church). There was talk of a new liberation theology but it was all in a quasi-clandestine atmosphere, as though we were under surveillance.

Toward the end of that same year, I participated in a meeting in Antigua, Guatemala, sponsored by the Social Secretariat of the Central American episcopacy, with bishops, priests, religious, and laypeople in attendance. We followed a similar dynamic of sharing of analysis of society and church and the use of a Medellin-inflected vocabulary, including the word "liberation." However, we were doing so under the auspices of the institutional church. Analyses and ideas that Colonese assumed had to be discussed clandestinely were now public and becoming mainstream.

The first public use of the term "liberation theology" was apparently in a talk by Gustavo Gutierrez to priests in Chimbote, Peru, in August 1968. In 1969 Archbishop McGrath passed me a small book in French by Gutierrez on the topic, based on a presentation in Switzerland. His book *Teología de la Liberación: Perspectivas*, published in Lima at the very end of 1971 (and in English in 1973), was a map of a newly emerging theological territory, which grew out of years of listening to clergy, religious, and active laity, in Peru and elsewhere. The first half of the book was a theological reading of the "signs of the times," with a focus on political developments. The second half offered sketches of major themes in theology (God in history, salvation, Christ, Eucharist, poverty) from this new angle. The book captured the hemisphere-wide ferment, highlighting emerging theological themes and providing a rationale for the kinds of pastoral work being done, particularly in solidarity to address poverty.

Other maps of this new theological territory appeared almost simultaneously with that of Gutierrez. In 1972 Jesuit Ignacio Ellacuria gave me a copy of *Teología Política* (Political theology) in mimeographed form, which is similar in themes to the second half of the Gutierrez book, although the last section deals with violence to a degree not common among others. Brazilian Hugo Assmann likewise published *Opresión-Liberación: Desafío a los Cristianos* (Oppression-liberation: Challenge to Christians) in 1971. He was then in Chile, having fled from his native Brazil and from Bolivia. Living under the elected socialist government of Salvador Allende, Assmann was more concerned about questions of praxis, particularly that of Christians committed to revolution, and of critiquing the use of Christianity to support the present unjust order. Alex Morelli, a French theologian working in Mexico, published *Libera a Mi Pueblo* (Liberate my people), which explicitly advocated nonviolence as a spirituality and a method of struggle. These early overviews were largely focused on issues of Christians in politics, not pastoral activity in a parish. Gutierrez, for example, did not mention Christian base communities in his book.

From Chorrillo I sought to interpret these developments for Catholics in the United States. In 1972 I published an article in *Commonweal* on Camilo Torres as a kind of proto–liberation theologian, in the sense that he had anticipated some of the major themes of the emerging theology—for example, the Eucharist, which should be a sign of unity, is problematic in a divided society. I then prepared an overview of this theology for the Jesuit review *Theological Studies*. Although I wasn't an academic and didn't have library resources, I had the advantage of being in a poor barrio myself and knowing a number of the theologians personally. The article, which appeared in 1973, surveyed the Medellin documents, the experience of conflict throughout Latin America, the theological critique of capitalism, the stress on praxis, and what was new about this theology and the challenges it raised. It was a very early scholarly survey in English of Latin American liberation theology.

* * *

Like many of my contemporaries, I found myself radicalized, at least intellectually. If I asked why people in Chorrillo lived in housing that was dehumanizing, my questioning moved from the landlords and their companies, to the inequalities in

Panama, and to the world itself. The roots of the problem seemed to be systemic and to call for systemic responses.

Marx had pointed out that wealth was *produced socially*—by large numbers of people working in complex organizations—but that it was *appropriated privately*—by the owners of capital. The logical step was to assure that what was produced socially was also appropriated socially. That was what socialism would be about. History itself seemed to be moving toward a qualitatively different kind of society; revolutions seemed to be a driving force of that history. Half the world was under some form of socialism (not only the USSR, China, and other communist states, but also India and a number of African countries). Socialism had a plausibility that is difficult to even imagine today.

Seen from the United States, the contest between capitalism and socialism was the heart of the Cold War. Latin Americans, however, objected to being thrust into a cold war; they insisted that the future society they had in mind was not a carbon copy of any model, not even Cuba, but rather a "Latin American socialism." In speaking of Latin America as the "Patria Grande" (Great Homeland), intellectuals meant that the new society would unify the continent, which had fractured after independence, contrary to the dream of Simon Bolivar.

To these utopian visions, Christians brought the biblical image of the equality exemplified by the first Christians in Jerusalem, who "held all things in common" (Acts). If the roots of poverty were systemic, and what was required was systemic change, then Christians should take their stand. To those who said that the church should not be involved with partisan politics, the reply was that the church is already committed—but to the status quo. Neutrality is impossible.

Similar radicalization was taking place in Europe and North America, politically in antiwar protests, and culturally. My alienation from the United States was reinforced by an experience in 1971 during a monthlong visit to my family. I was sitting in the Greyhound station in downtown L.A., on Skid Row, at 3 or 4 AM, reading a book on the Vietnam War—or perhaps dozing. A policeman came by and asked me what I was doing there. When I explained that I was waiting for a 6 AM bus to Covina, he told me to get up and go downstairs to where I would catch the bus. After taking the bus to Covina, I was walking toward my parents' home in the hills. Two police in a patrol car came by, stopped, and asked me what I was doing: a pedestrian at 7 AM in Covina was apparently suspect, especially if he was unshaven and looked vaguely Mexican. I explained and continued walking, and the same patrol car later cruised by, presumably checking to make sure that I was going where I said I was. I had been harassed twice the same morning, simply for my appearance. As trivial as the incidents were, they reinforced my sense of estrangement from the United States and gratitude for being in Panama.

As much as I gravitated intellectually toward a systemic critique, in Chorrillo we were working within the existing system, striving to address housing conditions.

Panama was not a candidate for revolution. Although Torrijos claimed to be revolutionary, he was encouraging the expansion of Panama as a banking haven; by the early 1970s over a hundred banks had set up operations there. A lawyer from a traditional aristocratic family told me with some sense of irony that by depriving the traditional elites of the political game, Torrijos had freed them to pursue business without distraction, and they were making fortunes in the process.

* * *

The election of Salvador Allende to the presidency of Chile in 1970 seemed to herald the possibility of a "peaceful path to socialism": steps could be taken toward a more egalitarian society through a democratic process. However, Allende had won only a plurality in a three-way race and had nothing near a majority in the Chilean Congress. He also faced the hostility of the Nixon administration, which immediately set out to isolate Chile internationally and destabilize it from within through covert CIA actions. Domestically, Allende's presidency was marked by increasing polarization.

In 1971 a group of priests in Chile published a statement arguing that Christians should support socialism, and were soon joined by others in an organization called Christians for Socialism. That did not mean endorsing a particular organization or party; their stances varied from support for Allende's Socialist Party to the MIR (Revolutionary Left Movement), which assumed that armed revolution would eventually be necessary. The Chilean bishops accused them of being involved in partisan politics and tried to force the group to disband. Resisting this pressure, they announced a continent-wide conference for April 1972. I was asked to organize the Panamanian delegation, and I pulled together a group of five or six. As a gringo I stayed in the background.

Attending the meeting were over four hundred people, most from Chile, fifty from Argentina, and a few dozen others, primarily priests and religious, with a scattering of Protestant pastors and theologians. Gutierrez, Assmann, Dussel, and other prominent theologians attended. The Chilean bishops opposed the meeting, and the only bishop who ventured to attend was Sergio Mendez Arceo of Cuernavaca. The conference itself was several days of plenary sessions and smaller group sessions. Walls in the main auditorium bore posters with quotations from Camilo Torres and Che Guevara; well-known Chilean folk-protest groups performed their works. President Allende sent a message of welcome, and at one point we were visited by Clotario Blest, a labor leader since the 1920s and a firm Catholic.

At one workshop I attended, Jose (Pepe) Alvarez Icaza, a Mexican who with his wife had been a lay observer at Vatican II, gave an introduction to *análisis coyuntural* (conjunctural analysis), a technique for reading the signs of the times. It entails taking information primarily from conventional news sources and organizing it by economic sector (agriculture/mining, industry, services) and actors (government, business, armed forces, church, popular movements, etc.) and summarizing it in a grid. The assumption is that doing so makes it possible to visualize the forces at work in society objectively, and thus to situate one's work more effectively. Conjunctural analysis subsequently became common throughout Latin America.

The general mood of the week was triumphalistic, as expressed in the final document: "The revolutionary process is in full swing in Latin America." That statement reflected the confidence of Chileans and Argentines. However, no one from Brazil, Bolivia, Paraguay, El Salvador, Guatemala, or Nicaragua could attend the conference openly, given the repressive regimes then in power; anyone attending from those countries was either there discreetly or already in exile. In a caucus of Central Americans I heard Salvadorans say that they were disguising the reason for their trip as tourism by making stops in several countries. Thus I felt a tension between the confident language about the "unstoppable advance of history" toward socialism and the reality that more than half of Latin America was living under brutal military repression.

The final document expressed a firm conviction that there are only two alternatives: dependent capitalism or socialism. It stressed the need for Christians to expose the ideological exploitation of faith and its symbols. Sunday at midday we gathered at a *quinta* (farm or rural getaway) outside of Santiago, where Bishop Mendez Arceo presided over the Eucharist, which segued into a farewell meal.

I stayed ten more days in Chile trying to understand what was happening, hosted by young Panamanians who were doing graduate studies in economics. Chile was then a magnet for young Latin Americans from around the hemisphere. It was a heady atmosphere: workers were organizing takeovers (*tomas*) of factories, and committees were being organized to distribute essential goods to overcome stoppages by distributors and truckers. I visited one such *toma*, where a community had set up an encampment on a riverbank and had organized their own collective business of digging sand and shoveling it onto trucks to be sold for construction.

Chilean society was already polarized, and signs of crisis were evident. Unable to have legislation passed, Allende was forced to use executive orders based on existing legislation, for example, accelerating the existing land reform program. The right wing was organizing protests, and Allende's economic policies were triggering inflation. Exchanging dollars at the unofficial rate I bought records and books at fraction of their normal price and mailed them back to Panama.

Despite the long tradition and present examples of military coups elsewhere in Latin America, Chileans of all persuasions were convinced that they were different, and that their democratic institutions would be maintained.

* * *

Stopping in Lima on my way back, I went to see Villa El Salvador, a settlement then less than a year old. Unlike the common pattern in which poor people invaded land, fought off the police, put up makeshift houses, and then spent years struggling to obtain electricity, water, schools, clinics, and so forth, Villa El Salvador was an "organized invasion." After an initial confrontation in which one demonstrator was killed, and with support from the church and Bishop Luis Bambaren, the government and the community agreed on a plan to settle people on land on the outskirts of Lima. The entire settlement was planned, surveyed, and organized into blocks and larger units, with adequate streets, space for green areas and parks, and urban services to be delivered. What I saw was an initial stage; the land was sandy, nothing was growing. People had put up shelters with square woven mats, which were sufficient initially since it almost never rains in Lima and the ocean moderates temperatures. Within a few years, solid houses had been built and businesses were operating. The idea of working with rather than against poor people attempting to build their houses was new but gaining ground. Villa El Salvador soon had several hundred thousand residents.

I also stopped in Colombia partly to observe something of the Golconda movement and its methods. The movement was one of the national priest movements that had sprung up in the late 1960s. While not large in numbers, the group was influential for several years, particularly through several charismatic priests such as Rene Garcia in Bogota. As some of the Third World Priests in Argentina had opted to support Peron, these Colombian priests supported the 1970 candidacy of Gustavo Rojas Pinilla, a former dictator from the 1950s, on the grounds that he was beloved by "the people," and any movement for fundamental change had to be rooted in the people. Three of the Golconda priests, all Spanish-born, joined the ELN guerrillas.

The group was very much influenced by German Zabala, a figure similar to Paulo Freire—that is, a guru who developed a method of popular education. Under his guidance, teams of university students and other young people went to live in poor barrios and organize. Unlike Freire, who proposed a small set of general ideas, Zabala had a complex system for first doing detailed community study. He had been trained as a mathematician and could fill out a blackboard with grid schemes, typically in threes, reflecting the influence of structuralism.

While in Bogota I was hosted by Zabala-influenced young professionals who were living communally and doing community organizing. They were an instance of that generation of idealistic young people throughout Latin America who spent years of their lives working toward what they hoped would be a vast continent-wide transformation.

Besides organizing in poor barrios, Zabala had educational theories and methods, and they were being implemented in schools in various parishes. The method was not based on lectures, tests, and grades. Rather, the teacher began the day by posing a problem to the students as a group, after which they were to do research to solve it, working together, and then present their findings. These schools operated in parishes, and along with the Zabala method, they also covered the Colombian government school curriculum sufficiently for the students to pass national examinations.

On the day I visited a school in the prosperous northern part of Bogota, I happened upon a crisis: one of the students in the graduating class had come to school high on marijuana. Zabala decided to hold a *tribunal popular* (people's court), borrowing a term then being used in Chile. The whole student body, elementary and high school, assembled in the courtyard. The student's "attorneys" were young faculty members, and Zabala served as "prosecutor." The defense attorneys used different lines of defense, particularly blaming bourgeois culture and ultimately capitalism; Zabala argued that bad apples spoil the barrel and had to be thrown out. The attorneys countered that student should be credited for showing up; if he had stayed away he wouldn't have been caught. It was all great theater and pedagogy: in the end a solution was found whereby the student could remain, and conventional bourgeois justice systems were castigated.

* * *

After my return from Christians for Socialism, Alberto (Betito) Quiroz Guardia had me as a guest on his morning talk show on Radio Impacto, and from time to time afterward, particularly to speak about developments in the Latin American church. Betito was not an activist in any party and was primarily a gadfly; he wanted to stimulate discussion. He was a Panamanian nationalist, and he believed in individual freedom and hence opposed the military government, but he sympathized with independent leftists.

Although the church-state crisis precipitated by the disappearance of Hector Gallego diminished over the course of 1972, some of the networks and activities that had been triggered during that time continued. Three youth (Raul, Mireya, and Selma) and I formed a quartet to sing and play arrangements of protest songs I had bought in Chile, performing in Chorrillo and sometimes elsewhere. The songs were generally poetic and suggestive—for example, "A Desalambrar" (to "de-wire") called for barbed wire to be cut down "because the land is yours and his," and belongs to "Pedro, Maria, Juan, and Jose." The lullaby "Duerme Negrito" begins with soothing words, "Sleep, little black baby, because your mother's in the field—working," and goes on to mention the treats she's going to bring, alternating between lullaby feelings and a description of her hard life. Once we went to the university to see a performance by the Chilean protest singer Victor Jara. A year later, after the military coup, he was imprisoned in the stadium where soldiers broke his fingers and taunted him before killing him. This music spread around Latin America as an expression of solidarity and a yearning for a different kind of society.

An interdisciplinary team of Jesuits ran programs out of the Centro de Capacitación Social, and an associated magazine, *Diálogo Social*, similar to such magazines in other countries, with some original articles and reprints, presenting postconciliar and post-Medellin viewpoints and experiences. One of the Jesuits was Xabier Gorostiaga, a Basque who had returned from studying economics at Cambridge University, where he had done a thesis on the economics of the Panama Canal.

Gorostiaga went to work as an adviser to the Panamanian foreign ministry. Since 1964 the canal issue had remained largely dormant, but Torrijos now began to publicly campaign for the Canal Zone, including the canal, to be returned to Panama. The argument was simple: the U.S. presence was a colonial occupation. Torrijos and the Panamanian government were advocating a renegotiation of the 1903 treaties, aimed at eventually restoring Panamanian sovereignty. Since my arrival I had largely ignored the Canal Zone, even though I had to drive through it whenever I went to the interior, and I lived next to it. Now it began to be a live issue, even though matters were being handled between governments.

At one point I was asked to go to Santa Fe to attend a meeting of the cooperative that had been formed out of Hector Gallego's work. Under Bishop Legarra the diocese had retreated from its commitment. Three Maryknoll sisters who had worked there for years had to leave, and they went to other countries. One of the main leaders of the cooperative was Jacinto Peña, the man from whose hut Hector had been abducted. I found the campesino pace of the discussions excruciatingly slow, and I had no relevant qualifications or expertise to bring to the meeting, but as a priest I expressed solidarity and some sense of connection with the church, in lieu of support from the local bishop.

In early 1973 I began a discussion in one section of Calle 27 exploring what I hoped would be an adult catechism for people of Chorrillo. We held about ten sessions focused primarily on the life and message of Jesus. I must have felt that my attention had been too focused on responding to events, such as the Hector Gallego crisis, and that I should devote more attention to basic evangelization. However, I was only beginning when I left the parish and Panama.

* * *

Through Gorostiaga I met Arun Shourie, an Indian economist who was spending several weeks in Panama doing quick studies of particular problems for Torrijos. I accompanied him and his wife, Anita, on a visit to the San Blas Islands, partly to serve as a Spanish interpreter. San Blas is the home of the Kuna people, who occupy the Atlantic coast from the middle of Panama to Colombia. They have retained their distinctive clothing and way of life, primarily by remaining by themselves on the islands. Arun, Anita, and I spent a couple days in San Blas at the beaches and occasionally speaking with the people.

One example of the kind of study Shourie was doing was on the problems of small banana producers, particularly getting their products to market. He said that India had been a supposedly socialist nation for decades but that it was still poor. The effectiveness of an economy and a government in getting things done is more important than its label. Shourie returned to his job at the World Bank in Washington and eventually went back to India and devoted himself to journalism, where he became highly regarded as a kind of public conscience.

* * *

In 1972 Gary MacEoin came to Panama to help Fr. Harvey Steele write his memoir. Harvey was a Canadian Scarboro priest, who in 1964 had set up the Inter-American Cooperative Institute (ICI) to train rural leaders in the principles of cooperatives. Through Gary I got to know Harvey and several times went out to see him, usually with the sisters. As a young priest he had gone to China and had to leave with the outbreak of World War II, but he retained great respect for the Chinese. After some time in Canada, where he studied the cooperative movement, he went to the Dominican Republic, but he had to leave under pressure from the Trujillo dictatorship.

Harvey saw cooperatives not as a panacea but as a tool for leadership development among the rural poor. Throughout his life he was a maverick, which may have accounted for his migration toward a kind of work that was not obviously "priestly." Gary interviewed him extensively over a period of weeks and edited the result into *Agent for Change* (1973).

* * *

The group seeking housing solutions with guidance from the architect Jorge Riba eventually concluded that the costs of building even modest apartments in Chorrillo would make them unaffordable for most people, or that they would require enormous subsidies. The group then explored possibilities of obtaining land on which lots could be built with houses within their ability to pay. One proposal was a tract of land in a place called Cerro Silvestre on the other side of the Canal Zone. The land was held by the agrarian reform agency.

On one occasion the group, which the government viewed with suspicion, organized a march from Chorrillo to the agency offices. On the way back they were halted by Guardia troops and told to come back to see Colonel Rodrigo Garcia the next morning. The colonel told them that if he had been there when they went marching by, he would have jailed them, and warned them that if they continued to be advised by "that little priest," they wouldn't get anywhere. The case was sent to a government development agency. For most of the year they took classes in cooperatives and pursued the possibility of a new housing development in Cerro Silvestre, which would be called Nuevo Chorrillo (New Chorrillo). Meanwhile, a rival group connected to the president of the legislature, Elias Castillo, continued to advocate for building apartments in Chorrillo.

MEMENTO OF THE LIVING AND THE DEAD

* * *

On Christmas Eve 1972, at around 10 PM as we were anticipating midnight Mass, a fire broke out on Calle 26 in the middle of Chorrillo. It started from a stove on which a woman had been cooking and spread to some spilled paint thinner, and from there jumped to a propane tank that exploded. Because the houses were separated by alleys only a yard or so wide, the fire spread from house to house. People fled into the streets, taking whatever valuables they could carry, some coming by the church. When the firefighters had halted the blaze, one little girl had been burned to death, eighteen houses had been destroyed, and 289 families were left homeless. Some of the victims took refuge in a school building. Ironically, two days before the fire, we had organized a barrio-wide caravan through the streets to take up a collection for the people of Managua, which had been leveled by an earthquake.

An ad-hoc committee worked on channeling items donated, such as food, stoves, kitchenware, beds, and school uniforms. For months Joaquin Melgar and his family lived in the parish office below the sisters, and the Smith family lived in the space in the back of the church that the youth group occupied.

In the midst of this crisis, a tabloid paper ran a bizarre story about me, including accusations of an irregular Eucharist. While it was anonymous, it seemed to come from some political sector intending to undermine the work of the parish, most likely connected to the Partido del Pueblo, which viewed any independent progressive group as a rival.

The fire spurred efforts to resolve the housing problem but also increased political tensions. The day after the fire, Torrijos gave the order for earthmoving to start in Cerro Silvestre for housing for chorrilleros, but opponents led by Elias Castillo prevailed. Torrijos reversed his order. The sticking point was still the perception that the group that had emerged from the parish organizing effort was anti-Torrijos.

* * *

Angela Brennan and I had been working together for over two years as colleagues. Sometime in the first half of 1973 we realized that we were falling in love. I had found her attractive from the time she arrived but had ignored those feelings. At some point I suggested we take a walk to the Canal Zone (where we were unlikely to run into Panamanians who knew us). There we found that we were both attracted to each other. Within weeks we realized that we could not continue in the parish and made plans to leave and marry. We informed Archbishop McGrath, who said he would try to facilitate my laicization in Rome. I was to leave in July, and Angie would join me toward the end of the year.

We decided to have a farewell party and invited parishioners and some others. At that gathering, Jorge Riba said that if other efforts to obtain land failed, he owned a plot of land on the other side of the Canal Zone that he would be willing to sell, and that he would then donate the proceeds to be used for a school in the new neighborhood. It was a generous gesture and indicated that the years of efforts to address housing might not be fruitless.

8

Finding Our Way—With Twists and Turns

RATHER THAN FLYING, I returned to Los Angeles by bus, going capital to capital through Central America, then through Mexico to southern Texas, and along the southern border to California, staying with friends along the way. My unhurried return was partly because we had several months of waiting, but perhaps because I had no clear idea of another career or vocation.

In Managua I stayed with Gerri O'Leary, who had been in Chorrillo and was now married to Edgard Macias, a Christian Democrat politician. Both of them worked in development agencies, which were busy in the aftermath of the earthquake a few months before. The entire former downtown was rubble; I saw an iguana in the rapidly spreading vegetation. Many families were still without housing. One of the forms of aid from Europe was a kind of instant housing made out of a Styrofoam-like material and shaped like igloos. It may have been practical in some situations, but it was ludicrous in the tropics, an example of an inappropriate response to natural disaster.

Somoza was said to be profiteering amid the inflation and an influx of foreign aid. Because earthquake experts warned of a pattern of fault lines, no rebuilding was permitted in the former center. Offices and workplaces had been scattered to what had been the outskirts. To this day Managua remains misshapen, and the old downtown is made up of green spaces through which cars and buses speed toward other destinations.

Gerri connected me to some French development workers and amateur volcanologists whom I accompanied one Sunday to the Masaya volcano not far from Managua. It is not the typical cone-shaped volcano but rather a gaping crater in the ground a couple miles across and a thousand feet or so deep. These volcanologists regularly went down into it to monitor temperatures for gathering data to be used in predicting eruptions. We had to hike down, smelling sulfur dioxide and at one point rappelling perhaps seventy-five feet. When we reached the flat area, another nonvolcanologist and I hung around while the volunteer scientists took measurements. One of them descended with a rope ladder into the clouds of sulfuric steam to dangle a temperature gauge from something that worked like a long fishing pole. We climbed back up in late afternoon, and at dusk we observed a red glow in the deeper hole. The area is now a national park, and visitors can only view the cavity from the rim, not climb down into it.

In El Salvador I went out to see Chencho Alas at his parish in Suchitoto, a colonial town about forty-five minutes from San Salvador. In the four years since IPLA, he had been developing peasant leaders, particularly through intensive courses. He was encountering resistance from local landowners, but he had solid backing from Archbishop Chavez. Over ten thousand small farmers in the area were about to be displaced by a dam of the Lempa River, which would flood a large area and form an artificial lake for hydropower.

* * *

During my first three or four years after ordination, leaving the priesthood was simply inconceivable. That was the psychological effect of years in the seminary and the notion of the priest as a "man set apart," marked by a permanent sacramental character imprinted on one's soul and the acceptance of celibacy as a lifelong commitment. All of that made it psychologically difficult for many of the priests who began leaving around 1967. By 1973, however, resigning from the priesthood had become commonplace. Some had left in anger and even written books denouncing the church; others primarily wanted to marry, and organizations were formed to advocate for a married clergy.

Former priests who were teachers usually continued teaching, perhaps obtaining advanced degrees. Some became lifelong activists. On the whole they went into the caring professions, for example, counseling or social work, or perhaps administration. Some became programmers in the early stages of the computer revolution and made their careers as the information technology field itself developed.

During these months Angie and I stayed in contact with letters and by sending cassette tapes. We wanted to marry in the church, if possible, but we also had to find new vocations or careers. As this story makes clear, it took us many years to settle into something that resembled conventional employment. Meanwhile, I had to adjust to no longer being "Father Berryman" or "Padre Felipe."

* * *

When I expressed in a letter to Gary MacEoin some hesitation about continuing work on Latin America, he replied, "That's what I see written all over your resume." At that point I had only a vague idea of what a resume was.

Staff from the International Fellowship of Reconciliation (IFOR) in Amsterdam wrote me a letter, explaining that they were looking for a coordinator for a Latin America–wide network of organizations pursuing nonviolent change. Since 1968 I had been following incipient organized efforts at nonviolence in the region.

Although normally they would be seeking a Latin American, the IFOR staff thought that given the increasingly repressive atmosphere, being a gringo might provide a degree of protection. Because this seemed like a strong possibility, I didn't pursue other avenues for a number of weeks.

At the invitation of Juan Romero, a priest friend and the president of PADRES, the national organization of Chicano priests, I spent two weeks at the Mexican-American Cultural Center (MACC), a training center in San Antonio, Texas, that ran courses for priests, sisters, and laypeople, somewhat like the IPLA course in Quito that had been important to me. Some of the key figures of Latin American theology, like Gustavo Gutierrez and Enrique Dussel, gave courses at MACC. The driving force was Fr. Virgilio Elizondo, who was then working out his "theology of mestizaje." Juan had thought there might be a role for me at MACC, but nothing along those lines materialized.

One evening Juan and I went with Fr. "Mundo" Rodriguez to see the community organizer Ernie Cortes and his wife. Cortes was doing the initial preparatory work on a campaign in San Antonio sponsored by a number of church congregations. The walls of the den were covered with large sheets of newsprint with the names of board members of the city's civic associations. Among the many dozens of names, all were Anglo—except for the "Mexican Committee" of the Rotary Club—even though the city was 52 percent Latino. It was an illustration of the lack of representation in the power structure. Using the methods pioneered by Saul Alinsky in Chicago, Ernie and others formed Communities Organized for Public Service (COPS), a broad-based network of organizations with strong roots in the churches, which over time played a key role in empowering the city's Latino majority.

I also spent several days as a volunteer at La Paz, in the central valley of California, the headquarters of the United Farm Workers (UFW) organization, helping in the work of putting out the newspaper. In that pre–personal computer time, the text was coded onto punched tape, which fed into a typesetter machine. One evening after the work was finished, a few of us spent some time with Cesar Chavez in his modest living room.

In September I flew to Sacramento to interview for the position with the IFOR. My interviewer was a minister who was part of the Fellowship of Reconciliation (FOR), the U.S. affiliate. Early in the conversation, he asked me point-blank for my position on nonviolence. Whatever I said in reply was the wrong answer, and at that point the interview as such was over, although we continued to talk.

Nonviolence is the starting point for principled pacifists and the core of their life. Others may be practitioners of de facto nonviolence and organize and participate in marches, strikes, and other actions, but they do not necessarily rule out the use of violence in self-defense or condemn others who use violence in a legitimate cause. Like most Latin Americans, I was then more in the latter camp, and my interviewer did not believe I was sufficiently committed to nonviolence in principle. The staff in

Amsterdam regretted that I had not been chosen, and the position went unfilled at that point. In February 1974, grassroots groups from around Latin America met in Medellin under FOR sponsorship, and at that meeting they created a network that they named SERPAJ (Servicio Paz y Justicia [Peace and Justice Service]) dedicated to fostering and training in nonviolence. Argentine artist Adolfo Perez Esquivel was elected to be the coordinator. In 1980 he received the Nobel Peace Prize while imprisoned by the Argentine military dictatorship.

* * *

After that interview I became more serious about finding a job— as I should have been doing from the start. I went north to San Jose and spent a month job hunting in the Bay Area. My seminary classmate John McFadden was helpful with practical matters of lodging, contacts, and buying a car. It was a time of economic slowdown. I was told that the Bay Area had thousands of overqualified candidates looking for work.

One of the first places I applied was the Opportunities Industrialization Center (OIC) in San Jose, a job-training program started by the Reverend Leon Sullivan in Philadelphia. Its strength was its track record in helping low-income people—primarily minorities—find and hold onto entry-level jobs. The trainees and staff in San Jose were largely Latino. Several former priests were on the staff or the board. I was offered a job as a "follow-up counselor" in the electronic-assembly unit and accepted it.

When Angie arrived in December we had been separated for five months in order to allow time for the laicization from Rome. Most of the thousands of priests then leaving the priesthood did not marry in the church. The processes were cumbersome and somewhat humiliating (the implication was that one was incapable of celibacy and was being granted a dispensation in order to avoid sin). It was easier to marry civilly and then apply for laicization. We were fortunate in marrying at a relatively accommodating time under Paul VI and having Archbishop McGrath to use his contacts in Rome to move matters along. The papers arrived in the mail about two days before our wedding, which took place on a Friday night shortly before Christmas in a dark and empty church with Fr. Cuchulain ("Cuch") Moriarty celebrating and John and Georgia McFadden as witnesses. Angie was wearing a long, white Mexican embroidered dress. We went to Carmel for our honeymoon, and after a couple days there we decided to drive to Southern California so that Angie could meet my parents. After a quiet Christmas, we drove back to San Jose and both went to our jobs.

Angie had quickly landed a job teaching in a Montessori school and was also teaching English to immigrants, mainly those working in the canneries. My job was to stay in contact with newly hired people, almost all young women, mostly Mexican American. They were typically soldering parts onto circuit boards for Intel, IBM, and other manufacturers to be used in mainframe computers. My "counseling" services were largely unneeded, but OIC had learned from experience that staying in contact with newly hired people helped make the program effective. I worked from early afternoon into the night, driving from San Jose up through towns in the lower end of the peninsula: Santa Clara, Cupertino, Sunnyvale—before the area was widely known as "Silicon Valley."

We settled into domesticity, furnishing our apartment, and keeping our 1960 VW Bug running with regular trips to the mechanic. Through work, parish, and my former seminary mates we soon had circles of friends. We attended concerts and political rallies supporting the United Farm Workers and protesting the brutality of the Pinochet dictatorship in Chile and U.S. support for it. We could go up to San Francisco on the weekends, or to Yosemite, or hiking in the nearby hills, or to the coast below San Francisco.

It was a peculiar moment in the United States, one that in hindsight proved pivotal. Gas prices had skyrocketed after the oil embargo by the Organization for the Petroleum Exporting Countries (OPEC), and occasionally we had to wait in line at the gas station; the Watergate crisis was unfolding; the Vietnam War was in its final phases, with U.S. combat troops gone and the corrupt government in crisis. A major news item early in our marriage was the abduction of Patty Hearst, the newspaper heiress, who within weeks appeared as a gun-carrying member of the Symbionese Liberation Army—a loony caricature of the revolutionary nationalism of the late 1960s.

That period, 1973–1975, is now understood as the end of the post–World War II boom and the beginning of the decline of the industrial working class. The reaction to *Roe v. Wade* provided evangelical and Catholic religious conservatives an issue around which to organize politically, thereby fueling cultural polarization.

We might well have opted to remain in California, taking up new careers, buying a house, and settling in, particularly as the economic and political climate became more uncertain. However, around May 1974 we were contacted by Harvey Steele, the Canadian priest whom we had known in Panama and sometimes visited at ICI, which trained campesino leaders in forming and managing cooperatives. Harvey flew me to Panama and explained that he was looking for a way to retire and thought that with some easing into it, Angie and I could lead ICI. It didn't occur to me that he should be replaced through a formal search process, rather than personalistically.

It looked providential: we would be returning to Panama to work in a development training center. In short order we quit our jobs and disposed of most of our worldly goods—we emptied the waterbed by siphoning the water out the window with a garden hose and onto the lawn. We would drive east in our VW, and I would meet Angie's family before going to Panama.

We took a leisurely route across the country. We camped at the Grand Canyon and hiked down to the bottom and back up in one day. We went backpacking in the Rockies with my sister Claudia. We stopped in Nebraska to visit Marge and Bill Farmer, whom Angie knew from Montessori training in Panama, and in Detroit to see my relatives. The last leg of our journey took us on I-80 through the middle of Pennsylvania, arriving at

Angie's family home in West Pittston at twilight. I met Angie's parents, Tom and Catherine Brennan, and began to meet her brothers and sisters.

The day after our arrival, my father-in-law took us on an all-day tour around a number of the towns in the Wyoming Valley, made up of many small boroughs near Wilkes-Barre and Scranton. It had been the center of anthracite coal mining around the turn of the twentieth century and had been the country's third-busiest railway hub. By the 1970s it had come on hard economic times, and most of Angie's siblings moved away from the area for their careers, but for decades we have returned there for family occasions.

While we were staying with her sister in Cranbury, New Jersey—where we watched Nixon's resignation— Harvey called from Panama to say that one of his aides had heard credible rumors of political opposition to our return and hence the job was off. We had been blindsided: we had given up jobs and an apartment, and were now unemployed with no place to live and no immediate prospects. Harvey sent a thousand dollars, the equivalent of several thousand dollars today, but it could not compensate what we had left behind. Now what?

Our Jesuit friend in Panama, Xabier Gorostiaga, pooh-poohed the rumor of political opposition and in his ever-enthusiastic way encouraged us to go there and explore other possibilities, which he was certain would exist. At the National Council of Churches (NCC) building in New York, we met with Benton Rhoades, at Agricultural Missions, an NCC program, and Bill Wipfler, an Episcopal priest who worked on human rights issues in Latin America for the NCC. They told us that Misión de Amistad, a program of the Church of the Disciples of Christ in Asuncion, Paraguay, was looking for directors to replace the couple who had been there for some years. Under the Stroessner dictatorship in Paraguay, being Americans might be an advantage.

Rather than flying, we decided to travel by land to Panama and then to Paraguay, with the hope that in one place or the other we would find appropriate work in Latin America. We were now in our thirties, and yet rather than hustling to find new careers we were going to adventure around the hemisphere.

At the time it didn't seem so crazy and improvident as it does in hindsight. My similar trip five years earlier had been very meaningful to me, and we had concrete job possibilities in two places. I also thought I might do some writing or reporting along the way, so I bought a used Voigtlander 35 mm camera and made some inquiries with magazines and newspapers. Tom Quigley, the staff member for Latin American programs at the U.S. Catholic bishops conference, gave us some contacts.

* * *

Gary MacEoin happened to be moving to Tucson for the sake of his wife, Jo, who was in the early stages of dementia. We agreed to take his car while they flew. We started out from New Jersey and made our way to I-81 and down the western edge of

Virginia, detouring through Skyline Drive in Shenandoah National Park to enjoy the fall leaves. We arrived in Tucson a few days later. After a day or so, Gary drove us to the Greyhound station, where we caught a bus for the border.

With no detailed plan we had only two fixed destinations, Panama City and Asuncion. We ended up traveling by land in three portions: through Mexico and Central America to Panama; through Ecuador, Peru, and Bolivia and along the northern border of Argentina to Asuncion, Paraguay; and from Santiago, Chile, to Argentina, Uruguay, southern Brazil, then north to Belem at the mouth of the Amazon, then by air to Manaus in the Amazon, and Bogota, before returning to Philadelphia.

In many places, we were hosted by friends; otherwise, we stayed in cheap hotels, the kind found near bus stations, where rooms would cost the equivalent of a few dollars a night. Guatemala City and Bogota were cheap, while Brazil was relatively expensive. We carried duffel bags; backpacks weren't yet in vogue, at least in Latin America. In Quito we bought the *South American Guide*, published in London, which offered information in tiny print on every country, including remote places, and was updated annually based on reports from travelers.

In each country we cashed American Express travelers' checks into the local currency as needed. In four months we went through around three thousand dollars, including five plane flights. International phone calls entailed going to offices of the national phone company and were prohibitively expensive, so we sent postcards to our families from time to time.

* * *

As we traveled down the coast of Mexico, the desert gave way to the tropics. In Rosario, Sinaloa, where my father had been born, we contacted relatives using my grandmother's name, as I had done a dozen years before while a seminarian. A taxi driver said that "Berryman" was a familiar name in the town. Among signs of progress was an electric power plant in the city.

In Mexico City we were hosted by Margarita Navarro, a sister whom we had known in Panama (and who had given Angie the hand-sewn Mexican dress she wore at our wedding). She was in Netzahualcoyotl, a district actually outside Mexico City proper, which already had a million people. Netza wasn't a flimsy shantytown—the buildings themselves were of cement block—but the entire area was being built by the people themselves, part of the wave of migrants from the countryside. Land titles were insecure, and people worked in the informal economy. Margarita was part of a team of Jesuits and others who were attempting a pastoral response. At one casual evening gathering of the team, their friend Jose Porfirio Miranda came by. Because of his book *Marx and the Bible* (1971), he is sometimes associated with liberation theology, but he was primarily an intellectual polemicist. He soon left the Jesuits and continued for the next twenty-five years to write treatises against positivists and other philosophers.

We stopped in the town of Comitan in Chiapas not far from the Guatemalan border to see Karl Lenkersdorf and his wife. Lenkersdorf had studied theology and philosophy in Germany, the United States, and Canada and had been a Lutheran minister before coming to Mexico in the 1950s and getting an advanced degree in philosophy. He contributed to discussions of liberation theology around 1970, and in 1973 he moved to Chiapas at the invitation of Bishop Samuel Ruiz. Now in his mid-forties he was immersing himself in the Tojolabal culture and language. He told us about the first National Indigenous Conference, which had been held recently. That event, which Ruiz and others helped bring about, turned out to be a major advance by indigenous people in seeking their own voice in Mexican society. The significance of that work came to light in the wake of the Zapatista movement twenty years later. Lenkersdorf spent the rest of his life as a self-taught linguist, anthropologist, and indigenous rights activist.

Entering Guatemala we passed through Huehuetenango on the Pan-American Highway (a two-lane mountain road) and continued to the capital. There we were given an overview of the country by two Jesuits, Ricardo Falla and Juan Hernandez-Pico, covering history, the economy, current politics, the church, and grassroots movements. It became a rule of thumb for the rest of the trip: if possible, get a briefing from the right Jesuit. They were a team from different disciplines, known as the "Zone 5 Jesuits," after the working-class neighborhood where they lived and worked. Less than two years later when we returned to Guatemala, they became close collaborators and good friends.

In Managua we stayed with Gerri O'Leary and Edgard Macias, as I had the year before. Managua had not yet recovered from the earthquake. Edgard was involved in discussions with a couple dozen other people on the beginnings of a public civic opposition to Somoza.

From Managua I went back north to the Caribbean coast of Honduras, which had been hit by disastrous flooding some weeks previously. In reply to my query, an editor at the *Washington Post* had suggested that I inquire into what happens in a disaster area after the media have withdrawn. The city of San Pedro Sula was back to normal, but refugees a few miles away were still in camps. At one point I was in a muddy field watching a nun oversee the distribution of a large pile of donated shoes from the back of a truck. *How do people find their size?* I wondered. *What good are high heels in the mud?* Feeling like an intrepid reporter I banged out drafts in a cheap hotel in San Pedro, and back in Managua I worked them into a story that I mailed with some photos. My work probably looked amateurish, and I received no reply, but I was taking clumsy steps toward journalism.

* * *

In Panama we stayed at Fatima Parish, where our Maryknoll friend Ellen McDonald was still in residence. Jesuits were coming on the weekend, but the parish had no pastor. The Nuevo Chorrillo movement, which had its office on church premises, had many dozens of members and was moving along with its intention to start a new housing project on the land offered by the architect Jorge Riba, although the Torrijos government still viewed them with suspicion.

When we had been there about a week, we were standing in front of the church about to go to the movies with another couple. Two men in plainclothes asked me if I was Berryman, and when I said yes, they seized me and put me into the backseat of a large, dark sedan. Angie insisted on going along, so they put her in also. As we barreled up the crowded street, they reported by radio, "Tenemos el paquete" (We have the package). We were taken to DENI headquarters a few blocks away, where we were put in a waiting room under guard. No one interrogated us, but they called me "Padre." At one point Elias Castillo, the president of the Torrijos-engineered assembly who had gotten his start from our organizing work in Chorrillo, came by, said hello, and entered an inner office. At around 10 or 11 PM we were told we could leave, provided we went to the Migration office in the morning, and so with Ellen, Roberto Batista, and others we went back to the parish.

The next morning we went to Migration where we waited in an open office with various officials at their desks. Toward midday we were taken to the airport without our luggage, where our passports were stamped "Deported," and we were put on a flight to Miami in seats at the very back of the plane. Archbishop McGrath managed to get onto the plane and briefly offer us support and encouragement.

Harvey Steele's lieutenant had obviously been right about political opposition to our return, even though we were not accused of anything or even interrogated. The deportation order must have come from Colonel Noriega. He was probably acting at the initiative of some elements of the Partido del Pueblo (the Moscow-linked communist party), perhaps the youth group that had utilized the church facilities. Just what sort of threat we represented is hard to imagine; perhaps whoever did it was simply wielding power.

In Miami I phoned Ricardo Arias Calderon, the Panamanian philosopher and major figure in the Christian Democrat Party who was then in self-exile and teaching at Florida International University. We had become friends through church contacts when I was in Chorrillo. He picked us up, and he and his wife, Teresita, graciously hosted us for a week. Our duffel bags arrived, and we requested new passports because ours had been stamped "Deported." Consular officials weren't disturbed by our deportation; they said that the matter was between us and the Panamanian government.

* * *

With new passports we took an overnight flight to Quito and spent three weeks in Ecuador with Esperanza (Elsie) Monge and Laura Glynn, Maryknoll sisters whom we knew from Panama. Bishop Legarra had forced them to leave Panama in 1972, and they were now doing human rights work in Ecuador and would do so for decades to come. Elsie is from a prominent industrial family in Guayaquil. We spent some time enjoying the country. We went to the beach with Elsie's family; Elsie and I went to a bullfight (Angie didn't want to go); one Sunday afternoon we climbed the Panecillo, the hill overlooking Quito; and we danced with crowds in the street during the anniversary celebration in early December for the city's founding.

The country had changed since my time at IPLA. In 1972 the military had overthrown the five-term populist president, Jose Maria Velasco Ibarra. Oil export had begun shortly before the price rose 400 percent. What Americans were experiencing as higher prices and lines at gas stations was a bonanza for Ecuador. The oil itself was in the Amazon region, the sparsely inhabited portion known as the "oriente" (east). It was pumped over the Andes to the Pacific. Only a minuscule portion of Ecuadorians were working in the oil fields, and the Texaco headquarters in Quito was unmarked, but oil revenues were fueling a construction boom. We saw a hole perhaps thirty feet deep being shoveled by hand for a foundation, the dirt being dug with picks and shovels and removed by buckets and wheelbarrows; it was cheaper to hire indigenous men at a the equivalent of a dollar a day than to lease heavy equipment.

I began to gather materials and information for something I might write. At the U.S. embassy the political officer gave us an overview of the country from the standpoint of the United States. In passing, he mentioned that it is part of the embassy's job to provide information to American citizens, a bit of knowledge that proved useful in subsequent years.

The four of us decided to go to the Ecuadorian Amazon. The area had been inhabited by lowland indigenous people, largely out of contact with the rest of the country, except for missionaries. From Quito we took a night bus over the crest of the Andes and then down nine thousand feet to the lowlands from which all water eventually reached the Atlantic Ocean through Brazil. We hired a boat to go downriver where, except for occasional settlements along the banks, we saw few signs of habitation. After spending the night in a thatched hut, by Sunday morning we were in an area where the oil operations were under way, hitching a ride in the back of a pickup that hit bumps so hard that an axle broke. We could see oil pipes running over the surface through the trees. We then hitched another ride to Lago Agrio, which had a Wild West feel to it—even swinging doors on cantinas.

There we went to the Texaco plant and introduced ourselves. A middle-aged American man came out and gave us a tour. The presence of three English-speaking young women no doubt helped; ordinary Ecuadorians would not have been permitted entrance. The technicians—Americans and other Latin Americans—were unconcerned about the impact of the oil. They said that their work was similar to what it would be in Louisiana or Texas.

Few concerns were being raised within Ecuador. Some nationalist intellectuals thought that Ecuador's share in the revenues was too low, or that the government had to do the bidding of the oil companies or the U.S. State Department. Within a decade or so, the environmental destruction from oil spills and toxic chemicals and the devastation of the indigenous people's way of life would be revealed. Over the decades, oil operations have continued, settlers have come from the highlands, pushing indigenous people away; roads have been built; and tourists now come for rafting and jungle tourism. The Ecuadorian economy has undergone booms and busts, reflecting world oil prices; in the 1990s a large portion of Ecuadorians emigrated. In the late afternoon we boarded a bus and arrived in frigid Quito after midnight.

Angie and I spent several days in the city of Riobamba in the province of Chimborazo, named for the snow-covered volcano nearby. We stayed in Santa Cruz, the retreat center built with funds from German Catholics, where Bishop Leonidas Proaño, whom I had first met at IPLA, also lived with members of his diocesan team. Two thousand people a year were participating in training courses at the center. We had two long conversations with Proaño, who was one of the most advanced of the Medellin generation of Latin American bishops, alongside Helder Camara and Cardinal Paulo Evaristo Arns in Brazil, Sergio Mendez Arceo and Samuel Ruiz in Mexico, and Gerardo Valencia Cano in Colombia.

When he became bishop of Riobamba in 1954 Proaño organized a land reform of the diocese's extensive holdings. He believed that the gospel should be a liberating force and saw the work of the diocese as concientización to help people overcome their fatalism. About half of the priests in the diocese, he admitted, continued the usual type of work around administering the sacraments. With the others and with laypeople, he concentrated on formation. They were organized into teams working in Riobamba itself, and missionary and pastoral teams worked in the rest of the diocese.

Proaño was not supported by the other Ecuadorian bishops and had been investigated by Rome, although no action was taken. From time to time he was called a communist or Marxist, while some on the left wanted him to be more explicitly political. He and his collaborators insisted that the people should move at their own pace and not be pushed prematurely into action. The headline of two-page spread of the article I later wrote for the *National Catholic Reporter* was a quote from Proaño: "I Am a Stone on a Bridge That Others Will Finish."

On our way out of the country we stayed with Pepe Gomez, the priest who had invited me to IPLA in 1968. By this time he had become pastor of a new parish in one of the outlying areas of Guayaquil that was somewhat swampy, while continuing his radio program and magazine column. He remained at the parish—Cristo Liberador—for the next three decades as the area was gradually transformed and became an established neighborhood.

FINDING OUR WAY—WITH TWISTS AND TURNS

* * *

After crossing the border into Peru we had a twenty-four-hour bus ride along the Pacific coast to Lima. Our hotel was full of the smell of cement or plaster from repair work, and that added to a general morale crisis around the time of our first anniversary. We were well received at the Maryknoll house, but otherwise we weren't able to interview people because it was Christmastime. On Christmas Eve we took an overnight bus to Arequipa, a large city with a pleasant climate and a colonial look. There we boarded an unheated train with wooden benches that turned cold as we ascended into the Andes. We spent some days in Cuzco and went to Macchu Picchu. To get to Puno we took a nighttime taxi: a sedan with five passengers and a driver who was dozing off. Puno is on the shores of Lake Titicaca, twelve thousand feet above sea level. An indigenous Uros man took me on a reed boat out to small floating reed islands made by the people who live on them.

We attended midnight Mass on New Year's Eve, and the next evening we boarded a luxurious passenger ship and crossed the lake overnight, landing on the Bolivian side in the early morning. There we caught a train across the high mountain plain, stopping at the archaeological site of Tiwanaku and then descended into La Paz. We met with Maryknoll priests and sisters and through them were connected to Jesuit anthropologist Xavier Albo and an Oblate, Gregorio Iriarte, both Spanish-born, who gave us overviews of the country. For years thereafter both were important in human rights work, Iriarte more with miners and workers and Albo with rural indigenous people.

At the archdiocesan chancery office we met Eric de Wasseige, a Belgian Dominican who had taken refuge there, after an order had been issued for his arrest and deportation. He was the president of the Bolivian Justice and Peace Commission, which published some human rights materials and advocated for political prisoners, and was now accused of meddling in politics. We were surprised to run into him in an open-air market a couple days later, apparently testing the waters. He and a fellow priest were deported some weeks later.

At that time about 80 percent of Catholic clergy and religious were non-Bolivian. That helps explain why a foreigner could be chosen to head the commission and why, more generally, foreigners often had leadership roles in the church. The percentage was similar in several other countries: Panama, Venezuela, Peru, Honduras, Guatemala, and Nicaragua. Native priests might understandably resent the power and resources of the foreigners surrounding them.

From La Paz we descended to Cochabamba, a pleasant city, so small at the time that you could walk across it in a half hour or so. From there we continued to descend toward Santa Cruz. Our bus broke down at 3 or 4 AM, so we hitched a ride in the back of a truck, in which a Bolivian indigenous woman was chewing coca leaf. Today Santa Cruz is the economic powerhouse of Bolivia, but then it was a town of largely unpaved streets filled with dust from vehicles. We were surprised to see

Mennonite farmers in overalls on horse-drawn wagons in the middle of town. They had come to this area from Russia, most by way of Paraguay, Mexico, or Canada. Santa Cruz is in flat lowlands and in some ways feels more like Brazil, four hundred miles away, than highlands Bolivia.

We headed south by train through the Chaco, a large, sparsely inhabited area of brushland extending through Bolivia, Paraguay, and northern Argentina. Crossing into Argentina, we caught a train that ran along the border with Paraguay. It stopped for hours at a time, and the heat and mosquitoes were oppressive. Gauchos with leather chaps stepped on or off. It took thirty-seven hours to cover four hundred kilometers. Toward the end of the journey the brush gave way to grassland as we approached Formosa, the site of Graham Greene's novel *The Honorary Consul*, which I had been reading. The plot involves hapless guerrillas who mistakenly kidnap a British citizen, not realizing that he is only an honorary consul, for whom the British government will not pay ransom. To Greene, Formosa was an appropriate location for his tragicomedy of misfits. From Formosa we took the ferry across the Paraguay River to Asuncion.

* * *

We spent several days at Misión de Amistad, with the directors John and Renee Carter. Misión de Amistad had been founded by the Disciples of Christ Church in the 1950s and was devoted primarily to service rather than proselytizing. We had been told in New York that the Carters were thinking of moving on, and Angie and I might be apt for the position.

Paraguay has been marked by its geography and history. Like Bolivia, it is landlocked in the heart of South America. After independence it was first governed by a benign dictator, "Dr. Francia," who fostered economic development but also isolated the country. In the War of the Triple Alliance (1864–1870) against Brazil, Argentina, and Uruguay, it lost a large proportion of the population, especially adult males. In the 1930s Paraguay fought the Chaco War against Bolivia.

On our last night John and Renee took us to a restaurant where we heard wonderful Paraguayan music accompanied by harp and guitar, much of it sung in Guarani. A unique feature of the country is that 90 percent of the people speak Guarani, even though most are not indigenous.

Paraguay reminded me of Nicaragua: it was a small tropical country ruled by General Alfredo Stroessner, an old-style personal dictator in the mold of Somoza and Trujillo. He stayed in power until 1989, and during most of that time he enjoyed good relations with the United States. The U.S. embassy was a very large compound in Asuncion, adjacent to Stroessner's own compound, and it was said to be a major communications link for the U.S. military presence in South America.

John showed us some life-size puppets then in storage, which had been used in a puppet show, ostensibly a children's fable about a king ordering everyone to bow down to particular colors. Paraguayans would understand it as a reference to the country's two main political parties, Blanco and Colorado (white and red), the latter being Stroessner's. It was deft way to raise questions about the political system; directly repressing the puppet show would only make the regime look foolish.

The Carters were gracious and the project seemed interesting, but at this time it did not seem worth exploring seriously. In fact, the Carters remained at Misión de Amistad for many years more and retired in Paraguay. Years later John Carter was recognized for his role in promoting puppetry as a form of theater.

Since we had been out of phone contact with our families because of the difficulty and cost of international calls, in Asuncion we were taken to see a ham radio operator, who located a fellow operator in the United States near our families, and then used a phone patch to call them to avoid paying long-distance charges. We could then have a conversation, but one way at a time, while the two operators switched back and forth.

After our time in Asuncion, we were no longer actively exploring possibilities of work in Latin America, and in fact I was being urged to come to Washington to work on a slide show on the Panama Canal. We flew to Santiago and began a slow movement north, continuing to gather impressions.

* * *

We landed in the Santiago airport fifteen months after the September 1973 coup. Over half of the three thousand killings of civilians had taken place in the first few weeks and months, but people were still being abducted and killed. Tens of thousands of Chileans had gone into exile, including virtually all of the people I had seen in 1972. Superficially, things looked normal, except for the visibility of the military in a country that had prided itself on its tradition of civilian democracy.

Our only contact was Jose Comblin, who was working with the bishop of Talca. He had gone there after being refused reentry into Brazil in 1972. We took an eight-hour train trip south through Chile's central valley, only to be told that he was in Santiago—so the next day we returned. The seats were filled, so we stood much of the way. At one point I tried to make conversation with a man next to me, saying that I had been in Chile in 1969 and 1972. Those were different times, he said, not unpleasantly, but unwilling to talk to a stranger. The silence of the passengers suggested how spirits had been crushed in this country that had been so politically vital.

We caught up with Comblin in a working-class parish where the pastor was a friend. Having experienced the Brazilian dictatorship for years, Comblin had been cautious in Chile, keeping his distance from Christians for Socialism, for example. He was convinced that the new Latin American military regimes were more than temporary episodes that would lead back to civilian democracy; they were a new model of state that would last for many years. In another year or so, he began to publish articles on "national security regimes," based on his study of writings by military theorists themselves. Parishes like the one where we met him were quietly helping people survive. Given the climate of repression, we were not going to find people willing to talk to two American travelers.

It was the beginning of the Southern Hemisphere summer and buses to Argentina were largely sold out, so we opted to leave the next day. Starting from Santiago, which was like L.A. in July, we climbed up to the frigid pass over the Andes and then down to Mendoza, which was decades from being the wine country destination it is today. At that time Chile and Argentina produced ordinary table wines for domestic consumption. We took a bus across the pampas to Buenos Aires.

As in Chile, we had virtually no contacts in a country under repression, and it was January, the middle of summertime. Peron had died after serving as president for less than a year. His widow, Isabel, was nominally president, but the country was really being governed by her advisers. The "dirty war" against the left was under way. We were bewildered by the cult around the figures of Peron and Evita.

After an overnight steamer across the Rio de la Plata estuary to Montevideo, we went to see Juan Luis Segundo and his fellow Jesuits at the Centro Pedro Fabro. Uruguay was also under military dictatorship, but there the regime's typical method was not murder or disappearance, but imprisonment. Because the country was so small, at this time it had the highest ratio of political prisoners in the world, and many Uruguayans were in exile.

Like Chile, Uruguay had had a strong democratic tradition. The country had prospered as an exporter of beef, wool, and leather goods for decades, and President Jose Battle in his second term (1911–1915) had brought reforms (eight-hour workday, social security, unemployment compensation) two decades before the New Deal in the United States. However, after the Korean War, prices for the country's exports declined, and by around 1970 it was in political crisis. The Tupamaro urban guerrillas had attracted some attention with their tactics—for example, hijacking dairy trucks and distributing the milk in poor neighborhoods—but they had provoked a military coup. One sign of long-term economic decline was the decades-old cars we saw parked on the streets; Uruguay didn't have the revenues to import new cars. When a policeman saw me taking pictures of them, he told me to stop.

* * *

In Brazil we made stops in Porto Alegre, Sao Paulo, and Rio, and went to Belo Horizonte, where we stayed for a week with Felix Valenzuela, the Augustinian who had handled the Chorrillo parish while I was at IPLA. From there we went to the capital, Brasilia; headed north through the eastern end of the Amazon Basin to Belem; and flew to Manaus, where we spent about twenty-four hours. We saw portions of the country that most Brazilians, concentrated in the south or along the Atlantic coast, never visited. At that time the better-off in Rio or Sao Paulo were more familiar with Paris or Miami than with northern Brazil.

The military government was beginning a gradual relaxation of control. In an election the previous November, the opposition coalition had defeated the official party, in what was being read as a kind of plebiscite. The opposition was tame, within the parameters set by the military. The country was in something of an economic slowdown, but it was not yet clear that the high growth of the "Brazilian miracle"—close to 10 percent annual GDP growth from 1968 to 1973—was over. Hardliners in the military opposed any easing of control, and it took another ten years for a civilian presidency to return.

At an apartment in the fashionable beach area of Rio we talked to a man in his twenties who now regretted his earlier involvement with radical politics. He had been imprisoned for four months and tortured by being hung upside down from his knees, given electric shocks, and forced to drink water to the limit of his endurance; we learned that not from him but from his mother. Like other Brazilians he seemed to have accepted the military government as a fact of life. One person who did not accept it was the Presbyterian minister Jaime Wright, who was pursuing the case of his brother Paulo, who had been abducted and disappeared. Wright became a close ally of Cardinal Paulo Evaristo Arns of Sao Paulo. Later that same year Arns, Wright, and Rabbi Henry Sobel jointly celebrated the funeral of Vladimir Herzog, a journalist who died after torture in prison, attended by thousands of people. That massive nonviolent action turned out to be a major step in the return to democracy.

The church, including the Brazilian Bishops Conference (CNBB), was a focal point of the critique of military rule and particularly the human effects of the economic model, which was benefiting the urban middle classes but not the urban or rural poor. The CNBB had printed a flyer with the 1948 Universal Declaration of Human Rights, and for each of the thirty articles (e.g., article 5 against torture), it had added a scripture passage and another passage from Catholic social teaching. Copies were distributed clandestinely through diocesan and parish networks. The flyers were "subversive," but once they were out, the regime would look foolish if it acted to suppress them. The Vicariate of Solidarity in Chile borrowed the idea and distributed a Spanish version.

While in Sao Paulo, we took a two-hour bus ride out to the prosperous city of Campinas to see Rubem Alves, whose book *Tomorrow's Child: Imagination, Creativity, and the Rebirth of Culture* (1971) I had also been reading on this trip. Alves's first book, *A Theology of Human Hope* (1969), had linked him to the liberation theologians, but this new work, written in English while he was at Union Theological Seminary, seemed strange for a Latin American. His references were to Nietzsche, Freud, Marx, Weber, Alvin Toffler—and *The Little Prince*. What he opposed seemed to be technocracy, but his work sounded more like the sixties counterculture than the output of Latin American radicals.

As we approached his house in a pleasant middle-class neighborhood with small gardens, we heard "Jesu Joy of Man's Desiring" on a piano. When we rang the doorbell, he stopped playing to let us in. My strongest impression from our conversation was his bemused comment about Marxist professors at universities. He had asked his colleagues whether they didn't feel guilty about their 55 percent pay increase (primarily adjusting for inflation) at the expense of the poor; they agreed but were planning how to spend it. For decades Alves continued in the same vein, publishing short, poetic, elliptical works, urging that we not accept present reality as the final word, but that we hold out hope for our grandchildren. However, he clearly stood aside from those who were actively resisting and were struggling for human rights.

Spending a week with Felix Valenzuela in Belo Horizonte, Brazil's third-largest city, gave us a little respite from going to a new city every couple days. We got a sense of everyday life, and we had someone who could speak with more trust—although he didn't reveal any delicate secrets. As a small example, we realized that most Brazilians could now see the far corners of their country on a color TV.

Felix took us to Ouro Preto, the colonial city that arose in the gold rush of the eighteenth century. There we saw the work of the black sculptor and architect Alejadinho, who carved statues of saints in a distinctive distorted style, and who, according to legend, continued working even after losing his hands to a degenerative disease, with the chisel tied to his arms.

From Belo Horizonte we took an overnight bus to Brasilia, the futuristic capital built from scratch in less than four years and dedicated in 1960, seemingly proof that Brazil was becoming a developed country in one leap. A priest at the office of the papal nuncio recommended by Felix drove us around the capital and showed us the satellite cities of poor people, which arose shortly after construction was completed. The designers had assumed that they were erecting a city for civil servants and hadn't anticipated the presence of poor people. Otherwise we tramped around a city that had not been planned for pedestrians.

The bus ride from Brasilia north to Belem over largely unpaved roads took us through the eastern Amazon. In the middle of the night we crossed the Trans-Amazon Highway, then a major project of the military, which was obsessed with populating the country's interior. These and other roads led to deforestation, as the wealthy bought up land, had it cleared, and set up cattle ranches. We were in Belem for Carnival weekend, where the event was more participatory than in Rio, where it is a spectacle.

Manaus sits in the middle of the country and then could be reached only by boat or plane. We went to see the Amazonas Theater, built in the 1890s at the height of the rubber boom. Italian opera companies traveled a thousand miles upstream to perform in the tropical heat. When rubber plants were grown in Malaysia, Brazilian production collapsed, as did the Manaus economy. The theater had recently been restored. It seemed strange that the city also had a free trade zone where better-off Brazilians could go to buy electronic goods cheaply, as a stimulus to the local economy.

FINDING OUR WAY—WITH TWISTS AND TURNS

* * *

In Bogota I wanted to talk to Bishop Alfonso Lopez Trujillo, who in 1972 had traveled throughout Latin America visiting bishops, in effect lobbying, and at the end of that year he was chosen to be the executive secretary of CELAM, headquartered in Bogota. He wasted no time and closed CELAM pastoral institutes in Chile and Ecuador, and centralized all CELAM training in Colombia. By this time Belgian Jesuit Roger Vekemans had come to Bogota from Chile, and they were both leading a countercharge against liberation theology, or at least against some aspects of it. The fact that he had been able to take over the reins of CELAM suggests that many bishops felt that matters had gone too far in the aftermath of Medellin and wanted to reassert control. By 1975 he was understood to be an ambitious conservative prelate with an agenda. The backlash in the Vatican and the hierarchy began before the papacy of John Paul II.

Lopez presumably understood that I was not sympathetic to him, but he treated me cordially like a journalist, and he gave me a copy of a recent book containing the presentations to a CELAM-sponsored meeting on liberation theology, in which Gustavo Gutierrez participated.

* * *

In Chile, Uruguay, and Brazil, we had experienced what would soon be called "national security regimes," states ruled directly by a military force that believed they were at war with "subversives"—their own citizens. Argentina would join them in 1976, although it was already in a "dirty war." Nicaragua and Paraguay were old-fashioned personal dictatorships. El Salvador and Guatemala were under repressive regimes where the military was the real power behind a civilian façade. Panama and Peru were under left-wing populist military regimes, although Peru was about to shift rightward. In Ecuador, Bolivia, and Honduras the military also played key roles. In only three of the countries we visited (Mexico, Colombia, and Costa Rica) were civilian governments in charge—and Costa Rica had abolished its military.

In the 1960s, elected civilian governments had been the norm, although they generally served the landholding and business elites. Starting with Brazil in 1964, the military had intervened when they judged that the civilian governments were not maintaining order sufficiently. The series of coups was driven by the Cold War, and especially by fears of "another Cuba." Whether or not U.S. government agencies were directly involved in specific coups—the evidence is no more than circumstantial—tens of thousands of Latin American officers received U.S. military training in the 1950s and 1960s. That gave them an enhanced sense of mission, and at moments of crisis they stepped in. They practiced torture, murder, and disappearance, and eliminated independent sources of criticism (the press, labor unions, universities, professional organizations). Once they were in power, the U.S. government gave them military aid and technical assistance, and shielded them from human rights criticism. After our return I wrote "The Khaki-ing of Latin America" (the title a play on a best seller on the 1960s counterculture, *The Greening of America*) for *New Catholic World* magazine.

* * *

In 1972 Phil Wheaton, an Episcopal priest who had served in the Dominican Republic and become an activist in Latin America, had brought a group of people to Chorrillo as part of an educational tour to Panama. He now wanted me to do a slide show on Panama and on the canal. The Torrijos government was pushing to revise the treaties with the United States. Upon our return to the United States I spent two or three weeks in Washington writing the script.

Here I was, campaigning on behalf of a country that had just deported us. However, we hadn't been deported by the Panamanians, but by the Torrijos government. We agreed that the canal and the zone should revert to Panama, and at Gary MacEoin's suggestion I wrote a long article for the *St. Anthony Messenger*—"The Panama Canal: Time for the U.S. to De-Colonize"—citing my own experience of living in close proximity to the zone, and giving the reasons, moral and pragmatic, for a new treaty.

While in Washington, I stayed at what was called the Lamont Street House, where Phil and other people working on social change were living in a community. Nearby was Tabor House, which had been set up a couple years before by Peter Hinde and Betty Campbell, a Carmelite priest and Mercy sister, also to work for social justice. In 1974 a group had founded the Washington Office on Latin America (WOLA), which initially focused on Chile but soon expanded to other countries. WOLA was a key actor in the formation of the contemporary human rights movement.

The Lamont and Tabor Houses were focal points of a loose network in Washington working on human rights, particularly in Latin America, made up largely of people who had been radicalized by their grassroots experience in the region. Some were working "within the system," pressuring for changes in U.S. policy, or even as aides to Congresspeople. Others believed that dictatorship and human rights violations were inherent in "the system," and that more radical change was required. In practice, the lines between the two groups were blurry.

* * *

Before leaving for Latin America we had visited a cluster of communal homes in West Philadelphia that called itself the Life Center, and we decided that if we didn't stay in Latin America we would move there. The community had been started in 1971 by activist Quakers. Its core principles were nonviolence, simple living, and egalitarianism. It was affiliated with likeminded groups in other cities in a network called Movement for a New Society. The grandiose sound of both names reflected the conviction of many people at the time that what was needed was nothing short of a new type of society. Unlike those on the political left who saw the taking of state power as crucial, the Life Center was in the anarchist tradition, distrusting state power and top-down politics. Living at the Life Center brought us into contact with Quakers and their commitment to nonviolence.

Several dozen adults lived spread through a number of communal households in Victorian houses that had been purchased cheaply in a leafy neighborhood a few blocks west of the University of Pennsylvania. Each house included a number of adults. The idea was that by sharing household expenses and tasks we could be freed to engage in social and political advocacy. We lived in a household comprised of Jim and Ruth, who owned the house, an older woman named Florence, Joan, Allan, and ourselves. There was no male-female division of labor: all adults shared equally in household chores. For example, each of us had a night for preparing the evening meal; all food was vegetarian. A food co-op operated in the basement of one of the houses, and we each had to do two hours of work there a week.

I participated in a collective working on opposing the development of the B-1 bomber. We met periodically and carried out some actions, such as leafleting. I also took part in a Macroanalysis Seminar, a set of topics over approximately twenty sessions considering in turn ecology, U.S.–Third World relations, domestic issues, and visions for the future and how to get there—all intended to offer a broader context for social change work.

Life Center members got part-time jobs in order to make sufficient money to pay their way but to have time for work for social change. Angie did some substitute teaching and then got a job at Episcopal Hospital working on intake. My work turned out to be primarily writing and translating. I published seven or eight articles based on our travels, including overviews of the situation in Ecuador, Uruguay, and Brazil. The checks came nowhere near paying for our travel, but they bolstered my sense that I could do journalism. One job involved researching nonprofit organizations doing overseas relief and development and preparing a kind of introductory manual for donors. I also served as the staff writer for a working group of the American Friends Service Committee, which studied the proposal for a "New International Economic Order," then being urged in the UN and other international forums for more just economic relations between developed and underdeveloped (or Third World) nations.

During this time I took part in a two-day seminar on Brazil at the State Department, along with academics and businesspeople. The tenor of the meeting was that, with its industrial development Brazil was becoming a significant actor on the world scene. I was there representing the church and human rights community. I also took part in a meeting at the Aspen Institute in Colorado organized by Lester Brown, in a similar capacity. Participants were from churches and development organizations, and included the World Bank president, Robert McNamara, whom Richard Taylor, also from the Life Center, challenged for his role in the Vietnam War.

MEMENTO OF THE LIVING AND THE DEAD

* * *

In August 1975 I went to the Theology in the Americas meeting in Detroit, getting a ride with Ken Aman, a sociologist and former Maryknoll priest. On the way we spent a night at his family's grape farm in the Finger Lakes district of western New York. The idea of the meeting had been conceived by Sergio Torres, an exiled Chilean priest who had been prominent in Christians for Socialism. His initial aim was to introduce North Americans to this new movement from the south, not only academic theologians, but those working pastorally or for social change. That entailed making a critique of society part of theology, as was done in Latin America. An augmented version of my article on liberation theology in *Theological Studies* was background reading.

The meeting became an encounter between Latin American, black, and feminist theologians—all increasingly conscious of their distance from the (white, male) theological establishment. The Latin Americans were heavily Catholic; the black theologians were drawing on their church experience; the feminist theologians were more in tension with their churches and traditions, which largely excluded women from leadership, and even from their symbols, for example, a male God and savior. The choice of Detroit was not accidental: deindustrialization and white flight were well under way. Attendees included social scientists and activists as well as theologians Gustavo Gutierrez, Hugo Assmann, Jose Miguez Bonino, Beatriz Couch, Juan Luis Segundo, Enrique Dussel, James Cone, Gregory Baum, and Rosemary Ruether.

A three-way clash ensued: to Latin Americans it looked as though black liberation theology was simply about getting a fair share of the American pie, without questioning its imperialist basis; to black theologians the Latin Americans looked "white" and relatively privileged; neither group seemed to understand or appreciate the depth of patriarchy, according to the women. U.S. Latino theologians were present but did not identify directly with any of these groups. Rosemary Ruether was among those who most clearly focused on how these dynamics were "interstructured," as she put it. The conference marked a significant step toward recognizing that all theology is "situated."

* * *

From the outset Angie had misgivings about the Life Center and whether it was right for us. We got along well with our housemates, but she was never convinced of the pretensions of the movement.

We soon found out that she was pregnant and that the baby was due in October, and we began to take classes in natural childbirth at Booth Maternity Hospital. We also sometimes went to see her parents and other family members about two hours up the Pennsylvania Turnpike. On a night in October, our daughter Catherine was born at Booth, delivered by a midwife, with doctors on hand. For the next few months we were absorbed in caring for her and noting her progress in raising her head, looking at the world around her, smiling. That cast a glow over our lives. She was soon baptized, with Angie's parents as sponsors. Fr. John McNamee, the celebrant, became a lifelong friend.

Many people at the Life Center practiced co-counseling (or Re-evaluation Counseling). The mechanism was simple: two people meet for two hours; the first hour devoted to one and the second to the other. There are no professionals and no fees. The theory, developed by Harvey Jackins, is that we are impeded by inner hurts that we have suffered and internalized, and we can release them through this form of counseling, which includes shouting and weeping. Although it fit well with the anarchist and democratic spirit of the community, it tended to create an in-group and an out-group feeling. Most of the participants were younger than us, and many were engaged in personal and sexual exploration. We sensed a subtle if unstated bias against monogamy.

Although ostensibly we were not enslaved to nine-to-five jobs, members nevertheless had a hard time being available to spontaneously help others and found themselves having to schedule appointments. One example came when we had car trouble, and the young couple living next door offered to help, rather than anyone from the Life Center. For me a turning point came at an evening meeting of the Macroanalysis Seminar group, when participants were asked to envision a different kind of society: what they said sounded like the Life Center writ large. The absurdity made something click for me.

From this description, the Life Center may sound like a cult. However, although it had recognized leaders (George and Lillian Willoughby, George Lakey) it did not have a personality cult, and it made strenuous efforts to cultivate egalitarianism and take every member seriously.

By the end of the year, we were beginning to consider next moves, particularly in conversation with likeminded people outside the Life Center.

* * *

In early 1976 we learned that the American Friends Service Committee (AFSC), headquartered in Philadelphia, was looking for a coordinator or coordinators for its Central America program. The AFSC was founded during World War I to help civilians in Europe, and over the decades sought to apply Quaker principles in various arenas. In 1947 the AFSC and British Quakers were jointly awarded the Nobel Peace Prize for their work after World War II.

Its presence in Mexico and Central America dated back to the 1930s, with an accent on short-term volunteer programs. It began working in Guatemala in 1960 in one such program. Around 1970 it moved away from that model to a program in the remote Peten region of Guatemala staffed primarily by Guatemalan medical students, with the AFSC serving in a coordination role. This decision represented a realization that short-term foreign volunteers were themselves the primary beneficiaries of such programs, and that serious development work required expertise and experience.

In rethinking its goals in the mid-1970s and in the wake of the U.S.-supported repressive military dictatorships throughout the hemisphere, the AFSC decided that the program should pay more attention to the U.S. role in the region, and that the focus should move beyond Guatemala to Central America. Thus the position was posted as primarily one of interpretation of events in Central America, particularly for the peace and antiwar movement in the United States. We interviewed for the job in February 1976 and were notified that we had been selected. Guatemala had just been hit by a devastating earthquake.

Shortly before leaving we were given an orientation to the AFSC, the various components of the head office in Philadelphia, its relationship to Quakers, and so forth. What I didn't appreciate at the time was the strength of the AFSC at the grass roots. It had thirty or more offices around the United States, each having various programs, primarily in the local community, but some with international dimensions.

* * *

Viewed decades later, in a time when much concern is put on finding one's career and training for it, our story here looks somewhat aimless and driven by chance occurrences. We were now in our thirties, having left the Catholic priesthood and religious life. It would have been prudent to get training and degrees in some new career. Instead, we left our jobs in California, only to find that our job in Panama had evaporated. We then took a four-month trip around Latin America, ostensibly to investigate other work possibilities, but ended up back in the United States. There we joined an intentional community a half decade after the high point of such movements. We then happened to be available when the AFSC was looking for Central America staff.

Yet it seems providential: our travels gave us insight into Latin America in the repressive 1970s, and we joined the small networks of those raising public awareness. Although the Life Center ultimately did not work out for us, some aspects of its ethos, such as simple living, stayed a part of our lives.

9

Responding to Spiraling Violence

When we arrived in Guatemala City in May 1976, the signs of the earthquake three months earlier were still evident: collapsed buildings, piles of uncleared rubble, and traffic routed around bridges not yet repaired or replaced. The quake had struck in a U-shape running through the central highlands south to Guatemala City, and out to the northeast. Most of the twenty-three thousand dead and over seventy-five thousand injured were indigenous people crushed under their heavy tile roofs. A million people had been left temporarily homeless, and some families were still in camps three months later.

Jim Bradford, the young man whom we were replacing, met us at the airport and took us to the house of two American nuns in an outlying zone of Guatemala City, where we stayed while beginning to get a sense of things. He introduced us to representatives of foreign aid organizations, church people, local development workers, and labor union leaders. Within a month we moved to an apartment on the second floor of a house in a quiet neighborhood, not far from downtown.

We closed the AFSC office downtown and set up an office in the house—an electric typewriter, phone, bookshelves, and file cabinet. Mail was our main means of communication with the AFSC office in Philadelphia; international phone calls were prohibitively expensive. About twice a month we sent letters describing our activities, and we received a similar number of letters, which often crossed one another.

Our primary assignments, which had been determined before the earthquake, were to develop educational materials on Central America for concerned groups in the United States and to support local groups working for social change. However, the AFSC had raised over one hundred thousand dollars for earthquake relief and reconstruction, due to its decades of experience in relief and its presence in Guatemala since 1960. By the time we arrived, it had been decided that AFSC earthquake aid would be channeled primarily through a project named Vivienda Popular (People's housing), which worked in the indigenous town of Comalapa. The team running the project was made up of people in the town and Guatemala City and dealt directly with the Philadelphia office. We were not involved in administration, but participated in the project's educational component.

Our role as AFSC Central America representatives was in the tradition of Quaker International Affairs Representatives (QIARs). A QIAR program typically worked behind the scenes for peace in areas of conflict—for example, by arranging off-the-record contacts between mid-level diplomats of adversary states. Our assignment was different from that model insofar as we were expected to work primarily with those doing grassroots work, with no pretense, for example, of cultivating contacts in the Guatemalan armed forces or the Somoza dictatorship. Because U.S. government involvement had been thoroughly entwined with Central America's history—notably the CIA-engineered overthrow of the elected Guatemalan government in 1954 and decades of close association with the Somozas—our work was intended to develop awareness in the United States rather than to reconcile adversaries in the region. One QIAR position that was analogous to ours was that of Bill Sutherland, an African American Quaker, who in the 1970s and 1980s worked on issues in southern Africa, doing liaison with antiapartheid groups in the frontline states, and speaking tours in the United States. Our constituency was church, human rights, and peace organizations, especially in the wake of the U.S. war in Indochina, revelations about CIA interference in Latin America, and U.S. government support for murderous military dictatorships in South America.

We found ourselves in the midst of increasing political violence in Guatemala, El Salvador, and Nicaragua, and we struggled to find appropriate responses.

* * *

Guatemala City, then with less than a million people, sits on a relatively flat space in the midst of mountains, and is shaped irregularly by *barrancos*, sharp canyons dropping off on several sides. The barrancos had squatter settlements, and the city was spreading beyond them. The city is divided rationalistically into zones, and most streets and avenues are numbered: we lived at the intersection of Third Avenue and Third Street in Zone 2, not far from Zone 1, which includes the city's historic downtown. From there the main axis of the city went south toward the airport, passing through wealthier areas.

Geographically, Guatemala is divided roughly into four areas: highlands, coast, east, and north. The highlands are mountains several thousand feet high, running through the heart of the country to the Mexican border, home of most of the indigenous. The coast is a strip of land between the Pacific Ocean and the mountains, with large sugar and cotton plantations and cattle ranches on flatlands and coffee plantations in the foothills. The east is made up of relatively arid lands extending to the borders with El Salvador and Honduras, with a narrow opening to the Caribbean. The north was then sparsely populated rain forest jutting into Mexico and bordered by Belize (which Guatemala then claimed as part of its territory). The highlands, including Guatemala City, enjoy springlike weather all year round; the lowlands, particularly the Pacific coastal plain, are hot and muggy year round. The rainy season is from May to November or so; the dry season starts before Christmas and goes through Easter.

Roughly half of Guatemalans were then indigenous, speaking indigenous languages, wearing indigenous clothes, and living primarily in indigenous communities. Guatemalans used the word *ladino* to refer to everyone else, non-Indians. Some ladinos had predominantly European features, but most were mixed-race. The indigenous/ladino divide was sharp: even in heavily indigenous areas the local power structure (storeowners, labor contractors) was usually ladino. Virtually no indigenous faces appeared in the daily papers or on TV.

* * *

The nations of Central America form an isthmus, stretching in a southeasterly direction from Mexico to Colombia. All had dual agriculture systems: large farms producing coffee, sugar, cotton, beef, bananas, and a few other crops for export, and small quasi-subsistence plots producing corn, beans, vegetables, poultry, and livestock for domestic consumption. The large landholdings were the source of the elites' wealth. Industry was primarily for local and regional markets—foods and beverages, cloth and clothing, household items, cement and other construction materials—with little heavy industry or production of complex consumer items. In each country the elites consisted of a few dozen extended families. Costa Rica was a partial exception to this pattern because coffee was largely produced on family-operated plots, and that fact had laid the foundation for a more middle-class type of society.

Although the trappings of democracy (elections, legislatures, courts) existed, all countries except Costa Rica, which had disbanded its army after the 1948 civil war, were under de facto military control. Nicaragua had been under the Somoza dictatorship since the 1930s, and thus the power structure was defined by the relationship with Somoza; some landholders and business people were his allies, while others were increasingly in opposition to the dictatorship. Panama was under the populist, left-leaning rule of Gen. Omar Torrijos.

* * *

Among the first people we met in Guatemala were Miguel Angel Albizurez, the secretary general of the CNT (National Labor Confederation), originally of Christian Democrat orientation, and Frank LaRue, its lawyer. Although labor unions had been under repression since the 1954 coup, in the wake of the earthquake they became more militant, perhaps calculating that the large presence of international relief and development agencies would put some constraints on the government and military. When the local Coca-Cola Bottling Company, owned by an American named John Trotter, dismissed 174 workers as a union-busting tactic, the workers occupied the plant. This dispute, which took place a few weeks before our arrival, was ended through negotiation but the conflict continued for several years. Although only a small portion of the Guatemalan labor force was unionized, the labor movement saw itself as fighting for the working class as a whole, and in alliance with other forces in society. By the same token, the army and the economic elites regarded labor unions as a subversive force.

In June the National Police attacked the CNT headquarters, located a short walk from the presidential palace, first using a jeep to bash down the door. Miguel Angel managed to escape over neighboring rooftops and later turned himself in, accompanied by a large number of union members and journalists, and was subsequently released. We informed the AFSC's Philadelphia office of this conflict and asked them to share this information with concerned organizations. This was the first instance in which we sent out a kind of international alert over a particular human rights struggle. Church and human rights groups in North America and Europe began to support the ongoing struggle of the Coca-Cola workers in Guatemala as the spearhead of a larger movement. Providing materials for international solidarity soon became a regular feature of our work.

* * *

Today it is common to speak of Guatemala's "thirty-six-year civil war," understood to run from the appearance of armed guerrillas in 1960 to the signing of the peace accords in 1996, but that was not how it appeared in the mid-1970s. The guerrillas seemed to have been defeated in the late 1960s, at the cost of several thousand, mainly civilian, lives. The architect of that campaign, Colonel Carlos Arana, had been elected president in 1970, and murder continued to be used selectively as a political tool, especially in Guatemala City. When we arrived, the president was Kjell Laugerud, a general from the area of Alta Verapaz, where European names were common among coffee growers. The vice president was Mario Sandoval Alarcon, founder of the right-wing MLN (National Liberation Movement) in 1954, who was reputed to have headed death squads since the 1960s. Guatemala wasn't a Somoza-style dictatorship, but despite the appearance of democracy, the army was the ultimate arbiter, and political violence was practiced with impunity.

In July 1976 the Guatemalan Catholic bishops issued *United in Hope*, a pastoral letter in which they used the earthquake as the occasion for addressing the situation of the country more broadly, with frequent citations of the Medellin documents. They drew attention to situations of inequality and used terms like "oligarchy." Stating that the poorest and most marginalized Guatemalan is "worth more than all the country's riches and his or her life is sacred and untouchable," they noted that killing had become "a business," and that some think that through this crime they are defending "Western Christian civilization." This was understood to be a reference to death squads and state-inflicted violence. The letter was issued by the bishops' conference as a whole, but Cardinal Mario Casariego of Guatemala City was absent and had not signed it. Upon his return he gave rambling press conferences that diluted the impact of the letter on the general public.

Catholicism was institutionally weak in Guatemala: 80 percent of priests and sisters were not Guatemalan-born. In the early twentieth century there had been only around two dozen priests in the whole country, mainly concentrated in the cities. Foreign missionaries had arrived at mid-century, including Maryknoll, which staffed the diocese of Huehuetenango. In several places in the country, especially in some rural dioceses, teams of priests and sisters were seeking to take new pastoral approaches, particularly by training catechists and other lay leaders.

* * *

During this period we saw the Maryknoll priest Bill Woods a time or two. Angie had known him in Huehuetenango, and I had met him in Panama in 1967 when he flew two or three Maryknollers out of the country, when the Melville brothers and Sr. Marian Peter had brought the congregation under suspicion by opting to join the guerrillas. After working with indigenous people in a remote part of Huehuetenango for a decade and a half and seeing that their poverty was rooted in land tenure, he had organized a colonization project in the Ixcan lowlands, where he bought a large tract of land with funds he had raised. He had learned to fly and gotten a plane to serve the projects. Bill exemplified a type of can-do missionary who sees things in terms of concrete tasks rather than theology.

After the earthquake he had been helping with relief work near Guatemala City. Angie ran into him in early November and invited him to lunch. His pilot's license had been canceled, and he had been warned by the U.S. ambassador that some top military men wanted him killed. He had gone to the United States for a period, but had now returned and was full of enthusiasm and plans for the future.

Two or three weeks later we heard that while flying out to the Ixcan area he had crashed with four passengers aboard, all Americans. Despite rumors of suspicious circumstances, we initially assumed it was an accident: we couldn't conceive of even the Guatemalan army shooting down a civilian airplane to kill a priest. However, over time that became the most plausible and accepted explanation. Bill and his passengers were among the early martyrs of Guatemala.

Perhaps army officers justified this action as counterinsurgency. Around 1972 a guerrilla group had come to the northern lowlands and begun to move about clandestinely. In 1975 they killed a notorious landowner named Luis Arenas (the "tiger of Ixcan"); they labeled it an "execution" and announced themselves as the "Guerrilla Army of the Poor" or Ejército Guerrillero de los Pobres (EGP). In response, the army began to abduct, torture, and kill local leaders. Church-trained catechists, including some in Bill Woods's parish, were prime suspects. Bill had supported efforts by the people to draw attention to these abductions. Oil exploration was under way in Ixcan and army officers were acquiring land there, adding further motivation for getting rid of him.

Since the 1954 CIA coup that overthrew the elected government, murder had been a political tool in Guatemala, used primarily by the army, but also by the National Police and right-wing death squads. These murders were intended not only to silence individuals but to send a message to particular organizations and to society at large. Who was doing the killing was not clear: press accounts might speak of the action having been carried out by "armed men" or even "armed uniformed men," but did not specify further. What was clear was that the killers were not concerned about being caught and brought to justice. From the outset we kept the AFSC Philadelphia office informed of this officially sanctioned violence by sending clippings from the press, and when Corinne Johnson, the head of the AFSC Latin America program, visited us, we discussed how we might respond.

* * *

Our neighborhood, Zone 2, was residential and quiet, comprising two-story masonry or concrete buildings dating back many decades. The more substantial houses had survived the earthquake, but some had been reduced to rubble. Houses were in the Latin American style with walls up to the sidewalk and internal courtyards. Although neighbors might nod to one another in the street, they did not open up to strangers. That was partly out of natural reserve, but it was aggravated by the general attitude of suspicion after decades of repression. We were friendly with the middle-aged woman and her elderly mother who lived downstairs but never got to know them, and they had no idea of what we were doing. Jorge Sarmientos, the director of the National Symphony Orchestra, lived diagonally across the street from us, but as much as I would have liked to strike up a conversation, we merely nodded from a distance.

Our apartment was four rooms in an L-shape, plus a small kitchen area. Doors and windows were usually open, given the year-round springlike climate. The house had no water heater, so for bathing Catherine we had to heat water on the stove. We showered in cold water for a couple years before buying an electric shower head. We also hand-washed clothes, especially cloth diapers, a year or more before buying a washing machine. We hung them on clotheslines on the flat roof where they would dry quickly under the tropical sun.

Four blocks away was a supermarket, which was modest in comparison to the array available to U.S. shoppers even then. It had what we needed by way of vegetables, rice, beans, packaged foods like soups and cereal, and meat and dairy goods. Bread we bought in the form of rolls from a bakery across the street, and tortillas were sold fresh in the street.

When we arrived our daughter Catherine was a half-year old. As she moved beyond the crib stage we had her play on a large *petate* (woven straw mat) and had to keep the decorative tile floor clean enough for her to crawl around. We were concerned about what germs she might be exposed to and had to boil all our drinking water. We made a sandbox from an old jeep tire, and she entertained herself with a few toys there.

We initially avoided the common practice of hiring live-in servants, but eventually we brought in Juana Hernandez, who was attending high school. She lived with us and helped with childcare and other household tasks. Juana also traveled with us to neighboring countries. Later her sister Rosaura also came to live with us.

For getting around we inherited a noisy blue Land Cruiser that had been bought for traveling on dirt and gravel roads in the interior. We used it for doing errands around the city, and driving around the country and neighboring countries, as far as Panama and Mexico City. Because our tourist visas had to be renewed every three months, we organized our fact-finding trips to neighboring countries accordingly. One day while I was driving to a laundromat with Catherine in a car seat I made a turn and a loose door swung open. A tall wicker basket full of dirty clothes tumbled into the street; I had to pull over and scramble to get them back into the car under the gaze of armed troops guarding some public building. We had convenient bus service to other parts of the city, then at five cents per ride.

Although we were increasingly surrounded by political violence, we were not concerned for our safety in the streets of Guatemala City. When I came walking back from a concert at the National Conservatory a mile down Third Avenue from our house, I never feared getting mugged. That changed in the 1980s.

As AFSC overseas staff, we weren't paid a salary because we were regarded as volunteers in a temporary position. Our living expenses were labeled "maintenance," and we had to itemize every expense for monthly reports typed up in columns, which we tried to keep under five hundred dollars (the Guatemalan currency, the quetzal, was on a par with the dollar). We bought what we needed, but shopping wasn't much a part of our lives, nor did we accumulate many belongings.

We found ourselves frequently serving as hosts to Guatemalans and foreigners active in earthquake relief, church people, labor activists, organizers, and journalists. At the request of a priest, we took in an indigenous woman who was getting a divorce from an abusive and violent husband, and she stayed six or eight weeks.

* * *

We went regularly to Comalapa, the indigenous town where the AFSC was one of the main sponsors of the Vivienda Popular project. That meant driving an hour out of Guatemala City through the highlands past Chimaltenango and then another hour on unpaved roads past fields, down into a barranco, and up through pine forests to the town itself. In the center of the town, which then had several thousand people, was the surviving façade of the Catholic church surrounded by rubble.

The language in the region was Kakchikel, although most of the men and some women spoke Spanish, sometimes haltingly. Comalapa, which dated back to colonial times, was the municipal seat and a market center for this region, one of many dozens of such towns throughout the Guatemalan highlands. In the hills around the town were a number of *aldeas* or hamlets, some accessible only on foot, typically with fifteen or twenty families. Although it was not a tourist destination, Comalapa had some claims to fame. The composer of the Guatemalan national anthem was from Comalapa, and the town was known for its tradition of folk-style oil paintings of indigenous life, dating back to the 1920s.

The project was coordinated by a team made up of local people and Guatemalans from the capital, particularly recent university graduates, including several architects. Some had already been doing Freire-style popular education. It was also intended to foster comprehensive development, including agriculture techniques, and education of women.

The economy of Comalapa was based on subsistence agriculture; each family farmed a few acres on which it grew corn and beans and some vegetables, and perhaps raised some chickens or pigs. The most important cash crop of the area was potatoes, and the Potato Growers Association was the starting point for Vivienda Popular. One night I attended a discussion of land led by Jesuit anthropologist Ricardo Falla. What struck me was that the men attending had detailed memories of land ownership going back to the nineteenth century, thus attesting to how central land tenure was to their lives.

Drawing on his previous ethnographic experience, Falla spent four days walking around the town, observing, talking to people, and taking notes. He then presented his findings to the Vivienda Popular team, primarily those from Guatemala City. "Comalapa is a town of *comerciantes* [merchants]," he began. The town had an unusual number of small stores, selling everyday consumer items or agricultural supplies. The implication was that if we wished to understand Comalapa we had to pay attention to these *comerciantes* and understand their role. It was something that team members who thought in terms of abstractions like capitalism might not notice.

Although the project was aimed at rebuilding houses, the people's immediate postearthquake concern was fertilizer, since planting took place in May. Sacks of chemical fertilizer, on which the farmers were now dependent, were made available at subsidized rates. The project also obtained sheets of corrugated metal to put up as temporary roofs. Rather than rush into building permanent homes, Vivienda Popular moved slowly in order to assure that the housing reconstruction would be done by the local people themselves, at their pace, and using their labor.

Indigenous women were expected to serve their traditional functions: rising before dawn to start the fire, preparing tortillas by hand, washing clothes in a stream. During the first year, Angie went to Comalapa every Wednesday, working with Dora Miron, a young woman from Guatemala City, doing informal education with women.

Through Vivienda we got to know the head of the project, Nehemias Cumes, a recognized indigenous leader; Anastasio Sotz, a man in his early twenties; and Juana Apen, still in her teenage years, who sometimes stayed with us when they had business in the capital. Going regularly to Comalapa gave me a little sense of what Guatemala looked like from the standpoint of the indigenous half of the Guatemalan population, although there was undoubtedly much that I didn't understand.

* * *

Our colleagues and friends in Guatemala were a circle of people involved in broadly similar efforts for social change, some of whom we met through Jim Bradford in our first few days, most notably Guillermo Corado and his wife, Isabel. Guillermo had grown up in Guatemala City, working first in a government agency and then as a teacher and high school principal. He then worked with Bishop Gerardo Flores in the Social Secretariat of the Guatemalan bishops, and later he moved into informal education with a Jesuit-initiated program that had created a network of local rural leaders. In the mid-1970s, Guillermo and several others formed COEDUCA (Educational Community of Central America), a team that did informal education, such as short courses, especially working with pastoral teams of sisters and priests in rural areas of Guatemala. Isabel managed the books of the Association of Radio Schools, a church-related initiative that used radio broadcasting in indigenous languages for educational purposes. Guillermo and COEDUCA were thus networked into people around the country doing grassroots development and informal education.

Another such person was Mary Hamlin de Zuniga, who was originally from Minnesota, and had headed the Peace Corps in Nicaragua in the late 1960s. She was now living in Chimaltenango, while her husband, Marcelo, a Miskito Indian from the Atlantic coast of Nicaragua, studied veterinary medicine. Mary meanwhile was training village-level health promoters ("barefoot doctors," in the jargon of the time). A basic tool was the book *Donde No Hay Doctor* (Where there is no doctor), a manual developed by Dr. David Warner in western Mexico. Trained health promoters could do elementary diagnosis and administer some medicines.

Some of our colleagues were working for UK and European aid agencies: Margaret Rondo representing the Catholic Institute for International Relations (CIIR), Reggie Norton for Oxfam, and Ian Cherrett, a Scotsman who was a field representative for several European development agencies and lived in Honduras. Julia Esquivel, a Guatemalan Presbyterian who had studied in the seminary, edited the ecumenical magazine *Diálogo*, similar to other progressive Christian magazines in Latin America. Another journalistic contact was Violeta de Carpio at Inforpress Centroamericana, a weekly subscription newsletter primarily for business clients covering the six countries in the region. Frank LaRue, the labor lawyer, has already been mentioned.

On our 1974–1975 trip we had met some of the "Zone 5 Jesuits," named after the neighborhood where they lived. They were an interdisciplinary team working directly to serve grassroots groups rather than in the usual university setting. They included Ricardo Falla, anthropologist; Juan Hernandez Pico, sociologist; and Cesar Jerez, political scientist; along with Fernando Hoyos and Enrique Corral, who were doing informal education in conjunction with sympathetic pastoral teams. The Jesuit team had been planned while they were still in training, and they had chosen their social science fields to be complementary. Similar Jesuit teams existed elsewhere in Latin America. The main part of the Central America team was in Guatemala, but it included Jesuits as far away as Panama.

We became part of this loose network, composed primarily of faith-inspired activists working either directly with poor people or on their behalf. It was a somewhat limited circle; we didn't regularly engage with politicians or business leaders, and only occasionally did we go to the U.S. embassy, generally to see the political officer. In the increasingly repressive atmosphere of Guatemala, we had to operate with discretion; circulating too widely and too visibly would jeopardize the level of trust and confidentiality people expected.

All of us were of "the left" in the sense that we believed that Guatemala suffered from a systemic inequality rooted in history and enforced by violence and repression. The heart of the economic system was export agriculture on plantations owned by wealthy absentee families, while the majority of people were doing subsistence farming on an average of a few acres of land, exemplified by the people we knew in Comalapa.

We shared a conviction that development work had to do more than address immediate problems; it had to be in some sense a step toward deeper systemic change. Thus, for example, the project in Comalapa should address more than access to fertilizer or building new houses; it should also develop a critical awareness and leadership that could be part of broader movements for social change.

When we arrived in Guatemala, there was no sign of such systemic change on the horizon. All revolutionary movements since Cuba had been suppressed, and the Pinochet dictatorship was the response to an attempt to use electoral politics in Chile to bring about systemic change. Two-thirds of Latin Americans were now under some form of military rule. Guatemala and Central America were part of a continent-wide dark night of politics.

* * *

For several years before us, the AFSC had sponsored a program in the remote colonization area of the Peten in which medical students in their final year at the national university did their required social service with agricultural cooperatives. Jim Bradford had overseen the closing of the program, but in 1976 I went to the Peten as a gesture of solidarity from the AFSC and to inquire whether there was any help we might provide. Getting there entailed a sixteen-hour bus ride from Guatemala City, primarily on bumpy unpaved roads to Flores, the capital of the department, and then to Sayaxche, a small town on the river. There I could hire a boat for a two-hour ride to the cooperative. In Sayaxche, I stayed with John Breen, a Maryknoll priest, who enjoyed being out on the frontier.

The cooperative members showed me around their community. They had come as settlers from the highlands years before, with the help of Maryknoll fathers. Everything here was their work: their homes and meeting places with woven palm roofs. They did not have electricity, but one of the cooperatives had a generator for a freezer. At one point I observed two men using a crosscut saw to cut planks from a thick log, which was suspended horizontally about eight feet above the ground. One stood on top of the log and the other underneath, with the blade vertical. Despite the sharp teeth it must have taken an hour or so for each plank, requiring skill and patience under the tropical sun.

Mary de Zuniga and Margaret Rondo accompanied me on another visit. Mary was able to line up training for the health promoters in the cooperatives and link them to a grassroots healthcare network. Going to the Peten gave me a glimpse of what life was like in these areas, where transportation was by river, similar to what Angie and I had seen in the Ecuadorian Amazon, and people's link to the outside world was at most a transistor radio. On one of my last visits I saw a small black-and-white TV in a roadside restaurant being run by a generator. I also saw how roads had led to rain forest destruction, where after a few years the red clay soil could barely support some cattle grazing.

* * *

Starting in mid-1976, we made regular visits to El Salvador and witnessed the growing level of confrontation over the next year. Although structurally similar to Guatemala, El Salvador differs in significant ways. The country is small: from the capital, San Salvador, the Pacific Ocean is a half hour away; the western and northern borders with Guatemala and Honduras, each an hour; and the eastern border with Honduras, three hours. There were no longer any significant groups of indigenous people; Salvadorans are mestizos. All cultivable land was in use, and in fact as the population grew, there were more and more "landless peasants," rural people who were dependent on what they could earn during the relatively short harvest season. Land tenure was extremely unequal, and the best lands were in the hands of a few (the so-called Fourteen Families). A 1932 peasant uprising had been put down with gratuitous violence, commonly believed to be thirty thousand people killed. Since the 1950s, presidents had come from the military, put forward by the official party, the PCN (Party of National Conciliation). The electoral fraud against the Christian Democrat Party in 1972 was still a fresh memory.

Some analysts had concluded that El Salvador's agroexport model was becoming nonviable; the economic basis of the country should shift from agriculture to industry, as had occurred in Taiwan where a land reform was the prelude to export industrialization. Thus, in June 1976 the military government announced an "agrarian transformation," which would begin in a fraction of the countryside: land would be taken from large farms and distributed to twelve thousand peasants. The owners would be compensated at market value and given incentives to invest in industry. The plan was called an "insurance policy for our grandchildren," with the implication that otherwise the peasantry would sooner or later revolt.

The plan was immediately denounced not only by landowners but by the private sector as a whole, led by ANEP (National Private Enterprise Association), the umbrella organization representing business, and also by most of the left. Supporting it were the U.S. embassy, the Communist Party, and the Jesuit University (UCA), which under the leadership of the rector, Ignacio Ellacuria, S.J., threw itself wholeheartedly into the debate, especially through serious studies in several issues of its journal *ECA* (*Estudios Centroamericanos*).

Waging an aggressive campaign, especially in the newspapers, ANEP forced the government to back down, and in October the national assembly issued a law eviscerating the reform. Ellacuria wrote a scathing editorial, "At Your Orders, Capital," mimicking a soldier snapping his heels and saying, "At your orders, captain." His interpretation was that the state, including the military, had attempted to gain some autonomy from the moneyed interests to do what the country needed, and had been squelched by the oligarchy. Five or six bombs were set off at the university or near Jesuit residences. In an editorial, "Why Do They Plant Bombs against Us?" Ellacuria answered that it was because the UCA Jesuits were striving to carry out their mission as a university in service to El Salvador. The visceral animus against Ellacuria, the Jesuits, the university, and the church would continue for a decade and a half.

Tensions heightened over an event in Aguilares, a town a half-hour north of San Salvador where Jesuits had been working for several years under the leadership of the pastor, Fr. Rutilio Grande. When a peasant organization gathered in late 1976 to make demands of two landholder brothers, a shot was fired and one was killed. Circumstances indicated that one brother may have accidentally shot the other, but in the minds of the landholders it was the work of the "peasant hordes," as they called them, in yet another barrage of paid ads.

These events formed the context as the February 1977 election approached. The official PCN had nominated General Humberto Romero, who had turned against the land reform plan he had earlier supported. Mindful of the 1972 fraud, the Christian Democrats and Social Democrats united around a retired military officer as candidate. In visits to El Salvador during this period, my informants were diocesan priests I had known, and young professors at the UCA, especially Ruben Zamora, a political scientist, and Hector Dada, an economist.

RESPONDING TO SPIRALING VIOLENCE

* * *

In early 1977 I wrote an analysis of the situation in El Salvador and then one about Guatemala marking the one-year anniversary of the earthquake. Both noted the growing level of political violence, especially state-sanctioned violence against civilians, and both were attempts to provide context, grounded in the recent history of the countries. The analyses were sent to the Philadelphia office, which then sent them to church, human rights, and development organizations as background. The recipients understood who was preparing these reports, but they agreed not to cite them. We had to be quite careful because from the standpoint of the Guatemalan or Salvadoran military such activity would be labeled "subversive."

At this time Central American countries received virtually no attention in the international news media. An academic study later found that the newspaper coverage of these countries was scarce and was limited to natural disasters, coups, elections, and visiting U.S. celebrities. A Guatemalan journalist told me that the *New York Times* had a source in Guatemala, someone who did not write news items but only indicated potential stories, for which a reporter could be sent to inquire.

The region was beginning to attract attention within the incipient human rights movement. In 1976 Bill Wipfler, the Episcopal priest who headed the human rights office of the National Council of Churches, gave congressional testimony on human rights in Nicaragua, Guatemala, and El Salvador. Amnesty International published a report on Guatemala in late 1976. The North American Congress on Latin America (NACLA), headquartered in Berkeley, had published a book-length study of Guatemala in 1974, with emphasis on the economic roots of the regime and on the role of U.S. military and intelligence advisers.

As our work evolved in response to events, we provided periodic documentation and analysis, which we mailed to the Philadelphia AFSC office. Dick Erstad, who was now working on the AFSC Latin America program, was in touch with organizations concerned about Latin America and shared our materials with them.

* * *

When visiting Nicaragua we stayed with Gerri O'Leary, who had worked in the parish in Chorrillo. Her husband, Edgard Macias, was a significant figure in the Christian Democrat Party and a member of UDEL (Democratic Union for Liberation), which had first formed to urge a boycott of the 1974 elections and had continued as a focus of anti-Somoza opposition. The president of UDEL was Pedro Joaquin Chamorro, editor and owner of *La Prensa*, and the most respected opposition figure in the country. Gerri worked in various development projects, particularly those sponsored by CEPAD (Evangelical Committee for Aid and Development), the umbrella evangelical organization that had been created to deal with the 1972 earthquake and had continued in development projects.

At Gerri's house in mid-1976 we met with Jesuit Fernando Cardenal, whom I had known since 1970 when he visited Panama. He had recently returned from the United States, where he had given testimony to a committee in the House of Representatives on human rights violations in Nicaragua arranged by WOLA. He presented data on the abduction and disappearance of many peasant leaders in the countryside. Those actions were Somoza's response to an action in December 1974 when the Sandinistas took a number of high government officials and Somoza relatives hostage, forcing the dictator to pay ransom and meet other demands. Fernando was astonished at the resistance he encountered from some congressional representatives. The Capuchin Fathers working on the Atlantic side of the country had compiled their own list of human rights violations, which they also made public. By early 1977 the Nicaraguan bishops, seconded by the conference of religious orders, also publicly criticized the regime for human rights violations.

Many years later Fernando revealed that he had joined the Sandinistas in the early 1970s. The Sandinistas, who took their name from Augusto Cesar Sandino, the leader of guerrilla resistance to the U.S. Marine occupation of Nicaragua in the 1920s and 1930s, had existed since the early 1960s but were not a major presence. At this time their numbers were probably only in the hundreds; they were also divided into three factions, with differing strategies. I happened to be in Nicaragua when *La Prensa* published verbatim court testimony by Tomas Borge, an imprisoned Sandinista leader. It was a confession and provided a history of the Sandinista movement and an account of its activities. The testimony occupied many pages printed over the course of two or three days.

Nothing like this would have happened in Guatemala, where there were no political prisoners; "subversives" would be killed either by death squad or the army or police. From Somoza's standpoint Borge's account served to show that the Sandinistas, who otherwise might seem shadowy, really existed. For *La Prensa* it sold papers, but likewise demonstrated the existence of an armed opposition to Somoza.

During this time we regularly went to see the Maryknoll sisters in OPEN 3, a barrio that had been formed on the outskirts of Managua by people who had lost their homes in the 1972 earthquake, particularly Peg Dillon, who was both irreverent and enthusiastic.

* * *

In 1976, world coffee prices rose sharply as result of a frost in Brazil, triggering a spike in the cost to consumers. The Philadelphia AFSC office suggested we look into the impact in Guatemala, particularly whether the workers benefited at all. That meant first trying to understand coffee production and trade. To do so I went to the Pacific Coast region, to visit coffee plantations and a coffee cooperative, and got a sense of the process itself for the first time in my life, despite the many gallons of coffee I had imbibed.

Coffee is grown on bushes generally in the shade of larger trees, in Guatemala primarily in the foothills and lower elevations of the mountains. The plants require more direct care than other export crops, such as sugar. Coffee is picked in berry form, then soaked in water to soften the outer part for removal by machinery, leaving the "beans," which are then dried either in the sun or in a drying machine. After removal of a thin outer film, they are bagged for shipping. Although coffee was grown on many plantations and small farms, export was in the hands of a few large companies.

Harvesters pick each berry by hand, choosing only those that are ripe, and drop them into a can hanging from their neck, emptying each can into a larger container. They were then being paid about a dollar for a hundred pounds, roughly a day's work. For the harvest season, they were hired by labor contractors, who brought them down from the highlands in trucks—women and children as well as men. Like sugar and cotton, coffee was picked in the slack time between harvest and planting in the highlands. It represented a chance for indigenous small farmers to earn cash, but at a dollar a day they could accumulate little. They were typically housed in open-air barracks where they hung their hammocks.

My inquiries brought me to an interview with the executive director of the Association of Coffee Exporters in his office in Guatemala City. On his desk was a red phone with direct connections to London and New York, impressive technology at that time. He explained that coffee prices could fluctuate at any time due to weather fluctuations or a dock strike in Colombia. "I'm in about ten or twelve businesses," he said, "and this one is the toughest of all. I can make ten thousand dollars in the morning and lose it in the afternoon," he said. *An enviable problem*, I thought to myself.

At that time Brazil was by far the largest coffee producer in the world, followed by Colombia. Guatemala and El Salvador were each less than 5 percent of world production. Coffee was then a commodity sold to large companies like Folgers and Maxwell House. The coffee exporters representative praised the discriminating taste of Germans and other Europeans, by contrast with Americans who were willing to drink anything black. The rise of specialty coffees was still a decade or more in the future.

Out of these inquiries I wrote a piece that Dick Erstad at the Philadelphia office placed as an op-ed in the *Washington Post*, "The Cost of Coffee." Consumer concern over high prices was a takeoff point for explaining the coffee production process, and particularly the plight of the harvesters, who were not sharing in the bonanza.

* * *

For the February 1977 Salvadoran election, the opposition coalition, headed by the Christian Democrats, had chosen a retired military man, Colonel Ernesto Claramount, as their presidential candidate, hoping to allay the fears of the military and the oligarchy. As the election approached, the level of violence escalated. Three foreign priests were deported in the first few weeks of the year, others were picked up and tortured, bombs were set off against others, and right-wing forces threatened still more. The head of the government tourism office was abducted by guerrillas. When the election results were announced giving the victory to the official party, the opposition claimed fraud and occupied a public plaza for several days. In the early-morning hours of February 28, troops surrounded the demonstrators and fired, killing some. Claramount and other figures took refuge in a church; the rest were forced to run a gauntlet through lines of police who beat them. An unknown number, perhaps many dozens, were killed, and the blood had to be fire-hosed off the street. Through the mediation of bishops, the party leaders were able to leave the church and go into exile. A state of emergency was declared.

In the middle of these events, Bishop Oscar Romero was made archbishop of San Salvador in a hasty, low-key ceremony. Based on their previous experience of him, my contacts regarded Romero as conservative and would have preferred Bishop Arturo Rivera Damas. The morning after the bloody ending of the opposition rally, Romero had his first scheduled meeting with his clergy. Rather than taking up the agenda, he suggested that they return to their parishes to be ready to assist people who might need it.

About two weeks later, Fr. Rutilio Grande, the Jesuit pastor of Aguilares, was shot dead on a Saturday afternoon while driving to say Mass, along with his two passengers. Romero went to Aguilares where he saw the body of Grande, who had been his friend. As a sign of repudiation, the following Sunday all Masses in the archdiocese were canceled, except a single one intended to rally Catholics. That action was opposed by the elites; a phantom landowners' association said that the church was being taken over by the Jesuits.

In May the body of the foreign minister, Mauricio Borgonovo, who had been kidnapped by another guerrilla organization, was found. Fr. Alfonso Navarro, who had said Mass for the opposition occupiers, was gunned down at his parish the next day; his murderers obviously intended it as retaliation. A murky organization calling itself the White Warriors Union announced that it would start killing the Jesuits one by one unless they all left the country. I was following these events with frequent visits to San Salvador. When I went to see Ruben Zamora at his house, I found him about to leave for the airport to flee the country as a result of death threats. He then spent two years in exile in Britain.

At around this time I went to see William Walker, the political officer at the U.S. embassy to get his analysis. He praised the ambassador, Ignacio Lozano, a Mexican American Republican newspaper owner from Los Angeles, and a political appointee of the Ford administration. Lozano took human rights seriously and saw through the subterfuges of the Salvadoran government. Both Walker and Lozano had become personae non gratae with the elites and government.

Walker urged me to meet Leonel Gomez, a coffee grower whom he called a "Renaissance man" who wanted to reverse what was happening. Gomez had angered fellow coffee growers by providing better living conditions for his workers. When Gomez and I met and talked, he took me to the modest house of a Salvadoran military officer and introduced me as a Quaker who wanted to understand the problems of El Salvador. It was midday and the officer was eating lunch in his boxer shorts. Gomez then left the two of us and said he would come back. I don't remember our conversation in detail, but the officer spoke of subversion and political meddling by the church.

Gomez circulated in various strata of Salvadoran society, from left to right, thereby arousing suspicion among some. Not long afterward he arrived unannounced on a motorcycle at our house in Guatemala City. He had come for some event: an exhibition of his paintings—or perhaps a shooting competition, since he was also a competitive marksman. We assumed he had come by to check out the veracity of my story.

Walker and Lozano left El Salvador at the moment the new government was being inaugurated on July 1, taking death threats seriously. After a considerable delay, the Carter administration appointed as ambassador a career officer named Frank Devine, who told me when I went to see him that he was going to take his time in making up his mind about El Salvador. He in fact said little over the next two years.

These events showed a kind of polarization in El Salvador, focused on land and property, with threats and violence against church people, and also growing militancy by mass political organizations, as well as assassinations carried out by leftist guerrillas. Salvadoran society was in crisis. In response to all of this, I wrote an article centered on Rutilio Grande, spelling out the context around his murder, which the Jesuit weekly *America* published under a pseudonym.

* * *

Our assignment from the AFSC was to monitor developments in the region as a whole. In the 1970s the population of all the Central American countries was less than 20 million, a fraction of Mexico, then over 60 million. That division into tiny countries was an accident of history—the factional fighting in the decades after independence (1821). The Central American Common Market (1960) was created to lower tariff barriers so that investors could set up operations aimed at the entire region. By the mid-1970s, the consumer products we bought, like detergent or cooking oil, were being manufactured and marketed on a regional basis. Having a head start, Guatemalan and Salvadoran industrialists had reaped the benefits disproportionately.

Even though the countries were small and close together, with capitals a few hours' drive away, relatively few people traveled outside their own country. The effects of the brief 1969 war between El Salvador and Honduras could still be felt.

The history of Honduras was different from that of its neighbors, because it had not had a coffee boom in the nineteenth century. American entrepreneurs had established banana plantations on the northern Caribbean coast, but they did business directly with New Orleans, and the rest of the country remained a backwater. One result was that San Pedro Sula became the business and industrial center of the country, equal in size with the capital, Tegucigalpa, in the interior. It was only in the mid-twentieth century that Honduras developed its own business and agricultural elites. Small farmers were poor but did not feel the land pressure as was the case in El Salvador and Guatemala.

In 1977 I went to La Ceiba with two solidarity journalists, primarily to talk to workers who were in a labor dispute. While there we got a view of a classic banana company town, where managers lived in an enclave with well-maintained lawns. We entered the grounds, walked to an office, and had a conversation with a Standard Fruit executive without an appointment, in a way that no Honduran would have been able to do. He was involved in experimentation with new products such as tomatoes and cucumbers, in order to diversify away from bananas and pineapples, and he was enthusiastic about the prospects. The banana companies were moving away from direct production toward contracting with Honduran producers, who would handle labor matters. In passing he remarked that from his standpoint it would make sense to develop citrus export in Cuba, if relations were ever renewed. This was over forty years ago, at the height of the Cold War.

It was always pleasant to be in Costa Rica. By comparison with its neighbors, the country had a modest prosperity, and it seemed to work reasonably well for its citizens: children were in school, and health care was available to all. The people were proud of their institutions, their democracy, and their peace. A major factor was that Costa Rica had disbanded its army after the 1948 civil war. However, I found the smugness of Costa Ricans toward their neighbors annoying. In hindsight I should have been more curious about what made the country work and what aspects of it might be replicable.

Although Panama is geographically the end of the isthmus of Central America, Panamanians did not identify as Central Americans. The heart of the economy was around the canal, the U.S. bases, and increasingly, international banking. The Torrijos government was renegotiating the canal treaties with the Carter administration, and our Jesuit friend Xabier Gorostiaga was working as an economic adviser to the Panamanian negotiating team. A few Panamanians continued to oppose the military government on principle, and some endured harassment and went into exile. We had some reservations about the treaties, particularly whether U.S. bases would remain, but did not devote major attention to the issue.

U.S. conservatives, notably Ronald Reagan, regarded the Carter government's renegotiation of treaties with Panama as a giveaway of a precious asset to an unreliable country. Archbishop McGrath, working in concert with the U.S. bishops conference, helped to prepare a favorable climate for the treaties. He was instrumental in enlisting the support of John Wayne, who enjoyed fishing off Panama, had investments in shrimp operations, and considered himself a friend of Panama. Wayne wrote a letter to all senators on behalf of the treaty, to the consternation of conservatives. McGrath made a pastoral visit to California to visit Wayne, who became a Catholic late in life as he was battling cancer. The treaties were signed in 1977, but the transfer itself would unfold over two decades.

* * *

In the early to mid-1970s, Leo Mahon and the San Miguelito team had continued to face harassment from both state and church. Phones were tapped, and team members were periodically under surveillance. The team was accused of heresy, but in an extensive trial-like procedure they defended themselves to the satisfaction of recognized theologians invited from Colombia. The papal nuncio intrigued with Rome and with Cardinal John Cody in Chicago. Meanwhile, the territorial scope of the team expanded as adjoining areas were included. Leo was vicar of the region, overseeing a team of over two dozen between priests, sisters, and laypeople.

Leo returned to Chicago in 1975, and when we visited Panama, Don Headley was in charge in San Miguelito. What had been innovative in the mid-1960s (priests not in clerical dress, Christian base communities, use of the Bible, folk music at Mass, development of lay leadership) were now enshrined in the Medellin documents, even if they were not always widely implemented.

In 1978 the Chicago presence was abruptly terminated, by an arrangement between Cardinal Cody and Archbishop McGrath. A Panamanian monsignor was appointed to replace Headley and took a more traditionalist line of work, dismantling the existing parish programs or letting them expire.

For approximately a decade, the San Miguelito experiment had served as a catalyst of church renewal, and was emulated or adapted in parishes in El Salvador, Nicaragua, Honduras, northeast Brazil, and elsewhere.

* * *

In conjunction with the Philadelphia office, we had decided to do a slide show on reconstruction from the Guatemalan earthquake. In early 1977 I visited a number of reconstruction projects, 35 mm camera in hand, and interviewed development workers to see what could be learned.

Perhaps in order to avoid what had happened in Nicaragua after the 1972 earthquake, where Somoza centralized relief and reconstruction aid and profiteered from it, the Guatemalan government and army set up the National Reconstruction

Committee, which brokered direct agreements between towns and development agencies. The upshot was a mosaic of approaches across the country.

Because their relatives and neighbors had been killed by falling tile roofs and adobe walls, the survivors strongly inclined toward abandoning traditional adobe houses and moving toward cinder-block construction, with reinforced concrete columns and corrugated metal roofs. That was the option of Vivienda Popular in Comalapa. In Tecpan, a major indigenous town off the Pan-American Highway, I visited a Salvation Army project where sixty people were employed building over five hundred such houses between mid-1976 and mid-1977.

The preference for cement-block housing was understandable. However, some pointed to the disadvantages of that model, namely the cost (around one thousand dollars per house), which poor families could accept only with a hefty subsidy, and which even so excluded the very poorest. Adobe houses were made with local materials by the people themselves. Aesthetic considerations no doubt played a role, especially with foreigners. Poor Guatemalans by contrast viewed a cinder-block house as a sign of modernity.

Three projects used different techniques to build safe houses using traditional techniques. The structures built under the World Neighbors project in San Martin Jilotepeque supported a lightweight roof on four wooden posts; the walls were not structural, were built of adobes stacked vertically, and were held in place by wire in such a way that in an earthquake they would fall away from the house, leaving the roof standing. World Neighbors was a long-term project focused on improved agricultural techniques and leadership development, directed by Paul and Mary McKay. The World Neighbors house model had been developed by Fred Cuny, an engineer from Texas who made a career as a consultant in disaster situations around the world, until he disappeared mysteriously in Chechnya in 1995.

A project sponsored by the Mennonite Central Committee used traditional *bajareque* (wattle and daub) construction: build a framework with sticks and fill it with clay, sand, straw, and other materials. When plastered over it can be quite pleasant, as we could see in the house that our friend Mary de Zuniga had built in Chimaltenango. In the town of Salama, in Baja Verapaz, I found a third technique led by a Swiss architect, Kurt Rhyner: square adobe blocks were made and then laid in a careful pattern in thick walls that would be earthquake-proof. We became friends with Kurt and his Canadian wife, Kathryn, and their twin sons, who were the same age as Catherine.

Visiting the projects and organizing and writing the slide show gave me a glimpse into what happens after a natural disaster and the problems of housing reconstruction. However, the deepening crisis of Guatemala and the region made the topic seem irrelevant, and the slide presentation was not widely used.

* * *

At the suggestion of the Philadelphia office and activists elsewhere, I delved into two other issues, free trade zones and the Latin American Agribusiness Development Corporation (LAAD), a consortium headed by Bank of America and supported by the United States Agency for International Development (USAID). In both cases researchers and activists suspected that these were economic schemes being foisted upon Latin American countries by corporations, the U.S. government, and international banks to bolster the capitalist system.

The Colon Free Trade Zone had operated in Panama for decades, and other zones were being set up in El Salvador, Honduras, Nicaragua, and Guatemala, located near ports or airports. They were fenced-in enclaves with some assembly factories. Companies could utilize cheap labor, and host countries got some jobs; otherwise, there was no connection with the local economy.

In Managua, the manager gave me a tour of the Bailey jeans factory. Imported cut cloth began at one end of a very long open building and passed through various stages where women sewed the cloth together and added buttons, loops, zippers, and so forth, Completed jeans emerged at the far end where they were boxed for shipment. Bailey was not a name known to consumers, but its dozen or so plants in the United States manufactured for Levi's and Lee and other brands.

LAAD was set up to provide lending to innovative agricultural enterprises that found it difficult to obtain loans from conventional banks. Among those I visited were a flower export operation in Costa Rica and an American farmer who was growing cantaloupe near Zacapa in the arid eastern part of Guatemala. I found him on his tractor, and after he cleaned up we had supper and a good talk.

A factory manager outside Managua remarked in the course of our conversation, "How much does labor represent of the total cost of production—15 percent? Twenty percent?" I was surprised since I had assumed that labor costs were a much larger proportion. My surprise reflects the fact that I had no sense of business from inside. In hindsight I wish I had been more curious about how commercial farming and business worked, rather than assuming, as did our colleagues and friends, that we knew all we needed about capitalism, namely that it is inherently exploitative.

After some initial investigation, we concluded that, at least for the present, neither of these proposals was as nefarious as some thought and did not merit further investigation on our part. For a decade or more the Nicaraguan revolution and the Central American crisis overwhelmed such schemes. Later on, many assembly plants were set up in the region, especially in Guatemala.

* * *

Starting in early 1977 we began to meet with a group of a half-dozen people at the site of the Zone 5 community of Jesuits to do conjunctural analysis, as was then common in Latin America. The idea was to examine the economic, political, and social forces at work in society, so as to be able to situate one's pastoral or popular organizing work in a realistic context. We each chose a topic area and read all relevant newspaper items for the period in question—the previous month or two. The topic areas included the economy, divided into sectors (agriculture, industry, and services); politics (Congress, the government, political parties, the armed forces); popular organizations (labor, peasants, slumdwellers); and events abroad (the United States, Europe, the Soviet bloc, etc.). A young indigenous university student working with the Jesuits clipped stories from six or so daily Guatemala newspapers and assembled them in topic folders. Participants arrived at the meeting having prepared a digest of developments in their particular area and presented them. Those were summarized on large sheets of newsprint in the form of a grid. If done well, this methodology, which I had seen in Chile presented at Christians for Socialism, offered a way of visualizing the forces at play in society. It forced participants to pay attention to data and move beyond impressionistic ways of understanding.

My topic was political violence. I went through thick folders of newspaper clippings with accounts of murders, abductions, and related news items and then organized the incidents into three columns: name of the person and date, location, and a brief description of the incident, arranged chronologically day by day. In September 1977 I wrote a report in Spanish, "Political Violence in Guatemala: June–August." The digest description of each incident was often very brief: "So-and-so was gunned down by several assailants who fled in a vehicle," or "A body found with ten bullet wounds and signs of torture." That report had sixteen pages of such digests followed by two pages of tabulations. The number of people killed was 111; the vast majority, 89, were poor; 8 or 9 were landowners or other wealthy or powerful people; 6 were students or professionals; and 5 were police or army.

The initial purpose was simply to provide one component for our conjunctural analysis group, but I sent it to the Philadelphia office accompanied by an analysis in English of the overall situation in Guatemala, with emphasis on political violence. Dick Erstad sent it to human rights and church groups, which found it helpful for their work, and from then on I continued to prepare similar reports in Spanish. They also circulated discreetly to others in Guatemala. Although I let the facts speak for themselves and did not accuse the Guatemalan army or police, such documentation was clearly "subversive" activity and would have endangered us if the intelligence services traced it back to me.

* * *

On our first trip to Costa Rica we were graciously hosted for several days by Hugo Assmann and his wife, Melsene Ludwig. Hugo had fled the military dictatorship in Brazil in 1968 and had lived successively in Germany, Uruguay, Bolivia, and Chile, where he published one of the early book-length treatments of liberation theology.

He had now taken refuge in Costa Rica, where he and fellow exiles Pablo Richard and Franz Hinkelammert had founded a research and training institute to which they gave the anodyne name Departamento Ecuménico de Investigaciones (DEI [Ecumenical Research Department]). DEI provided pastoral courses of roughly three months, based on the Bible and on social analysis. The participants were priests, sisters, and pastors in Central America and Mexico. To a degree DEI supplied what CELAM training institutions had provided before the purge carried out by Bishop Lopez Trujillo. DEI had close ties with the Seminario Bíblico, a nondenominational evangelical seminary in San Jose.

DEI also operated as a think tank based on different disciplines: economics (Hinkelammert), sociology (Assmann), and scripture and theology (Richard). A key early work was Hinkelammert's *Las Armas Ideológicas de la Muerte* (The ideological weapons of death; 1977), which is a critique of capitalism directed not so much at its effects as its underlying but hidden ideology. In that spirit, DEI organized a conference of theologians and social scientists in 1978 and published the papers in two volumes: *Capitalismo: Violencia y Anti-Vida* (Capitalism: Violence and antilife; 1978). DEI played a major role in bringing the topic of idolatry into theological currency, that is, that the capitalist system sacrifices victims like the ancient divinities that demanded human sacrifice.

A second DEI publication was *Carter y la Lógica del Imperialismo* (Carter and the logic of imperialism; 1978), a compilation of pieces likewise published by theologians, social scientists, and politicians from Mexico, Brazil, Chile, and elsewhere, many of them now exiles. From the DEI standpoint, there was little difference between the Carter administration, with its professed concern for human rights, and that of Nixon and Ford. In that collection, for example, Juan Luís Segundo took the United States to task for criticizing the military of his own country, Uruguay, for human rights violations, when they were simply playing their assigned role in the international system. As a system, capitalism denied the majority their basic right to a decent life; torture and murder of those who sought to change that system were a consequence of that more fundamental violation. Many on the Latin American left, including theologians, were suspicious of the international human rights movement and of (bourgeois) democracy. For a time, DEI was influential in Latin American theological circles, a kind of school within liberation theology.

Hugo and Mel hosted us and our daughter for several days on our first visit, and I stayed there later. They were always gracious hosts, and we had spirited conversations at night.

* * *

When General Humberto Romero (no relation to the archbishop) assumed the presidency of El Salvador in mid-1977, the White Warriors Union (known only through their communiques) did not carry out its threat to assassinate Jesuits one by one. Over the next year, though, clashes continued: kidnappings by guerrilla organizations, occupations of public buildings, marches in the streets.

In my visits to El Salvador I regularly stopped at the chancery office, which occupied a portion of the seminary complex, located near the major landmark statue of Cristo Salvador del Mundo (Christ, savior of the world). I was usually inquiring about human rights violations with Roberto Cuellar of Socorro Jurídico, or with Rafael Moreno, a Mexican Jesuit. When I went to see Archbishop Romero, inevitably I encountered several peasants on the plain wooden benches also waiting to see him. My recollection of Romero is someone soft-spoken and thoughtful, always in cassock. From his earliest years and throughout his life he was always striving to be a good priest. If I was in town Sunday morning, I attended his Sunday Mass and homily.

On one visit to El Salvador in 1977 I saw Chencho Alas as he was about to leave the country in his pickup truck. In consultation with the archbishop, Alas had decided that because of death threats against him, he needed to leave the country. He drove to the United States, lived for several years in Washington, DC, and did not return until after 1990.

While a militant organization was occupying the Ministry of Labor in November 1977, an industrialist was killed under mysterious circumstances, which served as a trigger for a barrage of accusations against the church and militant organizations. One of my regular contacts, Jose Siman, the manager of an ADOC shoe store and a lay adviser to Archbishop Romero, handed me a thick dossier of such accusations. In late November the government published a draconian "Law for the Defense and Guarantee of Public Order," which gave sweeping powers to security forces and in effect outlawed strikes and demonstrations. I began one of my confidential reports, "A new law in El Salvador makes it punishable by one to three years in jail to send out of the country information such as that contained in this article." International human rights organizations drew attention to the implications of the law.

Around Holy Week 1978, ORDEN, a right-wing paramilitary organization in the countryside, and FECCAS (Christian Federation of Small Farmers of El Salvador), a peasant group that to some degree grew out of pastoral work, had a series of clashes that left some people dead. A commission from the archdiocese investigated the events and prepared a report, attributing most of the violence to ORDEN. From that point on, the archdiocese began regular systematic human rights monitoring.

One evening I went to the National University to talk to representatives of the mass organizations. I found a dozen or more tables, each with representatives of one of these organizations. They were taking advantage of university autonomy—a tradition in Latin America by which security forces are not permitted on campus premises—to distribute literature openly. The multiplicity of organizations reflected the fracturing of the Marxist left into four or five ideological lines as well as the various sectors of society: peasants, labor, teachers, slumdwellers, university, secondary school, and so forth. The strongest confederations of mass organizations were the BPR (Revolutionary People's Bloc) and FAPU (United People's Action Front). They demonstrated for concrete issues like a raise in the minimum wage, but their ultimate aim, at least at the leadership level, was to create a different type of society by taking state power.

In beginning an interview with the executive director of ANEP, the private-sector umbrella group that led the opposition to the land reform in 1976, I asked a general question about the situation in the country. He replied, "To understand El Salvador you have to start in Moscow," and lectured me along those lines. Actually the major guerrilla organizations in El Salvador had arisen in opposition to the communist line from Moscow, but that did not matter.

In its publications, the UCA defended the legitimacy of the popular organizations and insisted that they should be allowed to operate legally. Romero, who had met some of their leaders in visits to the countryside, regarded the popular organizations as legitimate.

* * *

Ernesto Cardenal, a priest and poet who had been a monk at the Trappist monastery in Gethsemani, Kentucky, with Thomas Merton in the 1950s, had gone on to create a community of young people on the island of Solentiname in Lake Nicaragua, near the Costa Rican border. The people on the island made their living from fishing and farming, and a kind of artist colony developed, producing folk-style paintings. When he celebrated Mass, Cardenal led the people in discussions of the texts of the day influenced by liberation theology. These dialogue sermons, in which the local people gave their reflections, were recorded, and in 1975 they were published as *El Evangelio en Solentiname* (The gospel in Solentiname), and were soon translated into other languages, thus putting the island community on the international map.

In September 1977 the Sandinistas launched what was intended to be a set of simultaneous attacks against the National Guard. The attacks were poorly coordinated and the National Guard repelled them. Some of those attacking an outpost near the Costa Rican border were members of the Solentiname community. National Guard troops came and destroyed the community's dwellings, and Cardenal went into exile in Costa Rica. A few days later, a group of prominent Nicaraguan men—writers, businessmen, and priests, including Maryknoll father Miguel D'Escoto, and Ernesto and Fernando Cardenal—calling themselves *Los Doce* (The twelve), published a statement denouncing the abuses of the regime and recognizing the importance of the Sandinistas as part of the solution for the country.

La Prensa was publishing exposés particularly about a company named Plasmaferesis, which was exporting blood sold for cash by desperate Nicaraguans. In December 1977, priests and sisters at the shantytown OPEN 3 were beaten by the guardia for protesting treatment of youth, and a photo of Maryknoll sister Peg Dillon with her face bandaged became an international news item. After appeals from Archbishop Miguel Obando y Bravo and the political opposition, a commission for dialogue was set up, but was rebuffed by Somoza. Late in the year, Gaspar Garcia Laviana, a Spanish Sacred Heart priest working in Nicaragua, wrote an eloquent public letter to announce his decision to join the Sandinistas as a combatant. In early January the bishops issued a pastoral letter denouncing the abuses of the regime far more forthrightly than they had done previously.

This was the context in which Pedro Joaquin Chamorro was gunned down by a hit squad while driving to *La Prensa* in January 1978. He had opposed the dictatorship since the 1950s and was the most prominent opposition figure. The killing was apparently linked to the exposure of Plasmaferesis. Tens of thousands of people turned out for the funeral, and afterward Somoza-linked properties, including Plasmaferesis, were attacked and some were burned. Business associations organized a work stoppage. Different church bodies made eloquent statements denouncing the regime's abuses. Young people in the town of Monimbo organized an uprising that was put down by the National Guard. What drew attention was that for anonymity, they wore masks associated with a traditional indigenous celebration.

In March 1978 I was in Nicaragua when *La Prensa* carried the story of the killing of Reynaldo Perez Vega, a notorious Somocista general and reputed torturer. He had been lured to the house of Nora Astorga, in what he thought was an amorous liaison. She was a clandestine Sandinista, and he was killed while resisting being kidnapped. Her photo in Sandinista fatigues appeared in *La Prensa*, and the killing was called an "execution."

* * *

In October 1977 our daughter Maggie was born in Guatemala. We now had a two-year-old and an infant. Our original commitment was for two years. With two young children we might have prudently decided to return to the United States and put down roots. However, in discussion with the Philadelphia office, we agreed to renew our contract for two more years. A major reason was that, in Guatemala, establishing trust with people required a great deal of time, and having achieved that, it would be better for us to stay another term.

However, as we prepared reports for human rights and church groups, we became increasingly dissatisfied with simply mailing them to be distributed through the Philadelphia office. We wanted to hear some feedback from people using the materials and doing educational outreach in Central America. We also felt a strong need to communicate the urgency of the accelerating crisis of violence in the region.

In spring 1978 we spent a month in North America, combining visits to our families in northeastern Pennsylvania and Southern California and elsewhere, with AFSC-arranged meetings and presentations. We conferred with AFSC staff in Philadelphia and met with Tom Quigley at the U.S. Catholic bishops' conference in Washington, Bill Wipfler at the National Council of Churches, and staffers at WOLA. In addition we traveled to speak to small groups in Philadelphia, Washington, New York, Boston, Toronto, Denver, San Francisco, and Pasadena. (On the flight from San Francisco to L.A., Maggie, then a few months old, had a high fever, which we kept down by applying cold washcloths and ice.) We had dozens of meetings, but audiences for public presentations were small, such as a few people in a Quaker meeting. We felt impelled to try to alert our audiences to the rising tide of violence that was all around us. Central America aroused little interest: at a noontime brown-bag lunch organized at the University of Colorado Denver campus, only one person showed up. The organizers, Art and Natalie Warner, who had been AFSC staff in Chile after the Pinochet coup, joked that he was probably CIA.

Within a year a revolution would come to power in the region, U.S. government involvement would deepen, and the Central America crisis would be in the headlines for a decade.

10

Point of No Return

SHORTLY AFTER RETURNING FROM our month in North America, we attended the founding meeting of the Guatemalan Justice and Peace Commission, along with three or four dozen priests, sisters, and laypeople, as well as a few Protestants. The Vatican itself had encouraged forming such commissions. The usual model was an advisory group serving the bishops' conference or the archbishop of the capital city. No such group had arisen in Guatemala, primarily due to the resistance of Cardinal Casariego. This commission was founded independent of the hierarchy.

This meeting in early June 1978, held at a Catholic girls' school, was intended to discuss the study document for the CELAM conference scheduled for later in Puebla, Mexico. Although this Guatemalan group had no official recognition from the hierarchy, it had good ties to CONFREGUA (Conferencia de Religiosos de Guatemala [Conference of Religious of Guatemala]), the umbrella organization for religious orders and congregations. Many of those attending were doing pastoral work in the countryside.

Before the meeting, a brief news item appeared in the Guatemalan press, stating that thirty-four people had been killed when they attacked an army garrison in the town of Panzos. The area was relatively remote, and reporters could not go there immediately, but another account began to emerge. A priest from the diocese of Coban came to our meeting and reported what had actually happened. The root of the problem was the encroachment of local landowners on traditional lands of the Kekchi-speaking indigenous people. Employees of an agricultural company owned by a large nickel mine in the area had fired from a pickup and wounded seven local people. Summoned by the mayor, several hundred people came to the town on the morning of May 29. The local army detachment and heavily armed landholders were on hand. At some point conflict broke out, and the army and landholders began shooting. The people fled and over a hundred were killed, some drowning in the river. The Justice and Peace Commission issued a statement condemning the attack, and a government official retorted, calling it a "phantom group."

Because international news sources had no permanent presence in Guatemala, initially there was no alternative to the army's version. Labor and other organizations took out paid ads in the newspapers to denounce the massacre. We put together an account, beginning with the official version and then summarizing what was known through other sources, and mailed it to Philadelphia for distribution. When the journalist Marlise Simmons arrived from Mexico, we helped her make connections. Her report came out in *Newsweek*, including a photo that she had obtained of bodies in the back of a truck.

CNUS (the National Labor Unity Committee) organized a protest march. As foreigners we could not take part, but I went to observe and saw a Justice and Peace delegation a half-block long, including sisters in habit, within a far larger demonstration. The group's participation seemed to associate it with the Guatemalan left and made even sympathetic bishops reluctant to be associated with it. A Spanish nun working in the same diocese as Panzos was expelled from the country, accused of unspecified political involvement.

* * *

These events took place shortly before the transfer of the presidency from General Kjell Laugerud to General Romeo Lucas Garcia in mid-1978. On the day before the transfer, Fr. Hermogenes Lopez, the pastor in a town not far from Guatemala City, was machine-gunned to death. He had supported the people in their struggle with a company seeking to divert their water supply, and had protested forced recruitment of youth into the army. He had even placed a small paid ad in the press praising Laugerud and naively asking him to disband the army, saying that was what the people wanted. Lopez wasn't part of our circle, and we hadn't even heard of him before he was killed.

At a protest downtown in Parque Central I ran into Wiwi; his formal name was Mario Mujia, but everyone called him Wiwi. Angie had known him when he was a youth participating in the Maryknoll program in Huehuetenango. When I first met him in 1976, at a course at a Catholic retreat house, he criticized the legions of anthropologists who had done research in Guatemala, written their dissertations, received their degrees, and published their books and articles, but had not given anything back to Guatemala, analogous to those who exploit natural resources. That was a little unfair to anthropologists (many of whom have been involved with human rights for Guatemala for decades), but it attested to Wiwi's concern. He was a friendly, outgoing guy, liked by everyone. When I mentioned my interest in buying a guitar, he arranged to have a craftsman in Huehuetenango make me one by hand, which I then used in my fruitless nighttime attempts to teach myself classical guitar.

Wiwi was now a labor organizer for the CNT in Huehuetenango. In late 1977 he had announced plans for and organized a march of miners in Ixtahuacan protesting dangerous working conditions and low wages. They started near the Mexican border and headed toward Guatemala City. Despite threats from the government, over nine days the miners were given hospitality along the route, particularly from parishes.

As they entered the capital they were joined by workers who had been fired from the Pantaleon sugar mill on the coastal plain. An estimated one hundred thousand people gave them a tumultuous welcome.

When we met at the protest for the killing of Lopez, Wiwi and I agreed we should get together soon. Less than a month later, however, he was gunned down in his office in Huehuetenango. He didn't die immediately, and after receiving emergency treatment he was helicoptered to the Herrera Llerandi Hospital in Guatemala City, where surgeons tried to save his life. Angie and I were on the patio of the hospital on Sunday morning with others, including his wife, when we were told that he had died. At a memorial Mass for Wiwi, I realized that many of the liturgies we were attending now were funerals like this one.

A small press report at the time indicated that one of the guerrilla groups, the FAR (Revolutionary Armed Forces), had made a statement praising Wiwi as a fallen member of their organization. If true—something we could not verify—the statement suggested that the networks of revolutionary organizations extended to people working publicly and nonviolently. However, even membership in armed organizations did not justify assassination; if individuals had committed a crime, they should be arrested and charged, not gunned down anonymously.

Wiwi's murder, shortly after the Panzos massacre and the killing of Hermogenes Lopez, embodied what was happening all around us: people being killed with impunity for standing up for justice or attempting to organize.

* * *

In August 1978 a Sandinista unit boldly entered the National Palace and took two thousand people hostage, including most of the Nicaraguan Congress. Somoza was forced to meet their demands: release of political prisoners, publication of a statement, payment of a ransom, and safe passage out of Nicaragua. In September, in response to a call from the Sandinistas, uprisings took place in five or six major towns. Young people joined in the struggle, and National Guard garrisons were surrounded. It took weeks of aerial bombing and artillery shelling to put down the uprisings. Three thousand or more people were killed, and the Sandinista ranks swelled with many new recruits.

In Esteli three or four weeks later, I saw some of the destruction and heard about the uprising. Church groups, including religious orders and CEPAD, were delivering humanitarian aid and drawing up plans and stockpiling for future needs.

Somoza now looked vulnerable as he faced opposition not only from the Sandinistas but from political parties, business organizations, labor unions, and thousands of ordinary people willing to take a stand. After disregarding the anti-Somoza opposition, the Carter administration was now attempting to mediate a solution, including having Somoza resign, holding elections, and maintaining the National Guard—without allowing the Sandinistas to be part of any new government. One opposition coalition, the FAO (Broad Opposition Front), was seeking such a solution, while others believed that the National Guard had to be disbanded, some economic and political reforms had to be made, and the Sandinistas could not be totally excluded. Otherwise the result would be "Somocismo without Somoza."

In view of the unfolding crisis, the AFSC proposed sending to Nicaragua a fact-finding delegation of religious leaders. Dick Erstad put the delegation together in consultation with Catholic and Protestant church organizations, and I went to lay the groundwork in Nicaragua and Costa Rica. In San Jose I went to see Carlos Tunnerman, a university professor and member of the Twelve, then in exile, who was part of a network of people planning for a post-Somoza government. While waiting outside his office I found myself overwhelmed by the thought that in the midst of repressive dictatorships throughout Latin America, here was a group that sincerely intended to bring about changes in this tiny Central American country in order to enable the poor to have a more decent life. Around this same time, a well-known reporter, leaving our house in Guatemala on his way to Nicaragua, broke his objectivity to remark, "We just might win this one."

The delegation gathered at a hotel near the New Orleans airport: Wallace Collett, a Quaker businessman and head of the AFSC board; William Howard, president of the National Council of Churches; Dwain Epps, representing the World Council of Churches; Alan McCoy, a Franciscan and president of the umbrella organization representing Catholic male religious orders; Michael Czerny, S.J., of the Interchurch Committee on Human Rights in Latin America in Toronto; and I. We flew to Managua where we were met by a Jesuit, Fr. Roberto Zarruk, and taken to the Colegio Centroamericano, a Jesuit high school where we stayed.

With Zarruk as coordinator, we then spent two full days of meetings with Archbishop Obando, the militant women's organization AMPRONAC, academic analysts, and political party and business leaders. One afternoon we went to Masaya to see damage from the September uprising. We met with the Twelve, who had taken refuge in the home of the Mexican ambassador. At the U.S. embassy we met with Ambassador Mauricio Solaun and William Bowdler, an ambassador-at-large who was then pursuing mediation efforts. Bowdler came across as arrogant and condescending in his dismissal of the Twelve; he said they were a mixed group—some ideologically driven and some operating out of guilt or in an effort to stay in contact with their leftist children. He believed the FAO was far more representative of the Nicaraguan people. That impression was augmented by Bowdler's height and the sense of superiority that U.S. diplomats in Latin America generally exuded. In Costa Rica we met with representatives of the Sandinistas, who were still divided into three factions (called "tendencies"), in three successive one-hour sessions. Two of them used pseudonyms and seemed militaristic. Giaconda Belli, a well-known poet, made the best impression.

Upon their return, delegation members held a briefing for members of the press in Washington and had a meeting with State Department staffers, but not with higher-level figures, as the delegation had hoped. The fact that a long-standing U.S. ally was threatened by a serious insurrection movement had finally put Nicaragua and Central America on the media's radar.

In early December 1978 Angie and I drove to Panama with our daughters, stopping along the way. Leaving Managua in mid-afternoon we reached the border and managed to get through the Nicaraguan side but found that the Costa Rican border station was closed, and thus we had to spend the night between the border stations. We had an ice chest with food and beverages, and flashlights, but we were camping out alongside a waist-high loading platform. Nearby were two Nicaraguan men with a truck whose business was bringing in shoes from Costa Rica to sell. They had been at this location recently during a firefight between Sandinistas and National Guard troops. We left the keys in the ignition, ready to leave in a hurry. Rather than pass through there again with children, from Panama we had Juana take Catherine and Maggie back by plane while we drove back to Guatemala as quickly as we could.

* * *

Like most of our Guatemalan colleagues, we had been following preparations for the CELAM meeting at Puebla, particularly through discussions on the preparatory document that had been distributed and was being reviewed throughout Latin America. The political context had changed a great deal since 1968: most of South America was controlled by repressive military governments and Central America was in crisis, exemplified by the murder of priests and the growing anti-Somoza movement. In Mexico, Enrique Dussel published a book of country-by-country reports, titled *Década de Sangre y Esperanza* (Decade of blood and hope), and the Brazilian pastoralist Jose Marins compiled a book with a thousand pages of documents by Latin America bishops' conferences since Medellin, with critiques of what was happening in their countries. Theologians and pastoral specialists published articles analyzing the study document.

In March 1978, two documents written by an anonymous group of theologians were released in Venezuela with a view to contributing to the pre-Puebla discussion. One was written in first-person plural: "A Good News: The Church Is Born from the Latin American People." The "we" in this document seemed to be those working with the church. The authors recognized that they had been slow to enter into solidarity with the "world of the poor," and that they themselves had been evangelized by the poor, rather than vice versa. They denounced unjust structures and stated that human rights should be those of the poor. A second document, "Church Born of the People, Reflections and Problems," was more analytical and took popular organizing as its starting point, covering topics such as the participation of Christians in mass organizations, parties, and labor unions. Considerable discussion was devoted to ideologies, Marxism in particular. A central issue was "Latin American socialist projects" and Christian involvement in them, including working alongside Marxists. The assumption was that these developments were leading to something new in both church and society, a church from below arising out of struggles for a more just world that seemed almost ready to bear fruit. The authors were identified only as a group of theologians in Caracas, and their anonymity suggested that they feared reprisals from church, state, or both.

Although I was working for a Quaker peace organization, it seemed appropriate to go to Puebla to be present for an event that could have implications not simply for the Catholic Church but for society at large. Walking around the city shortly after I arrived by bus, I spotted Ernesto Cardenal, Rosemary Ruether, and Harvey Cox, and also ran into Pepe Gomez and Jose Comblin. Hundreds of journalists were accredited there to cover the event. A good number of representatives of European development and funding agencies were present, along with academics and activists.

John Paul II had been in office only two or three months. The crowds of Mexicans who lined the roads to see him challenged the myth of a secular state promoted by the PRI (Institutional Revolutionary Party) for a half century. Enrique Dussel was enthusiastic about the prospects for the church with the first non-Italian pope in several centuries.

Bishop Lopez Trujillo, who had held the reins at CELAM for over six years, was controlling the process. None of the well-known liberation theologians would be allowed into the seminary where the deliberations took place, as they had been at Medellin, even if invited by a bishop. An exception was Argentine Lucio Gera, whose "theology of the people" was somewhat divergent. It looked as though Lopez Trujillo might be able to achieve his goal of having liberation theology condemned, but his position was weakened when a Mexican newspaper quoted him gloating over his control of the process and speaking about the meeting as a kind of boxing match.

The excluded theologians and social scientists, including Gustavo Gutierrez, Enrique Dussel, Hugo Assmann, and Xabier Gorostiaga, met daily at a separate location and were in contact with sympathetic bishops inside and thus able to send in memos and drafts. As an outsider I initially felt that I had no function, but I was eventually doing some translation for nongovernmental organizations (NGOs) there. When I mentioned to Gorostiaga the difficulty of working in a climate of escalating violence, he told me to write it down and gave me the title: "Pastoral Ministry of Violence." The few pages I wrote then circulated among the friendly bishops.

Many activities took place outside the meeting itself. "Women for Dialogue" had sessions on the situation of women in church and society, but to little effect on the final document, which pays virtually no attention to women. Gary MacEoin organized press briefings that were far more informative than the official press conferences of bishops. When a journalist asked Comblin what the greatest problem facing the church in Latin America was, he replied, "Antibiotics." The journalist was puzzled, wondering whether he had misunderstood Comblin's heavily accented Spanish. He then received the explanation: "They keep bishops alive too long."

Efforts were made to have the assembled bishops make statements of support for Archbishop Romero in El Salvador and Archbishop Obando in Nicaragua. When that was blocked, around forty bishops signed statements of support. One afternoon I joined a group of writers and representatives of aid organizations on a bus tour of the churches of Puebla; for years I had been told that there were 365, one for every day of the year. While not literally true, it was an indication of the historic weight of Catholicism in Puebla and part of the reason the site was chosen.

The deliberations were a tug-of-war between the conservative faction, including the Vatican—which would have liked to see a condemnation of liberation theology and a general affirmation of church authority—and the progressive faction led by Brazilian bishops, who wanted a denunciation of violence and injustice, and an affirmation of the validity of the church opting to be with the poor. Between these factions was a large group of bishops concerned primarily with the unity of the church or the hierarchy. The result was a book-length document that reflected the contending positions. The expression "preferential option from the poor" comes from Puebla, although the idea of an "option for the poor" had been around for a decade. A passage about *rostros* (faces) initially drafted by the theologians "outside the walls" turned into an eloquent series of paragraphs on the faces of children, indigenous people, small farmers, workers, and so forth. Violations of human rights and the ideology of national security were condemned. Support was given for encouraging the poor to become organized to press for their rights, a point on which Gorostiaga had been insisting.

On the afternoon the meeting closed, I walked across the central plaza with Hugo Assmann, who was generally pleased with the result. Admitting that the document itself was mixed, he said, "We could collect a lot of good statements and make a little red book." He then chuckled, "Of course they could put together a little black book." As had been the case with Medellin, Puebla was cited selectively.

* * *

In El Salvador four more priests were killed between November 1978 and August 1979: Neto Barrera, Octavio Ortiz, Rafael Palacios, and Alirio Macias, all of them Salvadoran. I hadn't known any of them but had heard of them in Sunday sermons by Archbishop Romero. The circumstances of their killing varied. The government claimed that Barrera had been killed in a shootout. Romero was skeptical at first, but then guerrillas claimed him as one of their own. Ortiz was killed along with four youths at a retreat center; thirty-three others, including two nuns, were arrested. In 1978, church human rights analysts documented 147 people killed by security forces and 23 disappeared; 1,063 had been arrested for political reasons. Some, including

Romero, now spoke of a "persecution" of the church. The numbers were still low in comparison with what happened later, but the pattern of militancy by popular organizations and violent repression against them by official forces was intensifying. The murder of priests was intended to send a message.

In early May, Romero was in Rome for a canonization and sought to meet with John Paul II, then in office for less than a year. Romero had trouble getting an appointment with the pope, and when they met, the pope pointed to his own experience as a bishop under a hostile government, showed little understanding or sympathy, and stressed the importance of the bishops being united. In effect he was siding with the other bishops who opposed Romero and supported the government, the military, and the elites.

In late 1978, the Organization of American States (OAS) Human Rights Commission issued a report on specific violations by the Salvadoran government, citing a number of cases of named individuals. Torture of various kinds, particularly placing the victim laying on bedsprings and applying electric shock, was widespread.

* * *

In October 1978, bus fares in Guatemala City were raised from five to ten cents, so poor families that rode the bus multiple times in a day found their transportation expenses doubled. Protesters blocked traffic, high school students made barricades out of school desks, and protests spread. Unidentified gunmen fired into crowds. By the end of the week, thirty were dead, three hundred wounded, and eight hundred arrested; business losses were estimated at $4 million. The bus-fare hike was canceled for the moment. The ESA (Secret Anti-Communist Army) then published a death list with thirty-eight names, primarily labor leaders, but including university professors and journalists. Two days later Oliverio Castañeda, a high school activist whose name was on the list, was gunned down immediately after addressing a crowd in downtown Guatemala City.

We were in Mexico during the bus-fare disturbances, but we could sense the rising level of repressive violence in Guatemala when we returned. Several Coca-Cola labor union leaders were murdered. Continuing the systematic documentation of political violence case by case, I found that the number of victims rose from 374 victims in the first six months of 1978 to 505 in the second half of the year, coinciding with the change of the presidency from Kjell Laugerud to Romeo Lucas Garcia.

Two broad-daylight murders of moderate political leaders illustrated the escalation of violence. In January 1979 Alberto Fuentes Mohr was shot to death by assassins on motorcycles on a major avenue in the city. In March, Manuel Colom Argueta was gunned down while driving to teach at the university. Both men were in the process of founding social democratic parties and had been active in politics from a moderate left standpoint for years. (By chance I was introduced to the wife of Fuentes Mohr a day or two before his assassination.) General David Cancinos, who was reputed to have directed both murders personally, was himself assassinated by the EGP.

* * *

In January 1979 Somoza rejected all offers of mediation, and the Carter administration cut off aid, withdrew the Peace Corps and even military attachés, and for the moment took a hands-off position. In late May the Sandinistas launched what they called the "final offensive." Because the National Guard was still larger and had better weaponry, the Sandinistas sought to inspire mass popular uprisings. People in several major towns rose up and surrounded the Guard in their garrisons. The United States again dispatched William Bowdler, and various forces within Nicaragua considered transition formulas. Somoza had apparently indicated a willingness to resign.

We followed events from Guatemala on the radio and in newspapers. Somoza and his closest associates flew out on July 17, entrusting the presidency to Vice President Francisco Urcuyo for a short transition while negotiations were under way. When Urcuyo surprisingly stated his intention to remain in office, other governments objected, and the National Guard panicked: officers hijacked planes to flee the country, and troops shed their uniforms. The Sandinistas and their supporters were unopposed and entered Managua on July 19, in what looked like a reprise of Havana 1959.

A month later Angie and I drove to Nicaragua, along with my friend since seminary days, John McFadden, who wanted to work in the planned literacy campaign. Our jeep had been in the shop for almost a month, and we had to go to mechanics in El Salvador and Nicaragua (wires were smoking when we stopped to get gas).

In Managua we stayed with Gerri and Edgard—who was now vice minister of social welfare. In fact, many of the people whom our delegation had seen the previous November were now ministers or in other government positions. Our purpose was to get an overall sense of what was happening and to identify a project or projects that the AFSC might support with the money it was raising.

We got our first impression at the Nicaraguan border, which was no longer staffed by surly customs officers but by *muchachos* (kids), Sandinistas in ragtag uniforms. In fact, we saw muchachos with weapons guarding installations, running government offices, directing traffic, and taking joyrides in former Somoza regime vehicles. At night we heard occasional celebratory gunfire. We sensed great relief over the end of the war as well as enthusiasm for prospects under the new regime. A restaurant waitress replied to a customer harassing her, "Do you think we're still in the Somoza period?"

Along with the enthusiasm was a growing recognition of the problems ahead. Somoza and his cronies had looted whatever they could. Auditors were finding that his businesses, from rice fields to gold mines to factories, had evaded taxes. We went to see Jose Antonio Sanjines, who had been a Jesuit and had helped in the parish in Chorrillo after I left. He later joined the Sandinistas, left the Jesuits, and become a combatant. Now he was in charge of municipal street cleaning in Managua. He told us that they had only a couple of broken-down vehicles and scarcely any brooms. Somoza had taken the government's cash reserves.

The country was still in an emergency phase. Food aid was being sent from outside, primarily from the United States. A U.S. embassy staff person was annoyed that the Sandinistas didn't express more gratitude to the United States, but publicly thanked countries sending smaller amounts of aid. Some Sandinistas didn't like the fact that the aid was being channeled through the Red Cross rather than the government, but this was a practical matter: the Red Cross had a large staff and logistical experience. Directing the aid was Fr. Zarruk, the Jesuit who had coordinated our delegation the previous November and was in charge of the Red Cross. The hub of activity was the Hotel Internacional, the solitary downtown building that had survived the 1972 earthquake. The lobby was constantly full of Sandinistas in fatigues, civilian technocrats, journalists, and representatives of donor organizations.

We went to see Fernando Cardenal one night at the Jesuit house in the Bosques de Altamira neighborhood. He had gone from being constantly on the run during the final days of the war to now being responsible for planning the literacy campaign that was due to begin in a few months. John had done his dissertation on Paulo Freire and had worked in popular education with the United Farm Workers. Fernando agreed to take him into the team, trusting in our judgment and reputation with his fellow Jesuits. John and his wife and daughters soon came to Nicaragua, and he worked in the revolution for almost two years.

In choosing a project for the AFSC to support, we took guidance from CONFER, the umbrella organization of religious congregations that was serving as a kind of clearinghouse for outside aid. The project proposed was a training and clothing production program in Esteli. As a site they were given the Club Social, which had been a gathering place for local Somoza elites but was now abandoned. At this time, homes and businesses of Somoza and his allies who had fled the country were being appropriated by the revolution and put to other uses.

Somoza had not only plundered the country but increased its debt enormously in his last years. Xabier Gorostiaga, who was working in the planning ministry, said that Somoza had used those debts to keep himself in power, not for the development of the country; they ought to be cancelled, or at least there ought to be a five-year moratorium. However, it was unlikely that the banks would allow the precedent of even a bankrupt country to renege on its debts.

The first task was simply to reactivate the economy. Somoza and his cronies had owned a quarter or more of the economy when they fled, and thus the new government instantly held many farms, factories, and businesses. To run them, the Sandinistas needed technocrats and experienced managers. They could draw on people who had remained in Nicaragua, often their siblings, cousins, uncles, or in-laws. For example, a Nicaraguan economist whom we had known in Guatemala when he was working for a

Central American agency was now working in the Ministry of Agriculture. Although the private sector suspected that the Sandinistas intended to nationalize their businesses, that didn't seem likely in the short run.

The Sandinistas had entered Managua more or less as the Cuban revolutionaries had marched into Havana twenty years before. Until the very last days, that outcome had not been not foreordained; U.S. diplomats, political parties, business groups, and Archbishop Obando had engaged in negotiations seeking to ensure that the Sandinistas did not have a total victory. The confusion following Somoza's departure had nullified those efforts.

The Sandinistas did not intend to simply copy the Cuban model, and Castro himself had urged them not to do so. To avoid centralization in a single "Fidel," the Sandinistas named as their maximum authority nine *comandantes*, three from each of the tendencies. To run the executive they set up a five-person junta, including Violeta Chamorro, the widow of Pedro Joaquin Chamorro, and businessman Alfonso Robelo.

Business and political party representatives argued that elections should be held and Nicaragua should establish a normal democracy. The Sandinistas and their supporters believed that they had a mandate to carry out a social revolution—to organize the country around meeting the needs of the poor majority. However, they did not intend to set up a monolithic structure like that of Cuba or the USSR. They expressed this intention around three points (which Gorostiaga articulated): political pluralism (political parties besides the Sandinistas), a mixed economy (room for the private sector, provided it accepted the new "rules of the game"), and an independent foreign policy (relations with Europe, North America, the Soviet bloc, and the nonaligned countries). The overall idea was to move away from the Somoza system while not making the same mistakes as Cuba.

The Nicaraguan Catholic bishops were largely identified with anti-Sandinista forces: Archbishop Obando had been actively negotiating a transition without Sandinista participation in the days before Somoza fled, and the bishops soon made a strong statement that warned of dangers. Ernesto Cardenal upbraided them for not expressing gratitude and joy for the end of the war.

Jesuits and other religious order people were involved in relief work. Ernesto Cardenal was minister of culture, his brother Fernando was head of the literacy campaign, Gorostiaga was going to work in the planning ministry, and Miguel D'Escoto of Maryknoll was foreign minister (his father had been a diplomat). CEPAD, the evangelical umbrella organization, was careful not to endorse the Sandinistas politically or theologically, but was working in relief and reconstruction, channeling outside aid, and helping evangelical pastors adapt to the new situation.

* * *

"We're next," a taxi driver in San Salvador told me soon after the Sandinista victory. He wasn't necessarily expressing revolutionary aspirations but simply commenting on what seemed obvious. In fact the Salvadoran popular movements in some ways seemed stronger and more deeply rooted than the anti-Somoza movement.

In mid-October 1979 a group of army officers staged a coup, sent President Romero abroad, and set up a government with a five-man junta: two of the three civilians were from the Jesuit university, and ostensibly a reform faction now had control of the military. The initial pronouncements spoke of making needed changes and even of revolution. The logic was clear: if we don't do this we'll be facing a Sandinista-style revolution. The popular organizations denounced it as a gringo maneuver; Archbishop Romero insisted that the new government should be given a chance.

About a week after the coup I was in San Salvador with two AFSC staff people from Philadelphia, Jack Malinowski and Linda Ralph. On our first morning we joined a small number of journalists, including photojournalist Susan Meiselas, to follow a funeral for two FAPU militants killed two days previously. The procession began in Soyapango, a municipality in greater San Salvador. We were near the front of the march behind the pickup truck carrying the two caskets. We had not gone far when suddenly people around us dove to the ground—and we awkwardly followed suit. When I looked up I saw young people with various guns, which had been concealed in irregular cardboard boxes. It turned out to be a false alarm, and we continued on our way. I now realized that the line between popular movements like FAPU and the guerrilla organizations was blurrier than I had thought.

We reached the main highway and turned toward San Salvador. Not long afterward we heard gunfire from behind, as people around us were running forward, away from the shooting. We also ran and stopped when the sound of shooting seemed distant enough. We waited there an hour or two, and when the shooting had stopped we went partway back to see what had happened. The procession had been ambushed by uniformed troops, and those with guns had fired back. I saw two men dead; the toll I heard later was five. About a hundred people had been killed by government forces during the first week of what was supposedly a reform government.

In the early evening we went to the Jesuit high school, the Externado San Jose. The occasion was a meeting convoked by the church human rights organization Socurro Jurídico (Legal Assistance) of family members of those who had been disappeared under the previous government. Led by a young lawyer, Roberto Cuellar, the group had been keeping a record of disappearances and other human rights violations, similar to what the Mothers of the Disappeared had done in Argentina in the same period. The names of all 176 were read, and people shouted "Presente." Archbishop Romero then addressed the group, saying that those who had disappeared were either imprisoned or dead; the new government should investigate and let the families know their fates. If it couldn't or was unwilling to do so, that would be proof that it couldn't fulfill its promises. He spoke softly, but he was obviously presenting a serious challenge.

From the Externado we went to the presidential palace, where the new government ministers were being sworn into office. They included Ruben Zamora, who had returned from exile in England and was now minister of the presidency, and Jorge Villacorta, one of my informants at the UCA who was now vice minister of agriculture. They were unaware of the attack that we had witnessed in the morning.

* * *

Since our arrival, but particularly since 1977, we had observed the emergence in El Salvador and Guatemala of increasingly militant popular or mass organizations of peasants, labor, university students, and slum dwellers organized into larger coalitions, such as the BPR (Revolutionary People's Bloc) and FAPU (United People's Action Front) in El Salvador. They typically carried out large street demonstrations, but they also occupied churches and embassies. They were militant, and their rhetoric was Marxist. Governments and those representing business and landholders called them "subversives" and "terrorists." Archbishop Romero defended their legitimacy and devoted the last of his four pastoral letters to the topic of "The Church and the Popular Organizations."

I had wondered about their relationship to guerrilla organizations. For example, the BPR seemed to be aligned with the FPL in El Salvador, and the CUC (Committee for Peasant Unity) seemed to have affinity with the EGP in Guatemala. The alliances were murky. Perhaps some leaders in the mass organization were also in the armed organization, but most members would have no idea of that connection, and in any case their actions were nonviolent. People around us did not speak of any linkages, presumably because that could be used to justify violence against civilians engaging in legitimate activity. However, in late 1979 when Corinne Johnson from the Philadelphia AFSC office and I went to see Ignacio Ellacuria, he linked the popular organizations and the guerrillas. When I expressed surprise, he impatiently dismissed my objection, implying that the connections were obvious—that is, that the popular groups were the political wing of the armed organizations.

After the Sandinistas took power and it became clear that many people in Nicaragua had been working with them, including priests, sisters, and active laypeople, we wondered whether some people around us in Guatemala might have similar ties. The armed organizations seemed to have different categories of relationships: "members" were those fully under the discipline of the organization; "collaborators" were those who might knowingly carry out a task, such as transporting people, packages, or money; and "sympathizers" were those doing work for social change, but not necessarily consciously working with the armed organizations. In 1979 and 1980, some people we knew moved into membership and went underground.

Leaders of popular organizations assumed that they were working toward a qualitatively different kind of society, and that getting there would necessitate taking state power. Based on their observation of Allende's overthrow in Chile, for example, they did not believe that electoral democracy could bring about such a change.

In early January 1980 I suspected that at least one person on the Justice and Peace Commission steering committee might be a member of a guerrilla organization, and I went to his office to express my concern. I could hardly say, "I think suspect you're a member of the EGP." I spoke in hypothetical terms, using roundabout subjunctives and conditionals, along the lines of "It would be very unfortunate if anyone in Justice and Peace were secretly a member of a revolutionary organization and might thereby jeopardize the many people who would be unaware of such ties." I wasn't questioning his personal option, but the problem of consequences for others. He stroked his beard thoughtfully and said he agreed. I was powerless to change his mind, but I felt the need had to register my concern.

* * *

In August 1979 we hosted a meeting of all AFSC Latin America programs, from Chile, Mexico, Puerto Rico, and Colombia, and several people from the Philadelphia office, including Lou Schneider, the head of the AFSC board. The AFSC has a culture of consultation and dialogue, and of learning from experience, related to its Quaker roots. We were in charge of the logistics and organizing the meeting, which was held at a Catholic retreat house in Panajachel, along the shore of Lake Atitlan. Each program presented its history and the issues it was seeking to address: under the Pinochet dictatorship with indigenous people in Temuco and others in Santiago; in a variety of programs in Mexico; and in Puerto Rico, particularly around the island of Vieques. We presented an overview of Central America—a month after the fall of Somoza and with El Salvador heading toward insurrection and repression increasing in Guatemala. At some point in the proceedings it was noted that we were generally operating in a context of violence, with people and organizations that, while they typically engaged in nonviolent actions like protest marches, were not committed to nonviolence in principle, and might even have ties to armed groups. A key concern was that our commitment to people and groups should be complete, especially in Guatemala and El Salvador with the popular organizations. A subgroup drafted a statement articulating our concerns, which the group then refined and approved.

This "Panajachel Statement" became somewhat controversial within the AFSC and Quaker circles, and some pacifists raised objections to it. What drew considerable attention was the statement that we must remain committed to the people with whom we are working, even those who feel impelled to take up violence. That seemed to reflect a less-than-complete adherence to nonviolence. Some AFSC staff countered that if commitment to nonviolence meant never having anything to do with organizations that practice violence, we could never have anything to do with governments—especially that of the United States. For over a year AFSC committees debated the statement and sought to refine it. The discussion highlighted real questions of what it means to be nonviolent in situations of escalating violence.

* * *

In the midst of intensifying conditions, we continued to have a family life as our daughters went from being infants and toddlers to developing their own personalities. We had no TV and by U.S. standards not many toys—some dishes and pots, and a sandbox. Catherine could ride her tricycle in the patio area and on the flat roof. In 1979, with the help of Guillermo Corado, I built a bunk bed for Maggie and Catherine in their own small room. They accompanied us to meetings and were around when we had meetings in our house. When Catherine saw Isabel de Corado arranging chairs in her house, she asked whether a meeting was going to take place.

From the start we took them in our jeep to various parts of Guatemala and outside the country, from Mexico City to Panama. Sometimes it was in order to renew visas. Thus we spent some days in Copan, Honduras, the site of major Mayan ruins. In San Cristobal, Chiapas, where it was chilly, Catherine and Maggie liked a breakfast of café con leche served in tall glasses along with a sweet roll. We spent time at the beach in Panama, El Salvador, and Honduras.

For a while in 1977 when she was two, Catherine spent the mornings at a day care in Zone 7, with working-class Guatemalan children in a program overseen by an American sister. In early 1979 we enrolled her in a daycare center walking distance from our house called "La Casita de los Pollitos" (House of the little chicks), for which she had to be outfitted with a uniform and take a lunchbox. The daycare was directly across the street from the headquarters of the *judiciales*—plainclothes police who carried out many of the abductions. Newspaper accounts often mentioned that the perpetrators were seen driving away in a vehicle with license plates from Texas or another U.S. state. One day on the way to school we walked past a man in the street changing the license plate on one of their parked vehicles.

In Guatemala we occasionally went to the zoo, or to a park near us that had trampolines and modest rides. We also went to a few performances of children's theater in downtown Guatemala City, such as *Peter Pan*. They especially liked ice cream at a place called Pops.

As Catherine grew older and the level of violence increased, she inevitably became aware of some events. I once saw her explaining to Maggie the cover of *Newsweek International*, which showed the bodies in El Salvador after troops attacked one of the mass organizations occupying a church or an embassy. She told Maggie, "That's a campesino." Sometime in early 1980 the doorbell rang and she went to the corner balcony to see who it was. "It's Julia," she shouted back in, "and she has a wig." It was Julia Esquivel, the middle-aged editor of *Diálogo*, who was trying—not very successfully—to disguise herself as the surveillance and repression were increasing.

In April 1980, when Angie returned to the house after giving birth to Elizabeth, she was immediately plunged back into meetings and other activities, including hosting people on the run.

* * *

After our visit in the very early days of the Sandinista revolution, I returned to Nicaragua three or four times during the first year, before open organized opposition to the Sandinistas began. I viewed events mainly through my contacts with Gerri and Edgard, and other people who were working within the revolution, notably the Jesuits and other church people, but also Mary de Zuniga, who was working in health care, and Ivan Garcia, an economist in the ministry of agriculture.

A key question was the degree to which the Sandinistas would try to reproduce the institutions in Cuba and to what extent they would be independent, particularly in maintaining a private sector, and when—or whether—elections would be held. Ostensibly the country was governed by a five-person junta, including two Sandinistas. Government ministries and agencies were being staffed by employees who had remained, but also by Sandinistas and others who had no previous management experience. During those early months they put considerable energy into building and expanding mass organizations of workers, peasants, women, and youth.

The U.S. embassy under the Carter administration and Ambassador Lawrence Pezzullo, who had arrived during Somoza's waning days, wanted to work with the Sandinistas, but there were points of friction, for example, the Sandinista anthem spoke of the United States as the "enemy of humanity." As soon became clear, CIA operatives were already working with exiled Somoza National Guard troops to form what became the *contras* (*contrarrevolucionarios* [counterrevolutionaries]).

Two Jesuit social scientists, Ricardo Falla and Arturo Grigsby, carried out a number of quick surveys of communities, doing each in a few days, similar to what Ricardo had done in 1976 in Comalapa. They did this especially in communities on the Atlantic side, where people had not been deeply involved in the anti-Somoza struggle. Their aim was to present to the Sandinista leadership the situation of the communities and people's actual beliefs and desires—not what they should be thinking and desiring according to Marxist theory. It was a well-intentioned effort to get the Sandinista leadership to pay attention to real Nicaraguans, but the effect seems not to have been that great, judging by the opposition to the Sandinistas that developed in those regions, especially the traditionally isolated Atlantic coast, where the Sandinistas were seen as one more group from outside ("Spaniards").

Nicaragua seemed to present a new opportunity to the Catholic Church; many Christians and especially priests and religious had been involved in the anti-Somoza struggle, and now they were working within the revolution even in high government positions. Many others were working in parishes or in newly formed nonprofit organizations in relief and reconstruction. Think tanks such as CAV (Antonio Valdivieso Center) and IHCA (Central American Historical Institute), housed in the Jesuit university, were organizing conferences and elaborating rationales for Christian participation in the revolution. In November 1979 the Nicaraguan bishops produced a very positive document on the church and the revolution.

At around this time, I observed a political party meeting held outdoors at an upper-class home in Managua. The speaker was Alfonso Robelo, the businessman who had been a leader in the civilian opposition to Somoza and was now on the junta. He was asked questions and heard complaints about the Sandinistas and gamely tried to defend what they were doing. I noticed that the questions got more applause than his answers.

In March 1980, universities and other schools were closed, and tens of thousands of young people went to the countryside to engage in a mass effort at teaching people to read and write. About three hundred religious—sisters and priests—were involved in the literacy crusade, typically at mid-level management positions. The primary aim was to raise the literacy level so that poor people, especially in the countryside, could participate as citizens in the new Nicaragua that was being built. From the Sandinista viewpoint it was a political action, and the material used for teaching was ideological, a term that Sandinistas themselves used, since they saw ideological struggle as important at this crucial phase. The campaign was organized along military lines, for example, the volunteers were called *brigadistas* (brigade members). I observed a group of enthusiastic young people in the countryside at midday as a *torta* (potatoes, eggs, peppers, onions) was being prepared by Spanish volunteers in a very large pan. On another occasion I attended a dimly lit literacy session at night. At the end of the campaign the Sandinistas claimed that illiteracy had been reduced from 52 percent to 13 percent. Equally significant, tens of thousands of young people had gone to the countryside and come face-to-face with the poverty of campesinos.

In April 1980 Alfonso Robelo and Violeta de Chamorro resigned from the junta, thereby signifying the end of the honeymoon between the Sandinistas and business and other political parties. Less than a month later the Catholic hierarchy issued a document criticizing the Sandinistas and demanding that the priests in the government leave their posts.

* * *

In January 1980 a delegation of indigenous people from Quiche came to Guatemala City in order to draw attention to the many abductions of their leaders by the army. The delegation went to various Guatemalan government organizations and to international groups. I saw them make a presentation to a session of the Justice and Peace Commission at a Catholic school in Guatemala City.

A smaller group came to our house on a Saturday morning for an interview. I had begun to record and transcribe interviews of labor leaders and others, intending to compile an oral history, and I thought of adding them. Two men and two women arrived, and I recorded the conversation, which was largely about land disputes, although I couldn't really follow without knowledge of the local situation. The oldest among them, who did most of the talking, was Vicente Menchu (the father of Rigoberta Menchu, whom I only met a couple years later).

The following Thursday, January 31, a group comprising primarily indigenous people, but including labor and student activists, went to the Spanish embassy in a middle-class neighborhood in Guatemala City, entered by force, and took the ambassador and the staff hostage. The ambassador, Maximo Cajal, was familiar with Quiche and thought that the situation could be resolved without violence. When the police surrounded the building, Cajal pointed out to them that the embassy was Spanish territory and that its diplomatic immunity should be respected. Two Guatemalans who happened to be there, a former foreign minister and former vice president, echoed the ambassador. However, the police went up to the roof, began smashing windows, and attacked. A fire broke out, and when firefighters arrived, the police would not allow them to put out the blaze. A total of thirty-nine people burned to death, mainly the occupiers, but also staff people and the two Guatemalan dignitaries. In the melee before the attack, Ambassador Cajal managed to escape; after being held by the police for ten minutes he left with a U.S. embassy staff person.

After 10 PM, the government presented its version on TV: the occupiers were armed Marxist guerrillas, and they had started the fire. As it happened, one of the occupiers who had been buried underneath other bodies had survived. He was taken to the hospital, but the next day armed men entered and took him away by force; his body was dumped near the downtown campus of the national university, where students were gathering for a protest march.

At the time of the attack I was holed up in the apartment of friends, working on the report on political violence during 1979. Angie helped Stephen Kinzer, a stringer for the *Boston Globe* who happened to be in town, prepare an account, the only person from the international press to report on the event immediately and accurately. Meanwhile we gathered information from the newspapers and other sources and mailed an account of the facts to Philadelphia, with some press clippings. Spain broke relations with Guatemala, and the ambassador, who was under U.S. protection until he could fly out of the country, insisted that the problem could have been resolved without violence.

Despite the fact that several embassy staff members and the two foreign government ministers had died, many of the elites seemed to accept the government justification. "It was a terrible thing, but it had to be done," said someone at an upper-class social gathering, as a Guatemalan journalist who was present told me.

I went to observe the protest march of students and other militant organizations. As they processed through downtown they carried red carnations and chanted, "The color of blood is never forgotten." Just before the march, two student leaders were gunned down in full public view, obviously as a kind of message.

The Spanish embassy massacre, as it came to be called, was a watershed event in Guatemala—a point of no return. A revolutionary government had been in power in Nicaragua for a half year, and people sensed that something similar was under way in El Salvador and possibly Guatemala. Catholic religious orders whose provinces stretched across countries were especially aware of the chain of events in the different countries and how they influenced one another.

* * *

In El Salvador, despite the intentions of reformists in the government, the level of violence kept rising, as documented by church-related human rights organizations: in December 1979, more than three hundred people died in political violence. At the end of the year, the junta was disbanded and many of the reformists resigned, but the Christian Democrats as a party remained and formed a new junta including Jose Napoleon Duarte.

On January 22, 1980, the popular organizations, which had been ideologically and tactically divided, held a combined march with an estimated 140,000 people, said to be the largest in the country's history. When the marchers reached downtown they were ambushed by snipers from rooftops; 21 were killed and dozens wounded. Those who took refuge in a church and the university were surrounded by troops, but they were able to leave through the intervention of the Red Cross and others.

Roberto D'Aubuisson, a young retired major, presented on TV a list of people he called "traitors," including Ruben Zamora's brother Mario, who was mayor of San Salvador. A couple days later Mario was gunned down in his own home. In early March, I happened to encounter Ruben and his wife, Maria Esther, at the airport. Ruben was still in the cabinet and was flying to a neighboring country on government business. I offered to accompany him as we went through customs into the boarding area, as a bit of security against abduction there in the airport. My presence couldn't have prevented anything, but it suggests how anything seemed possible, including abduction of a civilian cabinet minister by death squads operating with impunity under a government that claimed to be reformist.

In February Archbishop Romero wrote a letter to President Carter urging that military aid to El Salvador be cut off, in view of the government forces' human rights violations. I was at the UCA in San Salvador in early March when it was announced that the country was under a state of siege in order to begin a land reform, as the United States had urged. Troops moved into the countryside, ostensibly to confiscate the 250 largest estates in the country. However, the land reform was used as a justification for militarizing the countryside, thereby generating the first flows of refugees, some of whom came to live on the seminary grounds.

As we had done in Nicaragua in late 1978 we decided to organize a religious-based delegation to El Salvador. I went to San Salvador to set up appointments with church and human rights groups. In the evening I explained the delegation to Archbishop Romero at the Divina Providencia Hospital where he lived.

A new U.S. ambassador, Robert White, had recently arrived. While serving as ambassador to Paraguay, White had earned the ire of the Stroessner regime by his criticism of human rights violations. While I was at the chancery office, White's wife was also there inquiring about those who had taken refuge at the church complex.

The delegation gathered in Guatemala on Saturday, March 22, and we flew together to El Salvador: Bill Wipfler of the human rights office of the National Council of Churches; Tom Quigley, Latin American affairs staff at the U.S. Conference of Catholic Bishops; Alan McCoy, the Franciscan head of the umbrella religious organization of male religious congregations; Betty Nute, representing Quakers worldwide; and Ron Young of the AFSC Peace Education Division.

The next day at the 10 AM Sunday Mass, Romero began his sermon by mentioning the members of the delegation who were present in the sanctuary. He also noted that his words were being transmitted once again by radio after repair of the transmission equipment that a bomb had destroyed. He had been preaching a Lenten series of related sermons in a kind of catechesis. This time he wove his comments around the theme of liberation. As was his custom he mentioned some incidents of violence from the previous week. Toward the end he said he wanted to address soldiers. He told them that they should not obey orders to kill innocent civilians, their own brothers and sisters. "No law is above God's law: Thou shalt not kill!" He begged, pleaded, and ordered them: "Stop the repression!" The sermon was halted by a long applause. Ambassador White and his wife attended the Mass and went to communion.

After Mass we attended a press conference with Romero held in the church. Journalists from the international media regularly covered the Sunday Mass because of the weight of what Romero said. After the press conference, the delegation had a closed-door session with Romero and a few key advisers, including Monsignor Ricardo Urioste and Jesuit theologians Ignacio Ellacuria and Jon Sobrino. As we were walking across a large yard to where the meeting was to be held, I said to Sobrino that the ending of the sermon was very strong: by telling soldiers to disobey orders—immoral orders, to be sure—he was challenging military discipline. Sobrino said that the group who met regularly with Romero on Saturdays to help prepare the sermons had collectively decided that the archbishop should include the statement. At our meeting Romero repeated his public plea for cessation of U.S. military aid until the armed forces halted their extreme repression.

That afternoon the delegation went to see refugees, some on the seminary grounds. Walking back to the hotel by myself that night in the nearly empty streets, I thought, *This might be it. They might kill him.* That foreboding was reinforced the next day when I picked up a mimeographed flyer in the streets comparing Romero to the Ayatollah Khomeini, the leader of the Iranian revolution.

Around dusk on Monday, March 24, as we were being briefed at the Human Rights Commission, a call came through that Romero had been shot. We went to the seminary/chancery office where priests and other close aides had gathered and heard that he had been shot while saying Mass in the chapel where he lived. We then went to the hospital and were there when he was pronounced dead. We were all stunned, but we also knew that he had long been receiving death threats, and with several hundred people a month now being murdered by official troops and right-wing death squads, the assassination was not unexpected.

Wipfler was in contact with the embassy, and we went to see Ambassador White there at around 9 PM. White had decided to spend the night at the embassy with some staff and his wife because they were anticipating a mass uprising, similar to what had happened in Nicaragua after the murder of Pedro Joaquin Chamorro. In our meeting White defended the U.S. position that the government was attempting to carry out reforms and had to be supported against both the armed left and the right. Toward the end of the conversation, Ron Young said that the delegation would be advocating for cutting off military aid, as Romero had urged. White indicated that he stood by the Carter administration's policy, but that the delegation should do what it saw fit. I interpreted that to mean that as ambassador he was defending the policy, but that part of him sympathized with our position.

Nothing happened that night, probably because the guerrillas and the mass organizations viewed the killing itself as a provocation and hence a trap. Given the national crisis, I expected our appointment with Vice President Jose Morales Ehrlich the following morning to be cancelled, but it wasn't. The fact that the Salvadoran vice president was able to talk with a visiting American delegation at such a moment was a telling indication of how little civilians mattered in the government. In an eerily calm tone, he maintained the position that this reform government had to be supported. Toward the end he said that, a hundred thousand people could be killed in a civil war, "and the worst part about it is that the right would win."

Later that day Wipfler and Quigley drafted a statement by the delegation. They returned to the United States and held a well-attended press conference at the National Press Club in Washington, stressing the gravity of the crisis in El Salvador and the problem of U.S. support for the Salvadoran military.

Back in Guatemala I made plans to return for Romero's public funeral on Sunday. Since many international journalists would be present, I assumed that it would be safe to attend, so I invited Bob and Elly Ledogar to come along. Bob worked for UNICEF, and Elly was an editor for the English edition of *Inforpress*, the Central American news service. Arriving Saturday afternoon we went to the cathedral and joined the line stretching far out into the street to view Romero in his casket. Sunday morning we walked from the hotel along Avenida Colon toward downtown.

The altar for the funeral Mass was on the steps of the cathedral facing out into the open plaza. The visiting bishops and clergy came in together in procession from the street. Notably absent were the other Salvadoran bishops, except for Rivera Damas. They had held a smaller, closed ceremony earlier and presumably regarded this public event as political. Around the beginning of the Mass we saw the BPR, the largest of the mass organizations, arrive in formation and process silently around the outside of the plaza and then take its place. We were halfway back in the plaza and off to the left side, facing the cathedral. The homily by the papal representative, Cardinal Corripio of Mexico City, struck me as rather ecclesiastical and safe, with no reference to Romero's courageous ministry.

Suddenly we heard an explosion, then saw a swirl of smoke from behind the National Palace. The crowd didn't react immediately, but after another blast from the same area, people began to move off to the right as what sounded like gunfire began. Some young people lifted their arms in the air and shouted, "Don't run!" These must have been members of the popular organizations who, on the basis of their previous experience, were prepared for something like this and were trying to prevent panic. The only way out of the plaza was off to the right from the cathedral. Because we were at the far end and tens of thousands had to evacuate, it took what seemed like a very long time for us to be able to flee.

Once on that street we hurried several blocks away from the cathedral area, and at that point participants began to disperse in different directions. We began a long trek of several miles, bypassing the downtown area, in order to return to our hotel. Those who had taken refuge in the cathedral, including the celebrants, endured a long wait in terror until they were allowed to leave, hands over their heads and under the eyes of the military.

Journalists reported that the Mass was attacked, and film footage shows people in the plaza shooting back; at least some members of the popular organizations carried weapons for self-defense. Government sources claimed that all official troops had been in their barracks, but during our walk back to the hotel we saw khaki troops seated in the back of a truck being driven somewhere.

Romero's murder and the attack on the funeral ended the possibility of public expression of opposition. The country was sliding slowly but inexorably toward civil war, which observers expected to be brutal and short, because of the lack of forest or jungle in which guerrillas could be concealed.

In July I met up with Bishop Ken Mahler, whom I had known as a Lutheran minister in Panama and who now had a position as a Central America overseer for the Evangelical Lutheran Church, and Phil Anderson, a young Lutheran minister. When we went for a morning appointment at the Jesuit high school, the Externado San Jose, we found it surrounded by National Guard troops who were carrying out a search operation, as was becoming common. Young people in one of the Protestant churches with whom we met were clearly involved in one of the mass organizations and were anticipating an insurrection.

On that same trip I went to Honduras to check reports of Salvadorans fleeing their country. That meant driving west from San Pedro Sula and eventually parking the vehicle and hiking the last several miles down to La Virtud, a small village on the river dividing the two countries, where people had indeed fled as refugees.

* * *

In Guatemala the level of confrontation and crisis continued, accelerated by events in Nicaragua and El Salvador. In February a strike organized by the CUC on one farm in the agroexport belt on the south coast quickly spread. Peasants blocked traffic and commandeered vehicles. It was toward the end of the harvest season, and their labor was needed. Some individuals were killed, but the government raised the minimum wage to \$3.20 per day, although not all plantations paid it.

In Comalapa, Nehemias Cumes, the Vivienda Popular director, was abducted at night as he stepped out of his car. A day or so later the vehicle was found abandoned and bloodstained, and he never reappeared. A few weeks later Anastasio Sotz, a younger Vivienda leader, was abducted as he was boarding a bus by army troops checking IDs against a list. Other Vivienda leaders went into hiding. I went to see the political officer at the U.S. embassy to express our concern over Comalapa and the general condition of the country, as I had done from time to time in the previous two years.

The traditional May 1 march of labor and other militant groups was large and seemed to take place without incident. Unlike El Salvador, where official forces attacked marches, in Guatemala they were generally allowed to proceed. In the aftermath, however, Conrado de la Cruz, a Filipino priest working on the south coast, was abducted along with a parishioner. Two weeks later, Walter Vordeckers, a Belgian priest from the same region and religious congregation, was gunned down in broad daylight. We knew both Conrado and Walter through the Justice and Peace network and our visits to the coast.

In May I was invited to a dinner with the U.S. ambassador, Frank Ortiz, along with about thirty other people, all Guatemalans concerned about what was happening in the country and the region. The occasion was a tour through the region by James Cheek, the assistant undersecretary of state for inter-American affairs. He spoke of developments in the region and particularly in El Salvador, where he accepted the government's assertion that the left had attempted to exploit Romero's funeral. The common thread of the meeting was concern over the increasing political violence in Guatemala. Notable among those speaking were the Christian Democrat politician Rene DeLeon Schlotter and the outspoken journalist Irma Flaquer. I didn't speak because I was a foreigner and

I didn't want to draw attention to myself. Some hoped that Guatemala might veer in a reformist direction, perhaps by the time of the 1982 election.

The next day I delivered to the embassy a memo addressed to Cheek that I had written in response to his presentation. I emphasized the problem of viewing events from the limited kinds of contacts that embassy officials had, and not being in contact with those who were suffering the brunt of the violence. I also questioned his view of Romero's funeral. I was then invited to the embassy, where I met with Ambassador Ortiz. He began by reciting the various posts where he had served; the subtext was that I was in no position to question the embassy's understanding of Guatemala.

At around this time a Spanish-speaking woman phoned the house where we and activists, especially CUC organizers, had a joint daycare center, first asking for Nehemias's brother and then asking for "Phil Berryman." The center was obviously under surveillance. We removed Catherine and Maggie, as did some others. Some of our acquaintances were leaving the country while others were going underground.

Months before I had been interviewed by a radio journalist preparing a story on Guatemala for National Public Radio (NPR). My understanding was that I was speaking primarily for background and that my voice would not be recognizable if it were used. In June a visitor brought a cassette of the program, and I was surprised at how much my voice was used, particularly to counter government and elite claims. A friend told Angie that the political officer at the U.S. embassy had said, "Phil Berryman's voice is clear." I went to see him, and he said that he was not aware of any specific threat to us and that the embassy would let us know if they did learn anything. Being a foreigner normally offered some protection, he said, but with three foreign priests recently murdered, that was no longer true. It also seemed likely that Guatemalan organizations like the Amigos del País, which were paying public relations firms in the United States to defend Guatemala's image, would get copies of the tape. One of the people on the NPR program was Tom Mooney, the head of the U.S.-Guatemala Chamber of Commerce, whom I had gone to see. In conversation he seemed reasonable, but he had recently been in the United States saying that communism should be handled in Guatemala the way it had been handled in Argentina, Chile, and Uruguay.

We saw further signs that we were under surveillance. A young man who appeared to be a plainclothes policeman was coming on average one day a week and standing on our corner for several hours. When Angie came out of the office of CONFREGUA, the umbrella network of religious congregations, she found a man taking her license plate number. In early July a man rang the doorbell, claiming to be delivering flowers that had been ordered. Angie refused to come down, but the man hung around for an hour with a woman companion.

In view of the increasing violence around us and the signs of surveillance, we bought tickets to the United States in case we needed to leave in a hurry, and we planned to go to the United States in late July regardless, for at least a month to allow things to subside.

In the second half of July, I began a trip through El Salvador, Nicaragua, and Honduras. Angie called me in Nicaragua to tell me that we needed to leave and that I should not return but fly from Honduras directly to Miami. Meanwhile she took our daughters to stay with Bob and Elly Ledogar. Expecting police or military searches, she and our friends gathered boxes of our papers, which they burned at a house in the hills some miles away or had buried.

When they arrived at the airport, Angie was told that the Aviateca flight had been cancelled, so she switched to a Pan Am flight for later that day. She went to the parking lot with our daughters and as she got into the jeep, she saw two men get into a vehicle and follow her. She made evasive twists and turns in the parking lot, and they kept following her. Bob Ledogar saw what was happening and pulled in behind her with his car, which had diplomatic plates since he worked with a UN agency. They went to our house, parked the jeep, and all went to the Ledogars. That afternoon he took her and the children to the diplomatic entrance to the airport. That night we were reunited at the Miami airport.

Just what had brought us under surveillance and into danger was not exactly clear, and was probably a combination of several things. Like others we assumed our phones might be tapped. People had phoned us saying that they represented Amnesty International or asking for details on the killing of a priest. Our church connections, particularly Justice and Peace and the Zone 5 Jesuits, would be known. Our ongoing work in Comalapa and with people involved in CUC were other indications, as was the fact that for four years we had helped visiting journalists. It was also possible that they had traced the source of the reports on political violence in Guatemala that I had been preparing, along with other confidential reports. Likewise, our frequent trips to other countries, especially El Salvador and Nicaragua, could be given a "subversive" or "terrorist" interpretation by army or police intelligence.

11

Solidarity and Resistance

HAVING ARRIVED IN PHILADELPHIA with only our suitcases, we lived with our AFSC supervisor, Dick Erstad, and his wife, Gladys Fenichel, for some weeks in Powelton Village, a neighborhood of Victorian houses in West Philadelphia. With the AFSC we agreed to work for another year to complete our existing contract, doing public education on Central America in the United States. Our status remained that of volunteers.

After some weeks we moved into a third-floor apartment a few blocks away. We bought a used Datsun station wagon and obtained some furniture. We didn't put much attention into décor: one of the beds was a mattress on the floor, and the bookshelves were cinderblock and planks. We enrolled Catherine in kindergarten in Powel School, and Maggie and Lizzy in daycare at Friends Center, the Quaker-owned building where the AFSC headquarters was located.

The AFSC arranged for two people to fly to Guatemala to empty our apartment and dispose of its contents, much of it AFSC property. They hired a Guatemalan lawyer, who arranged for the sale of some items, including the car, and had some shipped back to us.

We weren't thinking much of our living arrangements or our longer-term future; our attention was on the plight of Central Americans. We hoped that the violence could be ended soon, and we assumed we might return. We had no idea that we and many others would be combating U.S. policy for a decade.

* * *

That fall we learned that Kai Yutah Clouds had been abducted and murdered. We first met him in Philadelphia in 1978 at the AFSC office. He had been born in Germany (original name, Veit Nikolaus Stoscheck) and was brought to the United States as a child. When we met him in Philadelphia in 1978 he had taken on that Native American name and identity and wore hippie-style clothes. In Guatemala he made his way to San Jose Poaquil, an indigenous municipality adjoining Comalapa. He received his mail through our post office box, so when he came to Guatemala City he stopped by to pick it up. On those occasions I sometimes filled him in on current events. He struck me as unworldly and little cognizant of events outside Poaquil. Kai was a close associate with a shaman, and one day at their invitation we witnessed an initiation ceremony of an infant (a kind of indigenous baptism) in Poaquil, which took place over two hours or so in a large, dark room.

On October 10, 1980, Kai was kidnapped at gunpoint by five men, and his body was found a day later in Antigua, showing signs of torture, including a crushed skull. Because he had friends and acquaintances in the Native American movement in the United States and Canada, his case was presented to the Inter-American Commission for Human Rights, but no action was taken in Guatemala.

Repression was intensifying in Guatemala and El Salvador, to the point that it became impossible to publicly do work that the military would regard as in opposition. Activists changed houses or closed offices; some went into exile, usually to Mexico or Nicaragua; others went underground or joined the guerrillas. It seemed similar to the situation in Nicaragua two or three years earlier when the Somoza regime intensified its repression and was met with popular uprisings.

Not long after our return, a visitor to Philadelphia hand-delivered to us a letter from a guerrilla organization in Guatemala, recognizing our work and inviting us to collaborate with the organization. No name was mentioned, but we assumed that it was the EGP. Collaboration wasn't the same thing as membership, which would have meant being under the discipline of a revolutionary movement. In replying, we respectfully declined, pointing out that we worked for a pacifist organization.

* * *

Some weeks after returning we went to an AFSC Peace Education Division Roundup in Estes Park, Colorado, a town in the Rockies where staff from around the country came together— some, like us, with children—primarily to share with other people organizing on issues such as nuclear disarmament, the Middle East, military spending, and now Central America. Angie and I had been working with the AFSC for four years, but connection with the organization came through the Philadelphia office and from the speaking tour in 1978. We had been outside the United States for most of the previous decade and a half and tended to see things from our Latin American vantage point. As we undertook our new role of interpreting Central America, we had to understand our own country anew.

Over the decades, the AFSC had passed through various phases in response to changes in the country. Entering the 1980s, many staffers were veterans in the civil rights and antiwar movements. Most local organizers had been running programs for some years, and they were well connected in the local community, with religious congregations, universities and schools, and local media. They were part of the broader peace movement—a loose network of activists and organizations, some secular, some religious—radicalized since the sixties.

At the time, AFSC work was divided into three divisions. We were still under the International Division, which ran programs overseas. The Peace Education Division was engaged in issues like nuclear weapons and apartheid in South Africa, while the Community Relations Division dealt with domestic matters like racial discrimination, prison reform, and fair housing. At the local level, individual offices and organizers typically worked in more than one area.

While still in Guatemala I had been taking photos aimed at a slide show. In the fall of 1980 we put together *Central America: Roots of the Crisis*, with an accompanying analysis of the same title. It linked the common themes of land tenure, inequality, repressive governments, and historic interventions by the United States. Dozens of copies were distributed, and AFSC groups and others used them in the early months of what would become the Central America movement.

On a fall Saturday in 1980 I took a bus to upstate New York for several days of speaking on Central America, coordinated by Ed Griffin, who had previously served in Chile as a young Lutheran minister. My first stop was a Catholic parish in a small town, where I stayed with the pastor and spoke at the Mass the next day. I then went to Syracuse where I spoke to audiences that included classes at Cornell, a Native American organization, and the Syracuse Peace Council, an organization dating back to the 1930s. Later that fall I spent a week between Nashville, Tennessee, and Greenville, North Carolina. On these trips I also spoke on local TV and radio stations, was interviewed by local newspapers, and gave briefings to newspaper editors. These were the first of many speaking tours and engagements that the AFSC office coordinated. Topics were typically the situation in a particular country, an overview of Central America, or the role of the church.

* * *

At the time of our forced return from Guatemala, the 1980 electoral campaign was well under way. Not having been in the country for a presidential election since the 1964 Goldwater-Johnson campaign, I tended to see U.S. politics from the outside. I was appalled that Ronald Reagan, whom I associated with corny movies and hosting *Death Valley Days* on TV, was now a candidate. In many ways he foreshadowed Donald Trump: an old man who ignored details and uttered platitudes with a broad populist message. A campaign slogan was, "Let's Make America Great Again." One major difference was that he had long been active in the Republican Party and had served two terms as governor of my home state of California.

Seeking reelection, Jimmy Carter had to contend with several adverse circumstances: slow economic growth with inflation ("stagflation"); the 1979 Iranian revolution, including the ongoing hostage crisis at the U.S. embassy; a new gas crisis triggered by higher petroleum prices; and a general feeling of discouragement among Americans, following Watergate and defeat in Vietnam (although no one in public life for decades would dare call it a defeat). Ronald Reagan promised to reverse all of that, particularly by projecting strength in foreign affairs.

Central America was little mentioned in the campaign, but right-wing authors in conservative policy magazines were emphasizing ties between Managua, Havana, and Moscow and the geopolitical threat in the U.S. "backyard." An hour-long documentary appeared in prime time on a major TV network representing Managua as a pulsating red circle. A group calling itself the Santa Fe Committee issued a policy overview with these same themes: four of its five authors soon entered the Reagan administration. Right-wing groups in Guatemala and El Salvador were hoping for more support from a Reagan presidency.

Reagan won by a decisive popular majority and an electoral landslide. Salvadoran right-wingers fired guns into the air on election night. It was both astonishing and dismaying that a man who knew little of the world outside the United States and the film industry would have the power to wage nuclear war and was surrounded by people who intended to make Central America a test case for reasserting U.S. power.

* * *

In view of the deepening crisis, the AFSC decided to organize a tour of Central America and the Caribbean for a group of about fifteen national and regional staff and committee members. The aim was to give participants firsthand impressions as a basis for an anticipated long struggle, particularly in view of the historic pattern of U.S. intervention in Latin America. I went to Central America (except for Guatemala) to arrange for lodging and transportation, and to select local coordinators and people to meet.

To be less conspicuous, the delegation split during visits to Guatemala and El Salvador and reunited in Nicaragua. In Guatemala the group was taken to a safe house to which labor union activists, church people, and others could come discreetly. In El Salvador, when we met with Ambassador White, who had now been in the country for around nine months, around a thousand people a month were being killed, mainly by official troops, as he himself recognized. Nevertheless, he stood by U.S. policy of supporting the Christian Democrat junta headed by Jose Napoleon Duarte, because it was the only alternative to a government of the right or the left. Patricia Sellars, a young African American attorney, said, "Let me get this straight, Mr. Ambassador: are you saying that it is U.S. policy to support the military, which you yourself admit is out of control?" White had no reply.

At the Externado San Jose, the Jesuit high school, we met with two or three representatives of the FDR (Democratic Revolutionary Front), the political wing of the opposition, including its president, Enrique Alvarez Cordoba. He was a widely respected U.S.-educated dairy farmer who, starting in the 1960s, had urged agrarian reform and had served in the ministry of agriculture in three administrations, including the one that came in after the 1979 coup. Now he was part of the civilian opposition and thus regarded by the Salvadoran elites as a traitor. Given the danger to his life, I was surprised that he was willing to meet with us. We had seen each other in Philadelphia a few months earlier when he was on a speaking tour with the FDR, and one evening he and his group had gone to a Phillies game. When I reminded him of the occasion, he smiled and said he had had good instincts (the Phillies had gone on to win the World Series).

The whole group came together in Nicaragua, where we traveled around by minibus to appointments with government officials, the business opposition, and church figures, including a prison where an American nun was involved in an experimental program to make it more humane. Nicaragua stood in sharp relief to the situation in Guatemala and El Salvador, where official forces and closely linked death squads were killing activists and ordinary civilians with impunity. It seemed to be a grand experiment in building a new kind of society, one that was akin to Cuba twenty years earlier but was consciously seeking to do things differently—to have a mixed economy, political pluralism (opposition parties and media), and a nonaligned foreign policy. Internal polarization was only beginning, and the drastic shift in relations with the United States under Reagan was still a couple months away.

While we were at a former Somoza farm now in the hands of the state, I asked a Sandinista official about the situation of the workers, thinking of pay levels and working conditions. He claimed that their situation was entirely different. When I pressed for details, he said that the "relations of production" had been transformed. I was struck by how Marxist jargon could replace paying attention to reality.

In Costa Rica, local analysts expressed concern that conflicts in the region would spill over elsewhere in the region, particularly under U.S. pressure, and that their country's commitment to peace and democracy would be jeopardized. We then took an overnight trip to Monteverde, a place in the mountains where American Quaker conscientious objectors had settled in the 1950s and started a dairy operation in the cloud forest. Monteverde was an early example of preservation of nature in Costa Rica, which later became a pioneer in ecotourism.

After Panama I returned to the United States, while the rest of the group continued to the Caribbean. It was a whirlwind three weeks of visits and interviews from morning to night. Our hosts in each country understandably wanted to utilize our time to the maximum, but in hindsight we realized we had tried to pack too much in, to the point where participants became exhausted from continuous travel and nonstop encounters in Spanish with interpreters.

This was an early instance of what became a key element in the Central America movement, tours that allowed visitors to experience conditions in Central America firsthand, and to meet ordinary people and experts working in different areas. These encounters could be life-changing: John Ruthrauf, the executive director of a foundation in Philadelphia, was very much taken by the courage of Guatemalan labor leaders and others. Throughout the 1980s he organized eight tours to Central America, particularly among the progressive donor committee and on behalf of Guatemalan labor unions. Hundreds, perhaps thousands, of Americans made major life commitments as a result of their exposure to Central Americans and their struggles.

* * *

In late November, days after the delegation returned, Enrique Alvarez Cordoba and five other FDR leaders were abducted from the Jesuit high school where we had met with them, tortured, brutally beaten, shot, and dumped on a roadside.

Then on December 2, three U.S. sisters, Maura Clarke, Ita Ford, and Dorothy Kazel, and a laywoman, Jean Donovan, who were driving from the airport were stopped on the road by National Guard troops. Two were raped, and all were murdered and then hastily buried. Local peasants reported on the incident, and the bodies were soon discovered and disinterred. Kazel and Donovan had had supper with Ambassador White and his wife and stayed at their residence the night of December 1, before they had gone to the airport to pick up Clarke and Ford. At the sight of the bodies, White vowed, "This time they won't get away with it."

Angie knew Maura Clarke and Ita Ford through Maryknoll, and we both knew many other Maryknoll sisters of the same generation living and working in Central America. As shocking as the rape and murder of nuns were, it was part of the larger pattern of violence against civilians surrounding our friends and colleagues.

The long-awaited civil war formally began in January 1981, as the FMLN (Farabundi Marti National Liberation Front) launched what it hoped would be a general uprising that would present the Reagan administration with a fait accompli when it took office. Fighting took place over two or three weeks, but no mass insurrection occurred, perhaps because Salvadorans had been thoroughly intimidated. The FMLN withdrew to areas near the Honduran border.

On a Sunday in early January 1981 we went to Washington for a demonstration in solidarity with El Salvador, triggered by the murder of the churchwomen. Temperatures were below freezing; at one point I was stamping my feet on the snowy ground for circulation. Our three daughters, ages five, three, and eight months, were bundled up but were understandably not happy. Among the fifteen hundred protestors were a number of nuns and other church figures, particularly those who had been doing human rights work in Washington since the Chilean coup. Also present were peace activists and some long-standing critics of U.S. foreign policy.

This was the incipient Central America movement, driven by indignation over an administration that bankrolled those who would rape and murder nuns with impunity. We now faced a government whose Cold War–driven policy would inevitably aggravate conflicts in the region. "Stopping communism" in Central America seemed likely to entail sending U.S. combat troops. That might reactivate the U.S.

peace movement, said a Salvadoran activist, but Central Americans hoped we could prevent that from happening.

* * *

Rather than pressuring the Salvadoran government to solve the murders, Reagan administration officials maligned the churchwomen. Jeane Kirkpatrick, who had advised the Reagan campaign on Latin America and was now the U.S. ambassador to the United Nations, said that the women were activists supporting the guerrillas. Secretary of State Alexander Haig hypothesized that the women might have driven through a highway checkpoint.

The Reagan team expressly reversed the modest human rights emphasis of the Carter administration. Kirkpatrick had provided the rationale for this shift in a 1979 essay, "Dictatorships and Double Standards," in which she advocated supporting right-wing "authoritarian" regimes when threatened by left-wing movements whose likely outcome would be "totalitarian" regimes.

The administration sought to assure Congress that the Salvadoran government was making progress in terms of human rights. When Ambassador White refused to go along, especially on the case of the churchwomen, Secretary of State Haig had him recalled to Washington where he was given a desk job—the equivalent of a firing for a career diplomat of ambassadorial rank. He resigned and went on to devote the remainder of his life to advocating for human rights, starting with Central America.

The Central America movement prompted a clash of worldviews: the administration and its supporters appealed to the Cold War and geopolitical considerations, portraying the Salvadoran revolutionaries as part of an axis from Managua to Havana to Moscow. Critics of the policy questioned how the United States was supporting a government and a military that could rape and murder nuns. What few questioned was the assumed right of the United States to intervene in other countries. Among the critics were the U.S. Catholic bishops and Catholic religious orders, the mainline Protestant churches, and academics, especially social scientists who specialized in Latin America, as well as long-standing peace movements like the AFSC, and many peace activists.

Conservatives geared up to support the administration's policies, notably the Institute for Religion and Democracy, a Washington think tank founded in 1981, which in pamphlets and books claimed that church leadership, especially among mainline Protestants, had been taken over by doctrinaire leftists and Marxists, contrary to the will of the people in the pews.

* * *

Barely a month after Reagan's inauguration, the State Department issued a white paper titled "Communist Interference in El Salvador." Most of the document was a chronology of alleged contacts between Salvadoran guerrilla leaders and Marxist governments and movements elsewhere. I was astonished at the lack of historical sense of how the situation arose; the uncritical assertion that El Salvador had a "reform government" beset by extremists of right and left; the attribution of the violence in El Salvador to the left, rather than to the official forces and right-wing death squads; and the claim that the Soviet Union was carrying out a "well-coordinated covert effort to bring about the overthrow of El Salvador's established government and to impose in its place a Communist regime with no popular support." I could barely contain my indignation when the paper lamented the "brutal and still unexplained murders . . . of four American churchwomen"—using them as justification for sending money and weapons to the armed forces that killed them.

On March 11, 1981, I presented testimony to the House Subcommittee on Western Hemisphere Affairs on behalf of the AFSC and the Friends Committee on National Legislation. My written testimony was a critique of the white paper. Without questioning the authenticity of its observations on captured documents, I said that it lacked a historical sense of the roots of the crisis, and that few Salvadorans believed the fiction of a reform government beset by extremes of right and left. Disregarding Amnesty International and the Catholic Church in El Salvador, the white paper attributed human rights reports to an international communist campaign to discredit the government.

If the United States was determined to make a test case of El Salvador and if Salvadoran troops were unable to defeat the FMLN, then further U.S. involvement seemed likely, I said, despite declarations that the administration had no intention of making El Salvador "another Vietnam." I insisted that U.S. policy needed to take into account the history of El Salvador, the experience of its poor majority, the viewpoints of other countries, and the legitimacy of the FDR as a political force—and to be open to negotiation.

In itself my written testimony simply added to the thousands of columns in the *Congressional Record*. Before the committee I made a short oral statement, and when asked by Representative Michael Barnes (D-MA), I likened U.S. policy to a truck heading toward a cliff; the policy had to be turned around.

A few months later Jonathon Kwitny of the *Wall Street Journal* interviewed the author of the white paper, Jon Glanzman, at length, and found that the report was full of mistakes, guessing, and projections. The State Department nevertheless maintained that its conclusions were correct, and the administration sounded the same themes for years.

* * *

SOLIDARITY AND RESISTANCE

While on a speaking tour in Oklahoma and Kansas in early 1981 I met Stan Rother, a priest from Oklahoma City who had been in Guatemala since 1968, but whom I hadn't known during our time there. We met in Wichita at the home of Frankie Williams, who had done volunteer work at Stan's parish in Santiago Atitlan several times. Santiago is a well-known indigenous town on the shore of Lake Atitlan.

Stan was a diocesan priest in the Bill Woods mode, a farm boy with a practical bent, who had felt a call to go to Latin America. Angie had been with him in language school in the 1960s. He had gone on to learn Tzutuhil and then worked on translating the scriptures into that language and adapting the liturgy. He supported the radio school in Santiago but was not at all political. After guerrillas carried out an operation in the town, the army came in and occupied it. Parishioners began to disappear, including the head of the radio school, and Stan opted to withdraw temporarily to the United States. He attended one or another of my presentations, and our common experience of Guatemala gave us a bond.

He returned to his parish for Holy Week. In late July three men in ski masks entered the rectory, and when he resisted being abducted, they gunned him down. Rother was the tenth priest killed in Guatemala, starting with Bill Woods (three more would be killed by 1983). His funeral in Santiago drew a large congregation.

Amnesty International had published a report in January 1981 titled *A Government Program of Political Murder*, which estimated that three thousand people had been killed for political reasons from January to November 1980. A major finding was that rather than being the work of anonymous right-wing death squads, as often claimed, they were in fact coordinated by the army and police from an intelligence center in downtown Guatemala City. In April 1981, about fifteen organizations doing development work in the highlands had received death threats. These were all organizations seeking to be apolitical, like Rother and like World Neighbors, which had agricultural development projects in the department adjacent to Comalapa and were administered by our friends Paul and Mary McKay. Discreet inquiries indicated that the threats were serious. The army regarded even nonpolitical organizing among the indigenous as subversive.

All of this posed problems for the Reagan administration, which was seeking to renew military aid to the Guatemalan military. Frankie Williams gave congressional testimony about Rother and his work. The administration was limited to providing modest aid (e.g., fifty trucks), which was symbolically important to the Guatemalan military.

Investigative journalist Alan Nairn traced ties between Guatemalan right-wing groups and Reagan's inner circle. Michael Deaver was now Reagan's deputy chief of staff. His PR firm Deaver and Hannaford had done public relations work for Guatemala's image, financed by private Guatemalan right-wing groups. That personal connection helps explain persistent administration support for a regime that human rights organizations and anthropologists categorized as genocidal.

MEMENTO OF THE LIVING AND THE DEAD

* * *

Cesar Vera and his wife, Dora Miron, had been colleagues and friends, working with the project in Comalapa, he as an architect and she doing education and organizing with women. They were among the original organizers of CUC (Committee of Peasant Unity). Their son Javier was about the age of our middle daughter, Maggie. For some months we had shared an informal daycare arrangement with them and other activist couples, until we realized we were under surveillance.

In April 1981 Cesar's father and both of Dora's parents were abducted. Dora managed to flee with their children to Nicaragua and then Mexico, where she lived for many years. Although CUC was linked to the EGP, neither Cesar nor Dora was involved in armed activity, not to speak of their parents, who had little idea of what their children and in-laws were doing. Cesar was eventually abducted and disappeared in February 1982.

In June 1981 Guatemalan Jesuit Luis Pellecer was abducted off a street in Guatemala City. We were acquainted with him through the Zone 5 Jesuit community. I had last seen him when we ran into each other on the street in downtown Guatemala City and he informed me that several leaders of mass organizations in El Salvador had been captured. When nothing further was heard for many weeks, Pellecer was assumed to be disappeared. However, in late September he was brought out for a televised press conference at which he gave a long statement, first telling his own story as a Jesuit and then describing a vast left-wing network. He wove together the guerrilla organizations, the popular organizations, CONFREGUA (the umbrella organization of religious congregations), and a program in which students from a Catholic girls' school went out to the countryside. He repeatedly mentioned Marxist analysis, liberation theology, the option for the poor—and, at the center of it all, the Jesuits. He said he had repented of his involvement and arranged to have himself kidnapped.

Pellecer's statements had some elements of truth: church people had been crucial in starting CUC, and some young people had gone from church involvement to popular organizations and even joining the guerrillas. What was untrue was that all of this activity was connected and controlled by the guerrillas, the Jesuits, or anyone else. That assertion reflected the conspiratorial mind-set of army intelligence. His claim of a self-kidnapping stretched credulity. At several points, he repeated, "My name is Luis Eduardo Pellecer Faena. I am thirty-five years old . . . ," suggesting that he was reciting a prepared speech. Jesuits and outside experts concluded that his personality had been broken and remade by some combination of coercion, drugs, and psychological manipulation. Neither Jesuits nor journalists were allowed independent access to Pellecer. For a few months he made similar presentations to right-wing groups in Central America and then dropped out of sight. He is said to have married and worked in a series of government jobs, including in army security.

The Pellecer revelations came at a time when the army and police, aided by Argentine and Israeli intelligence experts, were succeeding in breaking various urban structures, such as safe houses, of the guerrilla organizations. The army then began to move through the indigenous highlands, region by region. Army intelligence classified communities according to whether they were sympathetic to the guerrillas, to the army, or in between, placing red, white, and pink pins on maps accordingly. They then had no compunction in slaughtering those whom they regarded as in opposition. By one count they carried out 440 mass killings in the early to mid-1980s. The aim was to separate the guerrillas from their civilian sympathizers. In 1982 the Guatemalan bishops estimated that a million people—one seventh of the population—had been forced from their homes.

We followed events through Guatemalan exiles whom we saw in Nicaragua, Mexico, or the United States, and through Guatemalan church and solidarity networks. Because there were fewer connections to U.S. policy, Guatemala had a relatively lower profile in the overall Central America solidarity movement.

* * *

In mid-1981 our term as volunteers in the International Division of the AFSC ended. Angie moved to the Peace Education Division, where she worked on Central American issues for the next several years. That meant representing the AFSC nationally in various coalitions and initiatives, and working with local AFSC staff people around the country. I began to work freelance, combining writing, translating, and occasional public speaking. We moved to a different house in the Powelton neighborhood in Philadelphia where we now had two floors and we began to furnish it with used items.

Powelton Village is located across the Schuylkill River from downtown Philadelphia and is part of University City, so named because of the presence of the University of Pennsylvania and Drexel University. It is filled with Victorian houses, built during the post–Civil War era as the city expanded. In the 1950s a group of Quakers made deliberate efforts to make Powelton a racially integrated neighborhood, and in the 1960s it was a center of antiwar activity, so much so that it came under FBI surveillance. One characteristic of the neighborhood is an attitude of tolerance, and hence gays and lesbians opted to live in the area. It also had significant numbers of architects and artists. Several of our AFSC colleagues also lived in Powelton.

Samuel Powel School had been founded in 1960 and had a cadre of dedicated teachers who worked together in a version of the open classroom, as well as parents concerned about their children's education. Our three daughters all attended Powel up to the fourth grade, and then transferred to another magnet-type school.

When Fr. John McNamee, who had baptized our daughter Catherine, was made pastor of St. Malachy's in North Philadelphia, we followed him there. The parish was founded by Irish immigrants in the mid-nineteenth century, who built a large church and a school in the style of the day. The ceiling is a massive painting of Jesus preaching the Sermon on the Mount; the Beatitudes are in Latin. In the twentieth century, the neighborhood became African American as whites moved out of North Philadelphia.

McNamee was a good liturgist and preached thoughtful sermons. When Dan Berrigan came to Philadelphia, he stayed with McNamee at St. Malachy's. McNamee's poetry, usually a reflection starting with an event in the parish, or perhaps in Ireland, was published in *Commonweal* and in collections. Two Catholic Worker houses were started near the parish, and the Catholic Peace Fellowship operated there. Many people like us found St. Malachy's to be a spiritual home in an archdiocese where a series of conservative prelates set the overall tone.

* * *

I felt impelled to tell the story of the church in Central America—"church," to me, still meant Roman Catholicism—the experience that we had been living. Presenting the story of church people might contribute to a better public understanding of what was happening and help counter the claim that these tiny countries were a security threat to the United States. Driving my project was a sense that the Reagan administration seemed headed toward deeper involvement in the region, in an Indochina-like effort to stop communism. I was uniquely positioned to write such a book because I had observed the unfolding of the conflicts in Nicaragua, El Salvador, and Guatemala and knew many of the actors. What I intended was a well-documented account, not a personal history.

With a fellowship from Maryknoll, in mid-1981 I traveled to the region to conduct interviews and gather materials and documentation. I couldn't go to Guatemala, and it didn't seem appropriate to be interviewing Salvadorans in the midst of a war, so I interviewed exiles in Nicaragua, Mexico, and the United States. I set up an office in the house of Dick and Gladys, two doors away, paying them a nominal monthly sum as I worked at an electric typewriter during the day. After doing rough drafts I went to the region again in early 1982 for further interviews and material gathering.

The largest portion of the book was a step-by-step account of the unfolding crisis of and Christian involvement in revolutionary struggles in Nicaragua, El Salvador, and Guatemala, and the early years of the Sandinista government. I also felt that I should distill issues in ethics and theology, drawing out some of the strands implicit or explicit in the previous narrative, such as the aims of the revolutionaries, the problem of violence (which was important to U.S. audiences, but scarcely discussed by theologians and others), the impact of division in society on the church, and theological themes emerging in Central America.

The manuscript, completed in mid-1982, was almost a thousand pages, which I paid to have retyped as a clean manuscript at a dollar a page; word processing programs were not yet in general use. After I delivered it to John Eagleson and Phil Sharper at Orbis Books, the lag between manuscript and published book seemed interminable, given my sense of urgency. *Religious Roots of Rebellion: Christians in Central American Revolutions*, published in spring 1984, helped activists and academics understand the experience of Central American Catholics, but it had no discernible impact on events.

* * *

While we were still in Guatemala I was able to attend the founding meeting in 1979 in Detroit of the National Network in Solidarity with the People of Nicaragua. In 1980 I was at the foundation of Committee in Solidarity with the People of El Salvador (CISPES) in Washington, DC (with a parallel meeting in Los Angeles); then I was in Washington at the foundation of the Network in Solidarity with the People of Guatemala (NISGUA) in 1981. Each had national offices and soon had local chapters across the country; individuals often participated in more than one network.

These three solidarity networks were just one part of an array of organizations and forces that arose to resist the Reagan administration's Central America policy: existing peace organizations, church bodies, and academics with research and expertise in Latin America. Small Marxist groups also gravitated to the movement, which ranged from nuns to Trotskyites.

In 1980 and 1981 the U.S. Catholic bishops and major Protestant denominations issued statements about Central America, supporting human rights, warning against direct U.S. military involvement, and questioning military aid to El Salvador and Guatemala. Thousands of sisters in dozens of religious communities across the country that had members serving in Latin America felt an affinity with the murdered churchwomen. Many sisters, priests, and pastors and some rabbis were active on the local level. For several years, the coordinator of the Nicaragua network was our friend David Funkhouser, an Episcopalian minister.

Most academics in fields like history and social sciences also opposed Reagan's Central America policy. Relatively few had done fieldwork in Central America— with the notable exception of anthropologists, many of whom had conducted ethnographic studies in Guatemala. However, many members of the Latin American Studies Association (LASA) had become radicalized in reaction to CIA interference in various countries, and especially efforts to undermine the elected Allende government in Chile, as well as subsequent support for murderous military dictatorships. LASA meetings, held every year and a half, became rallying points not only for academics but also for activists. At the 1982 LASA conference in Washington, Jaime Wheelock, the Nicaraguan minister of agriculture, received a standing ovation for several minutes. As the decade went on, a trickle and then a flood of academic books and articles appeared about individual countries and the region. Locally, academics were often activists taking part in coalitions, organizing teach-ins, and incorporating Central America into their courses.

Motivations for participating in the movement varied. Those in the solidarity networks sympathized with the Sandinista revolution and with the aims of the revolutionaries in El Salvador and Guatemala. They believed that Central America was spearheading a movement for a qualitatively different kind of society. Others were simply opposed to U.S. intervention in Central America out of principle or pragmatism. The U.S. Catholic bishops pointed out that they were expressing the wishes of their fellow bishops in Central America.

In order to approve appropriating military aid to El Salvador, Congress required that the State Department twice a year certify that the Salvadoran government was making progress toward constraining human rights violations. In fact, after 1981 the numbers of civilians murdered gradually declined. However, as Areyeh Neier of Americas Watch said in 1982, if a mass murderer kills only ten people in one year after killing twenty the year before, it shouldn't be called an improvement.

Being opposed to Reaganism as a whole, congressional Democrats were generally opposed to his Central America policy, not out of sympathy with the left but on pragmatic grounds and out of concern over the possibility of a Vietnam-like quagmire. Because of its grassroots nature, the Central America movement was able to impress on individual Democrats in Congress that this was an issue on which some constituents felt strongly. Human rights certification became a ritual: hearings were held, but Congress did not cut off military aid to El Salvador because Democrats would have been vulnerable to the accusation of being "soft on communism."

Journalists worked hard and often heroically in pursuing the truth about the events taking place. While in Guatemala we had known Alan Riding of the *New York Times*; his wife, Marlise Simmons; Ray Bonner; Stephen Kinzer; investigative journalist Alan Nairn; and photographers Susan Meiselas and Jean-Marie Simon. In the early 1980s they were joined by Alma Guillermoprieto, Julia Preston, Sam Dillon, Chris Hedges, Christopher Dickey, and others. Journalism could be dangerous: in 1982, four Dutch journalists were killed by Salvadoran troops, days after a death squad had issued threats against a list of thirty-five journalists.

Even under Carter the CIA had quietly begun forming an anti-Sandinista army in Honduras, which became known as the contras (*contrarrevolucionarios*). In 1982, after reporters began doing stories on contra actions, Congress passed the Boland amendment, prohibiting the use of U.S. funds to overthrow the Nicaraguan government. The administration then sought to devise ways to work around it. Because U.S. aid to the Guatemalan military was minuscule due to the Guatemalan army's human rights violations, Congress had few opportunities to vote on it, and activists had few legislative handles for solidarity work. The Reagan administration found back-channel ways to signal support to the Guatemalan military.

The Central America movement had to look for allies in Congress. Any achievements were piecemeal, and the conflicts continued inexorably on the ground. An inevitable tension grew between groups focused on legislation in Washington and those who were motivated by solidarity with the Sandinistas and with the Guatemalan and Salvadoran revolutionaries and the hope for the poor that they seemed to represent.

No central organization existed to coordinate the country-specific networks (Nicaragua Network, CISPES, NISGUA), peace organizations like the AFSC, Catholic religious orders, the Catholic bishops, Protestant denominations and the National Council of Churches itself, LASA, the human rights organizations, and independent journalists. Angie was the AFSC liaison to many of the national organizations. Ad-hoc coalitions were formed for several large national demonstrations held in Washington, as well as others in places like the Bay Area. Tens of thousands of people came to Washington, with many speakers and performers and protest groups like Peter, Paul, and Mary. Such national mobilizations became less frequent after 1983, when a consensus formed that energies could better be spent at the local level.

One response of the Reagan administration to this movement was the creation in 1983 of the Office of Public Diplomacy for Latin America and the Caribbean, headed by the Cuban American Otto Reich, formally housed in the State Department but actually working in conjunction with the National Security Council. It sought to shape public perception and influence the media by planting op-eds and stories—sometimes false—and pressuring media representatives, and lobbying for the contras and administration policy. It was taxpayer-funded domestic propaganda.

* * *

Paralleling the Central America movement was a mass mobilization in the nuclear freeze movement, calling on the United States and USSR to agree to halt the testing, production, and deployment of nuclear weapons. The movement grew out of antinuclear activities in the late 1970s and was accelerated by the stance of the Reagan administration and widespread public concern. In response, the U.S. Catholic bishops in 1980 appointed a committee to begin drafting a pastoral letter on nuclear weapons. The nuclear freeze proposal was raised in town halls and on many local and state ballot initiatives. In June 1982 we went as a family to a rally in Central Park with approximately a million people, one of the largest political demonstrations in U.S. history. At that time, polls showed a solid majority of the public favoring a nuclear freeze. In 1983 a made-for-TV movie, *The Day After*, portrayed portraying the effect of a nuclear attack centered on Lawrence, Kansas, and attracted 100 million viewers, the largest audience ever for a television film. I watched it in a Denver rectory with a youth group while on a speaking tour.

Reagan projected sunny confidence, untroubled by details or even facts. Early in his presidency, his aides had to explain to him that an arms proposal for deep cuts in land-based missiles was unfair from a Soviet standpoint, because U.S. nuclear weapons were more distributed around the triad of land, sea, and air-launched weapons, whereas the USSR was primarily land-based. The triad was common knowledge to anyone who read about such matters, but not to Reagan, who had built his political career on his staunch advocacy of U.S. military strength in the face of the USSR.

He dealt in anecdotes and stereotypes, such as the Chicago "welfare queen" who wore furs while driving a Cadillac to pick up her welfare checks—he didn't have to say she was black. His annual State of the Union messages were filled with lines intended to get Republicans to rise and applaud, and others intended to force Democrats to decide whether to applaud or not. The political and cultural polarization that began in the 1960s widened in the 1980s.

* * *

Into the mid-1980s I continued to do speaking tours and engagements, organized by local AFSC organizers or others, such as Catholic sisters. Besides the usual areas of Washington, New York, Chicago, Los Angeles, and the Bay Area, I traveled to Florida, the Twin Cities, Ann Arbor–Detroit, St. Louis, various cities in Ohio, Little Rock, Omaha, Denver, Atlanta, and elsewhere. I was hosted by AFSC staff or other activists and spoke in classrooms and auditoriums, and at Quaker meetings, Catholic parishes, and Protestant congregations; appeared on panels; had meetings with newspaper editorial boards or writers, and labor union leaders; and was interviewed on local radio or TV stations. Sometimes these occasions were in a format with opposing points of view, although exchanges were generally civil.

The head of the AFSC program in Vermont, David McCauley, hosted me in his snow-surrounded cabin and drove me around the state in his beat-up station wagon with a large mock-up of a cruise missile on the roof (another issue he was working on). I met many local organizers who were devoting years of their life to peacemaking activities with little pay, in addition to many devoted volunteers. In Los Angeles I spoke at the third anniversary of the murder of Archbishop Romero. Before the event we had a procession through the Pico district, which even then showed many signs of a Salvadoran presence in local businesses, as thousands had fled war and violence. In northern Virginia, I was on a national call-in radio show from midnight to 3 AM, hosted by Larry King, whom I had never heard of until that night. In 1984 my old friend from seminary days, Bill DuBay, who was working as editor of a magazine of native Alaskan peoples, arranged for me to speak in Anchorage. That enabled me to be there both for the wedding of my sister Claudia and the summer solstice, when darkness lasted only an hour or two around midnight.

By the mid-1980s I had made presentations on Central America in around thirty-five states. After living in Latin America for most of a decade and a half, these travels acquainted me with large sections of my own nation.

SOLIDARITY AND RESISTANCE

* * *

In the 1980s Nicaragua seemed to be an experiment of organizing a society around meeting the needs of all citizens rather than around the luxuries of a few. Nicaragua could carry out a better revolution than that of Cuba, I heard Enrique Dussel remark, and El Salvador's would be even better. That enthusiasm assumed that taking state power was a crucial step toward making the kinds of changes needed to build a decent society.

As already noted, after a honeymoon period of less than a year, the Nicaraguan bishops, and particularly Archbishop Miguel Obando, went into opposition against the Sandinistas, at the very same time as representatives of business and traditional political parties left the junta. A key point of contention was the presence of priests in high-level government positions: Miguel D'Escoto as foreign minister; Ernesto Cardenal, minister of culture; his brother Fernando, minister of education; and Edgar Parrales, minister of social welfare. The Nicaraguan bishops and the Vatican ordered the priests to leave their posts. These priests believed that the Sandinista revolution offered the chance to create a more just and humane society, and that for them to accede would constitute betrayal.

Each of these priests was in a somewhat different situation. As a poet, the leader of a religious community on the island of Solentiname, and then part of the anti-Somoza opposition, Ernesto had always been a free spirit. That continued now as he organized poetry workshops around the country. Fernando was a Jesuit and Miguel was in Maryknoll, so the Vatican applied pressure to their religious superiors. Fernando lived in community in the Bosques de Altamira neighborhood with other Jesuits, social scientists, and university professors, all broadly involved in the revolution. Parrales was a diocesan priest who eventually left the priesthood. The other three managed to temporize for a few years.

Xavier Gorostiaga, our Basque Jesuit friend whom we had known in Panama, founded two social science think tanks, CRIES and INIES, the first devoted to sponsoring and publishing research on Central America and the Caribbean, and the second on Nicaragua. The assumption was that a revolutionary process was under way in the region and that social scientists could learn from and assist it. They also published detailed month-by-month political and economic analyses, which amounted to a chronicle of events as they unfolded.

Religious controversies filled the newspapers. I was in Nicaragua in August 1982 during the "naked priest" controversy. As presented in the Sandinista media, Fr. Bismarck Carballo, an archdiocesan spokesman (whom I had interviewed), was caught on a TV camera running naked down the street in a Managua neighborhood, supposedly after a jealous husband caught him in a midday tryst. Carballo's story was that he had been having lunch with the woman when armed men entered and forced him to take off his clothes and go into out the street. Supporters of Archbishop Obando bused people in for a "mass of reparation" for this "suffering Christ." In a Managua neighborhood I witnessed a clash between pro- and anti-Sandinista factions; participants on both sides threatened each other with stones and sticks, while a nun and a Sandinista police officer tried to prevent them from tangling.

Where was the truth? The notion that TV cameras just happened to be on hand seemed implausible. Carballo's story may have been true, or Sandinista intelligence services may have discovered an affair or entrapped him. In any case, while listening to comments from ordinary people on a bus, I had the sense that both the hierarchy and the Sandinistas had been discredited and that many ordinary Nicaraguans were becoming disenchanted.

Initially when in Managua I stayed with Gerri O'Leary and Edgard Macias. He was vice minister of labor, and she was leading an NGO promoting breast-feeding. In mid-1982 they had a public clash with some Sandinistas and became convinced that they were under surveillance. While Gerri was in the United States, Edgard took asylum in the Venezuelan embassy and then went into exile with her. My contacts were skeptical of their story, which did not square with their experience of the Sandinistas. Gerri and Edgard were embraced by right-wing groups and the Reagan administration, and for the rest of the decade they told their story and accused the Sandinistas of being Marxists who had betrayed the revolution. We met at a couple of events in the late 1980s and were cordial, despite being on different sides.

I first heard of the contras in 1981 from an American priest who was working in rural northern Nicaragua. He called them *bandas* (bands or gangs), meaning former National Guardsmen based in Honduras who came across the border. Argentine military and intelligence advisers played key roles at this early stage. In 1981 Reagan authorized the CIA to train these forces on the grounds that Nicaragua was a Marxist threat. Another group, led by former Sandinista Eden Pastora, organized in Costa Rica. A third armed opposition force was that of some Miskito Indians on the Atlantic coast. Meanwhile the United States began building bases and stationing troops in Honduras. In my trips to Nicaragua I was mainly in Managua and other towns on the Pacific side, like Esteli, Leon, and San Juan del Sur, and hence the contra war was largely hearsay to me. Although the contras began as a CIA operation and their bases were in neighboring countries, they were able to tap into real grievances, especially among people on the Atlantic coast but also among Nicaraguan peasants in the more remote countryside who wanted land of their own more than they desired revolution.

Foreign Sandinista supporters tended to assume that because most Nicaraguans were poor, they supported the Sandinista revolution. Most of my contacts were involved in the revolution and viewed the internal opposition as representing the privileged, and the contras themselves as representing the United States. Many Nicaraguans, however, perhaps the majority, were neither active supporters nor opponents; they were trying to live their lives and survive.

Into this situation came Pope John Paul II, who visited Central America and Haiti in March 1983. Things went badly for the Sandinistas from the outset. As the pope stepped off the plane, Ernesto Cardenal was among various government officials lined up to meet him on the tarmac. As Cardenal knelt grinning to kiss the pope's ring, John Paul II waved a reprimanding finger and told him to straighten out his situation. D'Escoto had arranged to be out of the country on diplomatic business. The pope went on to various encounters in the country, urging crowds to be loyal to the bishops and saying nothing about contra attacks.

The visit closed with an evening Mass for which hundreds of thousands of people had been bused in or had trekked on foot to the vast open paved area known as the Plaza of the Revolution. Sandinista leaders were seated behind the altar. Some in the crowd wanted a condemnation of contra violence; a memorial service for seventeen young people whom the contras killed had recently been held at this site. Some began to chant, "We want peace!" The pope shouted back, "Silence!"—equivalent to "Shut up!" He added, "No one wants peace more than the church!" Opponents, including the Reagan administration, accused the Sandinistas of deliberately insulting the pope.

In October 1983 a crisis broke out on the tiny island nation of Grenada, then led by a self-proclaimed Marxist named Maurice Bishop, whom I had once seen address an outdoor rally in Nicaragua. When a hard-line faction overthrew and killed Bishop, the Reagan administration spotted an opportunity. Citing two justifications—concerns for six hundred American medical students there and a long runway under construction that they claimed was for military purposes—Reagan sent troops to overthrow the government and occupy the island. It was quite absurd; the entire Grenada population of ninety thousand could fit into a large football stadium. It was an instant victory for the United States.

To the rest of the world it looked like outlaw behavior (akin to Russia in Ukraine and Crimea in 2014). It also looked like a dress rehearsal for Nicaragua or El Salvador. The Sandinista leadership became more convinced that priority had to be given to national defense, both against the contras and in readiness for a possible U.S. invasion.

Living conditions did not improve much for most poor Nicaraguans under the Sandinista revolution. Schooling and health care were extended to poor areas, but the economy stagnated because businesspeople were reluctant to invest and complained about Sandinista policies and intentions. Small farmers and the urban poor saw little improvement, and rising inflation made their situation worse. These conditions weren't obvious to outsiders, including me, because our contacts tended to be through people involved in the revolution and its programs. The Sandinista government and the many NGOs working with it were highly dependent on outside sources of funding, particularly from European governments and aid agencies. That tended to shield them from the experience of ordinary Nicaraguans who didn't have dollars and depended on Nicaraguan currency.

MEMENTO OF THE LIVING AND THE DEAD

* * *

From mid-1980 to 1985 I didn't return to Guatemala or El Salvador, so for information I was dependent on reports from journalists, contacts with exiles, and occasionally people working in those countries. In both countries the government's primary agenda was defeat of the guerrilla coalitions, which was the task of the armed forces high command; the civilian governments were largely a façade. However, the Salvadoran military and government were highly dependent on U.S. aid and advisers, while the Guatemalan military rejected conditions on aid. The U.S. Congress was reluctant to approve large military aid to Guatemala, given the pattern of killing by the army and police.

In 1982 a group of Guatemalan army officers overthrew President Lucas Garcia late in his term, and General Efrain Rios Montt emerged as head of state. He attended the pentecostal Verbo church, which had ties to a parent church in California. Because of his flamboyant moralizing style—he gave Sunday-night TV addresses sounding like both a preacher and a parent—Rios Montt served as a symbol of what was happening in Guatemala. Church groups associated with the Christian right in the United States, including prominent televangelists, took an interest in Guatemala. Some churches sent volunteers to work in Quiche department, ground zero of the counterinsurgency campaign.

Meanwhile, targeted killings in urban areas and scorched-earth counterinsurgency in the countryside continued. During this time the army required all adult males—in practice, the indigenous—to participate in periodic "civil patrols," that is, to go out poorly armed looking for guerrillas. It was a way of forcing civilians to take sides and to use them as a buffer. The army moved systematically from areas near Guatemala City northward, frequently targeting villages judged to be sympathetic to the guerrillas.

In December 1982 Reagan met with Rios Montt in Honduras and said that he was being given a "bum rap" by human rights groups. The day after Reagan's statement, army troops entered the settlement of Dos Erres in the Peten, not far from the site of the former AFSC project that I had visited, and killed 167 people, including many children, some of whom they bayoneted. Decades later Rios Montt was found guilty of genocide by a Guatemalan court, but the verdict was nullified on a technicality.

Around this time we heard about the death of Fernando Hoyos in Huehuetenango. Fernando was a member of the Zone 5 Jesuit community in Guatemala City and did popular education in Quiche. He once officiated a wedding in our house. As repression increased and the Zone 5 community disbanded, Fernando opted to join the EGP and rose in the ranks. In a letter later published he said, "Even if I stop believing in God, he won't stop believing in me." Fernando was with EGP combatants fleeing an army attack when he and an indigenous youth both slipped down a steep embankment into a rushing river below and to their death.

SOLIDARITY AND RESISTANCE

Solidarity around Guatemala was largely a matter of making known what the army was doing. Because Guatemala was not prominent in U.S. policy, it received relatively little coverage from the mainstream press. Simply going to Guatemala was dangerous for journalists and anyone who would speak to them. Human rights organizations, such as Human Rights Watch, and anthropologists did especially heroic work. Photographer and journalist Jean-Marie Simon toiled courageously in the early 1980s, eventually publishing a volume with photos and text that told the story.

The disheartening fact is that the army strategy was effective. Targeted killings had eliminated any organized opposition in urban areas, and by 1983 the guerrillas had retreated to more remote areas, leaving most of the civilian population in the countryside under direct army control. The guerrillas continued to carry out actions and publish propaganda for years, but they had been eliminated as a threat to state power. Fifteen months after taking power, Rios Montt was overthrown in another coup. Under the new government headed by General Humberto Mejia Victores, the army began a phased program of gradual withdrawal from governance and a return to procedural democracy, although state terror was still used in smaller doses.

* * *

Before 1981, analysts had assumed that any insurgency in El Salvador would soon be ended, one way or another, given the lack of any extensive forest or uncultivated area in which guerrillas could hide. However, after the January 1981 uprising failed to spark a general insurrection, the FMLN guerrilla forces managed to hold territory in the northern part of the country in Chalatenango and in the east in Morazan, and even to carry out actions on the Guazapa volcano, not far from San Salvador. The capital and the Pacific coast area remained under government control, although guerrillas occasionally carried out actions such as destroying bridges.

In December 1981 the U.S.-trained Atlacatl Battalion came to the rural community of El Mozote in eastern El Salvador; rounded people up; divided them into men, women, and children; and killed them, eight hundred or more. Although it was in disputed territory and difficult to reach, journalists Ray Bonner and Alma Guillermoprieto and photojournalist Susan Meiselas managed to get to El Mozote and report on the massacre. The U.S. embassy and the Reagan administration denied the event and impugned the reporters' credibility.

The Christian Democrat junta headed by Jose Napoleon Duarte nominally remained in power until 1982, when elections were held for a constituent assembly, charged with drafting a new constitution. The right-wing Alianza Republicana Nacional (ARENA [National Republican Alliance]) party—the instrument of Roberto D'Aubuisson, the reputed death-squad leader responsible for the assassination of Archbishop Romero—won a majority in the assembly. In order to prevent him from becoming president, the U.S. ambassador pressured to have Alvaro Magaña, a banker, chosen instead. Meanwhile, the Reagan administration stepped up its military aid and training. In the 1984 presidential campaign, D'Aubuisson was a fiery speaker and employed U.S. political consultants; Jose Napoleon Duarte had his long public record and received a half million dollars in CIA funding, funneled through labor unions. Duarte won, thereby assuaging human rights concerns in the U.S. Congress. During his presidency Duarte functioned primarily as the civilian façade for the military and its U.S.-supported counterinsurgency efforts.

When Pope John Paul II visited the region in 1983, media attention was devoted to his encounters in Nicaragua. Less noticed was the fact that in Guatemala he physically embraced indigenous people at the time when the army was slaughtering them. In an outdoor address in San Salvador he urged "dialogue," using the word several times, when the Salvadoran right considered the notion treasonous. Ignacio Ellacuria published a ten-thousand-word essay distilling into a positive synthesis various themes from the pope's addresses to the region. His strongest criticism was that the pope had avoided the word "repression."

Starting in 1981 Archbishop Arturo Rivera Damas, Romero's successor, sought support for a negotiated end to the conflict in El Salvador. In 1982 Mexico and France recognized the FMLN as a representative political force in the country, thus countering U.S. efforts to delegitimize it. Fearing that the conflicts could become regionalized, as had happened in Southeast Asia during the U.S. war in Vietnam, the foreign ministers of the Contadora Group (Mexico, Panama, Colombia, and Venezuela) urged negotiations to end the conflicts in the region. All such efforts were rebuffed by the Reagan administration.

* * *

In March 1983 the AFSC published a fifty-page booklet of mine, *What's Wrong in Central America—and What to Do about It*, which reflected two and a half years of public speaking and writing numerous articles and op-eds. The argument proceeded in stages: a description of present U.S. policies, the origins of the crisis, the contradictions and costs, the possibility of a U.S. accommodation with the Sandinistas and revolutionary movements, and negotiations to end the conflicts.

Andre Shiffrin, the executive editor of Pantheon Press, invited me to New York to discuss expanding it into a book. Pantheon had been founded in the 1940s by refugees from Nazi Germany and had a distinguished list of books, both fiction and nonfiction. Working with Pantheon gave me an appreciation for the work of editors like Wendy Wolf, who oversaw the project through various rounds of editing. The resulting book, *Inside Central America*, which appeared in 1985, was a kind of handbook or primer for activists on the origins of the crisis, and an argument in favor of peace processes and for accommodation with the left. I was translating the viewpoint and experience of Central Americans and making a reasonable case for a change in U.S. policy.

In part I was appealing to common sense and proportion. Reagan portrayed Nicaragua as a threat to U.S. security, pointing out that Managua was closer to Harlingen, Texas, than Harlingen was to Washington. What he didn't say was that the United States had eighty times as many people as Nicaragua, and that its economy was a thousand times as large in dollar terms. That kind of logic was lost during the Cold War, when symbolism and fear outweighed common sense.

In 1983 the administration created the National Bipartisan Commission on Central America, chaired by Henry Kissinger, which, as its name suggested, was intended to draft a consensus policy framework to gain support across party lines. It was an implicit admission that its support for the murderous regimes in El Salvador and Guatemala and for the contras was not popular. I was one of about a dozen academics and policy specialists, calling itself PACCA (Policy Alternatives for the Caribbean and Central America), that met several times in Washington at the Institute for Policy Studies (IPS) to draft an alternative set of recommendations. The result was *Changing Course: Blueprint for Peace in Central America and the Caribbean*, which appeared at the same time as the Kissinger report. We critiqued the Cold War framework of the administration and urged a turn toward negotiation.

In that pre-Internet era, local newspapers were still important in shaping public opinion; on speaking tours I had sometimes briefed editors or editorial boards. At the AFSC we conceived the idea of offering materials on Central America for local groups to present to their editorial boards, and Betsy Berger and I were hired to prepare them. In the process we learned that there were about eighteen hundred daily newspapers across the country. The packet was called "Options for Peace in Central America," and it included the PACCA report and a set of conveniently arranged fact sheets. We didn't mail it to newspapers but provided it as a tool for local activists to use in meeting with editors. About 650 packets were distributed in this manner.

* * *

The Central America movement moved from season to season, responding to legislation and to Reagan administration actions. Significant new initiatives arose in the mid-1980s. A North Carolina group traveling in northern Nicaragua in 1983 heard local residents describe attacks by contra forces operating out of Honduras. On the way back to Managua the group wondered whether the presence of U.S. citizens might deter contra attacks and began considering some form of accompaniment in areas under assault. Within a few months Witness for Peace was under way, establishing a house and staff in Nicaragua to coordinate.

It soon became clear that a literal permanent "human shield" throughout the countryside was not feasible, and the movement evolved into a program whereby Americans arrived in groups; were given various presentations in Managua, including from the U.S. embassy and anti-Sandinista representatives; and then went to places in the countryside where they briefly experienced the life of the people exposed to contra attack. Their visit was a gesture of solidarity and an indication that some Americans were aware of their plight and seeking to halt the contra war. During the rest of the decade, close to four thousand Americans participated in Witness for Peace delegations and returned to their communities to speak from on-site experience of the harm that U.S. policy had done. In 1985 I accompanied a delegation from Southern California that went to an area where I was struck by the poverty of our hosts. When I returned to Philadelphia I found I had hepatitis and spent several weeks quite debilitated.

In response to the 1983 Grenada invasion, activists, mainly church-related, devised the Pledge of Resistance, whereby tens of thousands committed themselves to engage in nonviolent resistance, including civil disobedience, in the event of a U.S. invasion or similar action in Central America. A Washington-based "analyst group" would continuously monitor events and would provide input to a small "signal group" that would make the decision to activate the nationwide network through regional offices. Such readiness to engage in massive civil disobedience with tens of thousands of U.S. citizens, primarily members of religious congregations, willing to go to jail in protest was intended to function as a nonviolent deterrent.

A third initiative was the sanctuary movement. Hundreds of thousands of Salvadorans and Guatemalans had fled north to the United States, driven by violence. Some were being apprehended and deported back to situations of war. Calling on a tradition in which houses of worship were off-limits to the powers of the state, and thus "sanctuaries," congregations in Tucson and Berkeley in 1982 took in specific Salvadoran refugee families and declared public sanctuary. Soon dozens and then hundreds of churches and synagogues had followed suit. A Salvadoran or Guatemalan family in sanctuary was "adopted" by a religious congregation, so arresting them would entail violating "sanctuary"—which admittedly had no standing in U.S. law. In practice, those in sanctuary generally lived not on church grounds but in an apartment or house, and came and went normally. Sanctuary families told their stories to others and served to put a human face on what was happening in their home countries and the region. A young Salvadoran couple, Ernesto and Linda, were in sanctuary at Tabernacle Church in our neighborhood in Philadelphia, while Guatemalans Joel and Gabriela and their children were adopted by a Methodist congregation in the Germantown section of the city.

In 1983 I spent a week in Indiana in a statewide education campaign organized by the Interreligious Foundation for Community Development (IFCO), an organization founded in the 1960s by Lucius Walker, a black Baptist minister and activist. Walker and IFCO devised a model of a statewide blitz in which speakers, generally working in pairs, went to every corner of a state, addressing churches, classes, club meetings, and so forth, coordinated from an ad-hoc center. In Indiana I was paired with a Nicaraguan Assembly of God pastor, and we were given a rental car and a weeklong schedule of engagements in Terre Haute, Lafayette, and as far as East Chicago, in the northwest corner of the state. While the people-to-people methodology was common to the Central America movement, what made IFCO unique was the blitz aspect, reaching beyond the usual audiences. An early-morning breakfast meeting with six or eight Rotary Club members at a café at the intersection of two country roads stands out in my memory. We kept records of our meetings and estimated the numbers of people attending, all of it adding up at the end of the week to impressive numbers. IFCO organized such campaigns in a number of states; I participated in one the following year in Arizona, and toward the end of the decade in Virginia, where I logged in well over a thousand miles going to colleges and universities.

In 1985 the Central America Resource Center in Austin, Texas, published a directory of organizations doing solidarity work, listed state by state, totaling at that time 850 organizations, primarily local. All states had at least two organizations, and California had 175. A later edition listed over 1,000 organizations.

There was no single Central America movement but rather a series of parallel networks with considerable overlap: the country-specific networks for Nicaragua, El Salvador, and Guatemala; preexisting peace and justice organizations, such as the AFSC; church networks, including the many Catholic religious orders; Witness for Peace; the Pledge of Resistance; and the sanctuary movement. Coordination of the many local groups was provided by WOLA, which focused on legislation; the primarily Catholic Religious Task Force in Washington; and the primarily Protestant Inter-Religious Task Force at the headquarters of the National Council of Churches.

Angie was very involved representing the AFSC in coalition work with these various networks. My role in the Central America movement was not as an organizer but as a resource person, speaking at events. I took part in vigils and marches along with others and attended meetings of local Central America organizations. In downtown Philadelphia, as in other places around the country, the Federal Building was picketed weekly.

On a spring morning in 1983 I was one of many people involved in an act of civil disobedience, blocking the entrance to the State Department building in Washington over the issue of military aid to El Salvador. It wasn't a heroic act; dozens of others were also involved. Police warned us that if we didn't move, we would be arrested; when we didn't, we were duly handcuffed, led away to vans, taken for booking, placed in cells, and after some hours, released on our own recognizance. Many participants in the Central America movement regularly practiced civil disobedience.

* * *

In spring 1984 I was invited to London by the Catholic Institute for International Relations (CIIR), primarily for a conference on Central America. My visit happened to coincide with a visit of Ronald Reagan to Ireland, to see Ballyporeen, the reputed birthplace of his great-grandfather. I was sent to Cork, where I was first hosted by an activist priest, and then the next day, Saturday, I took part in an all-day march through the Tipperary countryside. The Irish peace movement was protesting the Central America policy and Reagan's recklessness about nuclear war. A man in a rubber Reagan mask was carrying a briefcase, like the one said to have the nuclear code.

In mid-afternoon while taking refuge from the drizzle, huddling around a truck we heard a news broadcast of Reagan speaking: "And it was William Butler Yeats who said...""; he pronounced it "yeets." One of the marchers burst out in exasperation, "My God—he's taken our Yeats!" That night we were hosted in modest houses along the way. Living standards in Ireland were still quite modest; I saw no sign of the Celtic Tiger that would be unleashed a few years later.

On Sunday morning the Reagan entourage flew into Ballyporeen in several large military helicopters. While he was visiting inside the town, we demonstrators were kept at a distance, where I was one of the speakers. After the fleet of helicopters noisily rattled away we were allowed to enter the town and march around it. I sensed that many Irish instinctively identified with Central Americans, given their long struggle under the British yoke.

Later that year I got a little glimpse into "real socialism" as a participant in a conference called "Toward a Theology of Peace" in Budapest, convened by Bishop Karoly Toth of the Reformed Church and Stephen Tunnicliff, an Anglican layman and peace activist. Among the dozens of participants were Hugo Assmann and Sri Lankan theologian Tissa Balasuriya. The sessions were held in a Reformed seminary, but we had time to stroll through the city on both sides of the Danube and hear gypsy music at night. I bought records, including the Bartok string quartets. Hungary was the most "open" and prosperous of the Eastern European societies, but I had few illusions. The Soviet military presence wasn't blatant, but it was there. When a Nicaraguan nun admiringly said that in Hungary a streetcar driver earned as much or more than a physician, I didn't share her enthusiasm.

On Saturday morning, after the conference was over, I had an informal breakfast conversation with some seminary students. When I told them of repression in Central America, they warmed up and identified with the victims. They were seeing things in terms of what governments did to people, not the ideologies they invoked.

* * *

Many Central America activists were veterans of the civil rights and antiwar movements, and shared the legacy of the New Left. With some exceptions, such as the 1972 McGovern campaign, that left had generally disdained electoral politics and did not identify as "liberal": it was liberals like Kennedy, Johnson, and McNamara who had escalated the war in Vietnam. The left believed that the problems of society were systemic and ultimately required systemic change, although their ideological frameworks varied from strands of Marxism to democratic socialism to anarchism.

The impact of the Reagan administration led many to reconsider their rejection of electoral politics. "Progressives," as they were now calling themselves, became more willing to engage in party politics. One vehicle was the Democratic Socialists of America (DSA), formed in 1982 through the merger of two previous organizations and associated with Michael Harrington, which worked within the Democratic Party. Bob Borosage, who had been in the PACCA group that prepared the response to the Kissinger report, was then advising Jesse Jackson, who ran in the Democratic primaries.

Former senator and vice president Walter Mondale ran against Reagan in 1984; the most novel element was a female vice-presidential candidate, Geraldine Ferraro. I took our nine-year-old daughter, Catherine, to the University of Pennsylvania campus for an outdoor large-screen showing of the vice-presidential debate.

The Republican campaign skillfully used symbolism in its "Morning in America" campaign ad, showing Americans going about their lives, secure under the Reagan presidency. Memories of the severe recession of the early 1980s were fading, and most voters were feeling more upbeat. Reagan won 59 percent of the popular vote and forty-nine states; Mondale won only his home state of Minnesota and Washington, DC. Central America was virtually a nonissue in the election.

Despite our strenuous efforts, Central Americans seemed doomed to further violence with no resolution on the horizon, and we would continue our Sisyphean task of resistance.

12

"Too Many Orphans and Widows"

DURING OUR FIRST TWO or three years in Philadelphia, Angie and I made no long-term plans or commitments because we thought that we would return to Central America, preferably to Guatemala. We assumed that conflicts would end soon; after all, the final phase of the anti-Somoza struggle had taken less than two years. However, as the conflicts in the region ground on, aggravated by U.S. interference, and as we put down roots in Philadelphia, such a return seemed unlikely. We began looking for a house to buy, concentrating on our neighborhood of Powelton, and managed to do so in late 1985.

It was a three-story row house built around 1885 that had been through various phases, including decades as a boardinghouse. A couple in the adjoining row house had bought it in the 1970s and combined the two backyards into a larger one. We undertook a number of renovation projects: laying cement on the dirt floor in the cellar, stripping paint from floors and coating the wood with polyurethane, putting up a divider in the large room on the second floor, adding a small room in the back as a dining area, tiling the kitchen and bathroom, building a deck on the third floor, redoing the flat roof. Some of this work I did, and some we had done.

Our three daughters attended Samuel Powel School in the neighborhood, which had a tradition of dedicated teachers, some of whom we knew; parent involvement; and a variant of open-classroom pedagogy. After fourth grade they moved to Julia R. Masterman, a magnet school three or four miles away where they attended middle school and high school. I continued to be self-employed, working at home, while Angie worked in the AFSC Peace Education Division, walking or taking public transportation to her office. I was able to be at home when our daughters and their friends came over after school, and I prepared the evening meal, which we ate as a family.

We weren't naïve about urban living. One night in our first year, as I was taking grocery bags from the car to the house, I was held up at gunpoint and forced to turn over what I had in my wallet; a dozen years later I was mugged by three guys with a knife in a supermarket parking lot. In the 1980s our house was broken into more than once, and our car was stolen twice. The second time, police located it in another part of the city, and when the driver tried to run over a police officer, he was shot and killed and the car was totaled. Nevertheless, Powelton turned out to be a fine place to live and raise a family.

* * *

I began translating books from Spanish and Portuguese, primarily for Orbis Books. Several were accounts of experiences of Christians in Latin America, such as *Witness to the Truth: The Complicity of the Church and Dictatorship in Argentina*, by Emilio Mignone, a lawyer who became a human rights activist after his daughter was abducted and disappeared in 1976. It was a pleasure to translate *Feet-on-the-Ground Theology*, by Clodovis Boff, a Servite theologian, and brother of the more famous Leonardo. After returning from doctoral studies in Europe, Boff opted to alternate between classroom teaching for half a year and spending the other half with sister-and-priest teams working in the state of Acre in the far western frontier of Brazil adjacent to Bolivia. The book is a journal of his observations on the life of the rubber tappers and other poor rural people in the area and pastoral work with them. At one point he rhapsodizes about hundreds of butterflies in a clearing in the rain forest.

The most challenging work was Franz Hinkelammert, *The Ideological Weapons of Death*. Hinkelammert and his DEI colleagues in Costa Rica believed that rather than simply denouncing the evils of the present order (poverty, military governments, torture, and murder), the nature of capitalism had to be exposed through a critique of its underlying hidden ideology. Translating it involved hours in libraries chasing down the passages in the original English (e.g., of Milton Friedman) or existing translations of *Capital* or other works of Marx.

Translation from Latin and Greek had been central to our seminary education, and I had translated from time to time in Panama and Guatemala. Without any formal training, I was now beginning to translate for a living, doing an apprenticeship on the fly. Translating entails more than knowing two languages: it requires knowing the source language, understanding the subject matter, and being a competent writer in the target language. Without that last element it is easy to fall into translationese.

* * *

John Ruthrauf, who had organized several tours to Central America particularly on labor issues, invited me in April 1985 to serve as a resource person on a delegation to El Salvador and Nicaragua, organized around the participation of two congressional representatives, Bob Edgar from the Philadelphia suburbs and Ted Weiss from Manhattan. Rounding out the delegation were state-level politicians, academics, and church people, including the Reverend William Sloane Coffin, totaling a dozen or so. A primary aim was to provide Edgar and Weiss with an experiential base for their positions.

The presence of the two congressmen made this somewhat different from other delegations: we stayed at the best hotels, and we had access to the U.S. ambassadors in El Salvador and Nicaragua and sessions with Presidents Duarte and Ortega. In other sessions Archbishop Rivera spoke of working actively toward a peace process in El Salvador, and Maria Julia Hernandez of the church's human rights office firmly refuted the rosy picture that Ambassador Thomas Pickering offered. We also met with refugees driven into San Salvador by the war.

Our sessions in Nicaragua included three with priests. In Esteli a local Sandinista commander outlined the military situation and stated that the Sandinistas had turned back the advance of the contras. Contra forces continued to kill and harass, but they were not a threat to the Sandinista hold on state power. While we were waiting in the U.S. ambassador's residence, Coffin sat down at the piano with utter aplomb and began playing Chopin from memory (he had trained to be a concert pianist). As Ambassador Harry Berghold entered the room, Coffin segued smoothly into the Yale anthem; Berghold was a fellow Yalie. He was also a career diplomat, recently arrived in Nicaragua, after having served in Hungary. At one point when pressed by someone in the group, he remarked that he didn't make the policy but only carried it out.

Although we weren't scheduled to go to Guatemala, Ruthrauf, Edgar, and I began the week in Mexico City being briefed by Ricardo Falla, the Jesuit anthropologist who had done careful studies of massacres by the army. Shortly before our trip, two leaders of GAM (the Mutual Support Group), made up of relatives of people who had disappeared, had been murdered in separate incidents. A protest march was planned for Saturday, April 13. We decided that Weiss, Edgar, Coffin, Rev. Ted Loder, and I would go to Guatemala as observers. Although our family had had to flee five years before, I assumed that the company of two congressmen would afford me sufficient protection.

When we arrived at the Managua airport Friday afternoon, however, we were informed through an embassy staff person that House Speaker Tip O'Neill was strongly urging—in effect, ordering—Weiss and Edgar not to go because of anonymous but serious threats in Guatemala against foreigners rumored to be coming for the march. The other three of us now had to decide whether to continue. Edgar and Weiss were cautionary and Loder was inclined not to go, but Coffin was determined, to the point where Loder became annoyed at his bravado. I suggested that we go to Guatemala to make up our minds there, and that we be met at the airport by U.S. embassy staff for some protection.

The embassy representative met us at the airport and took us downtown in a van to the Hotel Panamericano, where we joined a number of foreign observers, notably Canadians, including Peace Brigades International, which had been accompanying GAM. Also present was the longtime human rights advocate Areyeh Neier, then at Americas Watch. That night we were briefed on what was happening and what to expect. On Saturday morning, a carful of us, including Neier, went to the U.S. embassy and had lunch with Ambassador Alberto Martinez Piedra. Back at the hotel in the early afternoon, we had a press briefing in Spanish, where I was our spokesperson, contrary to my intention of keeping a low profile.

In mid-afternoon we went to the plaza where about a thousand marchers, including GAM members, trade unionists, and university students, were assembling a mile or two from downtown. When the march began, we were careful to follow it from the sidewalk—as observers, not demonstrators. Metal storefront doors came clanking shut as the march went down Quinta Avenida, a major commercial avenue. I noticed one of the embassy staffers also walking along the sidewalk. The march reached downtown without incident. When we arrived in front of the National Palace, there were no speeches; demonstrators silently threw carnations toward the palace.

A journalist with a cassette recorder came up to Coffin and asked, "Reverend Coffin, what do you think of Guatemala?" Standing alongside him to interpret, I thought, *Here we go, Bill doesn't understand how things work in Guatemala, and he's going to deliver a harangue on human rights violations.* But he said simply—and brilliantly—"There are too many orphans and widows!"

* * *

In the early 1980s exiled Chilean priest Sergio Torres, who had organized the Theology in the Americas conferences, brought the major Latin American theologians together with an ambitious proposal: to cover all of theology (Trinity, Christology, ecclesiology, sacraments, moral life, and so forth) from a liberation theology standpoint. Although theologians like Gutierrez, Boff, Sobrino, and others were being read in Europe and North America, seminaries in Latin America were still using translations of *Mysterium Salutis*, a multivolume work by German theologians from the 1960s. Torres assembled a group that besides the usual clerics included some Protestants and some female theologians. Volumes would be cowritten by more than one theologian, and sympathetic bishops were also involved—until the Vatican expressly prohibited them. They worked out a scheme with fifty-three titles, intended to be short books or booklets that pastoral workers could afford.

When titles began to appear in Spanish or Portuguese in the mid-1980s, they were book-length, did not break new ground, and seemed to overlap one another. Publishers found that sales were slow, especially in translation. The market for liberation theology seemed to be reaching a saturation point.

The theologians also faced opposition from the Vatican, energized by John Paul II's confrontations in Nicaragua. In 1984 Cardinal Josef Ratzinger, the head of the Congregation for the Doctrine of the Faith, issued a long critique of liberation theology on numerous grounds, faulting it for being too sociological, reductionistic, and secular, and for incorporating Marxism. In 1985 Leonardo Boff was silenced for a year, even though two Brazilian cardinals accompanied him to the Vatican. His primary offenses were apparently his critical observations in *Church: Charism and Power*, including sympathy for women's ordination.

Most Latin American theologians sidestepped the Ratzinger document, saying that it was a caricature and didn't really represent their work. That position was in keeping with their policy of avoiding confrontation with church authority, insofar as possible. However, Uruguayan Jesuit Juan Luis Segundo broke ranks and wrote a book-length reply to the Ratzinger letter. Besides contesting many of Ratzinger's individual criticisms, Segundo accused the future pope of expressing a dualism that had been left behind at Vatican II. To illustrate the point, he cited Paul VI, who in his closing address at Vatican II posed a question: "Will it not be said that the thought of the Church in Council has deviated toward the *anthropocentric* positions of modern culture?" The pope's answer was, "Deviated, no; *turned, yes*." The "turn toward the world" was endorsed by the pope himself. Segundo pressed home the point: "I understand that my theology (that is, my interpretation of Christian faith) is false if the theology of the document is true—or if it is the only true one." When I submitted a review to *Christianity and Crisis*, the editors titled it "Setting Ratzinger Straight."

* * *

Liberation theology and the role of progressive Christians in Latin America had begun to attract the attention of secular leftists. I was at a large gathering in a Manhattan apartment, primarily of secular Jews, that led to a special issue of the independent Marxist magazine *Monthly Review* on "Christianity and the Left," edited by economist Bill Tabb. My article, "How Christians Become Socialists," began with the radicalizing experience of living and working with the poor.

That year saw the publication *Fidel and Religion*, a book-length interview of Fidel Castro by Brazilian Dominican Frei Betto, in which Fidel told the story of his life and gave his views on religion. Since a solid portion of the world still lived under some form of socialism, collaboration between Christians and Marxists seemed relevant.

The editors of Pantheon Books asked me to do a book on liberation theology. The term itself had become shorthand for some pastoral trends in the church, understood as having a potential for mobilizing people for social change. The task I set for myself was to write a book that would be introductory but would not oversimplify—and not emphasize the political dimension at the expense of theology.

Early in the process, when I interviewed Jon Sobrino in San Salvador, he remarked that he had the impression that theologians were writing not about God but about other theologians. He had in mind the scholarly citations required in academic writing. I was struck by his stark conviction: whatever else he did—whether he invoked the experience of El Salvador, whether he cited other authors or not—was ancillary to that central task of speaking and writing about God.

From public speaking I was familiar with the questions people raised, but I tried to avoid structuring the book around those objections and stressed instead liberation theology's origins in pastoral situations and its biblical roots. Only toward the end did I take up the more controversial aspects, such as its relationship to Marxism. *Liberation Theology* was published in 1987 and was translated into Spanish and Japanese.

* * *

In that book, seeking to indicate to readers how unexpected and surprising Vatican II was to Catholics, I wrote, "In the 1950s, it would have been as difficult for Catholics to imagine the pope launching a broad reform movement within the church as it would be for Americans today to conceive of the Kremlin initiating a far-reaching democratization of the Eastern bloc countries. Yet that is what occurred with the Second Vatican Council." When I wrote that in 1986, Mikhail Gorbachev was calling for *glasnost* and *perestroika* (openness and restructuring), but he meant those terms as internal reforms; neither he nor anyone else anticipated what was to happen in less than three years. The Polish labor union Solidarity had arisen in the early 1980s but was now illegal. Timothy Garton Ash's reporting in the *New York Review of Books* gave fascinating glimpses into the lives of dissidents in Eastern Europe, but the "real socialism" of the communist world seemed as durable as the Roman Catholicism of my boyhood.

* * *

While the Reagan administration and activists both were fixated on Central America, two broad movements were taking place elsewhere in the hemisphere: a return to elected civilian government and the debt crisis. Under various circumstances the military regimes that had seized control, starting with Brazil in 1964, began to retire to the barracks.

A dramatic instance occurred in 1982 when the Argentine military invaded the Falkland Islands, three hundred miles out into the Atlantic Ocean, which Argentina had claimed but which were in fact occupied by a few thousand shepherds of British descent. The generals may have sought to arouse nationalism to divert attention from domestic problems. Because of their collaboration with the CIA and the Pentagon in Central America, the Argentine military assumed they would enjoy the support of Reagan administration and were surprised to see the United States stand with the Thatcher government, whose troops thrashed the Argentines. Humiliated by this defeat, the military allowed elections, on the condition that they not be subject to prosecution for human rights violations. In 1984 the Uruguayan military was forced to negotiate a return to democracy, and in 1985 Brazil held indirect elections for president, after a decade of a controlled decompression. Peru, Bolivia, and Ecuador now also had elected civilian governments. In 1988 Pinochet allowed a plebiscite vote on whether to continue military rule, and to his surprise the "No" vote won, leading the next year to an election in which by a center-left coalition emerged victorious. These civilian governments initially seemed fragile, as the military remained powerful actors behind the scenes and occasionally issued veiled threats.

In August 1982 the Mexican government announced that it couldn't meet its debt service payment. Brazil and other governments soon followed. After the oil shocks of the 1970s, Middle Eastern governments had deposited their rapidly expanding petroleum revenues in commercial banks, especially in New York. In order to use these deposits, the banks loaned to governments in developing countries at commercial rates, assuming that governments wouldn't default. The economic landscape changed when the Reagan administration raised interest rates to tamp down inflation, thus depressing the world economy and driving down demand for commodities along with the value of the governments' currencies in relation to the dollar. Many of the loans were short-term, and when the banks were unwilling to renegotiate, governments were hard pressed to meet their obligations. The Mexican default made the cover of *Time*—not out of concern for Mexicans but for the global financial system.

The International Monetary Fund (IMF) stepped in to help countries renegotiate, but it also imposed conditions on governments: they had to introduce austerity measures, reducing government expenditures and opening their economies to investment. In Latin America the 1980s came to be called a "lost decade" of slow growth, high inflation, rising unemployment, the expansion of the informal sector, and greater poverty. The IMF, as well as the World Bank and the United States, were viewed as responsible for these results. The poor were seemingly punished for the actions of their unrepresentative governments.

In 1985 Fidel Castro convoked a meeting in Havana of politicians, and other public figures to protest the IMF. Cardinal Arns of Sao Paulo and other church figures attended. Some floated the possibility of a "debtors' cartel" in which governments would band together to resist the conditions being imposed. For years afterward, left-wing intellectuals and activists called for a repudiation of the debt. The IMF and bank technocrats worked on a case-by-case basis, muddling through, seeking primarily to prevent a default that would threaten the world financial system.

In the 1980s Peru was shaken by the emergence of Sendero Luminoso (Shining Path), a Marxist guerrilla group that began in a university where students were largely indigenous and then spread into the countryside. Its key figure was Abimael Guzman, a philosophy professor who promoted his own version of Maoism and accused all other communists of being revisionist. I first heard of it from a visiting Peruvian priest who made a presentation to a small group of us in the St. Malachy rectory. What I found hard to understand was that he said they were terrorists. I had assumed that any guerrilla group needed to win the sympathy of the population. Sendero, however, did kill the peasantry. Initially the Peruvian army also violated human rights. Later human rights organizations estimated that almost seventy thousand people were killed in the conflict between 1980 and 2000, well over half at the hands of Sendero.

All this was of little direct relevance to Central America, but it was part of the regional context, paving the way for the response to globalization in the 1990s and 2000s.

* * *

While in Nicaragua in 1985 I went to a house where Miguel D'Escoto was on a fast and had been joined by Bishop Pedro Casaldaliga, who had come from Brazil. D'Escoto had taken leave from his duties as foreign minister to fast as a kind of appeal in the midst of the contra war, and particularly against Archbishop Obando's public sympathy with the contras. Casaldaliga was a Spanish Claretian who had been made bishop of the Diocese of Sao Felix do Araguaia, a rural diocese in the then-remote Pantanal region. Because the Brazilian government viewed him as suspect, Casaldaliga had not left Brazil for many years, out of fear that he would not be allowed to return. He now took that risk by flying to Nicaragua to join D'Escoto, who was fasting in a modest house, accompanied by a handful of others. In the heat of Managua, similar to the Pantanal, Casaldaliga was in light clothing and flip-flops.

After a couple days, he set out making pastoral visits, saying Mass in around twenty places. The Nicaraguan bishops accused him of meddling and not obtaining their permission; however, he had the backing of Cardinal Arns of Sao Paulo and regarded what he was doing as a gesture of comfort to those suffering Nicaraguans whom the local bishops were ignoring. Casaldaliga published a journal of his Nicaragua trip, which I was then asked to translate. What made the task enjoyable was his light touch and his ability to be prophetic without solemnity.

* * *

At this time I was generally writing a book, article, or review; translating a book; and sometimes making public presentations. Without having consciously chosen to be either a translator or a writer, I had drifted into it. Here I was, nearly fifty, and I didn't fit into any particular career path, unlike friends who now worked in policy think tanks or advocacy groups, or had entered academia.

In a bookstore I came across *The Independent Scholar's Handbook* by Ronald Gross. By "independent scholar" Gross meant an individual doing intellectual work but not as a tenured professor. The book, which reminded me of *What Color Is Your Parachute?*, presented stories about many such people, like historian Barbara Tuchman, and gave me a way of thinking of my irregular vocational trajectory.

I was slow to see myself as in business, however. It was only the mid-1980s, after attending a presentation on recordkeeping for self-employed artists, that I opened a separate checking account for my work. I hadn't realized that I needed to pay a city business tax, so I had to make arrangements to pay back taxes. It took me years to acknowledge that I was in business, perhaps because people on the left tended to see business as inherently exploitative. Only a decade or two later did self-employment became common and even cool.

* * *

In October 1986 a Sandinista soldier shot down a plane that turned out to be carrying weapons. The only survivor, an American named Eugene Hasenfus, said they were being taken to the contras, thus providing undeniable concrete proof of U.S. government involvement in illegal arms trafficking. As the affair unraveled, it led to the uncovering of the Iran-contra scandal: Reagan administration officials were selling weapons through third parties at inflated prices to the Iranian government, ostensibly an implacable enemy, in order to secure the release of hostages by Hezbollah guerrillas, and using the profits to buy weapons for the contras. That was a clandestine end-run around the Boland amendment, which had prohibited sending weapons for the overthrow of the Nicaraguan government. The ensuing months of revelations, hearings, and court cases put the Reagan administration on the defensive, although Central Americans didn't necessarily feel the relief.

Revelations also emerged about the dirty tactics that government agencies used against the Central America movement. The Immigration and Naturalization Service (INS) used paid informants to enter the sanctuary movement and gain information, and then launched two high-profile trials against sanctuary activists in South Texas (1985) and Tucson (1986) for conspiracy and harboring and transporting illegal aliens. In both cases the defendants argued on religious and constitutional grounds. Some were found guilty but received suspended or light sentences.

Details of other government harassment emerged. For years the FBI was using paid informants to surveil and seek evidence particularly against CISPES, the Salvadoran solidarity network. The Internal Revenue Service (IRS) zeroed in on activists and solidarity organizations for auditing. Dozens of church and solidarity offices were broken into and files and computers stolen, while other valuables were left untouched.

In April 1987 Ben Linder, a young American engineer who had been in Nicaragua for over three years, was attacked and killed by contra forces along with two Nicaraguans. About ten other foreigners had been killed, but he was the first American. Reagan administration spokesmen blamed Linder for having knowingly placed himself in a combat area, but his mother and other family members pushed back in congressional testimony.

As the Reagan administration was weakened and distracted, peace processes, which had been floated since 1981 and thwarted by the Reagan administration, took on new life. In July 1987 the five presidents of Central America met in Esquipulas,

Guatemala, to sign a peace proposal that Costa Rican president Oscar Arias had prepared. The Arias plan represented a consensus that the solutions the region needed were political, not military. It proposed a parallel treatment of the three conflictive countries: Nicaragua, El Salvador, and Guatemala.

This framework led to grassroots initiatives in the various countries. The Archdiocese of San Salvador organized an extensive consultation process, based on detailed questionnaires seeking the views of the citizenry. The UCA, under the strong leadership of Ignacio Ellacuria, was also holding public forums, to which representatives of all sectors were invited, including the right-wing party ARENA, associated with death squads. In Nicaragua, groups made up of pastors, priests, sisters, and other leaders fostered dialogue, especially in rural areas. In Guatemala I witnessed a similar session with mainly grassroots people held under ecumenical auspices. These were all efforts at consulting with civil society, a term then coming into currency.

* * *

In the mid- to late 1980s I continued to go to Central America regularly, sometimes as a resource person for a delegation or doing research for an article or book. My regular contacts were my friends, priests and sisters, journalists, and people working in human rights or development. Although I went out to other towns and the countryside, I tended to view things from the capital cities and through the eyes of my contacts.

In 1987 I made a three-day loop through the Guatemalan countryside with the director of a U.S. nonprofit organization that raised funds and channeled them to indigenous groups. Our trip was primarily to familiarize her with Guatemala. For the most part, priests had still not returned to Quiche since having to leave in 1980. I was particularly struck by the sisters who had remained as a presence in these areas, quietly accompanying the people and aiding them as they could. We went to one of the "model villages" set up by the army to concentrate indigenous people where they could be monitored, but we could only drive through and observe the physical appearance, not talk with any of the people. At a church center in Coban we saw Bishop Gerardo Flores and indigenous refugees from the violence seeking the aid of the church.

My 1985 and 1987 trips to Guatemala indicated that it was reasonably safe for our family to go there so that our daughters could experience the land of their infancy. The army had secured the countryside militarily; the guerrilla organizations still existed and carried out actions, but they had been pushed to remote regions and no longer had strong ties to the civilian population. Murder was still used as a political tool, but more selectively.

In the summer of 1988 we first spent some days in Mexico City, then took a bus to Oaxaca and flew to Tapachula near the Guatemalan border. There we had to carry our luggage perhaps a half mile in heat, humidity, and buzzing insects across a bridge to the Guatemalan side, where we went through immigration and customs and boarded a rickety bus to Guatemala City, passing through a tropical storm. Although our daughters, ages eight to twelve, weren't happy, it enabled them to see a little more than they would if we had flown directly.

Bob and Elly Ledogar, who had sheltered Angie and our daughters in 1980 as they escaped, allowed us to use their safe and comfortable house while they spent a month in the United States. That gave us a base for going to several places in the countryside. We were joined by their late teenage cousins, Mia and Angie Manley. The highlight was a trip to the Peten, where we ate exotic local foods in Flores, climbed the pyramids at Tikal, slept outdoors in hammocks, and swam in a lake at a biological reserve where the signs warned of caimans. Simply doing ordinary errands, such as buying tamales in the street or going to the local video store, was also part of the experience.

The Guatemalan presidency was now in the hands of Christian Democrat Vinicio Cerezo, the first civilian in two decades. During our stay, one military faction attempted a coup, with helicopters flying over the presidential palace; it was only put down because the more pragmatic wing of the army prevailed.

* * *

One evening in San Salvador I was present while church people made plans to escort a Salvadoran man under threat who had to leave the country. The meeting was by candlelight, so it must have been during an electrical blackout. The man and his foreign escort would go to the bus station the next morning but would sit separately, as though unaware of each other. If the person were apprehended, the accompanier would find a telephone and alert others in the capital. It was a small example of the everyday heroism required in a situation of war and human rights violations.

Perhaps a million Salvadorans—20 percent of the population—had fled the country, primarily to the United States. Classified ads in the daily newspapers carried offers to get people to the United States: so many Salvadoran *colones* up front, so many U.S. dollars upon delivery, and a phone number. The ads could be that telegraphic because movement to the United States was quite routine. Another indication of the Salvadoran diaspora was the symbol of an airmail envelope (a rectangle with diagonal red, white, and blue stripes around the edges), which could be seen on stores in small rural towns. It indicated a kind of parallel postal service whereby local residents could receive letters, gifts, and especially cash from abroad, primarily the United States, and correspond. Couriers flew back and forth to Los Angeles or elsewhere, where a network assured delivery.

In to El Salvador from the Philadelphia area in 1987, we passed through the town of Chalatenango, which was controlled by the army, and continued into an area controlled by the FMLN. As we arrived in the settlement, handwritten signs said, "Welcome, visitors from Finland." The words *Filadelfia* and *Finlandia* admittedly look alike, but the mistake suggested that the people here were used to welcoming international delegations. While there we sat in on a school class being held outdoors, understood perhaps as a seed of a new society yet to come. In San Salvador we met with labor and popular organizations, which were increasingly active.

The editors of the *Latin America and Caribbean Contemporary Record* asked me to do the article on El Salvador for volume VII, which would cover the 1987–1988 period. The volume was a type of publication that has largely gone out of existence with the Internet: a dozen thematic essays, articles on thirty-five countries of the hemisphere, followed by 350 pages of documents and statistical information—all told, over 1,000 pages compiled for library reference sections. For me it represented a chance to gather information and present it systematically.

At the outset I noted that the election of Duarte as president in 1984 had largely muted criticism of U.S. policy in El Salvador by Democrats. U.S. economic and military aid was on the same level as the tax revenues that the Salvadoran government itself raised, and moreover, a similar amount was coming in remittances from Salvadorans abroad, sent by those who had fled the war and emigrated to the United States. Indeed, President Duarte had sent Reagan a confidential letter asking that Salvadorans not be repatriated. Politically, the Christian Democrats were declining, partly as a result of Duarte's cancer, and the right-wing party ARENA, once linked to death squads, was rising, as was the FDR, the civilian wing linked to the FMLN. Labor militancy was also on the rise. The massacres of the early 1980s were a thing of the past, but civilians in the countryside were being attacked from the air, and individual political killings continued, primarily by the right.

In the course of my research I came upon a paper by four U.S. lieutenant colonels at the Harvard Kennedy School, using El Salvador as a test case. Most remarkable was their claim that the dependence of the Salvadoran government on U.S. military and economic aid was equivalent to that of the South Vietnamese government at the height of the U.S. involvement there; the country had an artificial "war economy." While recognizing some successes, they said that the "jury is still out" on whether the U.S. intervention would succeed. One of the authors was Andrew Bacevich, who soon retired and went on to a career as a professor of international relations at Boston University and became a major critic of U.S. foreign policy and the cultural impetus behind it.

In hindsight what is striking is what I and my fellow contributors didn't anticipate. When I submitted my study in early 1989 I mentioned the Esquipulas peace framework but did not envision any end to the conflict; neither did the authors on Nicaragua or Guatemala. Articles in the thematic section made observations on the end of the Reagan era, and on Gorbachev and Latin America; none foresaw communism's end, globalization, or the rise of China.

* * *

In mid-1989, when I stepped off a packed bus in Managua, I found that my wallet had been stolen. I canceled my next appointment; went to Telcor, the agency for making long-distance and international calls; and phoned Angie and asked her to cancel the credit cards. They couldn't be used in Nicaragua, but I figured that thieves might have a way of selling them and that the purchasers could fly them out. I had forgotten to include my phone card—a plastic card like a credit card used for long-distance calling from phone booths. Our next phone bill included twenty-eight hundred dollars in phone calls to Europe and elsewhere. Obviously, a well-developed network extended from petty thieves on the bus, to some place in Managua, to others in the United States, ready to take advantage. The phone company agreed to remove the charges from our bill.

Plainly there was another Nicaragua that I was little aware of, because I tended to see the country in terms of the Sandinista revolution and its internal and external enemies. I didn't have much contact with people in the middle, just trying to survive. By 1988 hyperinflation had set in—16,000 percent a year or more. People in the cordoba economy were having a very difficult time. The Sandinistas themselves and the NGOs working with them received funding in hard currency, so they were relatively shielded from the effects of hyperinflation.

* * *

For the 1988 election the Republicans chose Reagan's vice president, George H. W. Bush, who sought to ride on Reagan's popularity while subtly hinting at the distance between them. The Democrats chose Michael Dukakis, the governor of Massachusetts. The natural pendulum swing could be expected to favor the Democrats, but most Americans felt content with the status quo and seemed to respond more to symbol than substance. When Dukakis sought to offset his lack of military experience by donning a helmet and riding in a tank, he set himself up for ridicule. A Republican TV ad featured Willie Horton, a convicted murderer in Massachusetts who, during a furlough permitted under legislation that Dukakis signed, committed rape and other crimes; that he was black wasn't emphasized but played on white Americans' fears. During a presidential debate, Dukakis was asked whether he would favor the death penalty if his wife were raped and murdered; rather than showing indignation, he cited statistics. What stands out in memory is the Republicans' skillful use of symbolism and innuendo rather than substantive discussion of major issues. Bush won the popular vote handily and the electoral vote resoundingly.

* * *

In early 1987 I translated into Spanish "Economic Justice for All," the U.S. bishops' pastoral letter on the U.S. economy. As a rule, translators should work only into their own native language, no matter how well they know a second language. In this case I enlisted the help of a Uruguayan translator friend who edited my work.

With a contract from Pantheon I set out to write a book on the bishops' pastoral letters on nuclear weapons and peace (1983) and the economy (1986), along the lines of the one I had done on liberation theology. Both letters had been undertaken at the annual meeting of the bishops in November 1980 and were to some extent a response to the election of Ronald Reagan and what it portended. Each went through a very public process of hearings, publicly released drafts, and extensive discussion. Each document as written included an introduction that outlined the problem, a set of principles from scripture and from the philosophical-theological tradition, observations on policy, and a conclusion that presented a larger vision. Pantheon saw the letters as a significant development that deserved to be widely known. I had followed the development of the letters from their proposal until they were officially released. Now I studied the processes and read much of the discussion they generated. I also went to Washington in November 1987 to interview people on the fringes of the annual bishops' meeting.

What triggered the peace pastoral was the intention of modernizing nuclear weapons during the early Reagan administration. The letter was primarily about nuclear weapons, the morality of using them and of deterrence. The bishops considered just war theory, developed over the centuries in the West, but also the arguably older tradition of pacifism: the notion of Jesus pushing the nuclear button seems absurd. The U.S. bishops concluded that good ends, such as defending one's nation, "cannot justify immoral means (the use of weapons which kill indiscriminately and threaten whole societies). We fear that our world and nation are headed in the wrong direction . . . In our quest for more and more security, we fear we are actually becoming less and less secure." They went on to say that peacemaking is not optional: "We are called to be peacemakers not by some movement of the moment, but by our Lord Jesus."

Peter Rosazza, the goateed auxiliary bishop of Hartford, explained to me the origins of the letter on the economy. In 1980 the bishops had issued a letter on Marxism that attracted little attention. Two French priests who had been Rosazza's classmates suggested that a letter on capitalism would be more relevant to the United States. He proposed one and it was approved, but it was then decided to leave aside more theoretical questions and to examine the actual American economy. The specific policy areas the bishops examined in greater detail were employment, poverty, agriculture, food, and U.S. relations with developing countries.

In the book I situated the letters in the U.S. context and in the larger context of public discussion of nuclear weapons and economic issues, highlighting their content and the critiques of them. In each case, a group of laypeople, funded by conservative foundations and prominently including Michael Novak, did a parallel public critique and issued an alternative statement. They were convinced that the bishops' staffers, if not the bishops themselves, were too liberal.

In introducing the topic, I used Arthur Schlesinger Jr.'s notion that U.S. history moved in thirty-year cycles, and that the 1990s were likely to be similar to the 1930s and 1960s in that respect. If so, these letters could help move a reform agenda in both church and society. What neither the bishops, the commentators, nor I foresaw was the dramatic collapse of communism and the next phase of the computer revolution. Likewise, we did not foresee that some of the symptoms of the time—growing inequality, the decline of the Rust Belt, and bankruptcy of family farms—signaled longer-term trends.

At this time I explored two other possible book projects. For years I had been fascinated by priest and sociologist Andrew Greeley, who continued to produce social science, novels, and commentary, already well over a hundred books. Although some ignored or dismissed Greeley, partly because he was so prolific, I suspected he was saying something important about U.S. Catholic life, based on his decades-long friendship with Chicago Irish American middle-class laypeople and his sociological studies. I toyed with the idea of trying to pull together the various strands of his work, which I thought ultimately had theological value, although he insisted he wasn't a theologian. He graciously sent me a half dozen books, but I became absorbed in other pursuits.

In late 1988 I went to Los Angeles to explore a book about John Coffield, who had been an inspiration and a father figure to me and who was at that time living in a mobile home in semiretirement in Orange County but still doing pastoral work. I could tell the story of the Catholic Church in Los Angeles in the mid-twentieth century around Coffield and Cardinal McIntyre, who had died some years earlier. Aspects of Southern California (Hollywood) could make the story interesting, but L.A. could be a microcosm of U.S. Catholicism. In a six-hour interview I got Coffield to tell me his life story. On that visit I also interviewed a number of other people, primarily priests, including a half-dozen retired priests at the beach. One of them was the scripture scholar John McKenzie, who still enjoyed puncturing pious assumptions. When I described the story I had in mind, Frank Colborn, then teaching at the seminary, pointed out that Latino immigration was changing L.A. in ways that we would not have expected even twenty years previously. I concluded that it would not be practical to attempt to write such a book from Philadelphia, even with a publisher's advance.

On that visit I went to see Fr. Elwood Keiser, who as head of Paulist Productions since the 1950s had been producing TV dramas and films with moral and human value. His operation was in a ramshackle house where Sunset Boulevard runs into the Pacific Ocean. Keiser told me that the next week they were going to Mexico to film *Romero* with Raul Julia. When I saw the film a year or so later, it struck me as more or less true but considerably simplified. Some of the characters seem to represent types, and the film itself, most of which deals with events around the killing of Rutilio Grande and Romero's "conversion," feels small. In the film Romero goes to Aguilares, where soldiers have encamped in the church and desecrated the Eucharist; he picks the hosts up off the ground. When I saw Cesar Jerez, who had been the Jesuit superior in San Salvador at the time, I asked, "Romero didn't do that, did he?" Cesar chuckled good-naturedly, "No, I did." He was more willing than I to accept the fact that making a biopic required simplifying the story.

For writing and translating in the 1980s, I used a Kaypro computer (cost: eighteen hundred dollars), which was encased in a metal box, one end of which was the keyboard which came unclasped. The screen was a few inches across, green text on black. The five-inch floppy disks could hold perhaps forty pages of double-spaced text. My dot-matrix printer fed paper on a continuous perforated roll on which text was printed line by line. It was a considerable improvement over an electric typewriter, but for most of the decade I submitted my work in paper form. From there it was edited and eventually typeset.

At Pantheon I learned to appreciate the work of editors. After I submitted my first version, an editor read for consistency, pointed out problems, and made suggestions. My next revision led to line editing, with literal blue and red pencils, which I generally approved. Finally, I was sent a copy of the page proofs as a last chance to catch errors.

Sales of *Our Unfinished Business: The U.S. Catholic Bishops' Letters on Peace and the Economy* (1989) were quite disappointing. The most obvious reason was that readers were no longer interested in the topic. I had shown that I could write books and have them published, but that was not the same as making a living as a writer.

* * *

In the late 1980s I felt impelled to undertake another book on the church in Central America, to take into account developments since the beginning of the decade. In 1989 the Salvadoran government denied me a visa, as it had the previous year, when I applied in Guatemala. At around this time, Angie was in El Salvador on a delegation for the AFSC when the authorities gave her twenty-four hours to leave the country. In 1989 I went just to Guatemala and Nicaragua, leaving El Salvador for 1990. On my first trip the region seemed to be doomed to endless armed conflict; a year later the world had turned upside down, not through revolution but the sudden end of the Cold War.

Since my time in Panama I had been aware of evangelicals in Latin America but had paid little attention to them. The presidency of Rios Montt in Guatemala drew attention to their presence, but Catholics, as well as secular academics and activists, dismissed them as "sects" with an alienating theology; their success in winning converts was said to be due to foreign money or even the CIA.

To understand the phenomenon I interviewed pastors and researchers, read the academic literature, and attended worship. Church services typically lasted two hours: repetitive songs up to twenty minutes, emotional preaching with responses, and testimonies. It was clear that people around me were having an intense religious experience. Testimonies were often life stories of conversion away from alcoholism or infidelity or from Catholicism and an acceptance of Jesus as savior. More than once I heard stories about being persecuted by Catholics, for example, neighbors who threw stones at churches under the instigation of a priest. The settings varied from the distinctly upper-middle-class feel of the Verbo church (Rios Montt's), to the Elim church (what would later be called a megachurch), to small neighborhood churches.

I was entering a different religious world, one that had been there all the while. Protestants had been in Guatemala since the arrival of Presbyterians in 1882 at the invitation of President Justo Rufino Barrios. The evangelical but non-pentecostal Central American Church had likewise been present for many decades.

At a pentecostal church in Managua on a sultry Saturday evening, I had a sudden flash of insight. The church was spare and unfinished. Music was provided by an electric guitar and drums; some gauzy curtains hanging from the ceiling served as decor. As I sat on a bench it struck me that this church was very Nicaraguan—perhaps more Nicaraguan than a typical parish where the pastor was probably not Nicaraguan and the liturgy came from Rome.

Various reasons could explain evangelical growth: the institutional weakness of the Catholic Church, lively worship, personal testimony and especially dramatic conversions that enabled people to lead new lives, an emphasis on outreach, the sense of community.

The Catholic charismatic movement was similar in some ways, in emotional worship and testimony, but it entailed no break from Catholicism and retained some of its characteristic features, such as the rosary and the papacy.

* * *

Today it is difficult—practically impossible—to recapture the surprise at seeing communism collapse in Eastern Europe in a matter of weeks. The Solidarity labor union had become a mass movement in the early 1980s, but it remained illegal. Mikhail Gorbachev, who became general secretary of the Communist Party in 1985, represented a new generation of leadership after years of gerontocracy. He sought to open and modernize the economic system, engaged in nuclear weapons negotiations with Reagan, and—most significantly—indicated that the USSR would not intervene militarily to save regimes in Eastern Europe, as it had in 1956 and 1968.

In mid-1989, both Poland and Hungary moved peacefully toward parliamentary systems. Large numbers of East Germans seeking to cross into the West triggered the dismantling of the Berlin Wall. None of this was preordained: that same year, masses of Chinese protesters filled Tiananmen Square until troops killed several hundred or more demonstrators. The crucial events in Europe unfolded in a chain reaction over several weeks between November 1989 and early 1990. Communism was gone from Poland, Czechoslovakia, Hungary, East Germany, Bulgaria, Romania, Yugoslavia, and Albania. Dissident leaders like Vaclav Havel and Lech Walesa were elected heads of state.

Ronald Reagan is often credited with defeating communism, with his challenge, "Mr. Gorbachev, tear down this wall," or by accelerating an arms race that the Soviets realized they couldn't win. Some prefer to credit Pope John Paul II. Both views exhibit a simplistic "Great Man" theory of history. People living under Soviet control had long been aware that West Europeans had a far higher standard of living. Faith in official Marxist ideology had been waning for decades. The sudden end of communism in the second half of 1989 was nevertheless unexpected. It was a landmark event, although from today's perspective developments in post-Mao China, little noticed at the time, were at least as significant. Communism lasted in the Soviet Union for another year and a half, when its collapse was triggered by contingent and unexpected circumstances.

Although it is conventionally assumed that the United States and the West "won" the Cold War, in a larger sense everyone lost—especially in Latin America, Africa, and Asia, where the two superpowers sponsored proxy wars. In a subtler way it was also true in the United States with McCarthyism and its heirs, but also in the maintenance of an enormous military structure, capped off with the possession of a nuclear arsenal, ever at the ready.

* * *

In November 1989, as the Berlin Wall was falling, the FMLN launched a long-awaited attack in San Salvador, beginning in poor neighborhoods. Government forces attacked those areas from the air. Several days into the attack, in the middle of the night, troops of the U.S.-trained Atlacatl Battalion went to the residence of the Jesuit professors of the Catholic university on the opposite side of town, dragged six of them out, and shot them to death, along with a housekeeper who had taken refuge there and her teenage daughter. From those murdered, I had met with theologian Ignacio Ellacuria and social psychologist Ignacio Martin-Baro, and Amando Lopez had hosted our 1978 delegation in Managua; I had seen the others at the Jesuit residences over the years.

The military had regarded the Jesuits as "subversive" since the mid-1970s, and this action, which was directed from the top levels of the military, represented a long-felt desire to kill those whom they regarded as the "intellectual authors" of the insurgency—ignoring the fact that for a decade Ellacuria and the UCA had advocated peace negotiations.

Although the military, the government, and the U.S. embassy tried to portray this as an action by the left, that claim began to fall apart as witnesses appeared. The killing further exposed the bankruptcy of U.S. policy in El Salvador. Moreover, the end of the Cold War removed the claimed justification for U.S. support for the Salvadoran military and government.

* * *

In December 1989 President George H. W. Bush ordered an invasion of Panama to topple the government of General Manuel Noriega and bring him to justice in the United States. Even under Torrijos, as head of G-2 (Intelligence), Noriega had been the second most powerful man in the country. After Torrijos died in a plane crash in 1981 (which some suspected was not an accident), Noriega was the real power of the regime, but not the formal head of state.

For years he had been a CIA asset while keeping good relations with Havana. In the mid-1980s Noriega was accused of involvement in drug trafficking and money laundering. Late in the decade a political crisis unfolded, especially after the 1989 election, which outside observers said had been won decisively by Guillermo Endara, but which the regime refused to recognize. When Endara and the vice-presidential candidates protested, Noriega paramilitaries beat them savagely.

The United States still had several military bases with thousands of troops in the Canal Zone, which had not yet been transferred to Panama. The killing of a U.S. serviceman at a roadblock provided a trigger: U.S. forces literally had to only cross an avenue and advance a quarter mile to the Panamanian National Guard headquarters in Chorrillo. In the melee, Chorrillo burned down, either as a result of the attack or possibly set on fire by Noriega paramilitaries. Thousands of people were made homeless. In the early phases of the invasion and occupation, massive looting took place, as U.S. troops stood by and did not intervene. Noriega went into hiding and then sought asylum in the papal nunciature, where he turned himself in two weeks later, after U.S. troops surrounded it and blasted it with nonstop heavy metal music.

Few Americans questioned the invasion, softened up by media portrayals of Noriega as a thug. Virtually no one pointed out that although Noriega had blood on his hands, his victims numbered in the dozens, not the tens of thousands, as with the regimes in Guatemala and El Salvador, which the United States had supported for a decade and called "struggling democracies."

In January 1990 I went to Panama as part of a small AFSC delegation, arriving a day after Noriega surrendered, and went there again in the middle of the year, in both cases to assess the results of the U.S. invasion. In January, U.S. troops were still patrolling the streets and were in effect the authority, although they had installed President Endara. We went to see my old friend Ricardo Arias Calderon, who had hosted Angie and me in Miami when we were deported in 1974. He was now co–vice president in his office in the elegant Palacio de las Garzas, in the colonial part of Panama City.

We visited some of those left homeless in Chorrillo who were now housed in hangars at the former Albrook Air Force Station. They expected the United States or the new government to provide them with homes, preferably in Chorrillo. By midyear they were being offered a sixty-five-hundred-dollar voucher to be used on various new housing developments of the site-and-service model, that is, a concrete floor and roof, with water and sewerage, and construction materials with which to build a house, located miles from Chorrillo. Years later barebones apartment buildings for the poor were constructed in Chorrillo.

What shocked me above all was the reaction of most Panamanians. Few objected to the invasion in principle, perhaps because Noriega had so monopolized Panamanian nationalism that it became discredited. The upper and middle classes had been more frightened of the looting than the U.S. invasion, and I was told that many had bought guns and were learning how to use them. I found practically no concern for the fate of those who had been killed in the invasion, at least several hundred, perhaps more. At mid-year, a Jesuit and another old friend were trying to compile a list. For many years the fate of those killed was completely ignored. Only in 2016 did the Panamanian government appoint a commission to provide a report on the civilian victims of the invasion.

* * *

For the February 1990 Nicaraguan presidential election, the opposition coalition UNO chose Violeta de Chamorro, widow of Pedro Joaquin Chamorro, to run against Daniel Ortega. Polls gave the Sandinistas a ten-point lead, but as the results came in, UNO had won. Nicaraguans were stunned, including UNO, which had not even made plans for a victory celebration.

When I was in Nicaragua four months later to do research on the churches, the Sandinistas and their supporters were still having trouble coming to terms with the election results. Those who had worked in the government for a decade, confident that the revolution was permanent, now had to find ways of making a living. Many NGOs were quickly set up to work in health care, education, agriculture, and other types of development work.

One Monday evening at the monthly meeting of Christian base-community leaders from around Managua, I looked around at a circle of perhaps three dozen people and realized that they were weary and discouraged. Most were now middle-aged and had seen a decade of hopes for a better society dashed.

The mood in El Salvador was more upbeat, even in the wake of the Jesuits' murder, because it was clear that the war was winding down and would be ended through peace negotiations. With the journalist Gene Palumbo, I visited Ciudad Segundo Montes, a recently formed community of refugees returned from Honduras, where people had visions of a better life.

In Guatemala my last interview was at AVANSCO (Asociación para el Avance de las Ciencias Sociales [Association for the Advance of the Social Sciences]), a research institute in Guatemala City. About a month later Myrna Mack, an AVANSCO anthropologist, was stabbed to death by a military death squad outside the organization's office for her revelations about army violence.

We had begun the decade with a sense of urgency, hoping to prevent a Vietnam-like U.S. intervention in Central America, little imagining that the struggle would last so long. From small beginnings, a grassroots resistance movement had arisen and spread and constrained the administration. And then when the struggle seemed endless, the world changed.

The Central America movement had mixed results: the Reagan administration's support for the Salvadoran government and military and the contras had been slowed but not halted. On the other hand, U.S. combat troops had not been sent to Central America (with the exception of the Panama invasion). The realization that direct U.S. troop involvement would create a large grassroots opposition movement with strong roots in the churches had served as a significant deterrent.

* * *

Around 1990 Rosemary Ruether asked me to write a chapter on Latin America for a book she was compiling with Eugene Bianchi advocating the democratization of the Catholic Church. Although I sympathized with their aim, I replied that I was unlikely to submit the kind of article she was expecting. Through the 1980s theologians and others had written as though a "new church in a new society" was coming into being in Latin America. From my experience in Central America and what I was reading about other places, I sensed frustration and discouragement.

With his usual candor, Comblin had written me in a letter, "Liberation theology is in a crisis which reflects the state of crisis in all social movements on the continent, including Marxism." That crisis was largely unrecognized. "Partly it reflects repression from Rome, and partly it is the discouragement of pastoral workers who after twenty years have not seen any change in the political and social situation."

In my article I noted that the concerns driving progressives elsewhere, such as rethinking sexual morality or women's ordination, were not prominent in Latin America. Christian base communities had always represented a very small proportion of the population and were entering into crisis. The left, which had once disparaged "bourgeois democracy," was now learning to live in a democratic pluralistic society, which meant having to coexist with groups holding positions in vehement opposition to their own. Latin American Catholicism practiced considerable consultation between the hierarchy, clergy, and laypeople, but that wasn't regarded as democracy. Following my chapter was one by a Brazilian sociologist presenting the conventional view, with no hint of the crisis I sensed.

The fall of the Berlin Wall had ushered in a "new world order." While most of the world welcomed the fall of communism and looked forward to the prospects of what was now being called "globalization," the Latin American left experienced a crisis.

What were the implications for Latin America and for my generation's hopes and dreams? Such questions would occupy me for the next two decades.

13

Paradigms Lost

With a fellowship at the Kellogg Institute for International Studies, I spent the fall of 1990 at the University of Notre Dame writing drafts for a book on the churches in Central America that I had been researching. Michael Fleet, a political scientist at Marquette who also had a fall fellowship, and I rented a house from a faculty member on sabbatical. Through the semester I rode a bike four miles through farms down to an office on campus, worked into the evening, and then biked back through the dark for a late supper. Michael's research topic was the relationship between Catholicism and politics in Peru and Chile. The Kellogg Institute had been founded for interdisciplinary studies of democracy and development and had a strong emphasis on Latin America, reflecting the concerns of the Holy Cross congregation and Fr. Theodore Hesburgh, then recently retired after thirty-five years as president of Notre Dame.

Although I had spoken at dozens of universities and had taught a few adjunct courses in Philadelphia and New Jersey, this was my first ongoing experience of a university from within. I found the atmosphere collegial, but I saw the faculty and other Kellogg fellows primarily at brown-bag lunches and a few social events. When I posted a sheet on a bulletin board for signatures in protest against the recent murder of anthropologist Myrna Mack in Guatemala, I was dismayed at the slowness of the response. That was partly my unfamiliarity with the pace of life in academia. Only on my next-to-last day did the professor in the office adjacent to mine, a specialist in South Africa, and I discover that we had interests in common. My naïve belief in the university as a community of scholars collided with the reality of individuals pursuing their own specializations.

Narrating the story of the churches—now including evangelicals—was relatively easy. The larger challenge was how to make sense of it all. The dream of a qualitatively new kind of society had been thwarted. Had all the bloodshed, that of the people whose stories I have been telling here, been in vain? My provisional answer was reflected in the title *Stubborn Hope*. Theologians and others were refusing to simply submit to the new capitalist orthodoxy and were insisting on the need for pragmatism to be accompanied by utopia. Xavier Gorostiaga had quoted Pablo Neruda: "They can cut all the flowers, but they can't cut the spring."

Getting the book to publication brought problems of its own. I had a contract and advance from Pantheon, which had published three of my previous books. For years the Pantheon general manager, Andre Schiffrin, undertook worthy books while doing no more than breaking even, as had once been common in book publishing. However, Pantheon was owned by Random House, and a new CEO now forced Schifrin to resign with the aim of making Pantheon profitable. Andre's firing exemplified a shift in publishing in which managers increasingly saw books as commodities. Most of the editors resigned in solidarity with Andre, and hundreds of people, including Studs Terkel, Barbara Ehrenreich, and E. L. Doctorow, picketed Random House one noontime.

After long delays, the new editor in chief, Erroll McDonald, informed me that my manuscript was unacceptable, without explaining why. After some months he agreed to my proposal that I be allowed to take the manuscript to another publisher. *Stubborn Hope* was jointly published in 1994 by Orbis Books and the New Press, a nonprofit that Andre had set up with some foundation money. By that time, Central America—and Latin America as a whole—had dropped off the map in the United States.

* * *

One of the Kellogg fellows was Francisco Weffort, a Brazilian political scientist from Sao Paulo, who had been one of many who sought exile in Chile after the 1964 coup. His wife, Madalena, was a daughter of Paulo Freire. One day at lunch I asked him what had become of the dream of socialism. He began simply, "We're not talking about socialism any more, but about democracy."

The remark stayed with me because many on the left had not made such a step, including theologian Clodovis Boff, who in 1989 published *Cartas Teológicas sobre o Socialismo*, open letters he had published after extended visits to Cuba, the Soviet Union, and China in previous years, followed by an essay setting forth his own view of socialism. His vision in each case wasn't starry-eyed but was clearly intended to counter dismissals of socialism common in the West. He even included a postscript, taking into account the massacre in Tiananmen Square in May 1989, siding with the protesters and against the regime, but affirming that the demonstrators were calling for reforms within socialism, not its abolition.

The transition to democracy was Weffort's research topic. For him it wasn't simply academic; while at South Bend he sometimes spoke by phone with Lula, the labor leader who had been the Workers Party candidate for president in 1989.

As military rule gave way to elected civilian governments in South America (Peru, Bolivia, Argentina, Brazil, Uruguay, and Chile) in the 1980s, it wasn't at all clear that this democracy would last. Into the 1990s, high military officers in Chile,

Argentina, and elsewhere sometimes made threatening noises. Moreover, if these elected governments represented only the elites and were not really accountable to the poor majorities, they were at best formal or procedural democracies.

With the debt crisis, governments had become beholden to the IMF, the World Bank, and the U.S. government, which were making debt relief contingent upon undertaking major policy changes: reducing tariff barriers, reining in government spending, privatizing government enterprises, and fostering free trade. At a meeting of mainly Latin American economists in Washington in 1991, John Williamson summarized guidelines for economic policy in a document that became known as the "Washington Consensus." Its place of origin and nickname provided a convenient target. Opposition to "neoliberalism," a catch-all term for these policies, became a rallying point. Although Latin American activists and academic Latin Americanists moved away from yearning for a left-wing revolution based around a revolutionary party taking state power, they now put their faith in grassroots movements (e.g., peasants, labor unionists, women, indigenous, environmental activists).

Mexican public intellectual Jorge Castañeda took a provocative contrarian stance in the opening words of *Utopia Unarmed: The Latin American Left After the Cold War* (1993): "The Cold War is over and Communism and the socialist bloc have collapsed. The United States and capitalism have won, and in few areas of the globe is that victory so clear-cut, sweet, and spectacular as in Latin America." Although I didn't think anyone had "won" the Cold War, I appreciated Castañeda's blunt approach to facing the quandary of the left. His underlying argument was simple: there is no alternate economic system to capitalism, but capitalism exists in more than one form; Latin American nations should develop their own appropriate model. He advocated a strong welfare-state model as in northern Europe rather than an Anglo-American laissez-faire model. I thought his argument merited discussion and wrote a review in the *National Catholic Reporter*. Activists and academics were resistant to Castañeda's argument, as was clear at his presentation at the LASA meeting in Atlanta in spring 1994.

* * *

In the United States, Latin America was now being viewed through the lens of drug trafficking, particularly in view of the epidemic of crack cocaine and the associated rise in crime rates. For centuries, coca leaves had been grown in the Andes and chewed as a mild stimulant at work and for withstanding the cold. Now coca production expanded in remote areas because it was easy to grow and paid well. Coca leaves were processed into a paste in Bolivia and Peru and then transported to Colombia, where it was processed into cocaine powder that was transported to markets overseas.

In response to simplistic portrayals in which the producer countries were being blamed for U.S. addiction and crime, in spring 1992 the AFSC organized a speaking tour for three people from Latin American countries chosen by staff in South

America: Concepcion Quispe, an indigenous leader in Cusco, Peru; Eleuterio Romero, a Bolivian labor organizer from Cochabamba; and Ana Velasquez, a woman in her mid-twenties from Ciudad Bolivar, a large, poor barrio in greater Bogota. The tour took them to visit various local programs around the country. I was asked to go along, partly as an interpreter, but also to provide some continuity and assistance in the constant travel from city to city in a strange land.

One of the aims of the tour was to put a human face on the hemispheric drug crisis. They spoke at potlucks, to Quaker and church congregations, and in college classrooms, and were interviewed by local newspaper and TV reporters in Washington, Philadelphia, New York, New England, San Francisco, Austin—sixteen cities in all. The aim wasn't simply one-way communication; in a St. Louis hospital we were taken into the pediatric ward wearing gowns and masks and saw low-weight infants struggling to survive who had been born to addicted mothers. By being exposed to the effects of drug trafficking, these community leaders could help their colleagues appreciate the drug crisis in the United States. The emphasis was on contact with local community organizations. It was an example of the strength of the AFSC as a national peacemaking organization with strong local roots linking broader, even international, issues to local concerns.

* * *

Into the 1990s I had gone from project to project as a freelancer, translating and writing books, sometimes with an advance. I fancied myself a freelance writer and entertained the idea of making a career out of identifying a worthwhile topic, researching it, writing a book, and earning enough in the process to contribute my share to the family income. Spotting a small announcement in the *New York Review of Books*, in April 1991 I drove to Albany to attend a weekend conference of writers with a New York state connection, mainly nonfiction (Bill McKibben, Timothy Ferris, Steven Jay Gould, David McCullough, Maureen Dowd, Garry Wills) in panels organized around science, history, politics, and so forth. Also included was a Saturday-night panel with novelists William Kennedy (an Albany local), Mary Gordon, and Norman Mailer—the latter two clashing over Mailer's machismo. It was a bibliophile's delight.

During a break I had a few minutes' conversation with Taylor Branch, who had published *Parting the Waters*, the first volume of his trilogy on Martin Luther King and the larger context around him. Even though the first volume had won praise and awards, he said he was running out of savings as he worked on the second. That was a moment of insight: if Taylor Branch was having difficulty supporting himself, I was unlikely to make a living by writing. My books on Central America and liberation theology had sold in the tens of thousands, but the book on the U.S. bishops' pastoral letters on peace and the economy was a dud. Given the time involved in research and writing, and a year between the finished manuscript and publication, being a successful nonfiction writer meant identifying a topic that would be relevant in three to five years' time and producing a book whose royalties would repay the work of research and writing.

* * *

In October 1991 I spent a week in New York working with the cable network Court TV, which was then about a year old. They had obtained video of twenty hours of the trial of a half-dozen members of the Salvadoran armed forces for the murder of the Jesuits. From Monday through Thursday in a small side room, I gave a running translation of the trial to a young producer who took notes. She then selected portions totaling four hours, and on Friday I was joined by a freelance simultaneous interpreter who worked for the United Nations. We alternated doing simultaneous voiceover interpretation, and the program was aired shortly afterward.

The trial itself was eerie. Because of the danger to their lives, the jury members had to be hidden behind a partition. The eight troops placed on trial were among those who carried out the raid and murder; the colonel who headed the military school was found guilty, as was a lieutenant who had taken part in the killings. The other six were acquitted, even though some had also confessed to taking part. Higher officials who gave the orders were shielded from inquiry; this trial of lower-ranking troops was a sacrificial offering to U.S. public opinion. The two found guilty were released in an amnesty agreement in 1993.

During that week in the large open office area where most of the Court TV staff were working, monitors were carrying the Senate confirmation hearings for Clarence Thomas for the Supreme Court, at which Anita Hill accused him of sexual harassment and was harshly grilled by senators who dismissed her claim.

* * *

As one of his first acts in office, President Patricio Aylwin, who succeeded Pinochet in Chile, appointed a commission to investigate and compile a comprehensive account of the most severe human rights violations during the military dictatorship. The result was a two-volume report published in 1991, most of which consisted of chronological case-by-case descriptions of each instance of murder or disappearance, starting with the day of the coup and the death of President Allende himself. The commission used records of cases that had been filed with church assistance but ignored by the justice system, as well as interviews. Thus, the Chilean state was officially acknowledging what had in fact been previously denied or justified. The military and its civilian sympathizers pushed back.

I spent most of 1992 translating that report for the University of Notre Dame Press, at the behest of Fr. Bill Lewers, the head of the Center for Civil and Human Rights at the university's law school. Linguistically speaking, the translation was easy because the committee-written accounts used formulaic language and were repetitive. While working on it, however, I reminded myself that these events really happened and that, at a minimum, the victims should be publicly acknowledged by name.

A white South African law student working at the law school told me that the translation of the Chilean report would be useful to his own country when it confronted apartheid sometime in the future. By the early 2000s, such governmental and nongovernmental truth commissions had issued postconflict human rights reports in around three dozen countries.

* * *

Since the mid-1970s I have spent early Saturday and Sunday mornings drinking black coffee and reading and mulling over theology broadly considered—including scripture, history, ethics, philosophy, and religion generally—as well as systematic theology. My reading itself is unsystematic and is not driven by any teaching. It doesn't lead to prayer or meditation and may not make me a better Christian; I'm still mulling over questions I first encountered as a seminarian.

In order to teach an Introduction to Catholicism course at Rosemont College in Pennsylvania in 1989 I cobbled together a set of readings, including books by Lawrence Cunningham and Rosemary Ruether. That led me to conceive of gathering a representative set of readings in Catholic theology. Undertaking such a project would enable and even force me to read a great deal of material and sort it out. I mailed requests to around thirty theologians asking for their opinions—what they used in the classroom and copies of their syllabi. In their friendly replies, they welcomed my interest but cautioned me on the difficulty of compiling something that professors of theology would be able to use (as well as alerting me to the problem of securing permissions to reprint copyrighted material).

At that point, twenty-five years had passed since the end of Vatican II. Systematic theologians had quickly moved away from neo-Scholasticism and had made scripture central to their work. In writing about the various topics (God, creation, Trinity, Christology, ecclesiology, grace, sacraments, and so forth), they often focused on two poles: the scriptural texts and contemporary culture. Relatively little attention was given to historic controversies or even defined doctrine.

New questions were becoming central, notably "science and religion" and the relationship of Christianity to the other world religions. Various liberation theologies—Latin American, feminist, black, and so forth—were making praxis not a corollary but central to the way theological questions were posed.

How to make sense of the seeming cacophony of voices in theology? In *Method in Theology* (1972) Bernard Lonergan had proposed that theology be considered a vast collaborative enterprise. Rather than envisioning it as divided into fields and subfields, he proposed considering various "operations," which he called "functional specializations." Some of them seemed straightforward (research, interpretation, history, systematics, communication), but there were a total of eight, and they entailed adopting the cognitional theory that he had developed. His book had little influence outside Lonerganian circles.

After first providing an overview of Lonergan, David Tracy undertook to survey theology in what was intended to be a trilogy, publishing *Blessed Rage for Order* (1975), dealing with fundamental theology, and *The Analogical Imagination* (1981), with systematic theology. Both were wide-ranging surveys of the work of contemporary theologians, Catholic and Protestant. With the short volume *Plurality and Ambiguity* (1988), he signaled that his project had been interrupted. The book begins with reactions to a recent film portrayal of the French Revolution, followed by several pages of questions about the meaning of the revolution itself. If something like a revolution can lead to seemingly endless questions, much more must be the case of one who asks fundamental questions about life, as in philosophy and theology. Tracy now seemed overwhelmed by the endless possibility of questions and approaches. He dropped the earlier project and began to devote himself directly to the question of God. He presented his findings in 1999 at the prestigious Gifford Lectures, the forum in Scotland that leading thinkers about religion and philosophy have addressed since the nineteenth century. However, he did not prepare those lectures for publication, apparently unable to produce a text to his own satisfaction.

Tracy's travails illustrate the plight of theologians, caught between endless possibilities of interpretation, the need to speak, and the inadequacy of any human language.

* * *

In 1992 Latin America celebrated the five-century anniversary of the landing of Columbus, a key moment in the making of Latin America. Events were planned throughout the hemisphere, including a major UN conference on the environment to be held in Rio de Janeiro and a meeting of CELAM in Santo Domingo, following in the line of Medellín and Puebla.

What was being celebrated anyway? A "discovery"? That may have been true of the Iberians but not of the people they found. A "conquest"? That was certainly true, wrought by superior weapons and horses, but primarily by the diseases to which the indigenous peoples had no resistance, leading to a massive die-off. Some proposed the more neutral-sounding "encounter." In the preparations and celebration, Latin American identity was at issue.

Indigenous people were becoming more organized and militant. In 1990, indigenous groups had brought Ecuador to a standstill by blocking highways. Native American organizations were becoming networked and holding hemisphere-wide meetings. The 1992 Nobel Peace Prize was awarded to Rigoberta Menchu, the young

Guatemalan indigenous woman who for over a decade had denounced the military's human rights violations. I had interviewed her father and three other people a few days before they were burned alive in the Spanish embassy in January 1980 and met her when she stayed with us in 1982 while on a speaking tour. The Guatemalan military accused her of being a subversive.

I translated the 1992 CELAM document, which was bland in comparison to Medellin (1968) or even Puebla (1979). The document reflects a strong hand by the Vatican, after more than a decade of control imposed by John Paul II and the retirement and replacement of the Medellin generation of bishops. The CELAM text was organized around the figure of Jesus Christ and the themes of the new evangelization, human development, and Christian culture. The reading of the signs of the times was weak, with some remarks about democracy and market economies. The entire document had an ecclesiastical tone to it. Evangelicals were scarcely noted and were still called "sects," even though by this time they were on a par with Catholics in church attendance in Brazil, Guatemala, and elsewhere.

Perhaps the most positive side of the document was its treatment of culture and inculturation. Plurality of cultures (e.g., indigenous, mestizo, Afro-American, and modern) was recognized, and encouragement was given in principle to delving into indigenous cultures, appreciating their worldview, and using their symbols to "inculturate" the faith and the liturgy.

* * *

What was the situation of the churches in Latin America after the end of the Cold War and under globalization? To what extent was the "progressive" Catholic Church in crisis? Were expanding evangelicals now "coming of age"? I wanted to pursue these questions beyond Central America, and since the continent was increasingly urban, I wanted to focus on large cities. With a research grant from the Social Science Research Council, in February 1993 I set out to explore these matters in Sao Paulo and Caracas.

On the overnight flight to Sao Paulo I read a dissertation by anthropologist John Burdick, "Looking for God in Brazil." Doing field research in a neighborhood in greater Rio, he compared a progressive Catholic parish with an Assemblies of God congregation and practitioners of Afro-Brazilian religion. Burdick confirmed my hunch that a new religious landscape was taking shape.

Francisco Weffort, my colleague at Notre Dame in 1990, had arranged for me to rent a room in an apartment from Frei Betto, a Dominican lay brother and writer. As I had done in Central America, I interviewed church leaders and pastors as well as academics, and attended many church services, especially pentecostals'. I made my way around greater Sao Paulo on the metro and bus system, and sometimes just on foot. In Caracas I found a hotel in the neighborhood of Paraiso, a few bus stops from downtown.

Brazil and Venezuela were both in political and economic crisis. Brazil had suffered high inflation for many years, to the point where it was taken for granted. When I arrived, a strip of ten metro tickets cost fifty cruzeiros; when I left ten weeks later it was ninety. Since I had a dollar bank account, inflation didn't affect me much, but I observed price increases at grocery stores and restaurants. Growth was sluggish, and the country was only slowly opening to globalization.

President Fernando Collor had resigned under threat of impeachment the previous year, and Brazil was now in the hands of Itamar Franco, a traditional politician who was regarded as a caretaker president. Lula (Luiz Inacio da Silva), the labor leader and founder of the Workers Party (PT) who had lost to Collor in 1989, was the most popular politician in the country, and polls showed him to be the leading candidate for the 1994 election. PT mayors had governed a number of large cities, including Sao Paulo, where Paulo Freire had been secretary of education.

Brazil was also due to vote on whether to shift from a presidential to a parliamentary type of democracy. I attended a panel on the issue at the University of Sao Paulo, where Weffort was one of the presenters along with Fernando Henrique Cardoso, once an academic, and then minister of the economy in the Franco government. The next year he presided over a plan that halted inflation, which propelled him past Lula into the presidency. Meanwhile, the voters opted to retain a presidential model.

In Venezuela, demonstrations against President Carlos Andres Perez for corruption were constant, and he was forced to resign while I was there. The two-party system that had functioned since the 1950s had lost credibility. A major cause of the crisis was declining living standards, due to a drop in world oil prices. The Catholic university sponsored a weeklong seminar with panels of respected analysts on the situation of the country and possible ways out of the crisis, followed by discussion groups of ordinary citizens, many from parishes, presenting their conclusions in plenary sessions. As I went about Caracas, I was struck by the divide between the wealthy and the poor, whose barrios ran up the hillsides. In more than one parish I was told of gun battles between gangs and killings over sneakers.

One evening in the modest middle-class neighborhood near my hotel I came across a commotion: a pickup had been stolen and the driver shot in the leg as he was parking; a young woman, a sister or girlfriend, was screaming. After he was driven off to the emergency ward, a middle-aged woman approached the cluster of neighbors with whom I was talking and said that she had seen the pickup go careening around the corner. She was sure where they were going, pointing to the hills with poor barrios, and then added, "It's either them or us who will be left." She used this them-vs.-us language to a group of strangers, confident that we understood and agreed.

The previous year a group of military officers attempted a coup but failed. Hugo Chavez, one of the coup leaders, was now in jail. When he was released a couple years later, he skillfully exploited this polarization to be elected president, portraying himself as the champion of the poor over against the illegitimate elites, and won repeated elections for over a decade, aggravating divisions in the population.

* * *

My first interview in Sao Paulo was with a retired Baptist minister. Brazilian Baptists traced their origins to southern U.S. whites who, after the defeat in the Civil War, fled to Brazil where slavery remained. Although the church began among the poor, their descendants were often now middle class. Two pentecostal churches, the Assemblies of God and the Christian Congregation, had been founded around 1910; other major pentecostal churches had arisen in the 1950s; the newer pentecostal churches were thus a third wave. Venezuelan evangelical churches had arisen more recently, in the mid-twentieth century. Even though Catholics were only now noticing evangelicals in their midst, evangelicals themselves had a firm sense that they belonged.

One evening I attended the monthly meeting of Assemblies of God pastors. From my position in the choir loft in the large headquarters church, I estimated their number at eleven hundred, equal to the number of Catholic priests in greater Sao Paulo. Most were darker-skinned men, all in jackets and ties, making me feel self-conscious in the blue jeans that rendered me inconspicuous in the street.

To outside observers, pentecostals looked similar, but as I became familiar with the various churches, I encountered significant differences. The Christian Congregation, for example, did no proselytizing and had no clergy: it was guided by a belief that God directs everything, so much so that they did not prepare sermons but spoke as inspired by the moment. Men and women sat in separate sections, and at the end of the service I was surprised to find them kiss the people on either side, giving the "holy kiss," enjoined by St. Paul.

Most pentecostal churches were rooted in local congregations that grew as new members joined, and then split to start new congregations, sometimes after a dispute. In contrast, the Universal Church of the Kingdom of God first set up churches, often in old theaters, and held four services a day, every day of the week, inviting people off the street. Fridays, for example, were devoted to "liberation" (exorcism); those who were possessed by devils were invited up on stage where ministers prayed over them, telling the devils to "Get out!" as they writhed and shouted.

Some churches had a strict dress code, especially for women; others left it to the discretion of members. At a "God is Love" church I noted that everyone around me looked poor, including the ministers; other churches had a more middle-class feel. In the Renacer church in Sao Paulo I attended a Monday-night youth service, held in a former movie theater with the seats removed, which was a Christian rock concert with testimonies.

In Venezuela, the percentage of evangelicals was smaller than in Brazil, then estimated at 1 percent of Caracas and 4 percent of the country. I was impressed by the nondenominational Las Acacias church, which had a middle-class feel and many ministries, akin to what is now called a megachurch.

Considerable effort was devoted to church growth campaigns, such as large public rallies that went on for several days. One was held in downtown Sao Paulo during Holy Week, and another in an abandoned bull ring in Caracas. The ostensible aim was for people to come forward and accept Christ as their savior. However, church-growth specialists told me that growth was primarily through one-on-one influence on family members, work colleagues, and neighbors. Public campaigns and rallies served primarily as a show of force in society and gave evangelicals a sense of their strength.

As earlier in Central America, I appreciated the religious fervor of evangelicals and had some appreciation and sympathy for them, while not questioning my own Catholic identity. My Catholic and secular interlocutors were not very curious about the fast-growing churches around them. Bishops and theologians dismissed them; one recommended that I read a book by a Brazilian journalist that explained them away as the result of imperialism, and was based largely on U.S. journalistic sources rather than on-site observation in Brazil. Within a few weeks I knew more about evangelicals than my Catholic and secular friends, but they were little intrigued.

* * *

Progressive Catholics in Brazil were disconcerted by recent developments. "Five years ago we had many answers and few questions," said Father Alfredo Gonçalves, who was working in the crowded tenements of downtown Sao Paulo. "Today it's the other way around. We've got very few answers and lots of questions." I heard similar sentiments from several others. In the 1980s, church people had thought they were witnessing the birth of a new church of the people as part of a movement toward a different kind of society; now they were seeing neither.

Questions were being raised about the base-community model. Although it was commonly reported that there were eighty thousand or one hundred thousand of them; a more sober estimate was that the true number was probably closer to ten thousand. The Archdiocese of Sao Paulo had been split up by the Vatican, and although Cardinal Paulo Evaristo Arns was still in the central area, the bishops of the new dioceses were generally conservative and were dismantling what had been done under Arns.

The situation was especially troubling for Ana Dias, who had been active in church-related movements for over twenty years. Her husband, Santo Dias, had been a labor activist and church leader and had been shot dead by a policeman in the midst of a strike. The policeman had been found guilty but released after a year. Now thirteen years later she was still active, running a modest daycare center in the southern region of greater Sao Paulo, the widow of a martyr, but feeling the pain of loss and frustration, particularly over the lack of support from the institutional church. Church people in

Venezuela had less of a sense of crisis because they had not experienced such enthusiastic hopes as in Brazil.

Likewise, theologian Ivone Gebara said that she had always felt somewhat uncomfortable with the way theologians spoke of base communities and visions of a new church and a new society. That was a dream that was not rooted in the real conditions of the poor. Living among the poor and seeing the poverty, unemployment, and violence firsthand, she had felt that for years "we were using the poor to buoy up our own triumphalism about the poor." I encountered various examples of pastoral work among groups of women, which pastors and bishops largely ignored.

Vital pastoral work was being done, especially in two parishes in the east of greater Sao Paulo. I spent an evening in Praça da Se, the plaza in front of the cathedral in downtown Sao Paulo, in a ministry to street children. Priests, sisters, and seminarians stayed in the square from 8 PM until around 2 AM and were available to children and youth who came to them. Some youth were getting high by sniffing nail polish, which they had pilfered. This ministry, recognized by the archdiocese, offered help to those who wanted to get off the streets. Another ministry was to people living in crowded tenements, sometimes in abandoned buildings, in the now-decaying downtown of Sao Paulo.

In contrast with progressives, the Catholic Charismatic Renewal was confident. Over the four days of Carnival, it held continuous daylong prayer sessions in a large, open space in a Catholic girls' school, intended as a kind of spiritual antidote to the excesses and sin going on out in the street. A nun gave what amounted to instructions in glossalalia (speaking in tongues), encouraging us to try speaking nonsense syllables. A strength of the movement was its lay leadership in worship sessions and a national structure, although Edward Dougherty, S.J., an American priest who had brought the renewal to Brazil, was very influential. He was then developing a national TV network. In Venezuela the Charismatic Renewal was less successful. When I showed up for a gathering in a stadium, I was told that it had been cancelled, apparently for lack of attendees.

In both countries I obtained a manual typewriter from a repair shop and spent hours typing up my cassette tapes of interviews and my own dictated recollections. When I returned to Philadelphia I first had to complete that work and then organize the material. I opted to present much of my findings in the form of portraits or sketches of some of my interviewees, as well as descriptions of different churches and their worship.

In the closing chapters I proposed what Catholics and evangelicals might learn from each other. Rather than dismissing them as sects, Catholics could become curious about what moves people to join evangelical churches (sense of community, mutual support, overcoming of alcoholism and domestic violence, pastors from among the people, and so forth). Evangelicals could learn lessons of history from Catholicism and historic Protestant churches, particularly as they sought a more public role in society. I speculated that from time to time Catholics and evangelicals might join together in prayer or some public endeavors. It seemed to me that Latin American Catholics needed to acknowledge that they no longer enjoyed a cultural monopoly in their societies and should recognize and accept the reality of de facto religious pluralism.

* * *

Spending four months tramping around Sao Paulo and Caracas rekindled my fascination with cities, and Latin American cities in particular, that had begun during my years in Panama. Despite work done by Jorge Hardoy, Alejandro Portes, Bryan Roberts, and others, cities aroused relatively little interest among academic Latin Americanists and activists. Something similar was true of theologians; one could read the entire series done by the liberation theologians in the 1980s and not find any indication that most Latin Americans lived in towns and cities.

Yet urbanization was a fact: four the ten largest cities in the world were in Latin America (Mexico City, Sao Paulo, Rio de Janeiro, and Buenos Aires), all of them over 10 million inhabitants. When writing about cities, scholars and journalists tended to catalogue problems: slums, violence, lack of hygiene, and so forth. The larger the city, the more intractable the problems would presumably be. In the late 1980s Janice Perlman at NYU and others initiated the MegaCities Project with a different approach: assuming that people living in these cities must be devising solutions, the project sought to identify innovative groups in large cities around the world and link them in networks.

Delving into literature about cities around the world, I wrote a proposal for a study project called "Livable Cities?" The premise was that the future of the people of Latin America would largely be determined by the kinds of cities they lived in, particularly whether they would be safe. In a dash of bravado, I said that I wanted to do for Latin American cities what a number of recent books had done for the Amazon rain forest. I didn't get the grant (only one in twenty applicants did), perhaps because what I proposed looked more like journalism than scholarship.

* * *

When I returned from Brazil and Venezuela, our oldest daughter, Catherine, was about to start college, soon to be followed by her sisters. I needed to be able to contribute more reliably to our family income than I was doing as a freelance writer. Having translated some books, I decided to go into commercial translating, although I had only a dim idea of what that might mean. I began by looking up "translation" in the Yellow Pages for Philadelphia, Washington, DC, and New York, and mailing a resume to the companies I found there. These queries led to some initial jobs, particularly from some local translation agencies (in that pre-Internet era).

Joining the American Translators Association (ATA) and its local Philadelphia chapter, the Delaware Valley Translators Association (DVTA), and attending conferences, I began to understand how my adopted profession works. I passed the ATA accreditation exams for Spanish to English and Portuguese to English in the mid-1990s. Through the ATA I obtained lists of translation agencies and sent out my resume. In my query letter I emphasized my dozen years of living in Latin America and extensive travels, as well as the fact that I had translated books and written some of my own. Enclosed was a cartoon that I had found, showing two scruffy-looking men sitting at a table holding drinks. One of them, in a bow tie, is saying to the other, who is looking away with a frustrated expression on his face, "Do you not be happy with me as the translator of the books of you?"

Translation companies and their clients need more than competence in the source and the target languages; they expect expertise in the subject matter, particularly in technical areas, and for medical and legal matters. Thus, becoming a professional translator or interpreter has a chicken-and-egg aspect: how does a newcomer acquire the experience and expertise that clients and translation agencies seek?

In one of those early jobs I agreed to translate a document from Brazil about establishing telecommunications centers in rural Brazil. Although I could translate the apparent sense, I didn't have any real understanding of the technical vocabulary. Fortunately, our neighbor and friend Jim Parker did understand and could look at the original documents and my draft translation and walk me through an explanation. When I translated construction contracts or calls for bids, he could give me the correct term and assure me that it made sense. He has an astonishing background of experience in construction, the environment, telecommunications, and various other technical fields. Through Jim I eventually reached the point where I had relevant technical experience myself, including knowing when a particular translation was beyond my competence.

In the mid-1990s, translation agencies phoned me, and I delivered by express mail or FedEx, in WordPerfect. Soon translations were sent by file transfer protocol (FTP), and then email attachment became common. At ATA conferences I bought specialized (legal, technical, medical) Spanish- and Portuguese-to-English dictionaries. For over a decade they have languished on the shelf while I used online sources.

In translating a document I do an initial draft, then go through it a second time, correcting errors, resolving problems, and seeking consistency. I then print it out and do a hard-copy edit, enter the corrections, and submit the final version. A rule of thumb is that a translator can do about three thousand words a day finished copy, although some manage to do considerably more.

For decades, translators have heard others confidently assert that their function will be replaced by computers. Machine translation can give a sense of the content of a document, but except for very stereotyped domains (e.g., weather forecasts), the result does not look or sound like human speech or writing. Various forms of computer-aided translation (CAT) tools have been devised and translators use them widely. They divide up a text into units (sentences) and, drawing on databases of existing translations, propose translations of segments for the translator to approve or correct. I was slow to adopt these tools.

Translators and interpreters continue to struggle for recognition as professionals in the face of a tendency to think that anyone who knows two languages can translate or interpret. It is a major function of the ATA to achieve recognition for the profession, particularly by educating the public.

At an ATA convention in the late 1990s, I talked to a representative of the Foreign Broadcast Information Service (FBIS), a CIA operation that provided translations of newspaper stories in many countries to U.S. government agencies. For about a year I translated daily political stories from Brazilian newspapers. In doing so, I had to enter into the FBIS/CIA website, download the story, translate it, and upload the translation in the same fashion, via FTP. Doing so enabled me to follow political events in Brazil during the presidency of Fernando Henrique Cardoso, at a time when financial crises in Mexico and Asia impacted Brazil. One residue of that work is my CIA-assigned password, which I continued to use for other purposes. How could I cooperate in any way with an agency responsible for covert operations around the world, including overthrowing elected governments? FBIS was a legitimate intelligence operation; in fact, I learned of its existence when I saw a major human rights activist holding a fistful of FBIS reports.

Thus, in my fifties, after decades of being a priest, a peace organization staff member, an activist, and a writer, I learned a trade. When filling out forms, in the space for "occupation" I could write "freelance translator."

* * *

In fall 1993 I began adjunct teaching at Temple University, primarily Perspectives on Latin America, an interdisciplinary survey course in the catalogue, and occasionally Religion in Latin America. Adjunct teaching was a welcome complement to the solipsism of translation. Twice a week I drove or biked to Temple, four miles away in North Philadelphia to teach the class, and return. When I started, adjuncts were paid less than three thousand dollars per course (no more than twenty dollars an hour when preparation, exams, and grading were taken into account), a sum that grew only very incrementally.

Teaching forced me to keep asking myself: *How do I help eighteen- or twenty-year-olds understand and appreciate Latin America, and how do I help them integrate that into their lives and future careers?* I could have prepared a syllabus, chosen a standard survey text, and continued from semester to semester with only minor tweaks and telling "war stories" from Central America. From the outset, however, I decided that I should give due attention to the whole region, especially Brazil, Mexico, and the other large countries, and that I should incorporate ongoing developments. Each semester I looked for an overview book that would provide basic information and also books or articles that would give an experiential sense. A wonderful ten-part PBS series called *Americas* had appeared in 1992, the result of years of collaborative work by Latin Americanists. Each hour program combined a country and a theme. I frequently used Chile (human rights and women), Brazil (economic development), Mexico (rural-to-urban migration), and Bolivia–Dominican Republic (race/ethnicity), showing segments as a takeoff point for class discussion.

Existing survey texts reflected "dependency theory," which had gained currency as an explanatory paradigm starting in the late 1960s. Although the scholars differed among themselves, in broad strokes this approach focused on how Latin American nations had been incorporated into the international division of labor as suppliers of raw materials to the industrializing nations. The countries of the periphery (Latin America, Asia, Africa) were economically dependent on the center (Europe and North America); that dependence extended to politics and culture, and had been enforced by U.S. interventions in the region since the nineteenth century. The Reagan administration's meddling in Central America was only the latest instance. Survey texts as well as histories implied that Latin America needed to break free of U.S. domination or even of capitalism itself. By the 1990s that framework had lost some cogency, but it had not been replaced by any other paradigm, aside from resistance to U.S.-led globalization. While teaching I continually changed the assigned reading materials and waited for an adequate overview.

I had no illusions about my effectiveness as a teacher. For a few students the class was an introduction to Latin America that became part of their lives, but for most it was one of thirty or so courses and fulfilled a requirement. Students appreciated my decades of on-the-ground experience. Based on anonymous student evaluations submitted at the end of each semester, I fit into the middle of the bell curve with other professors.

Temple itself changed over my almost two decades of teaching. When I began, the students were mainly commuters from the Philadelphia area, and most were also working, sometimes thirty hours a week. Over time Temple became more of a residential campus extending into the neighborhood and attracting students from farther away. Initially I wrote with chalk on the blackboard, some students turned in handwritten papers, and I put books on library reserve for students to photocopy. Within a few years access to computers was taken for granted, although initially only a few could afford laptops, and I had to be vigilant to spot students submitting material plagiarized from the Web. I learned to use Blackboard, an education platform employed in many universities. Compulsive checking of handheld devices by students was only beginning when I taught my last course in 2011.

Having a Temple library card was a perk that I prized. I spent too many hours in the stacks, where there was a good collection of materials in religion and theology, partly as a result of Temple's strong graduate program in religious studies since the 1960s. I could check out materials and keep them through a semester if I wished.

Although as an adjunct I was marginal to the overall life of the university, I gained a glimpse of the aspirations and frustrations of students, professors, and administrators in a large urban university.

* * *

The 1990s in Latin America appeared to be another lost decade like the 1980s, with few signs of economic or political progress. In Brazil, inflation was finally halted in 1994 with a new currency implemented under Finance Minister Fernando Henrique Cardoso. That was a major development not only for business but for ordinary people. That achievement enabled Cardoso to defeat Lula in that year's election.

In Mexico the PRI establishment had been discredited by an electoral fraud in 1988 against the left-wing PRD. The Zapatista rebellion broke out in the southern state of Chiapas on January 1, 1994, the same day that NAFTA went into effect. Financial mismanagement by the PRI forced Mexico into a devaluation and economic crisis late that year. The Clinton administration provided crucial support, and the country's finances recovered. The PRI had been gradually allowing opposition parties to win elections for lower-level positions, and when Vicente Fox of the PAN (Partido Acción Nacional [National Action Party]) won the presidency in 2000, Mexico ceased being a one-party state.

In Peru, President Alberto Fujimori, who had run on a populist platform, abruptly embraced neoliberal reforms early in his presidency. The capture of Abimael Guzman, the cult-figure leader of the Maoist Shining Path insurgency that had terrorized the country for over a decade, boosted Fujimori's popularity, even after he disbanded Congress in a self-coup. His fortunes declined only late in the decade with revelations of corruption. Likewise in Argentina, Carlos Menem, who had run on Peronist populism, enacted some neoliberal reforms but enjoyed economic good fortune for most of the decade.

Seen from the outside, the Medellin drug lord Pablo Escobar seemed emblematic of Colombia, as he became a folk hero, was elected to Congress, was arrested and jailed, and escaped before finally being trapped and gunned down in 1993. Drug trafficking then became more decentralized but continued unabated, as did massive violence between official forces, right-wing paramilitaries, and guerrilla groups, forcing 4 million Colombians to flee the countryside into the cities.

Venezuela continued in political and economic crisis. Bolivia and the smaller countries of the region struggled to find relief from debt. Most of Central America stagnated under corrupt right-wing rule. A relatively bright spot was Chile, where the center-left coalition that had defeated Pinochet did not overturn the market-based economic model but instituted social programs aimed at addressing poverty and extreme inequality.

The grassroots organizations and NGOs that had emerged during the resistance to military governments and repression in Central America continued to expand into different areas (feminism, environmentalism, indigenous rights), constituting a vital civil society. Activists were learning how to lobby their legislatures and executive branches. However, the European funding agencies on which they had relied in the 1980s now turned their attention to the postcommunist societies of Eastern Europe and to sub-Saharan Africa.

After a decade in which Central America was a key foreign policy issue, Latin America largely faded from view in the United States. The two defining policy issues were free trade and drug trafficking. Activists in the region and their supporters organized around opposition to neoliberalism, as embodied in the debt crisis, lowering of trade barriers, and privatization of state-owned enterprises.

When I went into a supermarket in Cuernavaca in the late 1990s, what struck me was the fact that the customers looked like ordinary Mexicans, no longer the upper middle class and professionals whom I associated with supermarkets. A few years later, my impressions were confirmed in the work of agricultural economist Thomas Reardon on a "supermarket revolution" in Latin America and around the world. He found that in the 1992–2002 period, the supermarket portion of food purchasing in some larger Latin American countries had risen from 20 percent to over half.

On that same visit in Cuernavaca I began an interview with a reporter for *Proceso*, a respected independent left weekly, with a general question about the effect of NAFTA, several years after implementation, fully expecting him to catalogue the damage it was doing to Mexico. Instead, he told me stories of small farmers who had managed to supply tomatoes or onions to international buyers. To do so they had to meet requirements for delivery and quality. He also described how, after midnight, planes were taking off from the Mexico City airport for Europe and Asia loaded with strawberries and flowers. He wasn't making any ideological point but simply passing on what he had observed. It was a peek into the workings of globalization.

My translation work had included studies by the Inter-American Development Bank (IDB) economists on different topics related to development. One study noted changes in the demographic profile: with lower birth rates, Latin America was moving from a time in which children and youth were disproportionate into one in which people of working age were predominating. Within a few decades the demographic bulge would lead to large numbers of senior citizens. Countries should take advantage of the present and prepare for the future, for example, by reforming their pension programs to make them sustainable. Another study pointed out that economists had shied away from considering climate because of earlier stereotypes, such as the notion that people in tropical climates were indolent in comparison to the industrious populations in colder climates. However, the tropics presented some disadvantages to development, such as thin, poor soils and no annual freezes to kill pests. Another study examined school systems and experimental innovations in some areas. None of these studies offered an overarching theory of development, but they reinforced the importance of paying attention to specific conditions and of learning from successful innovations.

On a steamy August day in 2000, in conversation with two friends from El Salvador, I found myself questioning what I regarded as their conventional left analysis of El Salvador and Latin America, but unable to articulate a coherent alternative.

* * *

In the early 1990s, critics claimed that with the fall of communism, liberation theology had lost its relevance. The theologians replied that their loyalty had never been to Marxism but to the poor, and since there were at least as many poor people as ever, their theology was still needed. While admitting that the changing circumstances required some rethinking, they tended to echo the critiques of globalization and the neoliberalism of the left. Although the pace of publication slowed, several significant works appeared.

Gustavo Gutierrez worked for almost two decades on *Las Casas: In Search of the Poor of Jesus Christ*, which appeared in 1992. Las Casas went to Hispaniola in 1502 while a teenager and was the first priest ordained in the Americas. Initially a slaveholder, he was converted in 1511 and became a defender of native peoples for the next fifty years. Drawing on the large body of Las Casas scholarship, Gutierrez examines Las Casas on evangelization, the injustice of the wars against the native peoples, and the regime set up to exploit them. Although Las Casas was a man of action and his writings were prompted by what he had observed, he was a theologian, one who remains relevant. Gutierrez does not anachronistically claim Las Casas as a liberation theologian but presents him as a model of how the theological vocation can be lived.

Juan Luis Segundo conceived of *The Liberation of Dogma: Faith, Revelation, and Dogmatic Teaching Authority* (1992) in dialogue with his lay interlocutors in Montevideo. The book begins in the Old Testament, then moves to the New Testament, the patristic age, the conversion of the barbarians, and the modern age. At each stage Segundo inquires about dogma and at each stage sees a kind of pedagogy, a learning process in which error itself sometimes plays a role. Dogma—understood as static certainty—may inhibit learning. At one point Segundo brings up devotion to the Virgin of Guadalupe, which he sees as embodying pre-Colombian religion and not really being empowering or liberating even if it is part of people's identity. He then asks, "How can this theology liberate human beings if it does not liberate theology and dogma from their conception of exact information given once and for all, from something that closes the path to thinking and searching rather than opening the way? If theology does not liberate itself, how is humankind to liberate itself by means of theology?"

When I was translating Segundo's book, I was aware that he had submitted it to the multiauthor series coordinated by Sergio Torres in the 1980s, but it was not accepted. The reason was perhaps that it was "European" rather than "Latin American," or perhaps that it challenged church authority. Segundo dedicated it to his fellow Latin American theologians, insisting that it "was conceived and written to serve liberation." Segundo did not regard his work as ivory tower. I suspect, however, that the somewhat quirky and conversational way in which the book was written meant that it had little impact on academic theology or the church.

Another translation job of mine was Leonardo Boff, *Cry of the Earth, Cry of the Poor* (1995). After continued harassment from church authorities, Boff had left the Franciscans and married but continued to teach and lecture, especially on issues of spirituality and ecology. An opening chapter displays wide familiarity with contemporary cosmology and philosophy of science. Another chapter is similar to the "universe story" of Thomas Berry and other ecotheologians. One of the most interesting chapters is about the Amazon, dispelling some myths about it. Other chapters link care for the earth to liberation theology and take up other aspects of theology and spirituality. Over the years, Boff has been a kind of guru on the Brazilian scene advocating for the environment.

In an interview with a journalist, Ivone Gebara said that poor women who have abortions should not be condemned. Church authorities pressured her congregation, and she was ordered to a two-year period of silence and study abroad. She obtained a second doctorate and returned to Brazil where she continued to work with poor women and write on feminism and theology, as in *Longing for Running Water: Ecofeminism and Liberation* (1999).

* * *

In the mid-1990s I reencountered Ivan Illich, who now divided his time each year between Cuernavaca, Bremen (Germany), and Penn State in the middle of Pennsylvania when he taught each fall. While in the state he came to Philadelphia weekly to lead a seminar for grad students at the University of Pennsylvania. Lee Hoinacki, who had been his assistant in the 1960s but then had married and left Cuernavaca, was now again at Illich's side, assisting him with his thinking and writing. When in Philadelphia, Ivan and Lee stayed at St. Malachy, taking advantage of Jack McNamee's friendship and hospitality.

After being subjected to a grotesque Vatican inquiry and ordered to cease acting as a Catholic priest, Illich had published *De-Schooling Society* (1971), *Tools for Conviviality* (1973), *Energy and Equity* (1974), *Medical Nemesis* (1975), and other similar works. In an ironic, allusive, elliptical style, he questioned major institutions (schooling, medicine, transportation). He seemed akin to E. F. Schumacher, who called for an equitable human-level technology, and indeed Illich saw himself in the anarchist tradition.

The implication was that our lives would be more humane if we accepted our human condition, walking or biking instead of driving or traveling by jet, learning on our own rather than following straitjacketed classroom rituals, and accepting our illnesses as did traditional people rather than undergoing expensive treatments in hospitals in a vain attempt to stave off the inevitable. He had a lemon-sized tumor on the left side of his neck that was difficult to ignore. True to his convictions about institutionalized medicine, he had not had it removed. He did, however, inhale opium to dull the pain.

By around 1980 his writing had become darker and more opaque. It is impossible to summarize the position at which he had arrived. His stance resembled that of Jacques Ellul in *The Technological Society* (1950), namely that the technologies we think we control and utilize are in fact conditioning us. Ellul and Illich admired and appreciated one another. Invited to the inauguration of a reservoir project in Texas, he gave an address called "H2o and the Waters of Forgetfulness," which must have bewildered the audience. With many arcane references he told the audience that what comes out of our faucets isn't the same as the water that earlier generations experienced as powerful and mysterious.

Illich's work was now focused on tracing the deep historical roots of our present predicament. *In the Vineyard of the Text* (1992), a study of twelfth-century theologian Hugh of St. Victor, explored such developments as the movement to silent (as opposed to vocalized) reading and the technique of using the alphabet to organize information so that it could be indexed and retrieved. In the mid-1970s publishers had offered him large advances for whatever he intended to write next; now he was forgotten except by handfuls of devotees.

In a session or two at the school of design at Penn, I observed students make oral presentations on their dissertation work, to which Ivan gave virtuoso responses, on the Islamic sense of space as in the layout of cities, for example, or nineteenth-century German poet Novalis. A day-and-a-half-long seminar was held at St. Malachy's, with Illich enthusiasts in the Philadelphia area, mainly Catholics, but including Carl Micham, his host at Penn State, and David Cayley, a Canadian radio host, who had been interviewing Illich and later produced two edited books of those conversations, which became Illich's last testament.

Illich believed that the incarnation and life of Jesus had brought fundamental change: he repeatedly returned to the theme of the Good Samaritan and the revelation that we are to deal with our neighbor face-to-face, in the flesh. The church had institutionalized itself and turned gospel into law, instilling fear into people: *Corruptio optimi pessima*—the corruption of the best is what is worst. Lee hoped to interest Catholic theologians in this latter phase of Illich's thinking. although Illich had never had any interest in postconciliar theology in its concern for reform of ministries, or making the gospel intelligible to contemporary people, or the compatibility of religion and science.

Illich was fascinating to watch, but it was hard to know what to do with his ideas. Clearly he did not forswear all technology; he was quite attached to his laptop. Illich's simple answer to what to do was "friendship"—expressed in a simple spaghetti dinner and wine over which friends could enjoy one another's company.

Lee Hoinacki eventually ceased accompanying Illich around the world and lived in the St. Malachy rectory for several years, helping in the parish, standing in peace vigils downtown, and doing his own writing and editing work on Illich. Ivan died in 2002 in Bremen, surrounded by a small group of followers.

* * *

In late November 1997, through the AFSC, I took part in a delegation to Chiapas of about thirty people, including two members of the Mexican Congress, organized by Mexican civil society activists. It was then almost four years since the Zapatista movement had announced its existence by occupying San Cristobal and other towns. The movement dated to the early 1980s when Marxist guerrillas went to the Lacandon jungle area and began to establish ties with the local people, patiently laying the groundwork for an eventual revolution. Over time the movement evolved, and by the 1990s it no longer sought to take state power by force. Its face to the outside world was the ski-masked "Subcomandante Marcos," who wrote poetic commentaries on the movement and the larger political scene. For several years many Mexican leftists hoped that the Zapatistas were the spearhead of a renewed left. Negotiations with the Mexican state, still run by the PRI, under the mediation of Bishop Samuel Ruiz had come to a standstill.

With the mountainous city of San Cristobal as our base, the delegation went to various towns and settlements, sometimes hiking over muddy paths, on which I slipped and fell repeatedly. In one instance we met people driven out of their community and living under tarps exposed to rain and mud. We met with Las Abejas (the Bees), a cooperative that agreed with the aims of the Zapatistas, but not with any use of violence. One afternoon some of us drove down to the state capital, Tuxtla Gutierrez, in the lowlands, to express our concerns to the governor and other state officials, who didn't conceal their disdain.

The Mexican army and police had a strong presence in these highlands areas. In more than one place, local PRI paramilitaries were ostentatiously wielding their power. In the last place we visited, we realized that the local cacique regarded us with hostility, and as we warily drove away we were followed. The Zapatistas themselves stayed out of sight, except on the last night when several dozen indigenous men and women, their faces masked, processed silently into San Cristobal.

About three weeks later in Acteal, forty-five members of Las Abejas were slaughtered by a group of PRI paramilitaries, who obviously thought they could act with impunity. International attention was drawn to Chiapas, but the PRI government fended off criticism. International human rights courts took up the Acteal case, and in 2002 the Mexican government acknowledged that the state had been responsible. By that time, however, the PRI had lost the presidency.

Through this experience I realized that much of the PRI's strength was that it was a structure that extended down to the local level. It was also clear that as much as the Mexican national ideology exalted the preconquest indigenous heritage, actual indigenous Mexicans, over 10 percent of the population, were cynically disregarded by the power structure.

* * *

In the 1990s Westminster Abbey decided to install statues of ten martyrs of the twentieth century in a space over the main entrance. Among them were figures from all continents and from the major Christian bodies, including Martin Luther King; Dietrich Bonhoeffer, murdered by the Nazis in 1944; Esther John, a Pakistani Anglican; and Grand Duchess Elizabeth, killed in the Bolshevik Revolution. The decision to erect the statues was intended to emphasize that martyrdom was not limited to the early church but had continued into our day. One of them was Archbishop Oscar Romero, about whom I was asked to write a chapter for a companion book. I decided to attend the unveiling and a seminar held the previous day. I was housed in a small room on the grounds of the cathedral itself and attended a concert in the exquisite Anglican style.

Queen Elizabeth and other members of the royal family attended the ceremony, which took place in the late morning on a day in July. After scripture readings and music, the stylized statues, all by the same master sculptor, were unveiled.

Afterward at a reception with tea sandwiches in the grassy area inside the compound, I talked to Bishop Gerardo Flores of Guatemala. Two or three months earlier Angie had been present at the cathedral in Guatemala City for formal presentation of *Guatemala: Never Again*, the multi-volume human rights report of the Guatemalan Catholic Church that Bishop Juan Gerardi had chaired. Two days later Gerardi was bludgeoned to death as he was returning to the parish where he lived. Now the Guatemalan government was seeking to muddy the effort to reveal the killers.

* * *

My old IPLA classmate Chencho Alas had been outside of El Salvador during the war. He founded an NGO in Texas and raised funds for development in El Salvador. I was asked to write about him in conjunction with his being awarded the Tannenbaum Human Rights Award in 2000. Although I could have written primarily about his work in the 1970s, I decided I should go to El Salvador to see his current work, in the Bajo Lempa, an area where peasants were working land that they had been granted under the land reform in a sugar area on the coast. In the 1990s Salvadoran youth deported from Los Angeles had brought a gang culture that expanded into the countryside. Now youth from two different communities could not walk into each other's territory without the risk of violence. I watched Chencho bring together a couple dozen youths from the two communities where leaders of the rival groups shook hands. I don't know what happened afterward, but it was an indication of deep problems in postwar El Salvador.

* * *

At the LASA meeting in Washington, DC, in early September 2001, Jorge Castañeda addressed an auditorium of Latin Americanists. Once our fellow academic, he was now foreign minister of Mexico in the government of President Vicente Fox, the businessman who had become the first non-PRI president since the revolution. Two planeloads of Mexican officials had been meeting with their Washington counterparts. President George W. Bush had entered office promising a "humble" foreign policy; he had little interest in or knowledge of the world beyond Texas and as an adult had visited only two foreign countries, Israel and Mexico. He intended to emphasize relations with Mexico and Latin America in an otherwise unambitious foreign policy.

The September 11, 2001, attacks occurred a few days later. Our oldest daughter, Catherine, now in Minneapolis, had been working near the Twin Towers until a month earlier. We shared the shock, bewilderment, and fear of the nation. My September 12 flight to L.A. for a seminary class reunion was canceled. When we drove to see our daughters Maggie and Lizzy at Columbia University the following weekend, the Ground Zero area was still smoking. One of the victims was Johanna Sigmund, daughter of fellow parishioners at St. Malachy's.

Although I was apprehensive about what might happen next—a nuclear, chemical, or biological weapon, or a "dirty bomb"—I opposed the rush to war. At the very moment when Bush announced the start of the war in Afghanistan, I was marching in a demonstration up Philadelphia's Broad Street in opposition. The AFSC and other peace organizations organized to respond to the climate of fear and insecurity. Over the following months and years, Angie and I went to demonstrations and candlelight vigils at a time when polls showed three-fourths of the U.S. population supporting the wars in Afghanistan and Iraq.

In September 2002 the administration released "The National Security Strategy of the United States." Such overviews are issued periodically, but this document was the ideological justification for going to war against Iraq, albeit expressed in noble-sounding terms. Sensitized to ideology by my Latin American experience, I felt impelled to study it and prepare a critique. While doing so I read the works of the neoconservatives (William Kristol, Robert Kagan, Donald Rumsfeld, Richard Perle, Paul Wolfowitz,

Elliot Abrams, and various others), who had been pressing for a more aggressive foreign policy since the 1990s, specifically calling for overthrowing governments in Iran, Iraq, and elsewhere in the Middle East. Under the coordination of Vice President Dick Cheney, the Bush administration had begun making plans along these lines from the outset, while ignoring Al-Qaeda. They were now taking advantage of the concern and fear of the public to advance their preexisting agenda.

I had no direct knowledge of the Middle East, but for decades I had seen U.S. power used against a whole region, driven by Cold War ideology. These neoconservatives were preparing the public for a generation of conflict analogous to the Cold War. The very notion of a "war on terrorism" was misleading: wars are fought against nations, not clandestine stateless networks. Initially I circulated my critique privately; a shortened version of it appeared in *America* magazine in 2004.

* * *

I became aware of the clergy sex-abuse scandal first through reporting in the 1980s from Louisiana by Jason Berry in the *National Catholic Reporter*. Further reporting in the 1990s brought to light the existence of a surprising incidence of cases among Catholic clergy and a pattern of bishops moving priests around. A third round of reporting on notorious cases in Boston and elsewhere followed in the early 2000s.

At around that time my classmate Gerry Fallon and I were given a tour of the new cathedral in Los Angeles under construction by Fr. Carl Sutphin, who had been five years ahead of us in the seminary and was then in residence there with Cardinal Roger Mahony—the three of us going around in orange plastic hardhats. Not long afterward, Carl was defrocked, joining the many priests dismissed as a result of credible accusations of sexual abuse. The list of priest abusers from my seminary cohorts is long, including four of my classmates (from approximately twenty ordained), three of whom spent time in prison. Nothing in my years in the seminary or the priesthood prepared me for this; I was as astonished and puzzled as anyone else.

The Catholic priesthood seems to have attracted a disproportionate number of adolescents who didn't achieve sexual and personal maturity and in fact had the disorder of pedophilia and who took advantage of their position with children. We now know of high-profile cases of sexual abuse of children and adolescents by coaches, teachers, and family members, but that does little to explain its incidence in the priesthood.

With regard to cover-ups by bishops I can only guess that for many years, as cases came to light, church authorities viewed them as a problem or a weakness on the part of the priest, similar to alcoholism, for which clerical treatment centers existed. Priests were sent for treatment, and when deemed rehabilitated they were reassigned. Bishops were most concerned about protecting the image of the church, and later the prospect of lawsuits—hence the many out-of-court settlements, which eventually reached billions of dollars. Only very slowly did church authorities come to appreciate that victims often suffered trauma that affected them for years, and the church was very slow to recognize that abusers were criminals who should be turned over to the police and courts.

* * *

In 2002 I was finally able to satisfy my long-held desire to see Cuba for myself by adding it as a side trip when I traveled to Mexico City. Staying in a bed-and-breakfast near the University of Havana, I spent five days wandering and allowing for serendipity. After the fall of communism I had assumed that Cuba would reintegrate with the rest of the world, but Fidel Castro had decided that it was more important than ever to hold on to the socialist system.

As I walked toward Old Havana on my first afternoon, the sights and sounds, especially the Caribbean Spanish, were familiar. When I reached old Havana, I went into the Capitolio, the dome-shaped seat of government modeled on U.S. government buildings, and found some translators with whom I inquired about their work. Restaurants and businesses looked private but in fact belonged to the state, and they only accepted dollars. The country was clearly divided into people who had access to dollars and those who didn't.

A pentecostal church service Sunday morning seemed quite similar to services in other countries. I was unable to speak to Catholic bishops who were in session, but I interviewed a Spanish pastor of a parish, who said that he estimated that about 1 percent of Cubans were practicing Catholics.

My host, who was critical of the regime, noted that besides providing health care and schooling to all, it also enabled people access to sports and culture. Various times I happened across dance groups or musicians practicing. At the Book Fair in Havana I was impressed that tens of thousands of people had come out on a Sunday. Books were being sold cheaply, but I realized there were very few, largely classics in translation. Although Cuba had eliminated illiteracy early in the revolution, people had little worth reading: no real newspapers, and no serious magazines, and in fact I didn't see people reading.

My one venture out of Havana was to the city of Matanzas, known for art. While waiting for the train in the morning I came across the Dos Hermanos bar where I sat alone having breakfast of coffee and bread. On the dark paneled walls were photos of Lorca, Isadora Duncan, and Hemingway, who had hung out there. The train to Matanzas was slow and stopped various times, notably at a station named Hershey, after the chocolate company that had had a plantation there. In Matanzas I got into a conversation with a man with a guitar sitting on church steps who said he was a composer and offered to sell me a handwritten song. A guy in a passing pickup yelled, "*Compositor!*" at him.

Listening on the radio to a recorded speech given by Castro, I heard what sounded like a speech defect, as though his powers were failing. Two years later his sickness was announced, but he managed to live several years after that.

I had been asked by a Cuban outside the country to deliver a message orally to a person in an NGO. We went outside to a park where she felt we could speak beyond the earshot of others. However, Cuba didn't feel like a police state, at least in comparison to what I had experienced in Central America, but what I might call a "tutelary state," one that assumed it could decide in people's best interest. The Cuban state was making it difficult to get Internet access and to start businesses. The longer that continued, the harder it would be for ordinary people to enter the twenty-first century.

* * *

Orbis Books asked me to translate a work by Jacques Dupuis, a Jesuit theologian who had spent decades in India and then at the Gregorian University in Rome. It was a simpler version in Italian of a book he had published in French in the late 1990s on the relationship between Christianity and other world religions, to which the Congregation for the Doctrine of the Faith had raised objections and ordered him to reply.

Dupuis was yet another in a long line of theologians called on the carpet by the Vatican in the postcouncil years, often after anonymous accusations. Proceedings were behind closed doors, by officials who were both prosecutor and judge, with no means of defense. Hans Küng had been told he could not teach as a Catholic theologian. Leonardo Boff and Ivone Gebara had been silenced. Sri Lankan Tissa Balasuriya ended up being excommunicated by Pope John Paul II, after he refused to sign a profession of faith in the exact terms dictated by the Congregation for the Doctrine of the Faith. In the 1960s and 1970s the offending positions were questioning conventional sexual ethics or ecclesiology, not directly about God. By the 1990s they also included matters like Christology and the relationship between Christianity and other world religions. Almost all the theologians disciplined by Rome were people like Dupuis who had devoted their lives to the church. Their positions were generally not out of line with what was taught in theology departments at Catholic universities in the United States. The Vatican's aim was to make object lessons of them.

Dupuis did not offer bold speculations; he cited church documents and the work of contemporary theologians to argue that the Catholic Church could have an open attitude toward the saving function of non-Christian religions. His work looked timid beside that of Raimon Panikkar, who for decades wrote as a Catholic Christian, a Hindu, and a Buddhist, and whose observations were bold, and yet who never seems to have been disciplined, perhaps because he was hard to pin down, taught at secular universities, and was economically independent of the church.

When Dupuis gave an address at the Jesuit parish in Greenwich Village, I had a short conversation with him. He was soft-spoken and obviously pained by the bullying from Rome. The audience of progressive Catholics regarded him as a hero, but he was more professorial than prophetic. By the time he died in 2004 his name had been cleared, but the entire procedure was disgraceful.

* * *

Friends of Jose Comblin decided to celebrate his eightieth birthday in 2003 with a weeklong celebration in Joao Pessoa, and I accepted an invitation to attend. His birthday turned out to be the same as mine, March 22, exactly fifteen years earlier. During my overnight flight to Brazil, the Bush administration launched the war in Iraq. I was relieved to be in a relatively sane country for twenty days. Joao Pessoa is situated on the most easterly tip of Brazil; when I swam out into the ocean in the morning I was facing Africa.

Since the 1968 IPLA course with him in Quito I had stayed in touch with Comblin, through occasional letters and contacts. While working with Helder Camara, Comblin had developed a program for educating rural candidates for the priesthood in which they lived in small communities and didn't lose their peasant roots. Their studies involved exploring the popular culture around them and relating it to the Bible. In the 1970s he developed a similar program in the Diocese of Talca in Chile. When the Vatican ordered those initiatives closed, Comblin moved to training village-level lay missionaries. Dozens of them had come from all over northeast Brazil.

Comblin had written approximately sixty books and several hundred articles, in French, Portuguese, and Spanish. They included large theologies of peace, nationalism, the city, and revolution; biblical commentary and studies; reflections on pastoral action; and hard-to-classify works, particularly theological reflections on various phases of church history. His observations are often sharp and unconventional. He once advised me, "Always read the heterodox."

The event was titled "The Hope of the Poor Lives On" (despite discouraging developments in the church and society). A highlight of the week was the presentation of a Festschrift with around sixty-five contributors, from Brazil and elsewhere in Latin America, held in the gymnasium of a Catholic university. In my contribution, "The Medellin Generation and Its Successors" (written in Spanish), I argued that if there were such a successor generation, its social analysis and theology should reflect the world of the present, not that of thirty-five years before. As far as I know, my observations went unnoticed.

A few months later, when Comblin was visiting Maryknoll, I spent a day at the home of Tom and Mercedes Bamat, Maryknoll lay missionaries and good friends of Comblin, interviewing him on his life work. I then edited the transcribed tapes, hoping at the time to do follow-up interviews until I had an oral history, but I was unable to do so. Hoping to interest a new generation of theologians outside of Latin America in Comblin, I wrote an overview of his work for a theological journal in English.

The anonymous reviewers did not approve it for publication but encouraged revision, which I didn't get around to doing. Alerting the theological community to the value of his body of work remains unfinished business for me.

14

Consumption Democratized?

"Is Brazil a poor country with some millionaires, or is it a middle-class country with millions of poor people?" I asked a group of four or five Brazilian sisters of the Canonesses of St. Augustine after the end of the Comblin birthday celebration, apologizing for such a simplistic question. I was astonished at the changes I was seeing in Joao Pessoa. In 1969 it had struck me as emblematic of Latin American poverty, but now I saw definite signs of progress: poor neighborhoods had small supermarkets, and a modest freeway encircled the city.

The sisters, who worked with the poor, didn't treat my question as stupid or naïve; a similar question had recently been raised on TV. Appearances can deceive, they said: in a favela you can encounter two- or three-story houses with major appliances and computers, and you can go to a house that looks middle class and find that the people there have little furniture and nothing to eat.

From Joao Pessoa I flew back to Sao Paulo and spent a further two weeks looking for perspectives on what was happening in Brazil. From my base in an inexpensive hotel in Liberdade, the traditional Japanese district, I went around the city and state of Sao Paulo, and also to Rio and Curitiba. Signs of change were all around me and in newspapers and magazines. Sao Paulo had 9 million cars (for 17 million people); daily traffic jams were measured in kilometers. Agricultural productivity had risen 70 percent in a decade. Brazilian per-capita meat consumption was now 20 percent higher than Japan's. McDonald's had thirty-three thousand employees, more than any other private company. As ambiguous as such "progress" might be, it seemed to represent a significant change.

A decade previously Brazil had begun to enter the globalized world. For example, it had lifted the previous high tariffs placed on computers to protect Brazilian manufacturers, making computers expensive and years out of date. The country had now entered the Microsoft world. More generally, Brazil was shifting from manufacturing toward a service-oriented economy.

In Sao Carlos, a city two hours from Sao Paulo, a biologist met me at the bus station and drove me past a federal university entirely devoted to math and science, and then took me to his own university where 350 students were pursuing graduate studies in biology. He showed me examples of their research and took me to a university research station of a stand of Atlantic rain forest; one type of tree there has a greater mass in its roots below the surface than in the trunk, branches, and leaves above. He explained that decades previously Sao Paulo elites had determined that the country needed universities for both training and research. Three and a half million Brazilians were now enrolled in universities. A young man in a bus seat in front of me was reading the Brazilian edition of *Scientific American*.

This was during Lula's first hundred days in office. On his fourth attempt he had won over a considerable section of the middle class. While campaigning, Lula had proposed "Zero Hunger," arguing that in a country as big and powerful as Brazil, no one should go hungry. However, as the PT went about implementation it found some surprises, particularly that true hunger was not nearly as common as had been assumed. Debate swirled around whether the program should spend government funds or coordinate existing efforts, and whether it should deliver food or help people produce their own. Zero Hunger was eventually merged into a family allowance program that Cardoso had initiated.

On the whole, the Lula government was economically pragmatic, even conservative, particularly in cabinet positions. That disappointed the more radical sectors of the PT, but as it turned out, Lula presided over a boom in which ordinary people and elites both prospered. While I was there Lula raised the minimum wage 20 percent (from approximately sixty-five to eighty-nine dollars a month).

I went south to see the city of Curitiba, famed for its urban innovations, which had started in the 1970s under Mayor Jaime Lerner. In dealing with chronic problems of flooding during rainstorms, rather than diverting the water through culverts into a sewer system, the city decided to let the water flow to its natural basins, where it prohibited development and created green spaces. The city now had twenty-eight parks, thereby achieving a very high rate of green area per inhabitant. Some downtown streets were pedestrianized.

The most well-known innovation was in public transportation. Rather than opt for a metro system, the city developed five arteries of dedicated bus lanes, radiating like spokes from the city center: passengers entered prepaid, and the buses ran above ground on regular schedules, providing the advantages of a metro system at a small fraction of the cost. Eventually this bus-rapid-transit system was emulated elsewhere, especially in Latin American cities. For decades Curitiba has had a network of bicycle lanes, which are used for commuting and errands as well as recreation. The city also has a very high rate of recycling, fostered by programs whereby poor people receive groceries and school supplies in exchange for recyclables. Curitiba shows that significant change does not depend on the party in power nationally (Lerner was mayor during the military dictatorship), and that Latin Americans themselves can devise innovative solutions.

Upon my return I wrote my impressions in a long draft article. I ended by saying that the United States and Brazil have much in common; both are geographically large nations in which people are on the move; they are still dealing with their histories of slavery and racism; some day Americans would "discover" Brazil. My Brazilian friends felt that I had captured well the current developments in their country, but when I submitted it to a major Catholic publication, the editors weren't interested, possibly because it ran counter to their preconceptions about Latin America, which had been shaped by over a decade of attention to Central America.

* * *

Brazil's role in the world was on display a few months later at the World Trade Organization (WTO) summit in Cancun, Mexico. Almost 150 governments, five thousand journalists, and two thousand NGOs descended on the Mexican beach resort for what was intended to be a major step toward reducing tariffs and setting up a single trade regime for the world. I was there as part of an AFSC delegation and wrote short summaries of the events day by day, working in a huge hall full of reporters writing at computer terminals in the Convention Center. The meeting took place not in Cancun itself but on a barrier reef and could be approached only by causeways from the city with a credential. Large protest demonstrations took place in Cancun. At a mass protest at the start of the meeting, a Korean farmer committed suicide in protest over the WTO's impact in East Asia.

The actual deliberations took place between official government delegations behind closed doors, but lively meetings and presentations by NGOs were taking place elsewhere. The major fault lines were around two sets of issues. The wealthy countries (North America, the European Union, and Japan) wanted to have unfettered access for their agricultural products in developing countries, while reserving the right to protect or subsidize their own farmers. They also wished to impose conditions, in particular, intellectual property rights, for example, prohibiting developing countries from producing generic versions of patented drugs. Brazil, China, India, and South Africa formed a bloc as representatives of the developing countries. As the week unfolded, we could attend briefings by their diplomats.

The delegations failed to reach an agreement. On the afternoon of the last day in a packed auditorium, representatives of Brazil and the other Global South nations celebrated the outcome as a kind of victory; they had resisted being strong-armed into an unequal agreement. Since then no further advances have been made at the worldwide level, even as bilateral and regional trade agreements proliferate.

* * *

In 2005 I had a long phone conversation with Paul Mayer, whom I had known at San Miguelito in the mid-1960s, and who had gone on to a long career as a peace activist in the New York area. He was feeling gloomy about current events such as the Iraq War, and more generally what had transpired over our lifetimes. Based on what I was observing in Latin America, I said I thought it might be possible to establish a more decent world for all, and he replied, "Well, when you figure it out, let the rest of us know." That impelled me to develop my inchoate impressions.

I found myself at odds with the left-tending activists, writers, and church people who still took it for granted that "the rich are getting richer and the poor are getting poorer" as a result of neoliberalism. The slogan of the World Social Forum, "Another World Is Possible," implied that meaningful progress was impossible under the existing order. The one ray of hope seemed to be the advent of left-wing governments in the 2000s, ranging from the moderate versions typified by Michelle Bachelet in Chile and Lula in Brazil to the "twenty-first-century socialism" advocated by Hugo Chavez in Venezuela.

For over a decade "neoliberalism" had served as catch-all term for a number of changes being imposed on Latin American governments: bring spending into line with revenues; privatize state-owned companies, especially those losing money; reduce tariffs and open the economy to investment and trade. It is true that those policies were imposed by the IMF, the World Bank, and the United States as a condition for further lending during the debt crisis, and some people were losers, notably government employees. However, China in the late 1970s and India in the early 1990s had both moved from statist toward market economies and had seen remarkable growth. They had done so on their own, not under outside coercion. While much of the Chinese economy was opened to market forces, the state remained authoritarian and controlled the economy as a whole. In any case, the shift away from statist and toward market-driven economies was a worldwide trend.

I ended up with a long essay, "Fifty Years of Development—What Have We Learned?" My starting point was observable improvements in the lives of many ordinary people. In Chile three-quarters of households now had washing machines and refrigerators, up from less than 10 percent around 1960. That was especially helpful to women, increasing numbers of whom had jobs outside the home. Around the continent almost all children were attending elementary school, secondary education was expanding, and university enrollment had more than doubled in a decade.

In trying to explain how these positive developments came about, I discussed several trends, none of which was in itself conclusive or provided anything like an explanatory paradigm. As implied in the title, I was trying to distill lessons.

A simple point was the fact of urbanization. The typical Latin American was now a city dweller, whose grandparents were probably campesinos. That helped account for having drinking water and (possibly) sewerage, access to clinics, and higher rates of schooling. By the same token, land reform, seen as the crucial issue as recently as the 1980s in Central America, now seemed less so. Perhaps rather than traditional land reform, the aim should be to foster a model of family farming that could provide a decent living for those working their own land.

Activists and Latin Americanists still took it for granted that state control over natural resources was crucial to development, as exemplified by Hugo Chavez and petroleum in Venezuela. However, economic historians pointed out that (perhaps counterintuitively) countries with economies based on natural resources grow more slowly and are more unequal than those less endowed, for example, Saudi Arabia vs. South Korea. The apparent paradox can be grasped by realizing that societies with fewer natural resources are forced to rely more on human talent, whereas those with natural wealth tend to generate perverse incentives.

Since the 1980s Peruvian economist Hernando de Soto had been arguing that the key to development was to be found in entrepreneurialism, which he said was exemplified in the informal economy and off-the-books businesses, including construction. The main obstacle to the entrepreneurial genius of ordinary people was government regulation, particularly the many bureaucratic hurdles to establishing a formal business. De Soto had a point: all things being equal, making it easier to start and run businesses could spur development, but that was only one ingredient.

What was not so clear to me in 2005 was that a crucial element was controlling inflation, which had been tamed in Brazil and elsewhere, partly as a result of measures such as bringing government expenditure and revenues in line, a key component of neoliberalism. Inflation hurts almost everyone, but especially the poor who cannot put their earnings in property, as the middle and upper classes can.

In my explorations I didn't find any new overarching theoretical framework that could seem as explanatory as dependency theory once had. However, I did encounter the "new institutional economics," associated with C. Douglass North and others, which is sometimes summarized in the phrase "Institutions matter": it matters whether ownership rights are clear, contracts are enforced, corruption is punished rather than taken for granted, law enforcement and courts work, and people can be trusted to keep their word.

I ended up with a half-dozen or more general ideas, all of which seemed to be ingredients in successful development; none of them individually or even together amounted to a new paradigm. When I expressed this to an American social scientist who had spent years in Nicaragua in the 1980s, and later had evolved toward a pragmatic position on development, he answered in an email, "Why shouldn't Latin America muddle through? Isn't that what we do in the United States?"

Some of my hunches were bolstered by the findings of a team of Brazilian researchers who in 2005 did household studies in four Sao Paulo favelas and were surprised at what they found: communities were stable; houses averaged five rooms, and some had more than one bathroom; 29 percent of households owned a car; many had computers and cell phones; despite the reputation for violence, some described their areas as calm; when asked to rate themselves in terms of wealth on a scale of from 1 to 10, 70 percent chose 3, 4, or 5. That rang true to my impressionistic observations in the neighborhood of Vila Cisper in eastern Sao Paulo. The researchers titled their study "The Democratization of Consumption" and said that the changes had been taking place over the previous decade. At around this time, the respected Getulio Vargas Foundation estimated that 52 percent of Brazilians were middle class.

The titles of several books on Latin America published in 2007 showed no awareness of the positive signs I had been sensing: Patrice Franko, *The Puzzle of Latin American Economic Development* (third edition); Andres Oppenheimer, *Saving the Americas: The Dangerous Decline of Latin America and What the US Must Do*; Michael Reid, *Lost Continent: The Struggle for Latin America's Soul*; and Francis Fukuyama (ed.), *Left Behind: Explaining the Development Gap between Latin America and the United States*. All of these writers pointed toward what Latin American countries should be doing (develop more competitive economies, foster education, develop the rule of law, etc.), but they saw few signs that things were moving in that direction. My favorite title from this period was from Spanish economist Javier Santiso: *Latin America's Political Economy of the Possible: Beyond Good Revolutionaries and Free Marketeers* (2006). Santiso noted a turn away from ideology toward pragmatism in macroeconomic policies but saw few fruits in improved welfare for people.

* * *

Sometime in the 1990s I told a friend I felt "orphaned" by developments in the Catholic Church. I was expressing a sense of alienation, a feeling that the Vatican and the bishops had moved away from what I understood the church to be in the Council and its immediate aftermath. The backlash had begun under Paul VI, but it had become a program with John Paul II and Cardinal Ratzinger. Examples in Latin America were John Paul II's 1983 trip through Central America, and the 1984–1986 conflict with liberation theologians and bishops sympathetic to it. Elsewhere it was marked by rigidity on what the theologian Daniel Maguire called "pelvic issues" (contraception, homosexuality, abortion) and exclusion and treatment of women.

In the late 1980s I heard a Catholic college president express concern over an impending Vatican document on universities. For some years the Vatican attempted to insist that theologians would need to receive authorization, called a *mandatum*, from the local bishop. Catholic colleges and universities resisted, noting that this would violate principles of academic freedom and even threaten research funding. A respected ethicist told me that many of her peers were moving to non-Catholic institutions.

The *Catechism of the Catholic Church* (1992) exemplified the papacy. Ostensibly intended to reflect Vatican II, it was really an attempt to include every single item of defined Catholic teaching. The framework (creed, commandments, sacraments, prayer) was similar to that of the catechism I had been taught as a child and while it was dressed up with quotes from the Bible, in a deeper sense it wasn't really biblical.

The biblical symbol of "people of God," which emphasized the equality of believers, was eclipsed by an insistence on "communion" understood as submission to the hierarchy. John Paul II's worldview had been forged in his experience of decades under communism. He brought a combative spirit to very different situations and seemed to learn little from the rest of the world, despite his constant traveling to other lands. "Is the Pope Catholic?" went the old rhetorical expression. *Not enough for me*, I thought.

Under John Paul II, the Vatican made absolute loyalty to Rome on doctrinal and moral positions the sine qua non for even being considered for the episcopacy. Any priest who had ever expressed reservations about any official teaching, including the contraception ban, was ruled out: the upshot was that over time the episcopacy comprised company men.

None of this affected me directly since St. Malachy was a good spiritual home. I didn't feel called to participate in independent initiatives like Call to Action that were pursuing reform in the church.

By the 2000s, three of my seminary mates were cardinals: Roger Mahony, Bill Levada, and Justin Rigali. It wasn't entirely coincidental: Justin, who had spent most of his career in the Vatican diplomatic service and was a close confidant of John Paul II, had probably been instrumental in the choice of Bill and Roger, who were in the seminary class behind him.

After the death of John Paul II in 2005, fifteen or so of us who had been in the seminary together were in email contact. As the cardinals were scheduled to go to Rome to elect his successor, it struck me that we should try to let these three cardinals know what qualities we thought the pope should have. We weren't in ongoing contact with them, although some of us had seen Roger at a seminary reunion that he organized, and I had seen Justin briefly twice after he became archbishop of Philadelphia. I felt more theological and pastoral sympathy with Mahony than with Rigali or Levada.

We exchanged some ideas by email, and I did a draft of criteria for a pope, which after further discussion and light editing we all signed. We proposed that a pope for the twenty-first century should be grounded in human and pastoral experience, focus on communicating the gospel, and be especially sensitive to the poor. The subtext was that the emphasis should not be on a particular sexual morality or culture wars. It was surprisingly easy to come to agreement and we all signed the letter. Rather than mailing or FedExing it, we used personal contacts to deliver the letter. Roger in particular let us know he appreciated it.

We had no illusions about what influence we could have on these three cardinals whom we happened to have studied with, nor on what influence three of them could have; we simply thought we shouldn't neglect the opportunity. Cardinal Josef Ratzinger, who had been John Paul II's doctrinal enforcer, was elected, and he continued in the same direction, albeit with a lighter touch. It later turned out that the runner-up was Cardinal Jorge Bergoglio of Buenos Aires, who did match our criteria.

* * *

In April 2007 the Latin American bishops met at Aparecida, Brazil, for CELAM V, the successor to Rio de Janeiro (1955), Medellin (1968), Puebla (1979), and Santo Domingo (1992). In the second half of the year I translated their final document into English for CELAM and the U.S. Catholic bishops. While translating I concentrated on rendering each sentence and paragraph accurately, and so only after I had finished could I step back to examine and assess it.

My first strong impression was that it showed a more vigorous editorial hand than the previous CELAM documents. That hand turned out to be that of the head of the drafting committee, Cardinal Bergoglio. In 2013, as pope, Francis met with a representative group of Latin American bishops at Aparecida and reminded them of the document they had elaborated together.

The key words were "disciples" and "missionaries," sometimes combined as in "missionary disciples" or "missionary discipleship": the church had to go out of itself and needed to examine its structures and practices to do so. As admirable as that sounded, I wondered whether it would happen: for almost three decades, bishops had been chosen for their loyalty to Rome and their doctrinal orthodoxy, and to a considerable extent that emphasis had percolated to the clergy and laity. How would a church that had turned inward suddenly turn outward? What were "missionary disciples" to do? Bring back those who had become evangelicals or Catholics who were not practicing? Or was it to provide disinterested service to those most in need?

Liberation theologians were pleased that Aparecida had returned to the see-judge-act methodology practiced at Medellin, but less so at Puebla (1979) and even less at Santo Domingo (1992). I detected a difference, however: Medellin examined economic and political structures, assuming that they needed to be changed, perhaps radically. Aparecida put the emphasis on "sociocultural" analysis, seemingly on the grounds that the church needed to understand the society it sought to address.

As with previous CELAM documents, statements were made on many topics: parishes, dioceses, Christian base communities, catechesis, Catholic schools, the option for the poor, the environment, indigenous peoples, the family, the mass media, social media, and so forth. Aparecida could be cited to justify many pastoral options.

Early in their analysis, mentioning various contemporary trends (globalization, genetic manipulation, communications, etc.), the bishops commented that "reality has become ever more opaque and complex for human beings . . . This has taught us to look at reality more humbly, knowing that it is greater and more complex than the simplistic ways in which we used to look at it in the not very distant past which often introduced conflicts into society, leaving many wounds that have still not been able to heal." People like me had certainly been chastened by events, but that passage sounded as though those who had stood up for human rights were being blamed for having introduced conflicts, as though the victims and their victimizers were somehow equally responsible.

Although acknowledging the growth of evangelical churches and admitting that it was partly due to Catholic shortcomings, the bishops were still reluctant to fully recognize the de facto religious pluralism of Latin America. They admitted the positive side of contemporary pluralism, but then immediately added, "On the other hand, this same pluralism of a cultural and religious nature, forcefully spread by a globalized culture, ends up making individualism a dominant characteristic of contemporary society, responsible for ethical relativism and the crisis of the family."

A passage on urban pastoral ministry had a strikingly different feel: "Cities are places of freedom and opportunity. In them people seek the possibility of knowing more people, and interacting and coexisting with them. Bonds of fraternity, solidarity, and universality can be experienced in cities. In them the human being is constantly called to ever journey toward meeting the other, coexisting with those who are different, accepting them, and being accepted by them." Those words make more sense in the light of Jorge Bergoglio's lifelong devotion to Buenos Aires and its people.

Although the document made some interesting observations about economics, I could find no inherent logic: it seemed to me that one could cut and paste their paragraphs randomly and it would make just as much sense. That was not surprising since social scientists had not yet devised a new paradigm for economic growth and development.

In their chapter on the family the bishops spoke as though pluralism did not apply. As legislatures in some countries were responding to calls for greater reproductive rights, the bishops were attempting to decree the limits of legitimate discussion as though they were its arbiters. In particular, they spoke as though abortion were a foreign imposition by NGOs, oblivious to the reality that abortion rates were considerably higher in Latin America, where the procedure was generally illegal, than in Europe and North America.

Aparecida was well received by the liberation theologians. Amerindia, a network of theologians and pastoralists, published an e-book with over twenty essays on the document. Several of the contributors complained about the process and said that important input from the grassroots had been ignored. Chilean theologian Ronaldo Muñoz found twenty-four important changes made by the Vatican after the document was submitted. Brazilian Pedro de Oliveira used passages from Aparecida to critique globalization and reject neoliberalism. On the whole, the liberation theologians felt that they had been vindicated and welcomed back into the fold.

* * *

Aparecida and the papacy of Pope Francis have constituted a vindication of some of the major themes of liberation theology. Francis has met with Gustavo Gutierrez and sought advice from Leonardo Boff, and several of the pope's theological inner circle are associated with the Argentine strand of liberation theology. The pope's own emphasis on the poor, migrants, and prisoners is yet another indication of that affinity. In February 2017 I took part in a three-day meeting of Latin American, Spanish, and Latino/a theologians at Boston College, seeking to articulate common themes in the era of Pope Francis.

In my view, Latin American theologians still have difficulty recognizing certain signs of the times. They are still slow to recognize that Catholicism has lost its religious and cultural monopoly. Evangelicals, whom they either ignore or dismiss, are now often on a par with Catholics in terms of church attendance. Likewise, the number of Latin Americans who describe themselves as not belonging to any church, while still low, is growing rapidly, especially among the university-educated. The theologians likewise do not seem to have come to terms with the signs of a changing class structure that I noticed in the early 2000s. Although there is a younger generation of theologians typically teaching in Catholic universities, they largely repeat the positions of the founding generation (Gutierrez, Ellacuria, Dussel, Boff, and so forth).

The largely male theologians acknowledged the oppression of women, but they have not internalized the feminist critique of patriarchy. Women theologians teach in Catholic universities, but they cannot publicly discuss reproductive issues. That separates them from secular feminists who have advocated legalization of abortion. Some participate in Conspirando, a network of ecofeminist theologians with no ecclesiastical ties headquartered in Santiago, which holds positions akin to those common to feminist theologians in North America and Europe, but it is marginalized from mainstream theological institutions. This situation can perhaps be traced to the early 1970s, when the initial liberation theologians agreed that they should be wary of the European "progressive" agenda (then birth control, celibacy, and papal authority), because such "bourgeois" issues could be an impediment to bringing the institutional Catholic Church, including the hierarchy, onto the side of the poor.

* * *

It seemed obvious that someone would write an overview of Latin America taking into account the positive developments I was encountering. Each semester I expected to see such a book by a journalist or academic, or a Latin American intellectual, and each semester I was disappointed. Why wasn't I seeing panels about this at LASA conferences? Did my fellow Latin Americanists see something that I didn't?

My hunches were confirmed in brief visits to Lima and Santiago, on the way to our daughter Maggie's wedding celebration in Argentina in November 2008. One indication was that Latin Americans weren't greatly affected by the recession roiling North

America and Europe (with the exception of Mexico, whose economy was closely tied to that of the United States). A Chilean economist explained to me that by law the Chilean government was obliged to invest excess profits from copper in sovereign wealth funds to prepare for a future downturn, and that it was now beginning to draw on those. Previously governments would have spent the windfall revenues. It was an example of Latin Americans doing things right. More generally, pragmatic macroeconomic policies (which some might have labeled "neoliberalism") were now paying off.

When the book I was expecting didn't appear, I began sketching outlines and drafting chapters, drawing on my years of teaching, and went into further depth in books and articles, and reports by think tanks aimed at policymakers. One day in 2009 while running, it struck me that the two-hundred-year anniversary of Latin American independence was approaching. That anniversary would span a decade and a half because the independence struggle went from 1810 to 1824. That gave me a title: *Latin America at 200*. My writing accelerated in mid-2011, when I stopped teaching at Temple. I drew on trips to Mexico (2007), Central America (2011), and Colombia, Ecuador, and Bolivia (2012).

A surprising indicator of improved living conditions was life expectancy. In 1960 the figure for most Latin American countries was between fifty and sixty years; a few countries were higher, and Guatemala and Bolivia were under fifty. The corresponding figure for the United States was slightly below seventy. By 2010 all Latin American countries except Bolivia had life expectancies of over seventy, that is, higher than the United States when I was finishing my seminary career.

Two longitudinal studies of poor communities bore out my impressions that life was improving generation by generation. In *Favela* (2010), Janice Perlman examined what had happened to the individuals and families she had studied in Rio in the early 1970s, and in *Ordinary Families, Extraordinary Lives* (2009), Carolyn Moser wrote about the fortunes of people in a Guayaquil barrio from the time it was constructed on stilts above the swamp in the 1970s into the 2000s. In both cases, shacks had become solid homes, and children and grandchildren had better lives. On the other hand, people lamented crime and the lack of the kind of community they had experienced when they were young. I had similar impressions in interviews in poor neighborhoods in Cali and Guayaquil in 2012.

Three-quarters of Latin Americans were now urban, and so it seemed important to highlight issues of cities, and to take into account the decline of subsistence farming. After tracing some developments in large-scale agriculture, especially in Brazil, I proposed that the aim of policy should be to foster family farms—farms on which a family could make a decent living, selling crops, with the support needed in inputs, insurance protection, and so forth.

Instead of speaking of economics in abstract terms like capitalism, I opted to devote a chapter to businesses, ranging from corner stores to *multilatinas*, Latin American multinationals, which had operations in neighboring countries and even in

Europe, North America, and Asia. The chapter included sections on malls, franchises (which are major employers), and tech innovators.

Researchers were finding evidence for the emergence of a "new middle class" for which the Inter-American Development Bank offered a framework. Using a relatively high daily four dollars per capita as the cutoff point between poor and nonpoor, it found that two-thirds of Latin Americans were nonpoor. In between the third who were poor and the third who were middle-class, it proposed a "vulnerable" class (four to ten dollars a day), comprising people who could slip back below the poverty line. These are per-capita figures; thus, a family of five receiving four dollars a day per capita has an income of twenty dollars a day. The middle class, for example, families of five with combined monthly incomes between fifteen hundred and seventy-five hundred dollars, are definitely in the consumer economy. These figures demonstrated that what had surprised me in Joao Pessoa reflected more general trends in Latin America. Toward the end of his presidency Lula boasted that 30 to 40 million Brazilians had risen out of poverty. That still left a third of Latin Americans who were poor, especially subsistence farmers and indigenous and Afro-Latino people.

Rather than simply cataloguing problems, I put the emphasis on what Latin Americans were doing about them. On gender, that meant considering not only traditional machismo but advances by women in local and national politics, in the workplace, and in combating domestic violence and struggling for reproductive rights. On race, I considered the rise of indigenous organizations and affirmative action policies in Brazil. On the environment, I noted slowing of deforestation, efforts to curb mining, and urban initiatives such as bus-rapid-transit systems, in which Latin American cities lead the world.

A pragmatic shift could be seen in "conditional cash transfers," modest government payments to the poorest households, on the condition that children are vaccinated or remain in school, which were begun in Brazil and Mexico in the 1990s and spread to many countries, which have helped reduce poverty and have stimulated local economies. The longest chapter was on crime and corruption and efforts to combat them, such as professionalizing police forces, dealing with youth gangs and combating organized crime, and reforming the justice system and prisons. Corruption is not new; what is new is that at least some major perpetrators have been brought to justice.

While working on the book I found similar perspectives in *Americas Quarterly*, published by the Americas Society, and *ReVista*, a review from Harvard. Chilean businessman Raul Ramirez published *Nuestra Hora* (Our moment; 2011), arguing that Latin America's time was coming, with a bit too much of inspirational speaker for my taste. In September 2010, commemorating the two-hundred-year anniversary of the initial proclamation of independence in Mexico, *The Economist* ran a special cover story, "Nobody's Backyard: The Rise of Latin America," written by Michael Reid. In *Forgotten Continent*, published three years previously, Reid had seen few signs of progress; now he pointed to a rising middle class and other indications similar to what I had been sensing. (In 2017 Reid published a new edition of *Forgotten Continent*, now subtitled *A History of the New Latin America*, so thoroughly revised that it amounted to a new book.)

In 2012 I took the outline and sample chapters to the LASA conference to discuss with publishers. In 2013 I reached an agreement with the University of Texas Press, whose editor Theresa May was especially enthusiastic. The press provided a sum for photographs and hence the book was handsomely illustrated. *Latin America at 200: A New Introduction* was published in 2016. Although I had written it with general readers as well as students in mind, it has been seen as a book for classroom use and sales have been modest.

By the time the book appeared, some clouds diminished the sunnier picture it presented. It became clear that the boom in commodities prices that had driven growth for a decade and a half had halted, and growth slowed. The impeachment of President Dilma Roussef in Brazil in 2016 aggravated problems there, and the Mexican government seemed powerless to deal with corruption and violence, exemplified in the disappearance and presumed murder of forty-three teachers in Ayotzinapa in 2013 by state agents operating with impunity. In 2018, populist politicians tapped into discontent and were elected president, from the left in Mexico (Manuel Lopez Obrador) and from the right in Brazil (Jair Bolsonaro).

* * *

In 2011 Angie and I took a monthlong trip from Guatemala to Panama traveling from capital to capital by bus. Our aim was to renew contact with old friends and colleagues and catch up on developments in the region, including assessing whether people's life situation had improved.

As soon as we left the airport in Guatemala with Guillermo Corado we could see new sets of highways and bridges where we remembered hills and *barrancos*. Twenty years before, Panama City had a few skyscrapers; now its skyline looked like Miami. Malls had been built in many places, even at the edge of poor barrios in Guatemala. Supermarkets were common, and many ordinary people were shopping there.

Downtown Guatemala City, which had been the center of the city when we lived there in the 1970s, had been abandoned to the poor. The major businesses were now concentrated at the other end of town. The municipality was trying to lure people back with a new pedestrian mall along what had been a major avenue, but we had a general impression that those who could were retreating into gated communities. The countryside also showed signs of change. The Pan-American Highway near the town of Chimaltenango was lined with businesses, mainly vehicle-related, for what seemed like miles.

Signs of remittances from abroad, especially the United States, were everywhere. In the indigenous town of Nahuala, we spent the night in an empty cement-block house intended to display the wealth of its owner and saw various others. In El Salvador a major driver of the economy was money from abroad, enabling people to buy consumer goods.

In the 1970s and 1980s, it was taken for granted that the conflicts were over land; now we saw signs of a shift away from agriculture. Over a million acres of agricultural land in El Salvador were now said to be uncultivated. The country was no longer self-sufficient in rice or other staples. Traditional subsistence farming was in crisis, perhaps because life in the twenty-first century requires cash.

The day before we arrived in Guatemala twenty-seven people had been murdered in the remote northern Peten region, apparently by former army troops now in the drug trade. Central America served as a drug delivery route to the United States. Even in the indigenous towns of the highlands, young people could earn money transporting drugs. People were afraid of street crime throughout the region.

The political scene was generally discouraging. In Nicaragua two decades of right-wing governments had given way to Daniel Ortega, who no longer had the support of many Sandinistas. Guatemala was in the midst of a presidential campaign with a dozen parties, all candidates smiling and offering vacuous slogans. In Honduras we watched large crowds gather to welcome the return of the populist Manuel Zelaya, who in 2009 had been unseated by Congress and the military, and sent out of the country in his pajamas. Human rights activists were being murdered there with impunity. In El Salvador, Hector Dada, whom I knew as a young UCA professor who had spent a decade in exile, was now minister of the economy in an FMLN government, which was attempting to work pragmatically with business the way the Lula government had done in Brazil.

We were encouraged by progress being made on coming to terms with the human rights violations of the past. In El Salvador we went to see the wall with the names of over thirty-five thousand victims of the violence in the war, similar to the Vietnam War Memorial in Washington, with each name by year and in order. The National Museum had incorporated the war into Salvadoran history.

In Guatemala, the archives of the National Police had been accidentally discovered in 2005 in an abandoned warehouse, A crew of 150 people was working to organize, clean, preserve, and scan these records starting with the 1975–1985 period, the time of the most vicious repression, seeking to possibly determine the fate of those who had disappeared, or to determine responsibility for criminal acts. Electronic copies of the scanned documents were being sent for safekeeping outside the country, with the concern that a change of government could close down the operation.

At the Verbena Cemetery in Guatemala City, mass graves of thousands of bodies buried anonymously had been found. Forensic specialists in orange jumpsuits were being lowered by harness into a pit over sixty feet deep where they gathered remains and sent them up to the surface. There the dark brown or black bones were being sorted, cataloged and placed in bags. Not all were victims of political violence; some may have been homeless or their families may have not kept up on payments to the cemetery. Posters read, "My name is NOT XX: your DNA may identify me," with the aim of finding matches between the DNA in the bones and family members.

In Panama we were hosted by Hector Endara and his wife, Nati. She worked at a shipping company in Balboa in what had been the Canal Zone but was now Panamanian. We visited a few old friends in Nuevo Chorrillo, the housing development that emerged from our work in the early 1970s. In Chorrillo we talked to the priest at the parish of Fatima, which had now been in the hands of the Mercedarian Fathers for more than twenty years. On the premises they had built a residence for the aged. The wooden houses were gone, replaced by concrete apartment buildings built by the government. We wanted to walk up the street, but Hector, who had grown up in Marañon, a barrio similar to Chorrillo, said gangs with guns made it unsafe for outsiders.

Hector, who had worked with the church agency Caritas for many years, took us to Santa Fe for the fortieth anniversary of the killing of Hector Gallego. We walked in a short procession and then attended a Mass celebrated by Bishop Oscar Brown (who had entered the seminary from San Miguelito in my time), and a series of speeches outside. In the Mass, Hector's memory seemed sanitized: there was no mention of why he had been killed. During the speeches I noticed some schoolchildren who had come up to Santa Fe from Veraguas and were absorbed with their smartphones. The campesino cooperative was still in operation, and we met with Jacinto Peña, the leader from whose house Hector had been abducted.

Our friends and their colleagues were still working on behalf of justice. In Nicaragua, Mary de Zuniga was assisting grassroots healthcare networks. Maryknoll sisters in El Salvador were getting antiretroviral medications to people with HIV/AIDS, attempting to slow the disease in its early stages. A Jesuit-sponsored program in the barranco near the Puente Belice had programs whereby older youth mentored younger kids. One organizer told us of her work raising awareness of domestic violence in indigenous communities, and helping its victims. At the radio school in Nahuala we saw a young indigenous woman broadcasting, and heard how the program was now incorporating social media and doing nonpartisan education around the election.

15

The View from Eighty

THE CONTOURS OF THE story told here are a mixture of circumstance, contingency, and choice: boyhood in Southern California; twelve years in the seminary and two as a young priest in Pasadena; eight years in Panama and Latin America in the wake of Vatican II and church renewal; marriage, travel, and four years in Central America in a time of crisis, repression, and revolution; a decade of opposition to U.S. policy in Central America; freelance translating, adjunct teaching, and writing.

In hindsight I can see that I owe much to several father figures: John Coffield, Leo Mahon, Jose Comblin, Paulo Freire, and Gary MacEoin. Each was ten or twenty years older than I, and they impacted me in my twenties or early thirties. All were male, three were priests, and the other two had church ties, not surprising because I was a seminarian and priest myself.

Had Angie and I been prudent early in our marriage, we would have earned appropriate degree credentials, become professionals, and settled down—in my case perhaps as an academic. But in 1974 we sold our worldly goods and set out from California to Pennsylvania on our way to a job in Panama—which then evaporated. We opted to travel through Latin America, spent a year in an anarchist intentional community, served as AFSC staff in Central America, and worked on the incipient Central America movement. I was in my late forties when we bought our house, and in my early fifties when I finally adopted a recognizable trade as a freelance translator while doing adjunct teaching, and continuing to stew internally about big questions.

From 1965 into the 1980s, I saw the world from Latin America. That is where I experienced the sixties—and for that matter the seventies and to a degree the eighties. I thus came to see the United States from the outside, and specifically from the standpoint of Latin America. That included an awareness of the long history of U.S. interference in the region, from the nineteenth century (Monroe Doctrine, Mexican and Spanish American Wars), to the Cold War with CIA interventions, and support for dictators and military governments. I also gained an appreciation of the way even poor Latin Americans enjoyed their lives and loved their countries, even while criticizing their governments and elites.

Based on that experience, I try to understand the United States not only from inside but from outside, and to view its actions in the world from the standpoint of people on the other side. That makes me curious about how the world looks in other societies, when Angie and I have traveled in China, Bangladesh, Israel-Palestine, Ireland, Italy, and Spain, and also the work of filmmakers in Iran, China, Japan, Korea, and elsewhere.

* * *

Portions of the story told here are a necrology of the fallen: Hector Gallego (Panama, 1971); Bill Woods (Guatemala, 1976); Mario Mujia ("Wiwi"; Guatemala, 1978); Pedro Joaquin Chamorro (Nicaragua, 1978); Oscar Romero, Enrique Alvarez Cordoba, Maura Clarke (El Salvador, 1980); Conrado de la Cruz, Walter Voordeckers, Kai Utah Clouds (Guatemala, 1980); Stanley Rother (Guatemala, 1981); Cesar Vera, Fernando Hoyos (Guatemala, 1982); Marianela Garcia (El Salvador, 1983); Ignacio Ellacuria, Ignacio Martin-Baro, Amando Lopez, Segundo Montes (El Salvador, 1989); Myrna Mack (Guatemala, 1990); Juan Gerardi (Guatemala, 1998). Some were friends and colleagues; others were acquaintances or people with whom I had dealings. Many were priests, and almost all were church-connected; all except Fernando Hoyos were noncombatants.

They were a small portion of a much larger cohort of victims of repressive state violence in Latin America, starting with the military dictatorships in South America in the 1970s and then in Central America through the 1980s. Subsequent truth commissions concluded that those killed or disappeared numbered somewhat under three thousand in Chile, over nine thousand in Argentina, seventy-five thousand in El Salvador, and over one hundred thousand in Guatemala; other sources give higher figures. Those doing the killing were either uniformed state agents or clandestine death squads operating with impunity. In some instances they were combating armed leftist insurgents, but they did so by abducting, torturing, and killing civilians. The killers may have felt justified because they were obeying orders or believed that they were on the front lines of "World War III": the battle against communist subversion, which was taking place in their societies. That view had been fostered by the general atmosphere of the Cold War and the sense of mission the armed forces and police had absorbed in training courses given by the United States in Panama and elsewhere.

Throughout the hemisphere virtually no one was brought to justice for these crimes. In a few high-profile cases, such as the murders of Archbishop Romero and the six Jesuits, low-level participants were tried and sentenced, but those giving the orders were not. The exception was Argentina, where generals were jailed but later given amnesty. Decades later, a few officers and even heads of state were at last brought to court, notably Presidents Pinochet and Rios Montt, but their trials were inconclusive and they died before justice was served.

When I prepared reports on political violence in Guatemala in the late 1970s, and later when I translated the official Chilean human rights report, I felt that my labor was at least helping to preserve a public record of the wrong done to these people. Several of the postconflict human rights reports bore the title *Nunca Más* (Never again). I would hope that a culture of human rights is taking hold in Latin America and would prevent a recurrence of massive state-inflicted political violence with impunity. That may be one of the fruits of the work of my generation. As I write, Archbishop Oscar Romero has been canonized and Stanley Rother may join him.

Decades ago we assumed that these deaths were the birth pangs of a qualitatively different kind of society. That has not come about, and I fear that they may be like other victims in history, such as those who died in the Spanish Civil War of the 1930s. Part of my reason for writing is to preserve their memory with the hope that *Nunca Más* becomes more than an aspiration.

* * *

Like others of my generation, through my experience over time, I came to believe that the causes of poverty were systemic and had to be addressed systemically. When I returned to Chorrillo after a year of study and travel in South America in 1968–1969, I had been radicalized. That didn't mean taking up arms but seeking to go to the root (Latin: *radix*) causes. Poverty in Panama and Latin America was not an accident but was systemic and structural. If the existing economic system, capitalism, was failing to bring social and economic progress for the majority, it ought to be replaced by another system, socialism—not a carbon copy of the USSR, Eastern Europe, or China, but a "Latin American socialism." In 1972 I organized the Panamanian delegation to Christians for Socialism in Chile.

In this memoir I could have elided this aspect of my past since state socialism has been discredited for several decades. However, I wanted to give some sense of how I and many of my contemporaries could be sympathetic to it. Into the mid-1970s about half the world population was under some form of state-led socialism, not only those run by communist parties (USSR, Eastern Europe, China, Vietnam, Cuba), but also in India, Egypt, and various other noncommunist countries, particularly in Africa.

The 1973 coup in Chile, along with coups in Argentina and elsewhere, signaled the end of any electoral path to socialism in Latin America. The elites, the military, and the United States were quite willing to overthrow elected governments that they viewed as threatening. The Sandinista victory in 1979 led to a decade of counterrevolutionary violence in Central America. The very violence of that era reinforced our convictions: if they were willing to kill so many of us in the name of capitalism, our vision must be valid.

By the second half of the 1980s I no longer saw Nicaragua and the revolutionary movements in El Salvador and Guatemala as harbingers of a different kind of society. My hope was for a soft landing through peace negotiations. By 1990 many Latin American activists and their academic sympathizers no longer expected guerrillas in fatigues to march into the capital to take state power in the classic fashion. They now put their faith in grassroots organizations and NGO efforts, such as indigenous peoples, Afrodescendants, women, and environmental groups, eventually brought together in the World Social Forum, whose motto was "Another World is Possible." "Neoliberalism" served as a unifying designation for what had to be overcome. I was skeptical of this fuzzy new faith, but I didn't have an alternative.

What changed my mind was not any new economic or political paradigm, but observing signs of a consumer economy among ordinary people in Mexico, Brazil, and elsewhere, starting in the late 1990s. A surprising number of Latin Americans, perhaps a majority, were no longer desperately poor and were even middle class in terms of their own societies. However, the emergence of this consumer society was not clear to my fellow Latin Americanists, at least judging by the topics at LASA conference panels. The analysis of the Latin American bishops at Aparecida (2007) gave little hint of the change I was sensing, admittedly at a time when books by social scientists and journalists on Latin America continued to have gloomy views. Around 2010 the beginning of the bicentenary of Latin American independence, the tone began to change. Evidence was mounting that a global middle class was emerging, and business was beginning to target it. The most notable example was China, as I could see in Beijing in 2002 when I visited our daughter Lizzy, who was teaching there.

Extreme poverty was declining. Meeting in 2000 under UN auspices, the nations of the world had pledged to cut extreme poverty in half by 2015 in the Millennium Development Goals. Those goals were further specified under headings like health care, schooling, and equality for women. At first I paid little attention to yet another grand scheme by governments. However, the goal was met in most countries before the deadline. In 2015, governments reformulated the goals and pledged to eliminate extreme poverty by 2030.

How are we to account for this progress and learn from it? It was not simply the magic of the market, nor was it due primarily to government programs or international foreign aid, and it occurred under right-wing and left-wing governments. It reflects a confluence of a number of developments, most of them incremental and undramatic: the move to the city and the decline of subsistence farming; advances in public health and expansion of schooling; infrastructure (roads, electricity, water, and sewerage); the taming of inflation; social policies targeted at the poorest, particularly direct cash payments; a commodities boom, benefiting countries that exported raw materials. Not least were people's own efforts to advance at the household and community level, improving their homes over the years, and sacrificing for the sake of their children.

These advances were by no means universal. People in dozens of countries, particularly in sub-Saharan Africa, but including Haiti and some Central American countries (the "bottom billion"), were seeing little progress, compounded by governments that were incompetent, unresponsive, and corrupt. However, the hopes for a better world that once seemed to be utopian were gradually—if unevenly—being realized. This has been a welcome development over the course of my lifetime for which I am appreciative—even if it runs counter to convictions that my contemporaries and I held for many years.

* * *

I am writing in the midst of the presidency of Donald Trump, when many people in the United States and abroad are astonished and chagrined, trying to make sense of our national political and cultural polarization. From my experience the situation isn't quite as unprecedented as it might seem. When Angie and I returned from Guatemala in 1980 we were astonished to see the presidency won by an aging entertainer who had little knowledge of the rest of the world. We spent the next decade resisting his Central America policy, which was implemented by ideologues supplied by neoconservative think tanks. The parallels to Trump are obvious, although Reagan had been active in Republican politics since his Hollywood days, and he had been a two-term governor of California.

George W. Bush also had no virtually no experience of the world outside the United States when he took office. His foreign policy team harnessed the fear generated by the September 11, 2001, attacks to invade and occupy Iraq, which the neoconservatives had been advocating since the mid-1990s. Three-quarters of the public supported the wars in Afghanistan and Iraq until around 2006, when it became clear they were failing.

The Clinton and Obama presidencies were pendulum swings from their polarizing Republican predecessors. Seen in terms of the cycles of the last four decades, Trump seems like a logical, if grotesque, outcome. Politics is too often driven by a "take our country back" animus.

The roots of this political and cultural tug-of-war can be traced back to the 1960s, when some Americans were angered by the civil rights and antiwar movements, which challenged authority and conventional patriotism, and by what they saw as the immorality of the counterculture. Nixon successfully appealed to the "silent majority" in 1968, and Republican strategists crafted a winning electoral coalition by stoking concerns about race and crime among whites, which with variations has proved successful. The opposing Democratic coalition began to take shape in the 1972 McGovern campaign.

For decades, when changing residence, Americans have gravitated toward people like themselves, to the point where zip codes are increasingly homogeneous culturally and politically. When I was a poll watcher at our polling place in West Philadelphia in 2004, the vote was eleven-to-one Democratic. All this has been augmented by a twenty-four-hour media environment, starting with CNN and full-time news in the 1980s, through the Internet, and up to the social networks of today, in which individuals limit themselves to sources that they find congenial to their worldview. Feedback loops aggravate polarization.

Trump's crude "America First" nationalism draws on the deep-seated sentiment of American exceptionalism held with quasi-religious fervor, as can be noted in State of the Union messages in which presidents invoke God and partisans chant "USA! USA!" American exceptionalism seemed more plausible during my childhood and youth when most of the world was poor, and Europe was recovering from the devastation of war. Americans were richer than others; the U.S. armed forces seemed all-powerful; American technology and manufactured goods led the world. It was easy to conflate U.S. economic and military power and the strength of U.S. institutions with cultural and moral superiority. The result is an unconscious ideology that might be called "Number-One-ism." I eventually realized that one reason for this attitude lay in geography: Americans can drive for days on interstates and see the same hotel and fast-food franchises. Citizens of smaller nations know that within a few hours they cross a border and the people there speak another language and have other sets of laws and traditions.

That ideology has less plausibility than it did decades ago. By most measures China has the world's largest economy, and the disparity is likely to grow. European nations have a standard of living close to that of the United States. At least thirty other nations have longevity equal to or longer than that of the United States, and thus have parity in health. Over half the nations of the earth are now governed democratically, and some democracies are at least as firmly anchored as our own. The United States remains large and powerful but it is only 4 percent of humankind and it is no longer—and perhaps never has been—number one. Neither is any other nation. The very claim or assumption is meaningless.

Whatever the outcome of the Trump presidency, the polarization that it has brought to the surface runs deeper than one individual or one political party.

* * *

For a half century one of the Catholic eucharistic prayers has echoed the biblical account of creation and covenant, and proclaimed the message and life of Jesus: "a man like us in all things but sin. To the poor he proclaimed the good news of salvation, to prisoners, freedom, and to those in sorrow, joy." He gave himself in death, "but by rising from the dead, he destroyed death and restored life. And that we might live no longer for ourselves but for him, he sent the Holy Spirit from you, Father, as his first gift to those who believe, to complete his work on earth and bring us the fullness of grace." The consecrated bread and wine are then lifted up, and in the name of the congregation the celebrant prays for the living and the dead, and invokes the saints in heaven where all will be reunited.

This prayer situates worshipers in a cosmic and historic drama, in which the earthly life, mission, death, resurrection, and ascension of Jesus encompass their own life and destiny with the Father and Holy Spirit. This vision is intensified in the Holy Saturday Vigil, which begins with the lighting of the Easter candle, a procession into the dark church, and the singing of the Exsultet, followed by readings from the Genesis creation account, the exodus from Egypt, and the prophets, culminating in accounts of the resurrection. The vigil is the climax of the Holy Week liturgies starting Palm Sunday.

Catholics who attend Mass regularly hear the major texts of the Bible over a three-year cycle of readings. Each year focuses on one of the Synoptic Gospels—Mark, Matthew, or Luke—with the Gospel of John inserted in each of the years, and with the first reading (Hebrew scripture) chosen for its connection to the particular Gospel passage. The Pauline and other Epistles run on an independent parallel three-year cycle.

In the homily the priest celebrant is expected to "open the scriptures" for the congregation, contextualizing and explaining the original meaning and their continuing relevance for individuals and for the community. Provided that the preacher has a solid biblical background, Catholics should understand Jesus as a first-century Galilean prophet as portrayed differently by each of the evangelists. Jesus is our path to God, but our own human experience is crucial to understanding Jesus in his time. Good preaching reflects awareness of recent explorations of the historical Jesus, without getting lost in details, but rather as a refocusing on the earliest origins of Christianity.

Biblical language is symbolic: We are sheep and Jesus is our Shepherd; this life is a seed that must die in order to have life; we are united in Christ like branches on a vine; Christ is our high priest, indeed a temple. Our destiny is variously portrayed as a mansion with many rooms, a banquet, or a city. These metaphors are manifold and cannot be reduced to a system.

All of this stands in sharp contrast to the Catholicism of my childhood and youth, which was presented as timeless truth, even though its characteristic features had been established by the sixteenth-century Council of Trent. We were taught that this life was a preparation for the next life; it was all-important to die in the state of grace, and for that purpose penance (confession) and the other sacraments were necessary. Life was a trial with very serious consequences, as indicated in the medieval hymn "Dies Irae," portraying the day when the trumpet will sound and all will be summoned before the Judge who will consult the book in which everything is written. Along with that came a lively sense of an invisible realm alongside this visible earthly reality, such as guardian angels, as portrayed in Catholic art from the period.

That system collapsed in the years immediately after Vatican II, when the practice of regular confession dropped precipitously. The notion of being condemned to hell eternally for missing Mass, eating a hamburger on Friday, or even for illicit sexual pleasure lost credibility, not least because of its portrayal of a God so obsessed over the pursuits and mind-set of his creatures. God is now assumed to be a merciful Father toward whom we are all journeying, Catholics and non-Catholic alike.

Catholicism since the Council has more of a this-worldly focus. Catholic funerals now tend to be a celebration of life of the deceased, similar to secular rituals. Although saints and angels are mentioned in the liturgy, we no longer conceive of a parallel supernatural world alongside this visible one. Our efforts to make the world more humane for all contributes in some fashion to bringing about God's reign.

Catholic parishes now encompass many ministries: various spiritual movements, food for the poor or homeless, sick visitation, music, deaconate, and in some instances schools. This represents not simply a quantitative expansion of the pre–Vatican II parish with its emphasis on sacraments, but a community intended to accompany parishioners in their life journey.

Such a portrayal of contemporary Catholicism is no doubt somewhat idealized. Preaching can certainly be uninspiring; music of various types may be banal or clash with the sobriety of the Roman liturgy; the worship experience can become routine. Parishes may constitute a community for the inner circle of activists, but not for most who park, go to Mass, and drive off to their Sunday pursuits. The never-ending clergy sex abuse scandal and cover-up have provided further justification for sincere people to walk out and slam the door. Large numbers of former Catholics have withdrawn from the church. Some have migrated to other Christian churches, while others have joined the ranks of the "nones," the growing number of Americans with no religious affiliation. All of that notwithstanding, my own experience told here motivates me to continue as a Christian in the Catholic tradition.

* * *

Circumstances have given me several points of contact with Pope Francis, who is a year and a half older than I. We both experienced the postconciliar period in Latin America, he in Argentina and I in Panama. Jorge Bergoglio's pastoral experience was urban, primarily in Buenos Aires where he was born and raised. He was much influenced by two decades as bishop and archbishop in which he spent a great deal of time in poor barrios, with people whose lives may have resembled those of the people of Chorrillo. I translated the Aparecida document (2007), on which he was the major editorial hand.

I believe my sense of his background offers me some clues into his approach to the papacy. For reasons indicated earlier, I felt increasingly alienated during the papacies of John Paul II and Benedict XVI, with their enforcement of what they regarded as doctrinal orthodoxy and their hostility to what they regarded as secular humanism. However, I didn't think that the answer would be a pope who would line up neatly with my positions. I wondered whether the pope could be a figure somewhat like the Dalai Lama, one leading by example and inspiration, not by issuing orders. To a degree, that is how I see Francis. He is still recognizably a pope, but he regards himself as a fellow bishop, rather than a monarch.

Without criticizing his two predecessors, Francis has attempted to redirect the Catholic Church to the agenda of Vatican II. He no longer portrays Christians as doing battle with secularists or relativists. He emphasizes what all human beings have in common, a clear emphasis in the Council, and especially the document on the church in the modern world. His style is not that of condemnation or issuing marching orders.

His "field" hasn't been theology or philosophy or another academic discipline, but spirituality, which can be sensed in "The Joy of the Gospel," an initial programmatic statement; "The Joy of Love," his reply to the synods on the family; *Laudato Si*, the encyclical on the environment; and "Rejoice and Be Glad!" on the call to holiness. His spirituality is the outgrowth of a lifetime of experience and meditation. That life hasn't been one of unalloyed success: made superior of the Jesuits at an early age under the murderous Argentine military dictatorship, Jorge Bergoglio then occupied other leadership positions in Buenos Aires until he was exiled by the Jesuits themselves, first to graduate study, which he didn't complete, and then to the city of Cordoba, hours away from the capital. He was then picked as auxiliary bishop in Buenos Aires, where he became archbishop and cardinal, and for two decades lived a simple life, spending as much time as he could with poor people and their pastors. The qualities we see in him were honed over decades of sometimes difficult experience.

* * *

The gleaming technological future I read about in magazines as a child—families with their own private helicopters—did not come about. Much of our twenty-first-century way of life is surprisingly similar to the way things were when I was young. Although students now carry laptops and mobile phones, they are still in classrooms from September to June; have homework, examinations, and grades; and advance by cohorts for twelve or sixteen years.

Yet the world is very different from what it was eighty years ago. Diseases that were still lethal when I was young have been conquered; surgeries and pharmaceuticals have extended lifespan a decade. Spectacular theoretical advances in physics and space exploration affect daily life invisibly, as in the satellite systems on which our GPS devices operate. Going to a supermarket is superficially similar to what it was around 1960, but today the produce comes from thousands of miles away and is no longer tied to local seasons. A modern farm is a complex operation in which irrigation allocation may be aided by drones.

When I see people fixated on their handheld devices in the subway, on the street—or even at the gym—I sense that they are experiencing a world that is different from my own. And the very proliferation of gyms as a regular part of twenty-first-century life attests to a far-reaching change: very few people do enough physical work to keep them healthy, and thus they must set aside time for exercise.

Based on my life experience I might guess that our grandchildren's experience would be similar to ours: periodic new developments would bring surprises, but when they reach my age they would look back and see primarily incremental changes in a world that remains familiar. However, I suspect that technological developments are disrupting the world in ways that we are only beginning to discern, particularly the set of innovations in the mid-2000s: smartphones and social media.

New combinations of technology may eliminate a large percentage of current occupations, such as vehicle drivers, retail clerks, and even some portions of professions such as routine work by lawyers. Will other fields of work open up to employ those so displaced? Alarms about mass technological unemployment—or predictions of a leisure society—in the 1950s and 1960s proved premature, because new jobs have generally opened in other fields, primarily in services. However, this time it may be different.

Ideally all adults would have work that is valued, fulfilling, and adequately remunerated. However, in our society we have a bifurcated labor situation in which some people are highly paid and often work long hours, and others do low-wage but necessary labor, especially in the service sector—and most disgracefully in agriculture. If jobs of all kinds become scarce, what can be done to assure people a living?

* * *

In *Populorum Progressio* (1967), Paul VI said that economic and social development called for a "new humanism"; he characterized that development as "the transition from less than human conditions to truly human ones." Those less than human conditions were material poverty, political and economic oppression, exploitation of workers; truly human conditions included rising from poverty, achieving education and culture, being aware of other people's dignity, taking an interest in the common good, and seeking peace. This endeavor is ultimately part of the human journey toward ultimate union with God. At Medellin the Latin American bishops likened that process to the exodus.

My generation drew inspiration from that vision, not because it came from the pope—the encyclical was in fact drafted by a French Dominican, Louis-Joseph Lebret—but because of how it helped us situate our own work and provided a criterion for genuine development. Economic growth must not be sought for its own sake; the aim is not simply "having more" but "being more." To illustrate with a mundane example, when a poor family replaces an outdoor latrine with an indoor flush toilet it advances toward "more human" conditions. But is that true of a second toilet? Perhaps, but it is not nearly as significant as the first one. At what point would another bathroom—or other extra rooms—not make for more human conditions at all?

Likewise, having access to motor vehicles allows for further possibilities not available to people limited to travel by foot. But at some point the number of miles driven does not make for possibilities of being more human. Are some societies already reaching a level of consumption—money spent, miles flown, fossil fuels burned—that is not a transition from less human to more human conditions? This is a far from idle question. Should Latin America or China strive to reach a level of consumption on a par with that of the West?

The signs from nature, particularly climate change but also the effects of toxic chemicals in freshwater and the sea, are that we are already reaching limits. For the present generation, moving from less human to more human conditions may involve more of reducing extreme inequalities—between nations, within nations, and within enterprises—than simply increasing output and the use of the earth's resources.

* * *

Decades ago I heard Jose Comblin say, "If we knew at twenty what we're going to know at eighty, we'd never do anything."

He was talking about the human condition: we must act in the present even though we don't and can't know the consequences of our actions—and yet we can't let that paralyze us. Events during my lifetime—what I and my contemporaries didn't and couldn't know in advance—bear out his observation.

When he made the remark I was closer to twenty and couldn't imagine being eighty. Having reached that point, I have offered this story and these further observations, primarily on changes over my lifetime, with the hope that they can offer modestly useful perspectives for the present.

Index

abduction, 114–16 116–17, 216
abortion, 293
Acteal, 277–78
AFSC (American Friends Service Committee), vii, viii, 153, 155, 165, 171, 185, 195–96, 208–9, 210–12, 217, 222, 252, 258–59, 287
Agent for Change, 129
Aguiar, Cesar, 100
Aguilares, 166
Alas, Jose Inocencio (Chencho), 91, 116, 133, 178, 278
Albizurez, Miguel Angel, 157–58
Albo, Xavier, 143
Alejadinho, 148
Algodones, 50–51
Allen, Steve, 45
Allende, Salvador, 124, 125, 260
Altafulla, Jorge, 75, 84, 117
Alvarez Calderon, Carlos, 89, 99, 100
Alvarez Calderon, Jorge, 99, 100
Alvarez Cordoba, Enrique, 210–11, 212
Alves, Rubem, 147–48
Amazon, 141, 148, 165, 275
Amazonas theater, 148
America, 280
American exceptionalism, 305
Americas (film series)
Americas Quarterly, 296
Amerindia, 293
Amnesty International, 167, 206, 215
AMPRONAC, 185
análisis coyuntural, 124–25, 175–76
anarchist tradition, 276
Anchorage, 222,
Anderson, Phil, 203
ANEP (National Private Enterprise Association, 166, 179
angels, 13, 81
Another World Is Possible, 288, 303

Antigua, 121
anti-Semitism, 81
Aparecida, 292–93, 307
Apen, Juana, 163
Aquinas, Thomas, 27
Arana, Carlos, 158
Arellano, Estuardo, 89
ARENA (National Republican Alliance), 227, 243
Argentina, 58, 99, 124, 144
Argentine military intelligence, 224
Arias Calderon, Ricardo, 140, 252
Arias, Arnulfo, 93
Arias, Oscar, 243
Arns, Paulo Evaristo, 142, 147, 240, 241, 266
Assemblies of God, 265
Assembly of Chorrillo, 112–13
Assembly of Deputies, 120
assembly plants, 175
Assmann, Hugo, 122, 124, 152, 176–77, 187, 188, 232 x
Association of Chicago Priests, 83
Association of Coffee Exporters, 169
Association of Western Colleges, 27
Asunción, 137, 144
ATA (American Translators Association, 269, 270
Atlacatl Batallion, 227–28, 251
Atlantic rain forest, 286
Audet, J.-P., 97
AVANSCO (Association for the Advance of the Social Sciences,), 253
Aylwin, Patricio, 260
Ayotzinapa, 297

Bacevich, Andrew, 245
Bachelet, Michele, 288
backlash (to Vatican II), 149, 290
Balaguer, Joaquin, 54, 74
Balasuriya, Tissa, 43, 232, 282
Bamat, Tom and Mercedes, 283

311

INDEX

Bambaren, Luis, 126
banana companies, 172
banking haven (Panama), 124
baptism, 40, 66, 67, 77
Baptists, 265
Barnes, Michael, 214
Barr, Charles, 18,
Barrera, Neto, 188
Barrios, Justo Rufino, 250
batida, 119
Batista, Encarnación de, 74
Batista, Roberto, 74, 112, 118, 140
Batlle y Ordoñez, Jose, 100
Baum, Gregory, 152
Beaman, Pete, 49
Belli, Giaconda, 185
Belo Horizonte, 146, 148
Beltran, Edgard, 121
bendiction of the Blessed Sacrament, 15–16
Benedict XVI, 307
Berghold, Harry, 236,
Bergoglio, Jorge (see also Pope Francis), ix, 100, 292, 293
Bernstein, Leonard, 23
Berrigan, Daniel, 44, 218
Berryman (Brennan), Angela, vii, viii, 110, 113, 130, 133, 135–37, 140, 142, 151, 152–53, 159, 162, 165, 183–84, 185, 190, 197, 199, 205–6, 208, 210, 215, 117, 221, 231, 234, 244, 249, 252, 279, 297–299, 300, 301, 304
Berryman (Butterfield), Katherine, 2, 10
Berryman, Edward, 2, 23–24
Betto, Frei, 238, 263
Beutler, Harold, 34
Bianchi, Eugene, 254
Bible reading, 22
biblical culture, 44
Birdland, 28
Bishop, Maurice, 225
Black Like Me, 49
Boff, Clodovis, 235, 257
Boff, Leonardo, 235, 237–38, 275, 282, 294
Bogota, 94, 121, 127, 149
Boland amendment, 220, 242
Bolivar, Simon, 91, 123
Bolivia, 143–44
Bolivian Justice and Peace Commission, 143
Bonner, Ray, 220, 227
Bonpane, Blasé, 84
border (Nicaragua-Costa Rica), 186
Borge, Tomas, 168
Borgonovo, Mauricio, 170
Borosage, Bob, 233

Bosch, Juan, 54, 74
Boston College, 294
bottom billion, 304
Bowdler, William, 185
Boy Scouts, 8, 9
Boyle, Greg, 25
BPR (Revolutionary People's Bloc), 179, 194, 203
Bradford, Jim, 155, 163, 164
Branch, Taylor, 259
Brasilia, 148
Brazil, 79, 98–99, 146–48, 151, 264–65, 285–87
Brazilian bishops, 188
Breen, John, 165
Brennan, Edward, 18
breviary, 35
Britton, Floyd, 120
Broderick, Joe, 104
Brulc, Lilian, 59
Buckley, William F., 45
Budapest, 232
Buenos Aires, 293
Bulnes Aldnuate, Jose, 74
Burdick, John, 263
burial of infant, 51
bus fares conflicts (Guatemala), 189
Bush, George H. W., 246, 252
Bush, George W., 279, 304
bus-rapid-transit, 286
Butterfield, Clark, 1, 17, 28

Cajal, Maximo, 199–200
Camacho, Juan, 2
Camara, Helder, 89, 90, 101, 142, 283
Camarillo, 14, 15, 19, 26, 50
Cambra, Maura, 63,
Campbell, Betty, 150
Cancinos, David, 189
Cancun, 287
canon, 68
Capitalismo: Violencia y Anti-Vida, 177
Caracas, 263–68
Cardenal, Beatriz, 63
Cardenal, Ernesto, 179, 187, 191, 223, 225
Cardenal, Fernando, 121, 168, 179, 191, 223
Cardoso, Fernando Henrique, 264
carnival, 99, 148, 267
Carpio, Violeta de, 163
Cartas Teológicas sobre o Socialismo, 257
Carter administration, 184, 190, 197, 213
Carter y la Lógica del Imperialismo, 177
Carter, Jimmy, 200, 209–10
Carter, John and Renee, 144–45
cartoon (translator and writer) 269
Carvalho, Bismarck, 222–23

INDEX

Casaldaliga, Pedro, 241
Casariego, Mario, 159, 182
Castañeda, Jorge, 258, 279
Castañeda, Oliverio, 189
Castillo, Elias, 120, 129, 140
Castro, Fidel, 102, 240, 280,
Catechism of the Catholic Church, The, 290–91
catechism, 3
Catholic Action, 95
Catholic church, 58, 91, 197
Catholic Worker, 28, 218
Catholicism, Roman, 9, 20, 66, 159, 305–7
CAV (Antonio Valdivieso Center), 198
Cayley, David, 276
CELAM (Latin American Bishops Council), viii, 87, 88, 89, 91, 93, 109, 182, 162–63, 292–93
celibacy, 20, 65, 82, 93, 97
Central America Movement, 212–13, 219–21, 229–31, 242, 254
Central America Resource Center, 231
Central America, viii, 132, 155, 157, 171, 210, 225. 241, 243, 257, 272, 273
Central American church, 250
Central American Common Market, 171
Centro Pedro Fabro, 100, 146
CEPAD (Evangelical Committee for Aid and Development), 167–68, 191
Cerezo, Vicente, 244
Cerro Silvestre, 129, 130
Chaco, 144
Chalatenango, 244–45
Chamorro, Pedro Joaquin, 167, 180
Chamorro, Violeta de, 192, 198, 253
charismatic movement, 250
Charismatic Renewal, 267
Chavez, Cesar, 134
Chavez, Hugo, 108, 264–65, 288, 289
Chavez, Luis, 117, 133
Cheek, James, 204–5
Cherrett, Ian, 163
Chiapas, 277
Chicago, 52, 56, 83
Childhood Development Center, 113
Chile, 98–99, 101–2, 124–25, 145–46, 261, 272–73, 288
Chimaltenango, 161, 163, 297
China, 288, 303
chorrilleros, 72–73, 103, 112, 130
Chorrillo, viii, 71, 72–80, 87, 106, 106, 107, 112–14, 118, 120, 122, 129–30, 252, 299
Christian base communities, 79, 96, 101, 122, 253, 254, 266
Christian Congregation, 265

Christian Democrat Party, 140, 165, 200, 227–27
Christian Family Movement, 31, 80, 87, 106
Christianity and Crisis, 238
Christians for Socialism, 124–25, 145
Church Against Itself, The, 82
church and "world," 25, 37, 43, 71, 238
church and politics, 69, 117, 123
church born from the people, 186–87
church history, 31
church in Central America, 218–19, 249–50
church personnel to Latin America (Vatican proposal), 34, 50, 52, 56
Church: Charism and Power, 238
CIA, 120, 124, 156, 160, 220, 224, 228, 238, 252, 270
CICOP (Catholic Inter-American Cooperation Program, 52–53, 121
CIDOC (Intercultural Documentation Center), 74, 86
Cien Años de Soledad, 92
CIF (Intercultural Training Center), 86
CIIR (Catholic Institute for international Relations), 163, 231
CISPES (Committee in Solidarity with the People of El Salvador), 219, 221
cities (Latin American), 268
Ciudad Bolivar, 259
civil patrols, 226
civil rights movement, 48
civil war, 158, 212
civilian governments, 257
Claramount, Ernesto, 169–70
Clarke, Maura, 212
Clavel, Tomas, 52–53, 59, 70, 87, 108
CNBB (Brazilian Bishops Conference), 147
CNT (National Labor Confederation), 157–58, 183
CNUS, (National Labor Unity committee), 183
coca (and cocaine traffic), 258–59
Coca-Cola (Guatemala), 157, 189
Cochabamba, 143
Co-counseling (Re-evaluation Counseling), 153
Cody, Cardinal John, 65, 70, 173
COEDUCA, 163
coffee, 168–69
Coffield, John, 25–26, 38, 47, 49, 51–52, 248, 300
Coffin, William Sloane, 235–37
Colborn, Frank, 40, 51, 248
Cold War, 123, 149, 172, 213, 249, 258, 301
collapse of communism, 250–51
Collett, Wallace, 185
Collor, Fernando, 264
Colom Argueta, Manuel, 189–90
Colombia, 57, 79, 93, 121, 126

313

Colonese, Louis ("Mike"), 121
Comalapa, vii, 155, 161–63, 204, 207, 216
Comblin, Jose, 87, 89–90, 145, 117, 187–88, 254, 283–84, 300, 310
Comitan, 139
Commonweal, 122
communion, 291
compadre (comadre), 77
company men, 291
comunidades eclesiales de base (see "Christian base communities")
Concientización and Evangelization, 102–4
concientización, 102, 110
Concilium, 67, 81
conditional cash transfers, 296
Cone, James, 152,
CONFER (Conference of Religious of Nicaragua), 191
confession, 3, 41, 306–7
CONFREGUA (Conference of Religious of Guatemala), 182, 205, 216
Congregation for the Doctrine of the Faith, 237–38, 282
congressional testimony, 168, 214, 242
consciousness, submerged, naive, critical, 103
consciousness-raising, 117
Conspirando, 294
Contadora Group, 228
contestation, 93, 100
contraception, 43, 82, 93, 100
contras, viii, 197, 220, 224, 242
conversion, 61, 66
cooperative(s), 114–15, 129,
Copland, Aaron, 22
COPS (communities organized for Public Service), 134
Corado, Guillermo, 163, 196, 297
Corado, Isabel, de, 163, 196
Coronado, Maria de la Cruz (Adela), 56, 63
Corral, Enrique, 164
Corruptio optimi pessima, 276
Cortes, Ernie, 134
Costa, Rica, 57, 80, 157, 172, 176, 185, 210
counterinsurgency, 159
countersixties, 105
coup(s), 107, 146, 149, 193, 226, 227, 244, 302
Court TV, 260
Covina, 10, 123
Cox, Harvey, 187
Cremins, John, 22, 94
CRIES, 223
crime and corruption, 296
crisis, 254–55, 263, 266
criteria for pope (letter), 291–92

Cross Currents, 68
Cry of the Earth, Cry of the Poor, 275
Cuba, 69, 86, 94, 108, 123, 172, 197, 281–82
Cuban Missile Crisis, 35
CUC (Committee for Peasant Unity), 194, 216
Cuellar, Roberto, 178, 193
Cuernavaca, 84, 85–86, 273, 275
cultural differences, 90–91
culture wars, 105,
Cumes, Nehemias, 163, 204
Cuny, Fred, 174
CURE (Catholics United for Racial Equality), 49–50
Curitiba, 285
curriculum (seminary), 17–18
cursillo, 60
Cushing, Cardinal Richard, 52, 99
Czerny, Michael, 185

D'Aubuisson, Roberto, 200, 228
D'Escoto, Miguel, 179, 192, 223
Dada, Hector, 166, 298
Dario, Ruben, 74, 85
Daspit, Arthur, 18
Davis, Charles, 82
Davis, Wilbur, 35
daycare center, 196
De Colores, 61
de la Cruz, Conrado, 204
de Soto, Hernando, 289
death of God theology 81
death squads, 158, 160, 200, 227, 301
Deaver, Michael, 215
debt crisis, 240, 258, 272
Deferarri, Roy, 17
deforestation, 148, 165, 296
DEI (Departamento Ecuménico de Investigaciones), 176, 235
Dei Verbum, 81
delegations 185–86, 201–2, 244–45
DeLeon Schlotter, Rene, 204
DeLubac, Henri, 22
democracy, 118, 157, 172, 239, 254, 257
Democratization of Consumption, The, 290
demonstration(s), 212, 264
DENI (National Department of Investigation), 119, 140
dependency theory, 91–92, 271
deportation, 140, 170
De-Schooling Society, 86
development (economic and social), 83, 91, 95, 109, 112, 289, 309
development humanism, 83
Devine, Frank, 171

INDEX

DeVries, Bernhard, 27, 31, 34
diaconate, 60, 82
Diálogo, 163, 196
Dias, Ana, 266
Diaz, Gabriel, 96, 104
Dickey, Christopher, 220
dictatorship(s), 135, 154
Dies Irae, 13
Dillon, Peg, 168, 179
Dillon, Sam, 220
diplomatic immunity, 199
dirty war, 149
disappearance, 149
disbanding of army (Costa Rica), 172
Disciples of Christ, 137, 144
DNA testing, 115, 299
documentation of political violence, 167, 178, 186, 189, 199, 206
Dolan, Cecilia, 63, 63, 68, 118
Dolores Mission, 25–26, 52, 84
domestic propaganda, 221
Dominican Republic, 54, 74, 129
Donde No Hay Doctor, 163
Donovan, Jean, 212
Dos Erres, 226
Dougherty, Edward, 267
drug speaking tour, 258–59
DSA (Democratic Socialists of America), 233
dual agriculture, 157
dualism, 17, 238
Duarte, Jose Napoleon, 200, 210, 227–28, 236, 245
DuBay, Bill, 25, 44, 48–50, 52, 54, 222
Dukakis, Michael, 246
Dunne, Michael, 39, 41, 46, 51
Dupuis, Jacques, 282
Dusak, Bradley, 32
Dussel, Enrique, 89, 124, 152, 187, 223
Dutch catechism, 81
DVTA (Delaware Valley Translators Association, 269

Eagleson, John, 219
earthquakes 132, 154, 155
Eberhardt, Newman, 31
ECA (Estudios Centroamericanos), 166
Economic Justice for All, 247–48
Ecuador, 88, 92–93, 141–42
Edgar, Bob, 235–37
editors, 248
Education as the Practice of Freedom, 102
education, taking charge of, 26
Egan, John, 83

EGP (Guerrilla Army of the Poor), 159, 190, 194, 208
El Mozote, 227
El Salvador, viii, 84, 91, 116–17, 165–66, 169–71, 177–79, 188–89, 193–94, 200–204, 210–11, 214, 226, 227–28, 236, 244–45, 278–79, 298–99
election(s) (US), 166, 208–9, 233, 246
electoral fraud (1972), 165, 166
electric shock therapy, 48
elites, 157, 170, 199, 258, 286
Elizondo, Virgilio, 134
Ellacuria, Ignacio, 122, 166, 194, 228, 243, 251
Ellul, Jacques, 276
ELN (National Liberation Army), 69
Endara, Hector and Nati, 299
Enright, John, 63
entrepreneurialism, 289
environmental destruction, 142
Epps, Dwain, 185
Erstad, Dick, 167, 176, 185
Es Chile un País Católico?, 66
ESA (Secret Anti-Communist Army), 189
Escobar, Pablo
Esquipulas, 242–43
Esquivel, Jose Renan, 118
Esquivel, Julia, 163, 196,
Esteli, 184, 191
eucharistic prayer(s), 68, 305
evangelical growth, 250, 266,
evangelicals, 249–50, 293
evangelization, 64, 66, 67
experimental parish, 56, 57
export agriculture, 164
Externado San Jose (Jesuit high school), 193, 203, 212

Falla, Ricardo, 139, 162, 164, 197, 236
Fallon, Gerry, 28–29, 33, 84, 280
Family of God course, 56, 58, 59, 60, 64–65, 73–74, 79, 92
FAO (Broad Opposition Front), 185
FAPU (United People's Action Front), 179, 193, 194
FAR (Revolutionary Armed Forces), 184
fast, 241
father figures, 68, 300
favela(s), 101, 285, 289–90
FBIS (Foreign Broadcast Information Service, 270
FDR (Democratic Revolutionary Front), 210
FECCAS (Christian Federation of Small Farmers of El Salvador), 178
Feet-on-the-Ground Theology, 235

Fenichel, Gladys, 207
Fidel and Religion, 238
Fifty Years of Development: What Have We Learned?, 288–90
final offensive, 190
fire (Christmas Eve), 130
five-century anniversary 162
Flacquer, Irma, 204
flag riots, 58
Fleet, Michael, 256
Flores, Gerardo, 163, 243, 278
FMLN (Farabundi Marti National Liberation Front), 212, 298
FOR (Fellowship of Reconciliation), 134–35
Ford administration, 170
Ford, Ita, 212
foreign clergy and religious, 143
forest fire, 25
Forgotten Continent, 296–97
Formosa (Argentina), 144
Forty Hours, 16
France Pays de Mission?, 66
Francis, Pope (see also Bergoglio, Jorge), ix, 294, 307–8
Franck, Santiago, 96, 100
Franco, Itamar, 264
Franko, Patrice, 290
free trade zones, 175
Freire method, 101–4, 162
Freire, Paulo, 95, 101–4, 126, 300
Fuentes Mohr, Alberto, 189–90
Fujimori, Alberto, 272
Fukuyama, Francis, 290
funeral (FAPU militants), 193
funeral of Archbishop Romero, 202–3
Funkhouser, David,

G-2 (Intelligence), 115, 119, 252
Galilea, Segundo, 89, 121,
Gallego, Hector, viii, 114–16, 118, 127, 299
GAM (Mutual Support Group), 236–37
gang culture, 279
Garcia Marquez, Gabriel, 92
Garcia, Ivan, 197
Garcia, Jesus, 62
Garcia, Rodrigo, 129
Gaudium et Spes, 71, 81
Gazzaniga, Michael, 45
Gebara, Ivone, 267, 275, 282
Geist im Welt (Spirit in the World), 30
Gera, Lucio, 187
Gerardi, Bishop Juan, xi, 278
Getulio Vargas Foundation, 290
Glanzman, Jon, 214

Global South, 287
globalization, 254
glossalalia, 267
Glynn, Laura, 115
God is Love church, 265
Golconda movement, 126
Goldwater, Barry, 45
Gomez Izquierdo, Jose (Pepe), 87, 89, 92, 97, 105, 142, 187
Gomez, Leonel, 171
Gonçalves, Alfredo, 266
Gonzalez, Fidel, 62, 68
Gorbachev, Mikhail, 250
Gorostiaga, Xabier, 127–28, 137, 172, 187, 191, 223, 256
Gortaire, Alfonso, 89
Gospel According to St. Matthew, 46
Goss-Mayr, Hildegard and Jean, 96
Grand Tour, 105
Grande, Rutilio, 166, 170, 171, 248
great man theory of history, 251
Great Silence, 15
Greeley, Andrew, 83–248
Greeley, John, 65, 110–11
Gregorian chant, 15, 22, 32
Grenada, 225
Griffin, Ed, 209
Griffin, John Howard, 49
Grigsby, Arturo, 197
Gross, Ronald, 241
Grove Avenue Elementary School, 2, 3, 6, 7
Guarani, 144–45
Guardia Nacional, 73, 108, 110
guardian angels, 13
Guardini, Romano, 22
Guatemala City, 155, 156, 159, 183
Guatemala, vii, viii, 69, 84, 139, 156–57, 158–59, 168, 204–6, 226–27, 243–44, 297–99
Guatemala: Never Again, 278
Guatemalan bishops, 158–59, 217
Guayaquil, 92, 142, 295
guerrillas, 158, 170, 208, 227
Guevara, Ernesto "Che," 69, 91, 124
Guillermoprieto, Alma, 220, 227
Gutierrez, Gustavo, 87, 95, 100, 121, 124, 149, 152, 187, 274, 294
Guzman, Abimael, 240, 272

H_2O and the Waters of Forgetfulness, 276
Hacia una Teología de la Acción, 90
Haig, Alexander, 213
Halloran, Terry, 50, 52
Häring, Bernard, 83
Hasenfus, Eugene, 242

Havana, 281
Hawkes, Benjamin, 52
Headley, Don, 62, 67, 173
health committee, 118
health promoters, 163
Hearst, Patty, 136
Hedges, Chris, 220
hepatitis, 230
Hermanos, 59–60, 70, 79, 80, 82
Hernandez Pico, Juan, 139, 164
Hernandez, Gabino, 74, 80
Hernandez, Graciela, 63, 110
Hernandez, Juana, 161
Hernandez, Maria Julia, 236
Hernandez, Ramon, 107
Hernandez, Rosaura, 161
Herzog, Vladimir, 147
Hesburgh, Ted, 256
highlands, 91
Hinde, Peter, 150
Hinkelammeert, Franz, 177, 235
Hoinacki, Lee, 275–77
Hollydale, 1–2, 6, 10
HOLLYWOOD sign, 14
Holy Saturday Vigil, 306
Holy Year, 1
homosexuality, 20
Honduras, 172, 298
Honest to God, 44
hostage taking, 184
House Party, 6
housing discrimination, 48–49
housing reconstruction, 173–74
housing, 56, 72, 79, 106, 112, 117, 119,
Howard, William, 185
Hoyos, Fernando, 164, 226
Huehuetenango, 159, 183–84, 226
Human Rights Commission (El Salvador), 202
human rights, 143, 150, 158, 167, 177, 178, 188,
    200, 201, 220, 236, 240, 260–61, 278–79,
    293, 298
humanity of Jesus, 62–63, 65
Hungary, 232
Hurtado, Alberto, 66
hyperinflation, 246

Icaza, Jose (Pepe) Alvarez Icaza, 124
ICI (Inter-American Cooperative Institute), 129,
    136
ICIRA, 102
IDB (Inter-American Development Bank), 273
ideology of national security, 188
idolatry, as theological issue, 177

IFCO (Interreligious Foundation for Community
    Development), 230
IFOR, International Fellowship of Reconciliation,
    133–35
Iglesia del Carmen, 116
IHCA (Central American Historical Institute),
    198
Illich, Ivan, 57, 74, 86–87, 104, 275–77
IMF (International Monetary Fund), 240, 258,
    288
In Search of the Poor of Jesus Christ, 274
In the Vineyard of the Text, 276
inculturation, 263
independence of Panama, 58
Independent Scholar's Handbook, The, 241
indigenous people, 155, 156, 162, 228, 262, 278
inflation, 125, 225, 264, 272, 289, 303
initiation ceremony (indigenous), 208
INS (Immigration and Naturalization Service),
    242
Inside Central America, 228
Insight, 30
Institute for Religion and Democracy, 213
institutional church, 93, 100, 115, 121, 266
intelligence experts (Argentine and Israeli), 217
Inter-American Commission on Human Rights,
    208
Inter-Religious Task Force, 231
invasion of Panama, 252–53
IPLA (Latin American Pastoral Institute), 87,
    88–93, 97, 106, 117
IPS (Institute for Policy Studies), 229
Iran-contra scandal, 242
Ireland, 231–32
Iriarte, Gregorio, 143
Ixcan, 159
Ixtahuacan, 183–84

Jara, Victor, 127
Jerez, Cesar, 164, 248
Jerome, Gail, 109
Jesuit murder trial, 260
Jesuits murdered, 251
Jesuits, 127, 138, 139, 164, 166, 216, 251
Joao Pessoa, 99, 283, 285, 296
John Paul II, 149, 187, 189, 225, 228, 237, 251,
    282, 290–91, 307
John XXIII, Pope, 37, 43
Johnson, Corinne, 160
Johnson, Lyndon, 45, 55, 74, 194
journalists, 220
Jovenes Unidos, 110, 114
Juan XXIII Center, 115
Jubilee, 22

INDEX

judiciales, 196
Julieta, Sister, 85–86
Justice and Peace Commission (Guatemala), 182–84, 195, 198, 204, 205

Kai Yutah Clouds (Veit Nikolaus Toscheck), 207–8
Kaiser, Robert, 50
Kakchikel, 162
Kansas, 215
Kazel, Dorothy, 212
Keiser, Elwood, 248
Kellogg Institute for International Studies, 256
Kelly, Walt, 38
Kenneally, William, 31, 49
Kennedy, John F. 35, 45
King, Larry, 222
King, Martin Luther, Jr., 44, 48, 49, 79, 93
Kinzer, Stephen, 199, 220
Kirkpatrick, Jeane, 213
Kissinger, Henry, 229
Kremlin, 239
Kuhnhardt, Bill, 47–48
Kuna people, 57, 128,
Küng, Hans, 37, 43–44, 82, 100, 282
Kwitny, Jonathan, 214

La Ceiba, 172
La Prensa, 167, 168, 179, 180
La Virtud, 204
LAAD (Latin American Agribusiness Development Corporation), 175
labor movement, 158
ladino, 157
Lago Agrio, 141
laicization, 130, 135
Lake Titicaca, 143
Lakey, George, 153
Lamont Street House, 150,
LAMP (Latin America Mission Program), 50–51
land reform, 142, 166, 200, 288–89
landless peasants, 165
LaRue, Frank, 157, 163
Las Abejas, 277
Las Acacias church, 266
Las Armas Ideológicas de la Muerte, 177
Las Vegas (New Mexico), 34
LASA (Latin American Studies Association), 219, 258, 279, 294, 297, 303
Latin America (travels through), 97–104, 138–49
Latin America and Caribbean Contemporary Record, 245
Latin America at 200: A New Introduction, 295–96

Latin America, 54, 104, 167, 257
Latin American Catholicism, 66, 78,
Latin Americanists, 279
Latin, 17,
Laugerud, Kjell, 158, 169
Law for the Defense and Guarantee of Public Order, 178
lay missionaries, 283
Lebret, Louis-Jospeh, 83, 309
Ledogar, Bob and Elly, 202–3, 206, 244
Legarra, Martin, 115, 128
Legion of Decency, 5, 46
Leis, Raul, 113
Leite, Virgilio, 99
Lenkersdorf, Karl, 139
Lerner, Jaime, 286
Letter of Third World Bishops, 84
Levada, Bill, 291
Lewers, Bill, 260
Lewis, Ramsey, 28
Liber Usualis, 32
Liberation of Dogma, The, 274
Liberation Theology, 239
liberation theology, xi, 69, 86, 100, 121–22, 149, 179, 186–88, 237–39, 254, 274–75
Life Center, 150–53
life expectancy, 295
Lima, 126, 143
Linder, Ben, 242
Linkletter, Art, 6
literacy crusade, 198
literacy, 102
Liturgical Conference, 28, 43
liturgy, 43
Loder, Ted, 236–37
Lohle, Carlos, 97,
Lonergan, Bernard, 30, 261–62
Looking for God in Brazil, 263
looting, 253
Lopez Trujillo, Alfonso, 149, 187
Lopez, Amando, 251
Lopez, Hermogenes, 183–84
Los Angeles archdiocese, 43–44, 75
Los Angeles, 71, 82, 104–5, 132, 222, 248, 279
Los Doce, 179
lost decade, 240
lottery, 76
lowlands, 91
Lozano, Ignacio, 170
Lucas Garcia Romeo, 182, 189, 226
Ludwig, Melseme, 176–77
Lula (Luiz Inacio da Silva), 257, 286, 288
Lumen Gentium, 81

INDEX

MACC (Mexican American Cultural Center), 134
MacEoin, Gary, 111–12, 129, 133, 137–38, 187, 300
machismo, 60, 61, 98–99, 108
Macias, Alirio, 188
Macias, Edgard, 132, 139, 167–68, 190, 197, 224
Mack, Myrna, 253, 256
Macroanalysis Seminar, 151, 153
Maguire, Daniel, 290
Mahler, Ken, 70, 203
Mahon, Leo, 52–53, 56, 60, 61–65, 66, 67–68, 73, 75, 83, 107, 110–11, 115, 118, 173
Mahony, Roger, 280, 291
Malinowski, Jack, 193
Managua, 85, 117, 130, 132, 139, 246
Manaus, 148
mandatum, 290
Marins, Jose, 121,
Mario Mujia, ("Wiwi"), 183–84
Martin, Jay, 33
Martin-Baro, Ignacio, 251
Martinez Piedra, Alberto, 236
martyrology, 16
martyrs, 159, 278
Marx (and Marxism), 123, 148, 187, 197, 235, 239, 251, 274
Maryknoll sisters, 63, 109, 118, 128, 168, 212, 299
Maryknoll, 26, 62, 143, 159, 165, 218, 23, 283
Masaya volcano, 132
Masaya, 185,
mass killings, 217
mass organizations (see popular organizations),
Mass, 15, 17, 40, 63, 77, 201, 225, 306
Mass, Panamanian, 59
Matanzas, 281
May, Theresa, 297
Mayer, Paul, 63, 288
McCarthy, Joseph, 24
McCauley, David, 222
McCoy, Alan, 185, 201
McCoy, Bernard, 18
McDonald, Ellen, 106, 140
McDonald, Erroll, 257
McFadden, John, 47, 50, 52, 53, 101, 135, 190–91
McGlinn, Bob, 63
McGrath, Marcos, 56, 106, 108–9, 116, 121, 130, 135, 140, 172–73
McHenry, Henry, 1, 3, 4, 10, 32, 38
McIntyre, James Francis, 25, 38, 39, 48–50, 52, 54, 248
McIntyre, Thomas, 18
McKay, Paul and Mary, 174, 215

McKenzie, John, 33, 248
McNamee, John, 153, 217–18, 275
McNeil, Donald, 18
McTernan, Fred, 55, 63, 70
Medellin (bishops meeting and documents), 89, 93, 94–96, 106, 114, 121, 158, 173, 263, 292
MegaCities Projtect, 268
Meiselas, Susan, 193, 220, 227
Mejia Victores, Humberto, 227
Melgar, Gustavo, 120
Melgar, Joaquin, 74, 76, 80
Melgar, Leoncia de, 74, 76, 130,
Melville, Tom, Art, Margarita, 84–85, 159
Menchu, Rigoberta, 199, 262–63
Menchu, Vicente, 199
Mendez Arceo, Sergio, 85, 124–25, 142
Mennonite Central Committee, 174
Merlino, Hector, 96
Mersch, Emile, 30
Merton, Thomas, 21–22, 49, 179
Method in Theology, 271–72
Methol Ferré, Alberto, 100
Mexican national ideology, 278
Mexico City, 36
Meyer, Albert, 56, 65
Micham, Carl, 276
middle class, 290, 303
Mignone, Emilio, 235
Miguez Bonino, Jose, 121, 152
military (Argentine) 238
military aid and training (US), 149, 201
military governments, 147, 149–50, 164, 257
Millennium Development Goals, 303
Miller, Charles, 31, 36–37
Mingo, 120
Miranda, Jose Porfirio, 138,
Miron, Dora, 162
Misión de Amistad, 137, 144–45
Miskito indians, 224,
mission circle, 104–5
missionary disciples, 291
MLN (National Liberation Movement), 158
model villages, 243
Monge, Elsie (Esperanza), 115
Montani, Nicola A., 22
Montessori education, 113
Monteverde, 211
Montevideo, 89, 100, 146
Montezuma seminary, 34
Monthly Review, 238
Mooney, Tom, 205
Morales Ehrlich, Jose, 202
Morelli, Alex, 122

INDEX

Moreno, Rafael, 178
Moriarity, Cuchulain (Cuch), 135
Moser, Carolyn, 295
Mothers of the Disappeared, 193
Movement for a New Society, 150–51
muchachos (Sandinistas), 190
multilatinas, 295
Muñoz, Ronaldo, 293
music, 22–23, 32
mystique of priesthood, 13, 53

NACLA (North American Congress on Latin America), 167
NAFTA, 273
Nahuala, 297, 298
Nairn, Alan, 215
naked priest controversy, 223–24
National Bipartisan Commission on Central America, 229
National Catholic Reporter, 54, 81, 112, 142, 258, 280
National Council of Churches, 137, 167
National Guard, 107, 179, 186, 203–4, 212
National Indigenous Conference, 139
National Network in Solidarity with the People of Nicaragua, 219
National Police, 158, 293
National Press Club, 202
National Reconstruction Committee, 174,
national security regimes, 145–46, 149
National Security Strategy of the United States, 279–80
natural law, 43
Navarro, Alfonso, 170
necrology, 301
Neier, Areyeh, 220, 236
neoliberalism 258, 288, 303
Netzahualcoyotl, 138
new church in a new society, 254
new evangelization, 263,
new institutional economics, 289
New Left, 232–32
new middle class, 296
New Press, The, 257
Newman movement, 47
newspapers, 229,
NGOs, 225, 273, 287
Nicaragua, vii, 149, 157, 184–86, 190–92, 197–98, 211, 223–25, 236, 245 253, 298
Nicaraguan bishops, 192
NISGUA (Network in Solidarity with the People of Guatemala), 219, 221
Nixon administration, 124
Nixon, Richard, 35

Nobel Peace Prize, 162
nonviolence, 48, 96, 101, 107, 122, 133, 134–35, 147, 150, 195–96
Noriega, Manuel, 107, 115, 119, 140, 252
North, C. Douglass, 289
North, Monsignor William, 39, 41, 46, 47, 51, 53–54
Norton, Reggie, 163
Nostra Aetate, 81
Notre Dame (university), 256, 260–61
Novak, Michael, 247
NPR (National Public Radio), 205
nuclear freeze movement, 221–22
Nuestra Señora de Fátima, 71
Nuevo Chorrillo, 140, 299
Nuevo Veranillo, 69–70
Nugent, Peter, 32
Nute, Betty, 201

O'Brien, F. Patrick, 26
O'Donnell, Margaret, 47
O'Leary, Geraldine, 110, 112, 113, 114, 132, 139, 167, 190, 197, 224
O'Neill, Tip, 236
O'Reilly, Bernard, 32
OAS (Organization of American States), 189
Oath Against Modernism, 29
Obando y Bravo, Miguel, 180, 185, 188, 192
obedience, 10, 21, 44
Ode to Roosevelt, 74
Office of Public Diplomacy for Latin America and the Caribbean, 221
OIC (Opportunities Industrialization Center), 135
oil (Ecuador), 142
Olaya, Noel, 89, 94
Oliveira, Pedro de, 293
Omnibus, 21, 23
OPEN 3, 179–80
Oppenheimer, Andres, 290
Opression-Liberación: Desafío a los Cristianos, 122
Orbis Books, 219, 235, 282
ORDEN, 178
ordination, 34–35, 36, 38
original sin, 81
Ortega, Daniel, 236, 253, 298
Ortiz, Frank, 204–5
Ortiz, Octavio, 188
Our Lady of the Rosary Parish, 1, 10, 38
Our Unfinished Business, 249
outside the church no salvation, 13, 81
Oxfam, 163

INDEX

PACCA (Policy Alternatives for the Caribbean and Central America), 229
pacifism, 247
padrinos, 77
Palacios, Rafael
Palumbo, Gene, 253
Panajachel Statement, 195–96
Panama Canal Zone, 57, 58, 64, 70, 71, 73, 106, 108, 117, 128, 130, 131
Panama Canal, 58, 108, 128
Panama City, 57, 71, 76, 106, 112, 297
Panama, viii, 52–53, 55, 57–58, 96, 106, 123–24, 145, 172, 297–99
Panamanians, 58, 76
Panikkar, Raimon, 282
Pantheon Press, 228, 238, 247, 257
Panzos, 182–83, 184
papal authority, 82, 100
Paraguay, 137, 144–45, 202
Paraguay, 144–45, 149
paramilitaries, 277–78
parish census, 26, 39
Parker, Charlie, 15
Parker, Jim, 269
Parnassus, George, 32–33, 38
Parra, Angel and Isabel, 99
Parra, Isabel, 99
Parrales, Edgar, 223
particular friendships, 20
Partido del Pueblo (Panama), 108, 114, 120, 130, 140
Pasadena City College, 47
Pasadena, 39
Pasolini, Pier Paolo, 46
Passion Play, 59
Pastora, Eden, 224
pastoral institute(s), 55, 61–63, 67–68
pastoral letters, 221, 247–48
Pastoral Ministry of Violence, 187
Patria Grande, 91, 123
patriarchy, critique of, 294
patternmaking, 23–24
Paul VI, Pope, viii, 43, 50, 64, 82, 83, 86, 93–94, 111, 135, 238, 290
PCN (Party of National Conciliation), 165
Peace Brigades International, 236
peace movement, 208
peace processes, 242
peasant uprising (1932), 165
Pedagogy of the Oppressed, 102
Pellecer, Luis, 216–17
pelvic issues, 290
Peña, Jacinto, 115, 128, 299
Perez Esquivel, Adolfo, 135

Perez, Carlos Andres, 264
Perlman, Janice, 268, 295
Peron, Isabel de, 146
Peron, Juan Domingo, 146
Peronism, 99
persecution of the church, 189
Peru, 99–100, 143
Peten, 164–65, 244, 298
Peter, Paul, and Mary, 221
Pezullo, Lawrence, 197
Philadelphia office (AFSC), 155, 158, 160, 167, 168, 173, 175, 180, 183
philosophy (seminary), 26–27
Pickering, Thomas, 236
Pinochet dictatorship, 136, 164, 195, 239–40
Pinochet, Augusto, 260, 301
Pinto, Octavio, 57, 68
Pires, Jose Maria, 101
Pius XII, Pope, 1, 13, 37
plainclothes police, 205
Plasmaferesis, 179–80,
Pledge of Resistance, 230, 231
pluralism, 293
Plurality and Ambiguity, 262
polarization, 171
political officer, 204, 205
political prisoners 146, 168
popular organizations, 178–79, 194–95, 200
populism, 92–93, 108
Populorum Progressio, 83, 309
Portuguese, 97, 101
poverty, 36, 95, 285, 303
Powelton, 207, 217, 234
prayer (in seminary), 15–16
preaching, 36–37
preferential option for the poor, 188
Preston, Julia, 220
PRI, 272
priest groups, 93
priest shortage, 61
priesthood, 9–10, 13–14, 35, 71, 83, 97, 280
priests in government (Nicaragua), 192, 198, 223
priests killed, 188
priests retreat, 33, 50
priests, 18–19, 42.-3, 52–53, 78
private helicopters, 8, 308
Proaño, Leonidas, 88, 142
progressive Catholics, 266–67
progressives, 233
Proposition 14, 49–50
Puebla, 182, 186–88, 292
puppets, 144–45

INDEX

QIARS (Quaker International Affairs Representatives), 156
Quakers, 150, 151
Queen of Angels Junior Seminary, 14
Quiche, 198
Quigley, Tom, 137, 181, 201–2
Quiroz Guardia, Alberto (Betito), 127
Quispe, Concepcion, 259
Quito, 92, 93

racism, 92
radicalization, 122–24, 150, 208, 301
Radio Impacto, 127
Rahner, Karl, 30, 44, 87
Ralph, Linda, 193
Ramirez, Raul, 296
Random House, 257
Ratzinger, Josef, 237–38, 290
Ray, Mary, 106, 110
Ready, William, 18
Reagan administration, 212, 213, 218, 219, 233, 239, 242,
Reagan, Ronald, viii, 172, 208–9, 221–22, 226, 229, 230, 231–32, 245, 247, 251
real socialism, 232, 239
reality more complex, 292–93
Recife, 101
reconstruction, 173–74
recreation (seminary), 19
rectory living, 46–47
re-evangelization of the baptized, 67, 95
refugees, 201, 202, 204
Reich, Otto, 221
Reid, Michael, 290, 296
relations between men and women, 65
religious monopoly (end of), 294
Religious Roots of Rebellion: Christians in Central American Revolutions, 218–19
Religious Task Force, 231
Renacer church, 265
reports on political violence 167, 176, 178, 205, 301
repression, 196, 208, 228
retreat, 9
reverse culture shock, 71
Revolution Next Door, 112
revolution, 69, 83–84, 90, 94, 95, 96, 123, 124, 164, 180, 197–98, 223, 258
Rhoades, Benton, 137
Rhynor, Kurt and Kathryn, 174
Riba, Jorge, 119, 129, 130–31, 140
Rich, Buddy, 28
Richard, Pablo, 176
Riding, Alan, 220

Rigali, Justin, 291
Rio de Janeiro, 285
Riobamba, 142
Riordan, Thomas, 273
Rios Montt, Efrain, 226–27, 249, 301
ritual actions, 40–41
Rivera Damas, Arturo, 84, 170, 228
Rivers, Clarence, 45
Robelo, Alfonso, 192, 198
Roberts, Archbishop, Thomas, 44
Robinson, John A. T., 44
Rodriguez, Edmundo (Mundo), 134
Rodriguez, Jesus ("Chu"), 57, 62
Romero (film), 248
Romero, Eleuterio, 259
Romero, Humberto, 166, 177
Romero, Juan, 134
Romero, Oscar, xi, 170, 178, 188, 188–89, 193–94, 200–204, 222, 227, 248, 278, 301
Rondo, Margaret, 163, 165
Roosevelt, Theodore, 58
Rosario (Sinaloa), 2, 35–36, 138
rosary, 16
Rosazza, Peter, 247
Rosemont College, 261
rostros (faces), 188
Rother, Stan, 215, 301
Ruether, Rosemary, 82, 152, 254
Ruiz, Samuel, 139, 142, 277
rule (seminary), 21
Rumford Act, 49,
Ruthrauf, John, 211–12, 235–37

Sacramento, 134
Sacrosanctum Concilium (constitution on the liturgy), 43
Salesian Fathers, 9
Salvadoran election (1977), 169–70
San Blas islands, 128
San Cristobal, 276
San Fernando Mission, 14
San Fernando, 19
San Jose (California), 135
San Jose Poaquil, 207–8
San Miguelito team, 63, 79, 110–11, 173
San Miguelito, 55–71, 72, 73, 107–8, 110–11
San Pedro Sula, 139
San Pedro Sula, 172
sanctuary movement, 230
Sandinistas, vii, 168, 179, 180, 184–86, 190–92, 194, 197–98
Sandino, Augusto Cesar, 168
Sandoval Alarcon, Mario, 158
Sanjines, Jose Antonio, 190–91

Santa Cruz, 143
Santa Fe (Veraguas), 114, 128, 299
Santa Fe Committee, 210
Santiago Atitlan, 215
Santiago de Veraguas, 108, 114
Santiago, 101, 145
Santiso, Javier, 290
Santo Domingo Savio, 96
Santo Domingo, 263, 292
Sao Carlos, 285–86
Sao Paulo, 99, 263–68, 289
Sarmientos, Jorge, 160
Schallert, Eugene, 33
Scheeben, Matthias, 30
Schiffrin, Andre, 228, 257
Schillebeeckx, Edward, 83, 100
Schlesinger, Arthur, 248
Schneider, Lou, 195
Seamy Side of Charity, The, 86
see-judge-act methodology, 95, 292
segregation, 48
Segundo, Juan Luis, 66, 87, 89, 97, 100, 146, 152, 177, 238, 274–75
Seliga, Emil, 49
Sellars, Patricia, 210
Seminario Bíblico, 177
seminary, 12–38,
Sendero Luminoso, 240, 272
September 11, 2001 attacks, 279
sermon (on racism), 53–54
sermon (Romero), 201
SERPAJ (Peace and Justice Service), 135
Seven Storey Mountain, The, 21
sex-abuse scandal, 20, 280
Sharper, Philip, 219
Sheehan, Mark, 63, 110–11
Sheen, Fulton, 24
Shining Path (see Sendero Luminoso)
shooting (Caracas), 264
Shourie, Arun, 128–29
Silicon Valley, 136
Silver Moccasin Trail, 8
Siman, Jose, 178
Simmons, Marlise, 183, 220,
Simon, Jean-Marie, 220
simple living, 150–51, 154
sin, 41
sisters, 46, 65
sixties, 44, 93, 300
slide shows, 150, 173–74
Smiley, Glenn, 96
Sobel, Rabbi Henry, 147
Sobrino, Jon, 201, 238
Social Science Research Council, 263

Social Secretariat of the Central American Bishops, 121
socialism, 84, 123, 125, 187, 257, 301
sociodrama, 113
Socorro Jurídico, 178, 193
Solaun, Mauricio, 185
Solentiname, 179
solidarity, 158, 227
Somoza(s), 85, 117, 119, 132, 139, 156, 173, 180, 184, 185, 190, 191
Sosa, Guillermo, 72
Sotz, Anastasio, 163, 204
South America, 97–101, 141–50, 257
Southern California, 28, 48, 248
Southern Cone, 98, 121
Soyapango, 193
Spanish embassy massacre, 199–200, 263
speaking tours, 209, 222, 258–59
Splendour of the Church, The, 22
sports (seminary), 19
St. Emydius, 9, 10
St. Francis Hospital, 24
St. Gregory Hymnal, 22
St. James Society, 99–100
St. John Bosco, 9
St. John's Seminary, 14, 17, 26, 49
St. Malachy parish, 217–18, 240, 275
St. Philip the Apostle Parish, 39, 46–47, 51
St. Therese of Lisieux, 16
St. Vibiana Cathedral, 38
St. Vincent de Paul, 16
stagflation, 209
State Department, 186, 214, 231
Steele, Harvey, 129, 136, 137, 140
stipends (sacraments), 41
street children, 267
street crime, 298
street life, 72, 75
Stroessner dictatorship, 137, 144–45, 202
Stubborn Hope, 256
Subcomandante Marcos, 277
subsistence agriculture, 162, 164, 295, 298
Suchitoto, 116, 133
Suenens, Leo Joseph, 43, 100
Suhard, Emmanuel, 22
summer (in seminary), 24–25
supermarket revolution, 273
surveillance, vii, 196, 205, 242
Sutherland, Bill, 156

Tabb, Bill, 238
Tabor House, 150
Taylor, Richard, 151
Te Deum, 117

Tegucigalpa, 172
televangelists, 226
Temple University, 270–71
Teología de la Liberación: Perspectivas, 121–22
Texaco, 141–42
The Day After, The, 221
theologians (Caracas), 186
Theological Studies, 122, 152
Theology in the Americas, 152
theology, 16–17, 29–31, 43, 44, 62–63, 77, 86, 111, 121–22, 186–87, 261–62
Third World Priests, 84, 93, 100, 126
Tidings, The, 24, 39
Tom Jones, 45
tomas, 125
too many orphans and widows, 234–37
Torres, Camilo, 68–69, 104, 122, 124
Torres, Marta, 106, 110
Torres, Sergio, 152, 237
Torrijos government, 118–19, 120, 150, 172
Torrijos, General Omar, ix, 107–8, 114, 115, 116, 124, 157
tortillerias, 25–26
torture, 147, 149
Toth, Karoly, 232
tour (Central America), 210–12
Toward a Theology of Peace, 232
Tracy, David, 262
training rural candidates for priesthood, 283
Trans-Amazon highway, 148
translation, 235, 241, 246–47, 268–270, 292–93
treaties (Panama Canal), 172–73
tribunal popular, 127
Trotter, John, 157–58
Trujillo, Rafael, 54, 119
Truman, President Harry, 1, 9
Trump, Donald, 209, 304
truth and reconciliation commissions, 261
Tunnerman, Carlos, 185
Tunnicliff, Stephen, 232
Tupamaro guerrillas, 146
Tustin, 104–5
twenty-first century socialism, 288

U.S. ambassador, 159
U.S. Catholic Bishops Conference, 137, 172
U.S. Catholic bishops, 213, 219, 246–47, 292
U.S. embassy, 164, 166, 191, 198, 199, 204–5, 251
UCA (Central American University), 166, 179, 193, 200, 243, 251
UDEL, Democratic Union for Liberation), 167
UFW (United Farm Workers), 134
United in Hope, 158
Universal Church of the Kingdom of God, 265

Universal Declaration of Human Rights flyer, 147
universities, 286
University of Notre Dame Pess, 260
urbanization, 288–89
Urcuyo, Francisco, 189
Urioste, Ricardo, 84, 201
Uruguay, 100, 146, 177
us-versus-them, 264
Utopia Unarmed: The Latin American Left After the Cold War, 258

Valdes, Luis, (Caneo), 119
Valenzuela, Felix, 87, 106, 146, 148
Vanishing Clergy, The, 86
Vargas Llosa, Mario, 92
Vatican II, viii, 37, 41, 43, 64, 71, 80, 90, 94, 96, 97, 109, 111, 261, 283, 308
Vatican, 237–38, 282,
Velasco Ibarra, Jose Maria, 92
Velasquez, Ana, 259
Venezuela, 58, 264–65
Vera, Cesar, 216
Verbena Cemetery, 298–99
Vernaza, Alvaro, 115
Vicariate of Solidarity, 147
Vietnam, 45
Vila Cisper, 290
Villa El Salvador, 125–26
Villacorta, Jorge, 194
Vincentians, 16, 18–19
violence, 83–84, 122, 158, 179, 181, 195–96, 277
Virgits, Edward, 18
visitors (to San Miguelito), 57, 59, 64
Víspera, 100
Vivienda Popular, 155, 161–63, 174
volcanologists, 132
Von Der Ahe, Bill, 35
Vordeckers, Walter, 204

Walker, Lucius, 230
Walker, William, 170–71
Wallace, Henry, 4
wallet (stolen), 246
Warner, Art and Natalie, 181
Warner, David, 163
Washington Consensus, 258
Washington Post, 169
Wasseige, Eric de, 143
Wayne, John, 173
Weffort, Francisco, 257, 263, 264
Weiss, Ted, 235–37
Westminster Abbey, 278
Wheaton, Phil, 150
Wheelock, Jaime, 219

white paper ("Communist Interference in Central America"), 214
White Warriors Union, 170, 177–78
White, Robert, 201, 202, 210, 212, 213
Williams, Frankie, 215
Williamson, John, 258
Willoughby, George and Lilian, 153
Wipfler, Bill, 137, 167, 201–2
Witness for Peace, 229, 231
Wiwi (see Mario Mujia),
WOLA (Washington Office on Latin America), 150, 168, 180, 231
Wolf, Wendy, 228
Woods, Bill, 159–60
Workers Party, 257, 286
World Bank, 258
World Neighbors, 174, 215
World Social Forum, 288
Wright, Jaime, 147
writers conference (Albany), 259

WTO (World Trade Organization), 287

Young Christian Students, 25
Young Christian Workers, 25, 84
Young, Ron, 201, 202
Youth for the Improvement of Chorrillo, 114, 120

Zabala, German, 126–27
Zacchi, Cesare, 94
Zamboni, 7
Zamora, Maria Esther de, 200
Zamora, Mario, 200
Zamora, Ruben, 166, 170, 194, 200
Zapatistas, 139
Zarruk, Roberto, 185, 191
Zelaya, Manuel, 298
Zero Hunger, 286
Zone 5 Jesuits, 139, 164, 175, 205, 226
Zuniga, Mary de, 163, 165, 299

www.ingramcontent.com/pod-product-compliance
Lightning Source LLC
Chambersburg PA
CBHW082315230426
43667CB00034B/2737